NONVERBAL COMMUNICATION:

A Research Guide & Bibliography

by

MARY RITCHIE KEY

The Scarecrow Press, Inc.
Metuchen, N.J.   1977

R
016.0015
K 44

Library of Congress Cataloging in Publication Data

Key, Mary Ritchie.
    Nonverbal communication.

    Bibliography: p.
    Includes indexes.
    1. Nonverbal communication. I. Title.
P99.S.K4   001.56   76-53024
ISBN 0-8108-1014-X

Good Lord, what is man? for as simple he looks ...
All in all, he's a problem must puzzle the devil.

Robert Burns

ACKNOWLEDGMENTS

Thanks are expressed to the following authors and publishers for material reprinted with their permission in this book:

Istituto di Glottologia, Bologna, Italy for many of the ideas in chapter 2 which were drawn from my paper in the Proceedings of the Eleventh International Congress of Linguistics.

The Claremont Reading Conference for the illustration on page 39, which originally appeared in the Claremont Reading Conference 38th Yearbook.

The University of Michigan Press and Professor Kenneth L. Pike for the table on page 58, which originally appeared in The Intonation of American English by Kenneth L. Pike (Ann Arbor: Un. of Michigan Pr., 1945).

The editor of Language and Professor Pike for the illustration on page 61, from "Abdominal pulse types in some Peruvian languages," Language 33:1 (Jan.-Mar. 1957), p. 32.

Akademie Verlag GmbH., Berlin, for the musical notation on page 60, from "Emotional patterns in intonation and music," by Ivan Fónagy and Klara Magdics, Zeitschrift für Phonetik 16 (1963), p. 294.

David O. Watson, Jr. for the illustrations on page 66, from Talk with Your Hands (Menasha, Wis.: George Banta, 1964).

Chilton Books and Jerald R. Green for the illustrations at the foot of page 66 and the top of page 67, from A Gesture Inventory: for the Teaching of Spanish (Chilton, 1968).

The University of California Press, for the illustrations in the center of page 67, from American-Spanish Euphemisms by Charles E. Kany (Un. of California Press, 1960).

The University of Illinois Press for illustrations at the bottom of page 69 and on page 70, from "A model for the demonstration of facial expression," by E. G. Boring and E. B. Titchener, American Journal of Psychology 34:4 (Oct. 1923); for illustrations at top of page 69, from "Perception of another person's looking behavior," by J. Gibson and Anne D. Pick, American Journal of Psychology 76:3 (Sept. 1963); and for illustrations at the foot of page 68, from "Thresholds for the perception of difference in facial expression and its elements," by Frances W. Irwin, American Journal of Psychology 44:1 (Jan. 1932).

New Scientist and the authors for illustrations on p. 71, from "I see what you mean...," by C. R. Brannigan and D. A. Humphries, New Scientist 42:650 (May 22, 1969), p. 406.

North Holland Publishing Co., Amsterdam and Adam Kendon for the table on page 73, from "Some functions of gaze-direction in social interaction," by Adam Kendon, Acta Psychologica 26 (1967), p. 32.

The Williams & Wilkins Co., Baltimore and the authors for the table on page 74, from "Sound film analysis of normal and pathological behaviour patterns," by William S. Condon and William D. Ogston, Journal of Nervous and Mental Disease 143:4 (1966), p. 340.

The National Council of Teachers of English for the haptic notation on page 75, from "Nonverbal communication" by William M. Austin in A. L. Davis's Culture, Class, and Language Variety (Urbana, Ill.: NCTE, 1972), pp. 151-152.

Gallaudet College Press and the authors for the table of symbols on page 76-78, from A Dictionary of American Sign Language on Linguistic Principles by William C. Stokoe et al. (Washington, D.C.: Gallaudet College Press, 1965).

Professor Edward T. Hall for the illustration on page 80, from his Handbook for Proxemic Research (Washington, D.C.: Studies in the Anthropology of Visual Communication, 1974).

The Dance Library, Lincoln Center, New York, and Leticia Jay for the Jay Dance Notation on page 82, from "A stick-man notation" by Leticia Jay, Dance Observer 24:1 (January 1957), p. 7.

Pitman Publishing for illustrations on pages 83-84, from European Folk Dance: Its National and Musical Characteristics by Joan Lawson (London: Sir Isaac Pitman & Sons Ltd., 1953).

The Ronald Press Co., New York for illustrations on page 85 and at the top of page 86, from Dances and Stories of the American Indian by Bernard S. Mason. Copyright 1944, Renewed © 1972 by The Ronald Press Company, New York.

The American Psychological Association for the illustrations at the bottom of page 86, from "A study of postural-gestural communication," Journal of Personality and Social Psychology 2:4 (Oct. 1965), p. 594.

Munshiram Manoharlal, New Delhi, India for the hand illustrations on page 89, from Tandava Laksanam by Naidu et al. (New Delhi: Munshiram Manoharlal, repr. 1971).

Cambridge University Press and Professor David Crystal for the table on page 98, from Prosodic Systems and Intonation in English by David Crystal (Cambridge Univ. Press, 1969), p. 135.

Anthropological Linguistics and Gordon W. Hewes, for the chart on page 103, from "The Domain Posture" by Gordon W. Hewes, Anthropological Linguistics 8:8 (Nov. 1966), p. 110.

S. P. A. D. E. M. (12 Rue Henner, 75009 Paris) for the reproduction of Rodin's "La Cathédrale" from le Musée Rodin.

Harper and Brothers, for the illustrations on page 111, from Postures and Practices During Labor among Primitive Peoples (New York: Paul B. Hoeber, 1934), p. 44.

CONTENTS

ACKNOWLEDGMENTS   v

1. INTRODUCTION   1

2. CONSIDERATIONS IN NONVERBAL COMMUNICATION   5
   A. Motion and Sound--Structured Behavior   5
      Relationship of Nonverbal Behavior and Language   10
   B. Rhythm   10
   C. Relationship of Physiology to Communication   12
      The Brain and Nonverbal Behavior
   D. Relationship of Psychology to Communication   19
   E. Human Communication   20
      Interaction/Interlocution/Transaction   23
   F. Acquisition of Communication   27
      Innate and Learned Behavior   27
      Imprinting, Imitative Behavior   28
      Infant Development   29
   G. Animal and Human Comparative Behavior   36
   H. Extra-Terrestrial Communication   37
   I. History of Ideas   37
   J. Historical Reconstruction   41
      Origin of Language   45
   K. Theories and Models   46
   L. Universality and Future of Nonverbal Studies   50

3. REVIEW OF THE LITERATURE   52

4. NOTATION SYSTEMS   55
   A. Paralinguistic Notation   57
   B. Kinesic Notation   61
   C. Dance Notation Systems   71
   D. Annotating Both Paralanguage and Kinesics   72
   E. Annotating Interactional, Tactile, and
      Proxemic Behavior   74
   F. Kinds of Notation Systems and Recording
      Devices   76
   G. History of Notation Systems   89

ix

5. THE ELEMENTS OF NONVERBAL BEHAVIOR   92
    A. Paralanguage   92
    B. Kinesics   100
    C. Tactile Behavior   112
    D. Sensory Communication   113
    E. Proxemics (Space)   113
    F. Chronemics (Time)   114
    G. By-Elements: Artifacts, Clothing, Hair   116
    H. Silence   117

6. SPECIFIC NONVERBAL ACTS   119
    A. Outcries   119
    B. Mimicry--Baby Talk   119
    C. Descriptive and Symbolic Gestures   119
    D. Greetings and Leave Takings   120
    E. Deictic Gestures   120
    F. Affirmation and Negation   120

7. DIALECTS AND VARIETIES OF NONVERBAL
    BEHAVIOR   122
    A. Patterned Individual Behavior   123
    B. Patterned Group Behavior   123
            Geographic Varieties
            Temporal Varieties
            State-of-Being Dimensions
                Age
                Sex
                Status
    C. Cultural Dialects   125
            Rites of Passage
            Occupation
            Education
            Athletics
            Societies and Clubs
            Warfare
            Religious Ritual
            Folk Gestures
            The Arts and Performance
    D. Language Substitutes /Surrogates   133
            Lingua Franca
            Circumstantial
            Non-Normal
    E. Cross-Cultural Varieties   136

    BIBLIOGRAPHY   142

    NOTES   429

    INDEX   433

1.

INTRODUCTION

This volume has been long in the collecting and making. I started out to do one book and the files grew too large for one work. So the discussion on most of the topics has been published in a separate work (Key, 1975b), while this volume comprises the complete bibliography. I have tried to write both books so that they can be used independently, but they may also be used to supplement each other. This volume assumes some knowledge of the subjects involved; I have therefore intended not to repeat information contained in the first book. For a more thorough treatment of various ideas and topics, one can follow the sections of both books which more or less parallel each other.

The focus is communication, though I have pushed the limits in some cases--for example, in the sections on Sensory Behavior--in order to probe somewhat deeper into a little understood subject, from the point of view of human communication. The interaction considered will be concerned with direct communication--that is, person-to-person--without such mechanical devices as semaphore flags, smoke signals, or the tilt of the windmill to signal to neighbors. Nonverbal behavior is still far from being satisfactorily defined. Only in the last two decades have many scholars given it serious scientific attention. The study of meaning is even more baffling, and the correlation of nonverbal communication to language has only begun to be recognized as a cause worthy of study, though human beings from the beginnings of language must certainly have commanded both systems as vehicles of communication. The contradictions in language are resolved in nonverbal behavior, "You say 'no' as though it means 'yes'." Intention is also not understood in human transactions. It is often observed that little of what is meant is said, and little of what is said is meant. The delimitations of this study are difficult to set because of the intricate overlapping of many manifestations of behavior. For example, I do not attempt to cover the study of emotions per se, but do include

1

the communicative aspects of emotion in facial expression
and intonation. Intonation and hesitation (juncture) are only
touched upon in recognition of the difficulties in deciding how
much of them are linguistic in nature and how much are
paralinguistic. I have not used the term semiotics very
much in the discussions because it covers many other kinds
of communication, such as clothes and traffic signals.

> Giving a name, indeed, is a poetic art: all poetry
> ... is but a giving of names.
> --Thomas Carlyle, Journal, 1832[1]

Terminology is always a problem, but it is almost in-
surmountable when one is dealing with topics across disciplines. Nor are the dictionaries a help in these emerging
discussions. It is curious that the word pasimology, "the
study of gestures as a means of communication," is in the
Webster's Third New International Dictionary, while neither
paralanguage nor paralinguistics occurs in this or in The Random House Dictionary; pasimology rarely occurs in the literature and paralanguage is now a standard term. Terminologies
used in the various disciplines in nonverbal behavior make
discussions difficult and cataloguing and indexing sometimes
impossible. Important information may often be missing because of these differences in terminology. I have tried to
use the simplest vocabulary possible, without jargon, so that
a scholar in any discipline as well as an intelligent layman
can read the material--though there may be areas in which
a wider background or experience would be helpful. The ten-
dency to use abstruse words and phrases has long been with
us, according to Margaret Schlauch:[2]

> The tendency had begun in the fifteenth century
> and went to absurd lengths in the sixteenth. Ben
> Jonson satirized it in his Poetaster, a play in which
> a character guilty of pretentious verbal concoctions
> is made to vomit them forth in a basin, in sight of
> all. The victim, named Crispinus, is supposed to
> stand for the playwright Marston who actually com-
> mitted verbal atrocities of the sort. When the pill
> is administered Crispinus cries out:

> | Crispinus. | Oh, I am sick-- |
> | Horace. | A basin, a basin quickly, our physic works. Faint not, man. |
> | Crispinus. | Oh--retrograde--reciprocal--incubus. |
> | Caesar. | What's that, Horace? |

Horace.	Retrograde, and reciprocal, incubus are come up.
Gallus.	Thanks be to Jupiter.
Crispinus.	Oh--glibbery--lubrical--defunct; oh! ...
Tribullus.	What's that?
Horace.	Nothing, yet.
Crispinus.	Magnificate.
Maecenas.	Magnificate? That came up somewhat hard.

Among other words thus 'brought up' are 'inflate,' 'turgidous,' 'oblatrant,' 'furibund,' 'fatuate,' 'prorumped,' and 'obstupefact.' The ungentle satire concludes with admonitions by Virgil to the exhausted Crispinus: among other things

You must not hunt for wild, outlandish terms,
To stuff out a peculiar dialect;
But let your matter run before your words;
And if, at any time, you chance to meet
Some Gallo-Belgic phrase, you shall not straight
Rack your poor verse to give it entertainment,
But let it pass. ...

Complicated, "hard" words confuse what is known with what is unknown.

There are other difficulties in the research. Nonverbal studies are drawn from over a couple of hundred journals in addition to books, and from every discipline that is concerned with human behavior. The number of languages and kinds of publishing centers compound research problems. The studies made on whisper, for example, number only about a dozen, but they occur in over six journals or collections published in five countries. In the discussions, I have not mentioned the works of some authors in proportion to the importance of their studies. When the research is of major importance, the reader will want to consult the original work. This is a research guide, not a summary or survey on the work done.

I am acutely aware of the credits I should give. I first offered a course in Nonverbal Communication in 1968, and since then the exchange of information and drafts of bibliographies, course outlines, and articles that have gone in and out of my office have been remarkably large and unwieldy.

I wish it were possible to credit all of these sources.   My
debt is also to the authors listed in the bibliography.

        I close these introductory remarks with a quotation
which Konrad Lorenz used in his chapter "On the virtue of
humility" (1963):

        It is the greatest joy of the man of thought to have
        explored the explorable and then calmly to revere
        the inexplorable. --Goethe

CONSIDERATIONS IN NONVERBAL COMMUNICATION

A. <u>Motion and Sound--Structured Behavior</u>[3]

Human communication is body movement. Movement of the vocal apparatus results in <u>speech</u>, the verbal act, or <u>paralanguage</u>, a nonverbal act. Movement of other muscular and skeletal apparatus results in <u>kinesic</u> communication, another kind of nonverbal act. Language is refined, cultivated body movement with an elaborate system of sign and referent. The nonverbal systems are less elaborate, at times comprising a limited system of sign and referent, as for example, the lexical gestures which occur in the Spanish and Italian cultures. Or the nonverbal "language" may be highly sophisticated as in the nonverbal coded language substitutes or surrogates of language, such as deaf sign language, and to a lesser degree, the whistle, drum, and gesture languages which occur across distance or between various language groups.

The position that I have espoused since my interest in nonverbal behavior was first aroused, is that language and nonverbal events are inextricably related. One might consider the physiological systems as an analogy. The human body functions through several systems--the endocrine, circulatory, digestive, reproductive, respiratory, nervous, and lymphatic systems--all of which are interrelated. They cannot function alone and the total body cannot function without any one of them. They operate in a hierarchy of action; at times one system is predominant or in focus. Eating brings to attention the digestive system; mating highlights the reproductive system; illness or injury shows the lymphatic system in force.

The concept of the relationship between motion and sound is not a completely new idea, as browsing through the writings of past centuries indicates. But the rigorous analysis and descriptive devices now available make the possibility of discovering its interrelated structures very real.

Nonverbal acts occur in all direct interaction between

5

human beings, with a resultant effect on syntax. The meaning of the interaction, or of the communicative messages, can only be understood with reference to the nonverbal components of the communication items. One senses a merging of syntax and semantics in the descriptions of language, and concomitantly a merging of verbal and nonverbal systems.

Close observance of speech events shows the synchronizing of language structures and patterned nonverbal behavior. Openings and closures in the discourse are correlated with kinesic movement such as head nod, crossing the legs, hand drop, relaxed face, shoulder movement, and paralinguistic features such as intonation patterns, speed, loudness (Kendon 1967; Argyle and Dean). Research has shown eye movement to act as grammatical markers in speech behavior. Body movement signals to the listeners and speakers when the transfers back and forth should take place. Dittmann and colleagues have isolated specific body movement with grammatical behavior such as the phonemic clause. Kendon has worked with units of speech roughly equivalent to the "sentence" and the "paragraph" and found that for each unit of speech, at whatever level in the hierarchy of units, a clearly contrasting pattern of body motion was apparent (Kendon, 1969, p. 29).

There are occasions when nonverbal acts displace language altogether. A question may be answered by humming the intonation of a likely answer. "What do you call him?" mmmmmmmmmmmm, meaning "I don't know." During simultaneous conversations, one may take place nonverbally. Directions to a waiter may be given by gestures alone while one is talking to someone else--"More, please" ... "No" ... "That's enough."

Sentences may be completed by nonverbal acts. "After they get wet, they just go [p p ɬ ɬ ɬ ɬ]."

Word classes are identified by nonverbal accompaniments or lack of them. "That's the man!" A pointing gesture accompanying "that" indicates the object. "I didn't mean that." Without the gesture, "that" refers to something just said. Further, emotional language (resulting in paralinguistic acts) can change word order: "A hundred dollars that mistake cost me!" (Bolinger, 1968, 1st edition, pp. 57, 68). I have noted other examples of coordinated verbal and nonverbal patterning in preliminary remarks on paralanguage and kinesics (Key, 1970).

The semantic features in grammatical descriptions comprise various domains such as number, sex, positional, status, shape, proximate, visible, and definite. Of concern in this study is the feature ⟨+ nonverbal⟩.

One of the grammatical categories which is often referred to these days is the class of verbs which the philosopher, J. L. Austin, labeled "performatives." These are verbs which do not describe or report about something; they do not make statements which can be said to be true or false. These verbs express an action which is in the concept of being performed. Examples are 'I christen (or name) ... I give (or bequeath) ... I bet ... I promise ... I pronounce...." Performative verbs occur in the first person singular present indicative active. They contrast with "constative" verbs which make statements or describe something. Austin treats over 200 performative verbs and suggests sub-classifications.

The performative action may be indicated in various ways from a formal declaration to an informal expression. For example, 'I bequeath" may be expressed by 'I give," 'I bestow," 'I will to you," or simply, 'It's yours." Verbs that function as performatives may also function as constatives. "It's yours" can mean bestowing or bequeathing of a gift, or simply be a statement that it belongs to the person already. "There's a bull in the field" can be either a warning or a constative, describing the scenery. 'I shall be there" can be either a promise (performative) or a statement (constative), (J. L. Austin, pp. 9, 32-33, 42, 62).

Of interest to the purpose of this study is the occurrence of nonverbal accompaniments with the performative verbs, such as facial expressions, smiles, head nods, gestures, and vocalizations such as humming, hissing, shushing. Nonverbal acts may actually substitute for the performative verbals, as in the following. These may also occur concomitantly with the verbal.

bet = handshake
promise, vow = sign of the
    cross
warn = tsk, tsk
order = pointing
congratulate = handshake,
    kiss
condole = silence

permit = head nod
pronounce guilt = facial expression of disapproval,
    silence
reprimand = glare
consent, agree = vertical
    head nod, wink
dare = slit eyes, smirk

forgive, pardon = priest's
    blessing
apologize = hand gesture
bid = auction gestures
approve = smile, uplifted
    posture
greet, bid you welcome =
    smile, outspread hands
concede = shrug
approve = smile, head
    nod
thank = slight bow

censure = frown, finger
    snap
deny = horizontal head
    nod
reject = hands raised, palms
    out
protest = marching, sit-
    in
dismiss = stand up
toast = lift glass
challenge = throw down glove

These examples represent nonverbal acts that occur
in the English language. Presumably other nonverbal acts
would occur in other languages. Some of these are of a
ceremonial nature; others are informal expressions of performative actions.

There are some performative actions which do not
have a verbal component, as Austin points out (p. 65). The
act of insult or declaring vicious hatred, for example, is
expressed only in nonverbal ways, at least in adult behavior.
One doesn't say "I insult you" or "I hate you" but rather
sends the message by an obscene gesture, a stony silence,
the Bronx cheer, or a flatulent gesture. Among the Nava-
hos, hatred is conveyed by a slow, devastating blink (Landar,
p. 129).

Other nonverbal performative actions include a salute,
as for example, the military hand salute or a bow; obeisance,
as to gods, parents, and royalty. Certain conditions preclude the verbal performative. When speed is a factor at
an auction or a sports event, the performative is articulated
by the gestures of the bidders and the umpire. When distance or noise is a factor, the commands are given by gesture. When silence is obligatory, as during a funeral, greetings, welcomes, commands, thanks, and condolences are expressed by nonverbal acts. In crowd behavior performatives
are likely to be expressed by nonverbal means. The performative "applaud" results in applause; "criticize" is expressed by hissing; "consent" is expressed by smiles, head
nods, or clapping; "deplore" is expressed by glum silence
and frowns, throwing things, or walking out.

Another way to approach the understanding of the in-
terlacing of the verbal and nonverbal components is to look

at the syntactic constraints which occur in the use of words which depict paralinguistic and kinesic acts. Syntactic constraints are evidenced, for example, in the semantic features $\langle +$ animate$\rangle$ $\langle -$ animate$\rangle$, which designate that a construction such as "The rock laughed" is not permitted. Verbs such as "shout, scream, yell, holler, bellow, whisper, shriek, wail, lisp, hoot, growl, grunt, mumble, moan, howl, mutter, whine" have different restrictions in the syntax than verbs such as "say, tell, speak, ask," which represent the semantic notion of the speech act. For further discussions, see Key (1970, pp. 33-34) and Zwicky.[4]

The whole area of emotive or affective words and their place in the grammar is yet to be understood. Austin points out the difference between emotive words and conventional expressions or polite phrases. "I have pleasure ... I am sorry ... I am grateful...." (p. 81). Davitz has published a chapter titled "A dictionary of emotional meaning," and the definitions include a great deal of nonverbal behavior or expressions of it. Kiparsky and Kiparsky also discuss emotive classifications (p. 363):[4]

> The class of predicates taking emotive complements includes the verbs of emotion of classical grammar, and Klima's affective predicates [Edward S. Klima, "Negation in English," in Fodor and Katz, eds. The Structure of Language, Englewood Cliffs, N.J.: Prentice Hall, 1964] ... but is larger than either and includes in general all predicates which express the subjective value of a proposition rather than knowledge about it or its truth value....

The coordinate behavior of verbal and nonverbal acts is of crucial importance in understanding the differences between written and spoken language (Key, 1971). Consider what meaning is conveyed by tone of voice, lilt of pitch, dancing of eyebrows, tightening and extending of muscles, shift of torso, speed of movement and syllables, hesitation or interruption of gesture and vocalization. All of this is lost on a two-dimensional page where the skillful turn of a phrase alone must convey all that makes language alive and communicative.

As it is difficult to express performative actions by verbal means alone (written), so is it difficult to compose descriptions which seem real in writing. Consider, for

instance, the problems encountered in writing a description
of a spiral--without hand gestures curling through the air to
suggest measurement and shape.   For references to differences in Written and Spoken language see: Abercrombie,
1965; Blass; Crystal and Davy; Alfred Hayes, 1964; Key,
1971, 1974; Lefevre; Lloyd and Warfel, pp. 61-68; Mehegan
and Dreifuss; Vygotsky; Whitehall.

      For ideas and references on the Relationship of Non-
verbal Behavior and Language see: Abercrombie, 1965;
Agulera; Argyle and Dean; J. L. Austin; Mary C. Bateson,
1968; Bendor-Samuel; Bierwisch; Bolinger; Brodsky; Brosin;
Brosin and Condon; Browning; Bullowa; Bullowa, Jones and
Bever; Bullowa, Jones and Duckert; Cresswell; Davitz, 1969;
Delattre; Dittmann; Dittmann and Llewellyn; Dittmann and
Wynne; Elerick; Walburga Engel; Fillmore; Fónagy; Fouché;
Frahm; Gleason; Gruber, 1967; Hopkins; Hymes, 1961; David
Ingram; Jaffe and Feldstein; Janet; Kendon; Key; Kiparsky;
Kochman; Landar; Jonas Langer and Rosenberg; Leroi-Gour-
han; Levitt; Lieberman; Lindenfeld; L. Little; Lloyd and War-
fel; McCarthy; Malinowski; Marinus; Matarazzo, Wiens, Jack-
son, and Manaugh; Osgood; Postal; Quirk, et al.; John R.
Ross; Scheflen, 1963, 1964; Harry Scott and Carr; Scovel;
Sharpe; Sherzer; Smackey and Beym; Logan Smith; Karl
Stern, Boulanger, and Cleghorn; Takahasi; Teller; Vygotsky
(pp. 98-100, 142-144); Weeks; Wheeler; Zwicky.

                        B.   Rhythm

      Rhythm that is codified in some way, as in music or
chanting, is easily recognized.   Rhythm comprises elements
of timing, among other things (Fraser).   (See also the section on Chronemics, in Chapter 5.)   Rhythms of life and behavior, into which everyday events are cast in a seemingly
humdrum way, are not so readily identified; nevertheless
they are present.   Though they are obscured by their very
familiarity, we can eventually see them.   Some rhythms are
of an inner or idiosyncratic nature--associated with the individual; outer rhythms· occur in patterns associated with
family or society.   Condon speaks of "self-synchrony";
others have recognized "interactional synchrony"--for example, Kendon.

      Rhythms may be culturally learned or they may be
biologically based.   Since the advent of air travel, much has
been said about biological rhythms--the circadian rhythms,

or the biologic clock.   Moving across time zones disorientates
one as rhythms conflict.   See Bunning; Doob, 1971; Fraisse;
and Luce for statements on biological rhythms.

Lieberman (1968) shows a biological basis for rhythms
in intonation.   Abercrombie (1967, p. 36) believes that rhythm in language is one of the most fundamental properties,
and cites a study of a type of aphasia "in which brain damage
has caused every feature of the production of speech to be
lost except the pulse systems of the pulmonic air-stream mechanism, as if these were the most resistant to damage to
the speech-centres of the brain." (Italics mine, MRK.)
Superimposed on these basic rhythms are the culturally
learned differences in the rhythms of various languages.   The
following illustration from Delattre (1966, p. 197) shows syllable length (a component of rhythm) of four languages with
characteristic differences:

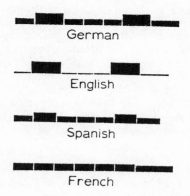

German

English

Spanish

French

Paralinguistic modifications in the rate of speech
(q.v. under paralanguage) should also be observed to understand rhythm.   For other examples in the rhythms of dialogue and other language behavior, see Jaffe; Jousse; Martin;
and Parrish.

It is thought that learned rhythms begin in utero
(Salk).   Condon and Sander have documented the neonate-
caretaker interaction which shows that the movement of infants corresponds to adult speech patterns.   Meerloo has
discussed infant rhythms with concern for communication

(for other references see his bibliographies).   See also Kestenberg; Lenneberg; and Lourie.

Meerloo observes that interaction rhythms may mean coercion, but can mean harmony and liberation.   Women who live closely together, for example in a dormitory or nurse's quarters, have noticed that their menstrual cycles may become synchronized.   Interaction between cultures may produce conflicts in rhythm.   Leonard studied films of greeting behavior of Black, Polish and American participants.   She charted the film at 24 frames a second, and showed that symmetric and asymmetric patterns resulted from crosscultural differences.   The symmetric patterns had an "even gait"; asymmetric patterns would either "stumble"--and subsequently recover--or "fall," when the out-of-phase interaction persisted.   For other remarks on cross-cultural rhythms, see Byers; and McDermott.

The Fine Arts give us many examples of ritualized and formalized rhythms.   Isadora Duncan notes that the feeling for dance may come from the environment: "My first idea of movement of the dance, certainly came from the rhythm of the waves."[5]   Montagu reports a relationship between body movement and music (1971, p. 119):

> ... it is of great interest to learn that Colin
> McPhee, the leading authority on Balinese music,
> found that the basic tempo of Balinese music is
> the same as the tempo of the women's rice pounding.

Abercrombie relates elements of paralanguage and poetry. For other references of rhythm and dance, see M. Davis bibliography (p. 199); Condon (1968); and Thie.

Rhythm or lack of rhythm in group activities is expressed in the verbs in an American Indian language, Itonama,[6] spoken by a tribe in the rainforest of central South America.   While verbs of Indo-European languages express tense and aspect, Itonama has a set of rhythm affixes which are attached to the verb base.

C.   Relationship of Physiology to Communication

The separation of the hard sciences and studies of human behavior was reinforced by the challenges of the space

age and the sweeping scientific discoveries.   Even medicine,
which is directed to the treatment of humans, became more
and more specialized and dehumanized.   Now, perhaps, we
will swing back to concern and involvement with human beings and their relationship to remarkable scientific advancement; the biological sciences and human behavior will be
seen to be more closely related than heretofore recognized.
As I said recently (Key, 1975b, p. 164), one of the great
surprises I had when I began seriously to study nonverbal
communication, was that so many physiological acts are
communicative, or at least contribute to communicative
events.

     It is a commonplace that tension, startle, anxiety,
joy, anger, and love all affect physiology, which in turn affects the vocal cords and muscular function.   The vocal apparatus produces language and paralanguage, and is also
used in the physiological functions of eating and breathing.
The body muscles and skeletal framework communicate by
gesture and other body language, and are also used in the
physiological functions of walking and sleeping.   LaBarre
speaks eloquently of the overlay of cultural semantics and
stylization on physiological modalities (LaBarre, in Sebeok,
et al., pp. 197-198):

> As for other physiological modalities in man--
> defecation, micturition, coitus, and even childbirth
> --these kinetic acts surely have their anatomical
> substrates, but they just as surely have their kine-
> mic contexts when they become loaded with cultur-
> al semantics and stylization, as every good and
> complete ethnographic monograph should indicate
> they do.   [Ellis, H., Studies in the psychology of
> sex, 4 vols. (New York, 1936), 3, 393ff., gives
> numerous examples indicating that coitus, micturi-
> tion, defecation, and walking are culture-conditioned,
> as also is childbirth.]   In the approved kinetic and
> parakinetic styles of these acts, Havelock Ellis,
> Malinowski and others have adequately edified us;
> and Kinsey has sufficiently adumbrated class-
> differences in these phenomena in America.   Ob-
> viously, like ballroom dancing, all the above have
> their sex-dichotomized aspects as well; and Kinsey,
> in one of his rare truly cross-cultural excursions,
> has stated that there are even preferred modalities
> in perverse acts among British (sodomy), Ameri-
> can (fellation), and French (mutual onanism) homo-

sexuals. In this section of the present paper, then,
the gamut from weeping to sexuality shows a complete range from the rather purely ethological to
the clearly ethnological. One's guess is that this
may be, in part, a function of the chronological
time of appearance of the phenomenon: the child's
cry at birth, at its first breathing, is most clearly
cut-and-dried physiology; whereas sexual behavior
already at adolescence has long since been sicklied
o'er by the pale cast of culture and ontogenetic
conditionings.

Nowadays one might argue with the use of the word "per-
verse" but one cannot doubt the communicative aspects of
cultural differences. Even such things as the physiology of
the inner ear have something to do with the perception of
movement and one's use of the body in space. Ostwald
(1960, pp. 121-122) brings to attention the affect of intense
sounds on the entire body of the listener: "The energy of
ultrasonic waves, if absorbed by the tissues of the body,
produces heat. " He goes on to say that high intensity sounds
can cause vibrations in the head which in turn can affect the
internal organs. Very loud sounds can produce feelings of
pain and pressure, in addition to the so-called auditory sensations. Ostwald (1965, p. 3) also reports on the work of
Leonard Rubenstein, who discovered that "the frequency pattern of the hummed tone changed regularly from day to night,
and that this diurnal fluctuation of the voice corresponded to
measurable biochemical changes. "

     For the Relationship of Physiology to Communication
and behavior, see: Allport and Vernon; Bailey; Sidney J.
Baker; Roy Coleman, et al. (relationship of voice quality and
heart rate); Eibl-Eibesfeldt, 1970; Feldenkrais; Kurt Goldstein; Hirsh (serial order); Hockett, 1942; Lashley (serial
order); Lenneberg; MacDougald (paralanguage in love-making);
Mazur and Robertson; Meerloo; Nattiez; Ostwald; Pollack;
Ruesch (cyclical rhythms, timing and results in disturbed
communication); Roland B. Scott, et al. ; Straus; Wiener
(sensory).

     For other references to physiology, see biological
rhythms (previously discussed in this chapter), and Chapter
5, under Kinesics and Sensory Behavior.

     Dominating all other functions and organs in physiolo-
gy is the brain, which guides human behavior as well as
physiology.

The Brain and Nonverbal Behavior[7]

It is possible that human beings are an evolutionary mistake, or at best, creatures who are still much misunderstood. As Konrad Lorenz (1963, p. 221) observed, "... the long-sought missing link between animals and the really humane being is ourselves!"

The brain--that marvelously intricate and mysterious organ which makes humans substantially different from all other animals--has the capacity for directing intelligent, rational behavior. Yet it would appear, from a study of history and daily events, that the human being makes decisions based on emotions, attitudes, and previously learned/structured behavior, rather than on factors that are logical in their implications for the future. Mankind, who is able to postulate in terms of the future, decides in the present. In every aspect of the lives of human beings--in government, in marriage and educational institutions, in economic negotiations--choices are based on emotional needs that often dominate the transactions. As we have seen, nonverbal behavior/communication gives the overriding meaning to the language of interaction between human beings. Both kinds of behavior are governed by a node in the brain, where thoughts are processed and where many physiological functions are guided.

Gross anatomy of the brain shows two hemispheres--the right and the left--and recent studies indicate that there are small but consistent anatomical differences between these hemispheres, especially locations near Wernicke's area (Geschwind, 1970, p. 944, for example). The right and left hemispheres are asymmetrical, at least in that speech-attributed area. Though this fact is widely accepted, it is by no means clear what the distribution of "duties" is for the right and left hemispheres, nor whether it is mutually exclusive. Over a century ago Broca popularized among neurologists the relationship of the left hemisphere and language. This premise has been widely accepted and has led to further declarations that the left hemisphere is the logical, intelligent, and analytic side of the brain which controls rational thinking. The left side is often referred to as the dominant or the major hemisphere. The right hemisphere is said to be minor and "primitive"--the one from which originate the emotional, intuitive, and artistic responses in the human being. Labeling has even gone to silly extremes, such as calling the dominant side "male" and the emotional right side the "female."

It might be seen that the nominal dichotomy of the
functioning of the brain is the origin of the apparent dichotomy of verbal and nonverbal behavior. Could it be that the
left hemisphere guides language (verbal) and the right hemisphere guides nonverbal acts? A review of the literature on
language and the brain gives many examples that lead to this
idea. If the extent and importance of nonverbal behavior is
recognized, it might subsequently be shown that the "dominant" side is not the left side.

The duties of the left hemisphere are said to special-
ize in the following: cognitive and propositional language;
sounds made by the speech apparatus (Kimura, 1973, p. 76);
some types of movement of the hand (Kimura, p. 76); speech
played backwards, foreign languages, and nonsense syllables
(Kimura, p. 71); consonants (Shankweiler); verbs (Gazzaniga,
pp. 117-121). Kimura (p. 76) makes other observations
about gestures and their relationship to speech. She notes
that the manual activity during nonspeech events is different
in kind.

The duties of the right hemisphere seem more numerous and varied and are difficult to delimit. The right
hemisphere, Kimura says, plays a dominant role in the human being's perception of the environment. This side processes melodies, timbre and tonal properties, "emotional
tone" of sentences (Gazzaniga, p. 104; Kimura, p. 71; Van
Lancker and Fromkin). The right side also is said to describe colors and objects (Gazzaniga, p. 65). It processes
visual tasks, such as spatial relationships and depth perception (Gazzaniga, p. 65; Kimura, pp. 72-76); emotional
behavior, such as humor, displeasure, profanity (Gazzaniga,
pp. 105, 117); environmental sounds and sonar signals (Van
Lancker and Fromkin, who review other research); non-
language vocalizations (Van Lancker and Fromkin); coughing,
laughing, crying (Kimura, p. 71); tactual behavior (Gazzaniga,
pp. 25 ff. , and passim; Kimura, p. 76); olfactory (Gazzaniga,
p. 106); abstract notions, ideation, mental concentration,
and high-order mental capacities (Gazzaniga, pp. 125, 128).

The right side qualifies statements which are made
by the left, by such modifiers as "if, and, but, however"
(Gazzaniga, p. 142; Geschwind, p. 942). The right side
recognizes faces and tells the face to frown, or to shake the
head (Gazzaniga, pp. 104, 107, 121). It also deals with the
negative/affirmative concept (Gazzaniga, p. 130; Gazzaniga
and Hillyard, pp. 273-274). This should be of interest to

linguists who have recently analyzed these concepts in a
"pre-sentence" construct. With regard to acquisition of
language and the negative/affirmative concept, is there a relationship between the brain development and children who go
through the "No" stage? (Gazzaniga, pp. 129-131). The
right side specializes in concrete nouns (Gazzaniga, pp. 120,
129). As far as gestures are concerned, Charlotte Wolff
(1945, pp. 198 ff.) noted a preference for the left hand in
expressive movement. She felt that the left hand, under the
control of the right hemisphere, has a closer link with emotional than voluntary impulses. (See this reference for other
comments on the right-left problem; see also Needham.)

    The relationship between the right and left hemispheres
is not clearly understood yet, in spite of all the impressive
research and publications (see also J. E. Bogen on split-
brain). There are difficulties in testing, and some of the
experiments seem even more ingenious than the brain itself.
For one thing, the brain manages to compensate (Geschwind,
p. 942), and the behavioral strategies, cross-cueing, inter-
locking, and cooperation between the right and the left can
only remind one that the human brain belongs to an "endless-
ly clever primate" (Gazzaniga, p. 126). In reviewing the
studies, one also becomes aware that the term "nonverbal"
is sometimes used in different ways than I am using it here,
and we are not always talking about the same behaviors. At
times the experiments are inadequate because they record
only the verbal response of the subject, though we know that
other interactions take place--such as eye movement, facial
expression, body movement--which add to the meaning of the
response.

    Nevertheless, there is enough anecdotal information to
hypothesize that the verbal and nonverbal systems have different origins in the brain. For one thing, the consciousness of control of these systems is different. Language is
voluntary and conscious, while nonverbal behavior is usually
out-of-awareness (except, of course, when it is brought into
awareness). For another thing, people do not react in the
same way to sounds which are in the sound system of language as to sounds which they use in the paralinguistic system.
A teacher in Germany once told me of the difficulty experienced by his students (from another dialect area) in pronounc-
ing a "z, " even though they used the sound freely to accom-
pany a certain gesture. English speakers use at least two
"click" sounds in their paralinguistic systems, but find it
difficult to use these sounds in a language such as Zulu,

where they occur in the language system. Also, there is a "perceptual" difference between singing and talking. While some people cannot carry a tune, they have no problem with pitch in intonation. There are differences between the singing and speaking behavior of aphasic patients (Geschwind, 1970, pp. 940-941) and people who stutter. For classifications of right and left behavior, we should again consider linguistic structures that show classes of words which reflect nonverbal categories, such as sensory verbs, and verbs which indicate paralinguistic activity, such as shout, holler, scream, yell, bellow, whisper, shriek, wail, growl, grunt, mumble, moan, howl, mutter (Zwicky, and Ross). Compare Gazzaniga's discussion of "smile, laugh, nod, frown" p. 121).

There are other curiosities which must be brought to light in discussions of specialities of the two sides of the brain; for example, male and female responses. Kimura notes that males tend to have a greater left-visual-field superiority for dot location and dot enumeration than do females, and that females tend to have more verbal fluency than males (Kimura p. 78). Someone has conjectured that females do somewhat better than males in music performance. In prelinguistic behavior one notes that infants coordinate seeing and reaching. Gazzaniga (p. 132) says that there is a clear link between eye and hand, and I am reminded of the remark by Juana Inés de la Cruz: "I hold in my hands my two eyes, and see only what I touch."[8] The matter of tactile interaction between humans is of concern in that some scholars have suggested that the act of touching and being touched is essential to the development of the brain, as well as to other physiological maturation.

For further references on studies of the brain, see Gazzaniga; for additional references on Kimura's important research, see Shankweiler. For other studies see: Bever, 1970; Joseph Bogen; Brain; Broadbent; Carterette; Curry; Curtiss, et al.; Gazzaniga; Gazzaniga and Hillyard; Geschwind; Gordon; Kimura; Krashen; Lenneberg; Luria; Mehegan and Dreifuss; Millikan and Darley; Penfield and Roberts; Roemer, Teyler, and Thompson; Shankweiler; Van Lancker and Fromkin; Whitaker.

D. Relationship of Psychology to Communication

The physical world is readily accessible to the awareness of human beings, but much of human behavior has to do
with abstractions and concepts which are out-of-awareness.
Much--perhaps most--nonverbal behavior lies out-of-awareness and, like an iceberg, it is deceiving in its "underwater"
influence. Kluckhohn speaks of "covert culture" and the
cross-cultural difficulties in understanding. We must dif-
ferentiate between those out-of-awareness behaviors which
can be brought to attention and those behaviors which are
not accessible to awareness. For the most part, people are
not aware of their own articulation of nonverbal behavior.
This was demonstrated in an experiment in which police offi-
cers responded to a sudden shot in order to record the
startle pattern. Even after repeated shots, every subject
showed an eyelid response to every shot. Other movements
of the head and face occurred, but the men had to be shown
the film before they were convinced that they had reacted
with visible motion (Landis and Hunt, pp. 35-37). There
appear to be gray areas where scholars simply do not know
how much the human being is capable of realizing. This
may have to do with critical periods in the development of
the brain and other maturation processes. For example,
animals raised in the dark are permanently blind.

Nonverbal displays of emotions, attitudes, needs, and
aptitudes are evidenced in many areas, from paralinguistic
intonational patterns to voice qualities, facial expressions,
postures, and quality of body movement. Studies of human
behavior and communication have dealt extensively with emotions and attitudes. Nevertheless, some needs, aptitudes,
and properties remain curiously unexplored--for example,
power and greed, and the need for achievement and triumph.
The place of power in human behavior, along with the need
for food, sex, and love, is not necessarily evil; it may
simply be the opposite of helplessness or lack of control.
It is dealt with in the realm of political systems so often
that we do not think of it as a basic human component.

Other emotions or needs are not even mentioned in
studies done in Western cultures. It is of interest to compare
the features discussed in various studies. The linguistic
study of Hungarian emotional patterns in intonation, for example, lists joy, tenderness, longing, coquetry, surprise,
fear, complaint, scorn, anger, and sarcasm (Fónagy and
Magdics). The Natya Shastra, which discusses the emotions

expressed in dances of India, lists love, humor, pathos
(grief), anger, heroism, terror, disgust, wonder, and serenity (Singha and Massey). These lists differ significantly
from the lists of items used in research in Western Europe
and the United States. Ekman, Sorenson, and Friesen, for
example, list happiness, anger, fear, disgust, surprise, and
sadness. Allport used pain-grief, surprise-fear, anger, disgust, pleasure, and attitudinal (in Guilford, p. 192). Dickey
and Knower included reverence and pity in their cross-
cultural study done in Mexico City. Izard included shame-
humiliation in his recent study. See Ekman and Friesen
(1972) for other comparisons in the studies. For a study of
emotion and movement, see Clynes.

     Perception is involved in the relationship of psychol-
ogy to nonverbal communication. We hear and see the message we want to see and hear, and smell and feel. See
Broadbent; Bruner; Miller, Galanter, and Pribam; Mol;
Peterson and Barney. See Broadbent for the effects of noise
on human behavior. See also the section on Sensory in
Chapter 5.

     The principle of antithesis has been observed and
commented on, particularly by Darwin. Open hands demon-
strate impotence; clenched fists indicate power. When drunk
a person may exhibit behavior opposite to that exhibited
when sober. The extremes of behavior follow the pendulum
syndrome. Aggressive behavior is much in need of careful
research--but again, this is a difficult area because of its
very nature. Opinions about the impact of violence on the
viewer of television are many and varied, but in no way de-
finitive. Violent scenes in drama almost certainly provide
a release mechanism for those who have actually experienced
extreme violence or torture--a safety valve of sorts. But
for children who have not had similar experiences the scenes
may be suggestive--appealing to their imitative behavior.

                    E.   Human Communication

          Man has great power of speech, but the greater
          part thereof is empty and deceitful. The animals
          have little, but that little is useful and true; and
          better is a small and certain thing than a great
          falsehood. --Leonardo da Vinci[9]

Perhaps in attempting to define communication we have tried too hard to wring meaning out of language, in terms of information content. Perhaps we will come to recognize that language is primarily a system of accommodation, to get from one point in time to another point in time and to get from one relationship or situation to another. As walking is a system to get from one place to another--in space, so language is a system to get from one place to another--in time.

Ogden and Richards (p. 226) observed that it is somewhat surprising that grammarians have paid so little attention to the plurality of functions of language. The emphasis on the cognitive and informative function, which came with education and the introduction of rhetoric and grammar studies, obscured the fact that language, starting with its autistic forms, has a very important role in human beings learning to survive in their environment. Communication can be seen then as a means of integrating self and developing a self-image in order to cope with relationships to the world and to other humans. In this sense nonverbal communication plays a large part, for example in autistic behavior. Communication is also a means of establishing and maintaining contact or interaction between people, as well as rejecting or breaking a relationship. It is possible that language is much more ritualistic and symbolic than we have heretofore realized, because of our preoccupation with predicates. It is possible that much of language has little "meaning" but is rather a "programmed" way of getting from here to there in time. The function of the integration of self, for example, can be seen in the importance one gives to one's own words. Often in a conversation, the only one listening is the speaker!

The proportion of people who read and have written books compared to the number of people who do not use language in this way is vastly unbalanced. This fact perhaps has distorted our understanding of what language is, and has led us in academia to believe that it is first of all a vehicle to convey ideas--a propositional artifact. It should be looked at again, to see that it is often just another means of passing the time. Haiku, a very special form of language, is frankly acknowledged as being a means of diversion, as well as a form of art.

Notwithstanding these considerations, it is still useful, in our discussions, to refer to the generally acknowledged functions of language: 1) Informative, 2) Directive,

and 3) Expressive (see Key, 1975b, pp. 19-21, for other discussion and references). It is also being noted these days
that nonverbal modalities at times have a higher rank than
the verbal modality, particularly in emotive communication.
This is easy to recognize because quality and tone of voice
lend themselves easily to the emotions, and facial expressions are seen as carriers of emotion, as well as regulators
in the interaction, or as a means of signaling changes in the
ongoing relationships. Nonverbal behavior, however, carries
a great deal of weight in directive communication. People's
actions and the nation's business are impelled by the extra-
linguistic concomitants of the directives. It is not the office
memo that causes John Doe to finish the report before his
supervisor goes to New York; it is the set of the supervis-
or's jaw as he inquires whether the report is finished.

Scholars have ignored some extremely important
events in discussions of history and elaboration of interactions and transactions of human beings, because these events
are expressed primarily in nonverbal ways and are more
difficult to document than language. If one were to measure
value and importance from the amount of space that scholars
and academic journals have given to certain activities of human behavior, one would have to conclude that the grain
market in Chicago, the stock market, and the tobacco auctions in the South are relatively unimportant events. The
following bibliography does not document (except by journalists) these events in the transaction of which a high proportion of nonverbal signaling takes place. And yet it is such
nonverbal acts that control the economy of the nation.
Comedians, humorists and journalists have caught the spirit
of the human condition at times when scholars have defaulted.
Perhaps this lack of information in certain areas has contributed to the difficulties scholars have in relating to meaning. For a comic approach to human behavior see Dali and
Halsman; D'Angelo; Halsman.

Other accounts of human events record situations in
which direction was given by nonverbal behavior. Mercy
deaths, for example, have probably rarely been ordered
verbally. A retired physician in England discussed how
these directives were given: "Usually this has involved no
more than a glance, an eyebrow partly raised and a barely
perceptible nod, confirmed as need be by discussions outside the door."[10]

Information which is overwhelming and too powerful cannot be conveyed by verbal means. An old friend of the Churchill family had to inform young Winston that his father was insane. Winston later recounted, "[The friend] patted me on the knee in a gesture, which, however simple, was perfectly informing."[11] Havelock Ellis comments on the use of language in marriage proposals (E. S. Turner, p. 219): "The recognition that direct speech is out of place in court-ship must not be regarded as a refinement of civilization.... Among so-called primitive peoples everywhere it is well recognized that the offer of love, and its acceptance or re-fusal, must be made by action symbolically, and not by the crude method of question and answer."

For studies on <u>Human Communication</u> and signs see: Gregory Bateson; Bram; Bronowski; Kenneth Burke; Carpen-ter and McLuhan; Chafe; Chao; Cherry; Macdonald Critchley; Flack; Gumperz and Hymes; Kluckhohn; Martinet; Charles Morris; Ruesch; Sapir; Sarles; Scheflen; Sebeok; Sinauer; Alfred Smith; Henry Lee Smith; Lee Thayer; Trager; Trager and Hall; Vendryes; Leslie White; Wiener and Mehrabian.

Interaction/Interlocution/Transaction

The meaningful unit in human communication consists of more than the utterance (the Verbal Act) or a Nonverbal Act. It comprises also the response or the feedback, that is, the <u>interaction</u> of the participants. Jonathan Swift (1667-1745), a brilliant observer of conversation, used the word "Dialogues" and gave careful attention to the "Answers, Re-plies, Rejoinders, Repartees, and Remarks." He also was keenly aware of body language contributing to the message and noted (Swift, p. 24) that the Dialogues required:

> some peculiar graceful Motion in the Eyes, or Nose, or Mouth, or Forehead, or Chin; or suitable Toss of the Head, with certain Offices assigned to each Hand; and in Ladies, the whole Exercise of the Fan, fitted to the Energy of every Word they deliver: By no Means omitting the various Turns and Cadencies of the Voice, the Twistings, and Movements, and different Postures of the Body; the several Kinds and Gradations of Laughter, which the Ladies must daily practise by the Looking-Glass, and consult upon them with their Waiting-Maids.

Recent scholars have used the terms "face-to-face" and "dyadic" to refer to the rhythmic exchange in conversation. The elements of interaction are rule-governed and are usually or often produced out-of-awareness. The meaning of a conversation can only be understood (if indeed it can be at all!) by looking at the response and elements of the communication beyond the sentence. The nonverbal elements can be "markers of units"; they may be major cues in the interactional behavior.

The speaker of the interactional event has two options governing his or her speaking-turn: he can either yield his turn at a certain rhythmical point or he can deny the other participant's right-to-speak. In this turn-taking activity, scholars ask, "Who speaks next?" along with "When?" The speaker may hold the floor by filling the hesitations with vocalizations, by keeping a level pitch in the intonation pattern, by head-turn away from the other participant(s), or by eye avoidance. Refusal to make eye contact is ritualized in parliamentary proceedings when a chairman does not want to give the floor to a member of the assembly.

The hearer/auditor/listener contributes to the interactional event by response signals. The hearer may indicate assent or disagreement, boredom, amusement, or a mask of neutrality. These response signals are variously called "accompaniment signals" (Kendon, 1967), "listener response" (Dittmann and Llewellyn, 1968), and "back channel" (Yngve, quoted by Duncan). Fries called these responses "signals of attention" and noted that in an inconspicuous and conventional way the hearer gives the speaker attention. He also noted that, 'In conversations that are not by telephone but face to face, the signals of continued attention are often made not by words but by nods of the head" (Fries, pp. 49, 52-53).

These signals have also been called "regulators" (Ellsworth and Ludwig, pp. 384 ff.). It has been shown that they do indeed have a regulating function (Gunnell and Rosenfeld; Smith, pp. 322-323) and can influence for good or for bad--in negative or positive ways (Gross). Several investigators have noted the rhythmical nature and the synchrony of interactional behavior (Condon and colleagues; Dittmann and Llewellyn, 1968; Jaffe and Feldstein, 1970).

The sociolinguistic variables should be considered in the analysis and description of interactional behaviors. One must consider the description of the speaker and hearer, of course, but also the description of the person(s) referred to and the audience and situation of the surroundings--the Context of Situation. The shared experiences and the length of time for which the participants have known each other will determine the choice and range of behaviors used. D. H. Lawrence and Jonathan Swift noted sex differences in conversational behavior and resultant imbalances between male and female participants (Key, 1975a, chapter 3). Very few recent studies have dealt with sex variables, but a few observations have been made. Argyle, Lalljee, and Cook's study focused on visibility in the interaction of two persons and came up with some unexpected findings (p. 15): "It looks as if males are motivated to dominate and do so largely by interrupting and talking more, especially when the normal cues for floor-apportionment are absent." Two other studies on interruption patterns (Zimmerman and West; Kester) show high incidence of males interrupting females, and husbands answering for their wives. Cross-cultural differences also show interesting contrasts in interruption patterns. Efron (p. 89) noted that traditional Eastern Jews touched their conversational partner to interrupt or capture his attention. In contrast, Italians did not use the tactile gesture to interrupt, but rather as a way to express confidence (pp. 119-120). Gallois and Markel, however, observed that some things were the same in English and Spanish, and interpreted this to be a "manifestation of larger cultural norms regulating the phases of conversation." Status differences may dictate who speaks first. In Latin American countries the inferior approaches the superior.

The inventory of nonverbal elements that can fill the slots of interactional behavior is very large. It comprises paralinguistic acts such as clearing the throat (ostensibly), laughing, snorting, changing speed, pitch, or loudness, inhalation, and other vocalizations. It comprises kinesic acts such as change of posture, crossing or uncrossing the legs, hand movements, raising the eyebrow, opening the mouth. Head nods as assenting signals have been described by Fries, as mentioned above; Birdwhistell; Dittmann and Llewellyn, 1968. Kendon (1967, p. 46) discussed change in gaze-direction. He noted that looking at each other increases in positive and enjoyable situations, and decreases in negative or disgusting reactions. Kendon (1967, pp. 37ff.) discusses the relationship of hesitation patterns and eye movement in conversation. The response may be of a physiological nature, often to express crude behavior; for example, a belch or flatulence (Key, 1975b, pp. 95-96).

Silence is another means of responding to and controlling interactive behavior. Bruneau calls this "interactive silence" and notes that it may be used "to share cognitions and
solve problems symbolically together" (p. 28). He notes that
it also promotes interpersonal closeness (p. 30), but that it
can also be a form of attack. (See also, Key, 1975a, chapter XIII, and 1975b, chapter VI.)

Simultaneous conversations may occur. One of them
may be articulated completely by nonverbal acts, such as the
side instructions to a waiter in a restaurant, or remarks to
children, or another conversation while talking on the telephone. Secret negotiations may be conveyed simultaneously
by nonverbal gesturing. Simultaneous conversations may both
be articulated vocally. Apparently cultures tolerate varying
degrees of simultaneous speaking (Efron, p. 10). Simultaneous speaking may be an asymmetrical behavior which indicates mentally disturbed behavior or a temporary upset.
Using sign language, the deaf may carry on simultaneous
conversation.

Informal behavior appears to involve more nonverbal
acts than formal encounters (Hodder). Imitative behavior is
displayed by the hearer's repeating or mimicking the speaker's last utterance or gestures. Attention-getters may be
expressed verbally or nonverbally: "Excuse me--do you
know where the Post Office is?" Raising the hand in the
classroom is a ritualized gesture, probably derivative of the
natural reaction of hand gesturing to get attention. The
speed and length of the interaction varies considerably. The
most rapid transactions occur at auctions, in sports, and in
emergencies; the slowest in courtship behavior, where time
stands still.

The responsibility in interactional behavior is more
requisite with the spoken word and still more with the written word (contracts for example). Responsibility may be
remiss in nonverbal behavior, which lends itself to derelic-
tion. "But I didn't say anything!" The raise of an eyebrow
or an exaggerated silence can cause irreparable damage,
but the participants cannot be held accountable. The "silent treatment" has been used effectively to psychologically
"speak" to a person. The motivation underlying interactional events would appear to be little understood. For the
most part people aren't really talking for the sake of the
subject matter. Recall Malinowski's "phatic communication,"
or is it "communion"? Actually people do not want to be

understood much of the time; they want others to believe the
image they present. I believe there is a fallacy in many
contemporary discussions of interpersonal relationships.
Mis-communication is not necessarily a breakdown of communication, but rather a rejection of the person or the message.
Something was communicated! People who are too intense in
their strong convictions are often rejected in conversations,
because the topic, or the subject matter, is not the real
reason for talking anyhow.

A delicate or sensitive transaction or relationship
may better be handled by a third party "advocate." The
third party may even be in the form of a written message--
anything to avoid a direct confrontation. A Japanese novel-
ist wrote a poignant account of a marriage, during which the
husband and wife communicated their intimate messages to
each other by their diaries. [12] The use of the third party
obviates the nonverbal concomitants which carry the emotional and attitudinal messages.

For studies on Interaction and Turn-taking see: Ar-
gyle, Lalljee, and Cook; William Austin, 1972; Dolores
Brown; Bruneau; Dinges and Oetting; Dittmann and Llewellyn;
Fraida Dubin; Starkey Duncan; Duncan and Niederehe; Efron;
Ellsworth and Carlsmith; Exline; Feldstein; Frahm; Fries;
Gallois and Markel; Geizer; Goldschmidt; Gross; Gunnell and
Rosenfeld; Hodder; Jaffe and Feldstein; Jaffe, Feldstein, and
Cassota; Jaffe, Stern, and Peery; Jefferson; Kendon; Kendon,
Harris, and Key; Kester; Luft; Malinowski; Markel, Prebor,
and Brandt; Martirena; Meltzer and Morris; Ruesch and Kees;
Schegloff; Schegloff and Sacks; Schenkein; Siegman, Blass,
and Pope; Siegman and Pope; Alfred Smith; Valsiner and
Mikkin; Stuart Vance; Wainerman; Yngve; Zimmerman and
West.

F. Acquisition of Communication

Innate and Learned Behavior

The ancient theological debate about predestination
and choice has not been settled, in spite of extensive scientific investigation of nature versus nurture. Nor will basic
problems of biology versus culture soon be settled. Ostwald (1963, Soundmaking, p. 48) has discussed the question
of whether crying has a genetic component, and suggests
that the study of soundmaking might be useful in the understanding of genetic patterns and human behavior.

A further complication in delimiting innate behaviors
is the now generally accepted idea that an unborn infant can
respond to stimuli from outside the uterine environment.
See Ostwald (1960, pp. 20-21) for some discussion of intra-
uterine babies. I discussed this problem with reference to
male/female differences (Key, 1965a, pp. 59-60).

Both innate and learned behaviors are usually out-of-
awareness and, like a great iceberg, are out of reach unless
brought to attention in descriptions of human behavior. The
arbitrary selection of the forms articulated depends on one's
culture and individual experiences--not on logical process.
Acquired behaviors are often referred to as conventional--
symbols with intent to express something (for example,
James, 1932, p. 429). Custom has, seemingly, a supernatural power over human behavior.

For Innate and Learned Behavior, see: Davitz, 1964,
pp. 18-20; Eibl-Eibesfeldt, 1969, pp. 9-14, and passim; Ekman and Friesen, "Repertoire..." p. 59; Hall, 1966, pp.
177-178; Honkavaara, pp. 9-13; William T. James, p. 429;
Lorenz; Ostwald; Schneirla; Sontag and Wallace.

Imprinting, Imitative Behavior

The concept of "imprinting" grew out of ethology--
studies of animal behavior (Lorenz, 1937). By extrapolation,
scholars then began to see imprinting in human beings. Is
imprinting irreversible? Can human beings learn and un-
learn after certain chronological ages? For discussions of
imprinting see: Martha Davis, index of bibliography, p. 183;
Foss; Philip Gray; Hess; Lorenz; Ruwet; Salk.

Aristotle is said to have observed that 'Imitation is
one instinct of our nature." There are at least two kinds,
or degrees, of imitative behavior. The kind that is out-of-
awareness can be observed when one notices that one infant
crying in the nursery will trigger other crying throughout
the nursery. A cough in an auditorium will be echoed
throughout the hall. Yawning, finger-tapping, leg-crossing,
all have been noticed in imitative behavior. Then there is
the deliberate kind of imitation when children mimic their
elders or each other, or when students imitate language sequences in learning a new language.

For Imitative Behavior see: Martha Davis, index to
bibliography, p. 183; Brazelton and Young; Guillaume; George
Mead; Miller and Dollard; Rashevsky.

Infant Development

> But what am I?
> An infant crying in the night;
> An infant crying for the light;
> And with no language but a cry.
> --Alfred Lord Tennyson[13]

A baby's first communicative and cognitive experiences
are nonverbal expressions. Vocalizations and motor activity
are precursors of language and gestures (Key, 1975b, pp.
140-147). A large portion of the work done on infant vocalizations is concerned with the cry, and most of the studies
have been done in medical centers, for diagnostic purposes;
for example, Call; Fisichelli, et al.; Karelitz; Karelitz and
Fisichelli; Lind; Michelsson; Ostwald; Ostwald, Phibbs, and
Fox; Wasz-Höckert, et al.

Various instruments have been used to record and
make fine analyses of infant vocalizations: The Scott Sound
Analyzer, by Ostwald, Freedman and Kurtz; sound spectrograph, by Bosma, Truby, and Lind (1965, p. 91); Lieberman; Lynip, 1951; Murai; Ostwald; Ringel and Kluppel; Wasz-
Höckert, et al.; Winitz; Wolff; cineradiography, by Bosma,
Truby, and Lind; volume-unit meter, by Fisichelli, et al.;
spirography or esophageal pressure analysis, by Bosma,
Truby, and Lind; phonograph and phonophotography, by Fairbanks; computer, by Lane and Sheppard; Sheppard and Lane.

In 1965 Bosma demonstrated with cinefluorography
the physiological and anatomical mechanism of normal swallowing and crying in thirty infants. Also, Truby and Lind
collaborated with Bosma to produce highly sensitive, complex medical recordings, or "cryprints"--visual-acoustic
characteristics of crying--which illustrate the uniqueness of
the individual infant. Cryprints are analogous to finger-
prints. See also section on voiceprints, under Paralanguage
in Chapter 5.

The studies on cry behavior isolate three or four different cries. Wolff worked with: hunger, anger, pain.
Truby and Lind used three "cry sounds": basic, turbulence,

shift. Wasz-Höckert, et al. used: birth, pain, hunger,
pleasure signals. These kinds of isolates are equivalent or
mostly equivalent across the studies. The cries were usually
elicited by artificial stimulation: a finger flick, Karelitz
and Fisichelli; mask and withdrawal, and removal of bottle,
Wolff; rubber band snap, Karelitz and Fisichelli; pinch,
Truby and Lind; Wasz-Höckert, et al.; pulling infant's hair,
Ringel and Kluppel; vaccination, by Wasz-Höckert, et al.
Peter Wolff and Lenneberg used a "natural history" approach
and also spoke of "naturalistic settings."

Linguistic studies have been made by transcribing
phonetic or impressionistic phonetic recordings of the vocalizations, using phonetic symbols; for example, the International Phonetic Alphabet (Irwin; Karelitz; and Lewis). Distinctive features (Jakobson, 1941) have been used in three
studies, but, unfortunately, the same features were not used,
so it is not always possible to equate the studies. Gruber
used four features: vocalic, sonorant, consonantal, grave.
Ringwall, Reese, and Markel used: vocalization (sound/si-
lence), length of sound (short/long), length of silence (short/
long), direction of air stream (egressive/ingressive), air
passage (oral/nasal), muscular tension (lax/tense), force of
air stream (soft/loud), vocal cord vibration (voiced/voice-
less).

Wasz-Höckert et al. used five melody types, continuity of sound, voiced/voiceless, oral/nasal, lax/tense. In
addition they recorded length and pitch, glottal plosives,
vocal fry, and subharmonic break.

Eventually the linguistic studies should be integrated
with the findings of the instrumental studies. Further, the
articulatory impressions of the phoneticians should be correlated with the analyses by distinctive features. It should
be noted, however, that not all sounds are described con-
veniently by the distinctive feature [+] and [-] choices.
Some features of sounds are better described in terms of a
continuum (Bolinger, 1961).

Non-cry vocalizations have been studied much less
than the cry. Irwin attempted to assess the acquisition and
frequency of use of English speech sounds, but says little
about other sounds and speech sounds which are not English
specific. Peter Wolff (1969) makes brief mention of non-
cry vocalizations, such as lalling, gurgling, and laughing,
and adds that his is a preliminary statement.

        The close relationship of laughing and crying is docu-
mented by Crystal and Quirk in their instrumental study with
respect to paralinguistic features. Though their study was
not done on infant behavior, it is of interest to the description of the cry. They identified a continuum of focal behavior: laugh--giggle--tremulousness--sob--cry. They qualify
this by saying (p. 42), 'It is not possible to say when giggle
ends and laugh begins, or when cry ends and sob begins....
All qualifications involve spasmodic air pressure, pulsating
breath out of phase with the syllable.... Articulatory cor-
relatives can be studied by setting up parameters for degrees of pulsation type, pulsation speech, oral aspiration,
nasal friction, air pressure, amplitude and frequency of
vocal cord vibration, and volume and tension of supraglottal
cavities. "

        Peter Wolff (1969, p. 100) discusses the meaning of
laughter and says that it is "neither the expression of a
'pure' affect nor an extreme form of smiling, but expresses
conflicting emotion" (he quotes others also). He indicates
that there may be "some indirect evidence for the hypothesis
that crying and laughter may have a functional relation. "

        It is probable that intonation is the first linguistic fea-
ture of language which the infant acquires (Key 1975b, pp.
143-144). Lieberman (1968, p. 38) makes a strong case
that "the linguistic use of intonation reflects an innately de-
termined and highly organized system. " See his chapter 3
for a review and history of studies on infant intonation.
For other studies of intonation see: W. Engel; Kaplan;
Lane and Sheppard; Lewis; Lieberman; Sheppard and Lane;
Tonkova-Yampol'skaya.

        Future studies of infant behavior with concern for ac-
quisition of communication should involve the total inventory
of vocalizations. While cry behavior features more of the
components of intonation, other vocalizations contribute to
the development of language, such as the air stream mechanisms which control the direction, source, amount and quality of air used in language. This aspect of the development
of language seems relatively untouched in the studies. Observations should note the order of appearance of the use of
the vocal articulators for producing sounds, the overlapping
of these features, the adding, dropping off, and later re-
establishing of features. In spite of a fairly large bibliography on infant vocalizations, few of the studies are made
from the point of view of articulatory phonetics. Even

though instruments give a valuable insight into vocal behavior, it is still true that the human ear hears accurately
everything that is needed for verbal communication. For
this reason, a study which focuses on phonetic, paralinguistic, and intonational features would contribute to the understanding of speech development in infants.

A longitudinal study would be desirous since the
growth differences could not then be attributed to idiosyncratic differences of the same vocal act, as might be interpreted in a cross-sectional study. A longitudinal study, or
rather several, should give some insight into the understanding of order and quantity of the events of an infant's vocal
development--important features of linguistic behavior. Investigation of the acquisition and function of particular acts
in sequence would remind us that acquisition of language is
more accurately understood as being a process (Bullowa,
1970, p. 191).

The relationship of movement to vocalization is also
of concern in understanding the acquisition of communication.
It has been claimed that the cry is basically a motor activity.
If this is so, and since we have already noted the expression
of intonation in cry behavior, all the more reason to study
the articulation of motor-acoustic correlates in infant growth.

Interaction between an infant and other participants in
the surroundings begins at birth. Various terms have been
used by researchers to refer to interactions: pair activity,
response, encoding-decoding, interpersonal, conditioning,
reinforcement, maternal-infant attachment, attention and
arousal. Middlemore spoke of the dance-like or not dance-
like behavior of the mother-infant interaction (Brazelton, et
al. , 1975, p. 152). There is still a need to have data on
natural vocalization and gestural behavior--without artificial
stimulus--in order to understand the beginnings of interactional communication. Various paralinguistic and kinesic
acts have been noted in the interactions of infants and others:
coughing, smiling, cooing, eye batting, tsk-tsk, tactual movements, facial movements, eye-to-eye movements. For
references to interactional behavior see: Mary Bateson;
Brazelton, Scholl, and Robey; Bullowa; Call, 1970; Caudill;
Condon; Friedlander; Gewirtz; Rheingold, Gerwitz, and Ross;
Schwartz, Rosenberg, and Brackbill; Todd and Palmer; Weisberg.

 Regarding <u>notation systems</u> for infant vocalizations,
relatively little work has been done, or is published.   Irwin
depended upon the International Phonetic Alphabet, which is
useful only for adult speech sounds.   Jakobson's distinctive
feature analysis could perhaps be called a notation system of
sorts, but because of its breadth and complexity, it cannot
be read off in linear fashion.   Truby and Lind devised three
"phonetic" symbolizations to designate the three cries which
they isolated:

 1. Basic cry

 [æ̃ ::] [æ̃ ::]

 2. Turbulence

 [æ̃ ::] [æ̃ ::]

 3. Shift

 ++   ++
 [i::] [i::]

 Bullowa, Jones, and Bever give a sampling of a notation system which they are devising:

W	whimper	B	labial
T	tremble	G	velar
C	cry		
S	scream		

$<$ opening

$>$ closure

 The <u>cognitive</u> and <u>cognitive-emotive</u> development of
an infant begin much earlier than speech development.

 These features are expressed in vocalizations and
kinesic behavior.   The infant relates to categories and

concepts in nonverbal ways.   The kinds of things which later
are articulated in language to give meaning are being developed before speech begins.   For example, infants begin
to distinguish between human and nonhuman (animate and inanimate categories in morphological or syntactical structures).   Infants gain control over: affirmation/negation;
deictic processes; demand/request/command; alternatives
(if, and, or); cause-effect (pushing, dropping, hitting).   The
infant relates to imaginative and pretend concepts by pretend-
ing to pick things out of the air, or dressing up in Mommy's
purse and shoes (legendary and fable linguistic categories).
The infant is defining categories by inserting or removing
certain objects from the toy box, a purse, clothes hamper,
wastepaper basket, dishwasher, and drawers.   Infants understand rejection and denial, as well as various question types:
Who? Where? What?

Infants make up vocabulary items to cover categories
which are meaningful to them.   One infant I observed said
[sísí] every time she heard a lawn mower, vacuum cleaner,
automobile, or any motor that sounded similar.   Infants also
use syntactic structures of more than one element before
speech develops.   One infant I know used a three-constituent
construction at one year of age.   It was composed of recog-
nizable syllables and a three-element intonation pattern,
which could be recorded something like the following:

[da-da-da   iiiiii   da-da-da].

It occurred while the family was out riding and a vehicle with a siren shrieking crossed their path suddenly.
Complete with uplifted facial expression and pointing gesture
toward the sound, it could be translated something like,
"Mommy, a siren went by!" or "Listen! The siren made
a noise!" Infants are often heard to make two-constituent
constructions, such as [da-da-da Ummmmmm], which might
be translated "These (are) good"--an equational construction.

Infants use conversational styles, "talk" in whole
paragraphs, and "tell" stories before they develop speech.
These are expressed with nonsense (to the adult) syllables,
using intonation patterns with breath groups and rising-falling
pitches as are heard in dialogue and paragraph structure.
Appropriate gestures and movement complete the "conversation," which may take place with a toy phone, with dolls,
or with other small children.   One infant I observed folded
her arms at the end of the "conversation," just as her
daddy did.

It seems that it would be profitable to investigate infant communication in much the same way that linguists record an unwritten language in a monolingual approach--when
there is no common language between the native language
and the linguist.[14] One would discover that before speech,
the infant uses communicative devices in a systematic and
meaningful way.

For infant development in the Acquisition of Communi-
cation see: Abecassis; J. A. Ambrose; M. C. Bateson;
Bever; Bloom; Bosma; Bosma, Truby, and Lind; Brackbill;
Brannigan and Humphries; Brazelton and Main; Brazelton,
Scholl, and Robey; Brazelton, Tronick, Adamson, Als, and
Wise; Brazelton and Young; Bruner, Olver, and Greenfield;
Charlotte Bühler; C. Bühler and Hetzer; Karl Bühler; Bullo-
wa; Bullowa, Jones, and Bever; Bullowa, Jones, and Duck-
ert; Call; Cameron, Livson, and Bayley; Caudill; Eimas,
Siqueland, Jusczyk, and Vigorito; W. R. Engel; Fairbanks;
Fisichelli, et al.; Friedlander; Gewirtz; Gleason; Kurt Gold-
stein; Philip Gray; Gruber; Illingworth; David Ingram; O. C.
Irwin; Irwin and Chen; Jaffe, Stern, and Peery; N. G. Blur-
ton Jones; Kagan; Kagan, et al.; Kagan and Lewis; Eleanor
Kaplan; Karelitz; Karelitz and Fisichelli; Key, 1975; Klaus,
et al.; Kumin and Razar; Kurtz; Lane and Sheppard; Lauren-
deau and Pinard; Lenneberg; M. M. Lewis; Lieberman;
Lieberman, Crelin, and Klatt; Lind; Luce, 1970; Lynip;
McCarthy; McNeill; Mehrabian and Williams; Michelsson;
Middlemore; Molyneaux; Ashley Montagu; Moss; Müller,
Hollien, and Murray; Murai; Nash; Ostwald; Ostwald, Freed-
man, and Kurtz; Ostwald and Peltzman; Ostwald, Phibbs,
and Fox; O'Toole and Dubin; Prescott; Rheingold, et al.;
Ringel and Kluppel; Ringwall, Reese, and Markel; Robson;
T. Schaefer; Schiefelbusch and Lloyd; Schwartz, Rosenberg,
and Brackbill; Sheppard; Sheppard and Lane; Slobin; Frank
Smith and Miller; Stechler and Latz; Stokoe, 1974; Todd,
Gibson, and Palmer; Tonkova-Yampol'skaya; Truby; Truby
and Lind; Vaughan; Vetter and Howell; Vygotsky; R. W.
Washburn; Wasz-Höckert, et al.; Weeks; Weir; Weisberg;
Werner and Kaplan; Winitz; Peter Wolff.

For additional references see sections on Cry and
Tactile in Chapter 5 and Age in Chapter 7. For other bib-
liography see N. G. B. Jones, in Hinde (1972) and the new
Journal of Child Language.

G.   Animal and Human Comparative Behavior

Some insights into human behavior are gained by observing animal behavior, without at all implying that animals
and humans are alike--in many pathetic ways they are different! Nevertheless ethologists have contributed significantly to understanding the communication systems of humans as
well as animals. Both animals and humans use signals for
warnings and protection, for social sounds of uniting groups
and mating couples, for indicating daily needs such as food
gathering.

Observations of chimpanzees show some similarities
to human behavior which are curious/humorous/mystifying/
quaint/tantalizing--depending upon your mood. I noted a few
examples while reading van Lawick-Goodall (pp. 44, 99, 115,
127, 206, 250). A female new to the group rushed up to a
large male and held her hand toward him. He reached out,
clasped her hand in his--drawing it toward him--and kissed
it. Some incidents displayed the relationship between sniffing and sex, which I gave examples of in an early study (Key,
1975b, "Sensory Communication"). In a confrontation, one
chimpanzee raised his hands high as if in surrender. In
play behavior chimpanzees tickled each other. When begging
for meat the chimpanzees stretched out their hands in a begging gesture. In greeting behavior, chimpanzees may bow,
crouch to the ground, hold hands, kiss, embrace, touch, or
pat each other, especially on the head, face, and genitals.

Touching or holding another male's genitals is a greeting in some societies; in Western societies lovers may greet
each other in this fashion. In Black culture, it has been observed that males greet each other by touching or approxi-
mating their own genitals. This has been called the "Short
Arm Salute" by an expositor of Black culture:[15]

> WHEN CONFRONTING A NIGGER ... in a public
> gathering. And you wish to establish full rapport
> as a Brother. Test him. Give him a 'Short Arm
> Salute.' Reach down, fingers of your hands to-
> gether and extended with thumb alongside, palm
> down, then salute him from the fly of your trou-
> sers. If he acknowledges to return it, then he is
> a brother. But, if he ignores the gesture to
> scratch his head, adjust his eyeglasses, straighten
> his tie or pretend to button his coat, then beware.
> It is evident that he is a would-be 'Negro' and
> wants no part of you.

Gestures of dominance and submission are similar in human and other primate behavior (Lynn O'Connor). The manner of communication between humans and animals also takes place by nonverbal communication. Pets react strongly to human body language. Animal calls and animal mimicry are referred to under Mimicry in Chapter 6. For animal communication see also Origin of Language in a following section of this chapter.

For references to Animal Communication see: Stuart Altman; R. J. Andrew; Benveniste; Berelson and Steiner; Bolwig; Bronowski; Roger Brown; Karl Bühler; Busnel; Chafe; Chance and Jolly; Chomsky; Condon and Ogston, 1967; von Cranach; Macdonald Critchley; Danchin; Darwin; Diebold; Eibl-Eibesfeldt; Gardner and Gardner; Griffin; Edward Hall, 1966; Hass; Hockett; Humphries; Phyllis Jay; Klima and Bellugi; Lawick-Goodall; Lenneberg; Lorenz; Lorenz and Ley-hausen; McBride; McNeill; Parkes; Pitcairn; Sarles; Sebeok; Sebeok and Ramsay; W. John Smith; W. John Smith, Chase, and Lieblich; Thorpe; Van Hooff; Vine; Young.

H.   Extra-Terrestrial Communication

If inhabitants from another planet came to visit earth, how would we communicate with them? If their communication system were cultural, as ours is, then we might have some clues that would lead to communication. If not, we wouldn't have the faintest idea how to tune in to their system. We even have trouble talking about anything that is not on our planet. For example, geologists have trouble labeling what they found on the moon. "Soil" is not an accurate term for loose material; "sand" and "dust" are no better. Nevertheless, some people, including linguists, have speculated about communicating with extraterrestrial intelligence.

For references on Extra-terrestrial Communication see: Cherry, p. 17; DeCamp; Golomb; Hockett; Hogben; Sagan; Shipman; Wooster, Garvin, Callimahos, Lilly, Davis, and Heyden.

I.   History of Ideas

"Nothing endures but change"
                    --Heraclitus, d. ca 480 B.C.

It is like reading Machiavelli--it was all there before,
now it has been brought to our attention. The current wave
of interest in nonverbal communication--the new terminologies, the spate of publishing--leads some to think of these
studies as a fad. But like ecology, whether ignored or at-
tended to, nonverbal phenomena will continue to be an inte-
gral part of human behavior. As we will see later, in the
review of the literature, nonverbal modalities have been recognized since classical times. When the printing press was
introduced, the verbal modalities of human interaction came
into focus. Differences between written and spoken language
became more evident as the written word was increasingly
made available to the masses. The teaching of Rhetoric in
the schools highlighted skills in written language and en-
couraged elegance in constructing the written phrase. In
some senses these skills were not unlike the ingenuity and
adroitness of the oral story teller or the orator. In another
sense, the contrasts between writing and speaking are very
great. Paralanguage and kinesics and the feedback, the controls, the regulators, by definition, are absent in the written
word. Writing is two-dimensional and linear; speaking is
accompanied by nonverbal embellishments. See the accompanying illustration (p. 39) which graphically represents various media and their modalities. [16]

The mystical belief in the power and truth of the
written word was easy to come by, of course, since early
writings were of a supernatural nature. Even today there
are those who believe everything they read--if it's printed,
it's true. This speaks to the history of ideas: some ideas
which should be abandoned, or at least modified, are perpetuated in print.

With the invention of radio, the spoken word came
into focus again. Oratory was revived. Skillful use of paralinguistic effects again became a necessary concomitant in
communicating with the public. Whole nations could be
roused to action by a Churchill or a Roosevelt or a Hitler,
men whose tone and quality of voice and timing lulled their
listeners into passive reception. Television added kinesic
behavior and brought us back to the complete use of human
expression present in face-to-face communication--almost.
The feedback is missing. Nevertheless, the speaker can
make full use of facial expression, tilt of head and gesture
to enrich the message and give the effect of total communication. Is it only coincidental that the invention of this
medium and the resurgent interest in nonverbal communication concur?

COMMUNICATION

Channels: acoustical, optical, tactual, chemical, electrical

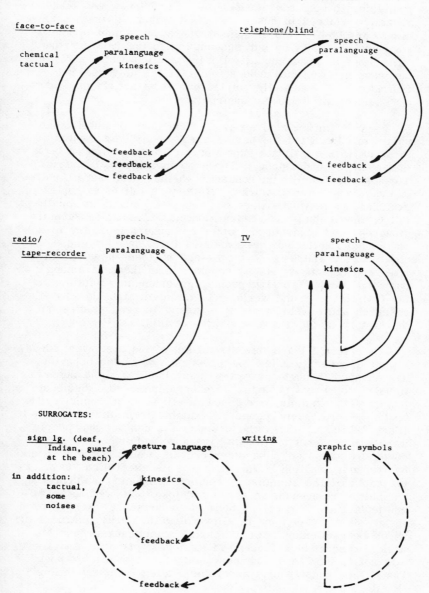

It seems trite, or too cute, to speak of this as being
an idea whose time has come. Nevertheless it does seem
propitious to take advantage of the interest now and make
great leaps ahead in research. But perhaps it is well to remind ourselves of the damage to the advancement of knowledge brought about by our succumbing to the fads and the
"in" things in academia. Following every whim can distort
our research and our understanding of the universe, as
Bolinger (1960) skillfully pointed out in an article on linguistic science and linguistic engineering.

Will Durant also spoke of "fashions" in intellectual
writings. He noted the period when "... it became the style
to speak with a delicate superiority of any non-fiction book
that could be understood. The snob movement ... began."[17]
To fads and fashions in research we must add the difficulty
of evaluating existing works. History is full of examples of
geniuses whose works were not accepted, and it is equally
full of intellectual and academic frauds. At times scholars
disagree, and students and other bystanders must try to sort
out honest intellectual disagreement from naked aggression
and attack. There is no more--and no less--honesty, integ-
rity, and objectivity among scholars than there is among
business people, working people, government officials, and
the Godfathers of the world. To maintain stability in one's
research and development, it is useful to read studies on
the history of ideas and scientific revolutions.[18]

Before I leave this discussion of the history of ideas,
I want to refer to a few examples of how human behavior
has changed through the years, and also how some observations of nonverbal behavior have been inherited. Some of
the funniest examples are found in etiquette or "courtesy"
books. I previously quoted an example from Amy Vanderbilt
(Key, 1975b, p. 138), who noted that a century ago people
were exhorted not to "fondle" the nose! Further, it was
noted that the nose, like other organs, would augment in size
by frequent handling. The nose and its execretions have often captured the attention of society, producing a surprising
number of references in songs and jokes, as well as in etiquette books. A courtesy book of Renaissance Italy, written
in the sixteenth century by Giovanni della Casa, instructs the
would-be gentleman against wearing a toothpick around his
neck, or scratching himself in immodest places. And above
all, not to look in his handkerchief after blowing his nose,
"as if thou hadst pearls and rubies fallen from thy brains"
(E. S. Turner, p. 49).

The history of gestures across time and cultures also reveals antithetical meanings expressed by certain acts. Handclapping has been and is used for applause, but can be used also for disapproval, and has been taboo in some instances (Francis Hayes, 1957, p. 257). The gesture of the uplifted two fingers representing "V" for Victory during World War II evolved in one generation from "Fight for Victory!" to "Peace--don't fight!"

Sometimes an idea has to wait for more information. Around the turn of the 19th century, the idea was set forth that thought and movement, particularly hand movement, were correlated. This idea has been revived recently in studies of brain and cognitive processes. For comments on Thought and Movement, see: Cushing; Sandor Ferenczi, 1919; Marshall Jones; Kirk and Burton; Schulman and Shantz; Tissie.

There are instances when an idea has been thoughtlessly copied from publication to publication. For example, the statement keeps cropping up again and again that there are some 70,000 distinct signs. Critchley (1939, p. 123) attributed the statement to Paget.

Some gestures are thought to be new because their history is not known. Contemporaries may think that the idea of blowing in someone's ear began in this generation, but Tylor gave an example in the 1860s.

The term "emblem" is used in a recent classification of gestures by Ekman and Friesen (1969, p. 63). One can trace its use through Efron, Leibniz, and still further back to Francis Bacon (Knowlson, p. 504; Efron, pp. 94-96). One is indebted to one's ancestors. Knowlson and Jules Paul Seigel traced the evolution of gestures and published these studies in a journal devoted to the history of ideas. Though their studies focus on the sign language of the deaf (see also Stokoe), their work shows the value of viewing ideas in relationship to their times. One final example of beliefs about the language of the body: Pardoe, in 1923, pleads for more emphasis on gesture in education, saying that gesture language is "the one language the good Lord did not confuse at Babel. "

J.   Historical Reconstruction

Comparative analysis of kinesic and paralinguistic events has the potential of reconstructing some aspects of

history, even as comparative studies of languages show historical connections and common origins.   Chen-Ming Chang
even spoke of "gestural etymons," in much the same way that
comparative linguists speak of etymons with regard to language relationships.   Jorio (1932) investigated modern Nea-
politan gestures in order to show their historical evolution
from ancient classical gestures depicted on vases and other
art forms.   See also Mallery (1972, pp. 294-296) and Efron
(p. 63) for further comment on the historical depth of Italian
gestural behavior.

     Anecdotal observations might lead toward ideas which
should be rigorously treated.   For example, items such as
the following might be investigated with profit.   The use of
falsetto voice in Africa could be compared with the use in
Black English in the United States.   American Indian deaf
sign language could be compared with that in Europe, to
identify common origins and observe changes necessitated by
the Indian languages.   I have heard that among educated Hun-
garians the polite way to approach the soup plate is to draw
in the first--and only the first--spoonful with audible friction,
reminiscent of the Asian manner of sucking in tea.   Does
this harken back to Hungarian origins from the East?

     Some history has been lost completely, but we don't
know how much.   The Rebel Yell, used effectively to terror-
ize the enemy during the Civil War, is no longer articulated.
But descriptions of it bear a striking resemblance to the
yelling heard at soccer games in present-day Scotland (Allen
Walker Read, and further comments he gave, Key, 1975b,
pp. 58-59).   Children's gestures include remnants of gestures which adults used centuries before.   The following illustrations show three gestures that children use today.
The first shows a leader of a parade crossing his two index
fingers.   While admittedly it is difficult to identify the gesture accurately, without indication of movement, it brings to
mind the children's gesture of "whittling" one index finger
against the other.   The second illustration is the familiar
"King's X," and the third shows the linking of little fingers
which children do to show loyalty or promise. [19]

     Comparative studies can also tell us something about
the origins of behavior, when history has been obliterated or
"edited" because of taboos or changes in behavior.   The
matter of male genital presentation or display has been discussed recently by Eibl-Eibesfeldt and discussants, along
with other expressive movements (in Hinde, pp. 306-14).

Leader of a parade crosses his two index fingers.

The familiar "King's X."

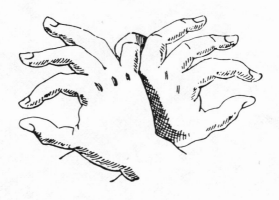

The linking of little fingers, used by children
to show loyalty or promise.

There are illustrations from several cultures and countries: Europe, Greece, Bali, Nias, Japan, Papua. The European sculpture shows the crucial material chiseled away! As previously noted, touching one's own or another's genitals is a manner of greeting in some societies. Barakat observes that a similar gesture is used among the Bedouins to require a witness to tell the truth: "The judge places his right hand near or on the phallus of a witness who is then required to tell the truth without bias." The Romans used the gesture of placing the forefinger on the testicles as an oath to tell the truth (Barakat, 1973, pp. 761-762). Lawick-Goodall noted that this gesture is referred to in the Bible, but that it has been translated as placing the hand under the thigh. Abraham, for example, told his old servant, "Put your hand under my thigh, and I will make you swear by the Lord, the God of heaven and of earth..." (Genesis 24:2-3). Goodland (p. 287) gives an example from Hoëvell, where showing the penis to an opponent in an argument lent force to the words.

In view of the great effect of the temporal, geographical, and cultural features of inherited behavior on the expressive language of today, it is difficult to imagine how one could think only in the "here and now" of human behavior and interrelationships--except in an extremely narrow sense of the word, and this might be almost useless.

For classical studies and those with historical depth, see Francis Hayes' bibliography, which has many more references which I did not repeat in this bibliography. For historical reconstruction see: Mary Austin; Blasis; Brilliant; Herbert Fischer; Henser; de Jorio; Jucker; Kapsalis; Mallery; Mawer; Moser.

Origin of Language

There was a time during the last century when scholars called a moratorium on reading papers which treated the origin of language. No new information was being added. Recent applications of scientific methodology to studies of animal communication and of paralanguage and kinesics have reopened these discussions and it is respectable once again to talk about the origin of language. Speculation that gesture language preceded vocal language is not a new idea. In 1956 Abercrombie pointed out that Henry Sweet, the great phonetician of the 19th century, discussed the

theory of the origin of language in terms of gestural language. Sweet believed that the hand gestures of primitive
people were accompanied by "sympathetic tongue-gestures,"
and when the cry for attention or other vocalization was
added, the hand gesture was eventually dropped as spoken
words developed (Abercrombie, 1956, pp. 82-83). During
the same period, Tylor maintained that there was an inter-
dependence of gesture and speech in the origin of language.

For references on the Origin of Language see:
Richard J. Andrew; Barrois; Karl Bühler; Chomsky, 1968;
Count; Edmund Critchley; Macdonald Critchley; Fouts; Hal-
dane; Francis Hayes, 1957; Hewes; Jane Hill; Hockett; Jó-
hannesson; Jousse; Susanne Langer; Lieberman; Lieberman
and Crelin; Lieberman, Crelin, and Klatt; Lucretius; Mc-
Bride; Mattingly; Paget; Paschall; Revesz; Harry Scott and
Carr; Swadesh; Thomas; Trojan; Tylor; Vendryes; S. L.
Washburn; Wescott.

K.   Theories and Models

"Where ignorance exists theories abound."
                        --Leucippus, ca. 460 B.C. [20]

All students of human communication, or of various
aspects of it, begin such studies somewhat naive about the
complexities and depth of the processes involved.   J. Robert
Oppenheimer made such an observation concerning studies in
science. He expressed the view that "units of analysis in
science usually turn out to be much larger and more inclu-
sive than one at first expects."[21] It may be that human behavior, with its element of "choice," is even more complicated than any of the sciences, and that actually we are at
the primitive stages of discovery at which our ancestor-
scientists were when they were dealing with earth, air, fire,
and water.

It must be acknowledged from the start that we do
not have an adequate theory of human communication to test
and validate. Perhaps the closest we can come to it is to
think in terms of a "general systems theory." We are dealing with many complex structures which correlate and inter-
relate to each other in a hierarchical setting (see Scheflen
[1966]). The medical field suggests an analogy that is useful
toward understanding what we have to deal with. The human

being is a single body made up of many different systems, none of which can function alone, but each of which can be studied separately--the respiratory system, circulatory, digestive, lymphatic, and all the rest. Each is dependent on the other; life depends on all of them. "Communication" is a complex organism, made up of interactional systems, thought processes, social systems, linguistic systems, as well as the nonverbal systems which are the concern of this book--that is, the paralanguage system, the kinesic, sensory, proxemic, chronemic, and tactile systems.

Several students of human behavior have suggested that a cross-disciplinary look at the theoretical approaches used in science might be useful in understanding communication. Specifically, a "unified field theory" has been suggested as an approach to human communication. Though physicists are still struggling to understand the four basic forces that hold the universe together, their present understanding has some appealing aspects for researchers who are trying to isolate the forces which attract and repel human beings. A colleague in the medical profession, Donald O. Walter, has put forth some thoughts on this in a brief communication, which I quote here in part:[22]

General relativity, in Einstein's hands, was a cosmological theory of the astronomical universe which attempted to bring together the not obviously amicable theories of gravitation and of other physical forces.

What does all this have to do with Kinesics et al. ? Well, the models used at various stages in the historical elaboration of this unified field theory include, for example, universes containing nothing but two attracting bodies and some signals between them; if you imagine two people and some signals between them as a microcosm corresponding to that macro-model, you will have some concept of the analogy I am urging. At the level at which I am able to grasp this model, the signals are somewhat discrete emanations from the two attracting bodies; but I have the impression that those who understand this model more deeply also understand how these signals could be evolved as an inseparable aspect of the bodies' dynamics. Therefore, I am urging us communications scientists to become students of at least the popularizations of

the advanced epistemologies and ontologies now being worked on by fundamental physicists. Maybe
then we can create a non-fragmented model of real
human communication.

Some attitudes that have been prevalent in the past
generation of research may actually have impeded progress
in human behavior studies. One such attitude is that only
theoretical research is respectable and anything that smacks
of applied work is to be disdained. I can only respond by
saying that we would not have landed on the moon if the
theories about space had not been tediously and rigorously
applied. An almost supernatural reverence for theory has
produced too much ersatz or pseudo-theoretical work, rather
than a substantial and reliable body of well-documented facts.
A resulting weakness is that some "scientific facts" are actually myths which continue to be perpetuated in the name of
science because these "conclusions" were "proved" by "scientific experiments" under "controlled conditions. " Human behavior, with all its variables, is not so easily measured;
but the present-day worship of instruments and technology
have superseded common sense, an open and creative mind,
and quiet reflective thinking.

Anecdotes have always been used as a heuristic device by scholars looking for truth, but sophisticated researchers today laugh anecdotes out the window. Curiously
enough, one person's "anecdote" is another person's "counter-
example. " Good scholars have always recognized the need
for fact-finding and applying the slowly unfolding theories.
Mandler and Kessen have noted the need for developing a vocabulary in using a scientific approach to human behavior
(p. 169):

> Dull on occasion, the refinement of the protocol
> language--the language of what you 'see'--is re-
> quisite to the nobler language of theory--the lan-
> guage of what you think about what you 'see. '

Classification is one step in theory-building which de-
mands a rigorous development and use of terminology and
categorization. Many researchers in nonverbal behavior
have dealt with this--some extensively and thoroughly. Interestingly enough, some classifications, of gestures for example, are quite similar in some respects. At times this
is because researchers have built upon the work of prede-
cessors, but at least some of these classifications have been

done independently. This says something good about the methodology used and the results put forth. Herein is a parallel to the linguistic situation, where two linguists, working separately in time and/or space, come up with the same, or almost the same phonological analysis of a language.

Classifications differ according to purposes. They may be based on functions--human goals and needs--or on meaning. They may be based on physical properties--the use of space, or the part of the body used. They may be based on spatio-temporal dimensions. The tools of analysis may influence the kinds of classifications. Videotape may bring about a classification different from sketches done in previous centuries. Basic to a good classification is an understanding of categories: categories of the physical universe, of language, or of human experience. See Bertalanffy for a discussion of categories.

Francis Bacon introduced the term "emblem" in his discussion of gestures and symbols and how they relate to communication (in Wallace, pp. 9, 158). In 1806 Austin made a lengthy study of rhetorical delivery, with attempts to classify. Since then, many classifications have been set forth. The following are a few examples: Birdwhistell; Carus; Efron; Ekman and Friesen (1969); Key (1970); Rabanales; Sanford (1942); Spiegel; Stokoe, Casterline, and Croneberg; West; Wiener, Devoe, Rubinow, and Geller.

The matter of interpretation continues to be of crucial importance in attributing meaning to nonverbal behavior. A clenched fist raised at a Chicago Board of Trade auction means something very different from a raised fist on a picket line. I have given several other examples and discussed the difficulties and complexities of interpreting facts that are observed (Key, 1975b, pp. 164ff.). The use of lie detectors and other recording techniques has highlighted the problems in making correct interpretations. We simply do not have a complete catalog of people's past experiences that now shape their responses to stimuli: the facts (hoolahoops), sorrows (assassination of a President), boredoms (having to wait for another plane), monotony (a factory job), joys (the return home of a soldier), sensations (the smell of lilac), and so forth.

The methodological use of "same" and "different, " which linguists have found to be indispensable, has entered into the analyses of other disciplines. Frijda has made

50 Nonverbal Communication

good use of the concept in his study of emotions: "One and
the same pattern of behavior may 'belong' to an array of different emotions; one and the 'same' emotion may manifest itself in several different ways" (Frijda, 1969, p. 3). These
concepts have to do with the notions "emic" and "etic"--con-
cepts which reduce the complexities and abstract the features
which are distinctive. Kenneth Pike has explicated these notions and, further, has extrapolated their use to larger units
of behavior. The New Yorker, though not academically oriented, seems to have grasped the concept in its succinct
comment on a psychologist's remarks:[23]

> "When a man wears red, it could be a sign he's
> restless. It may indicate his need for a change of
> job, a change of scene or a new romance."
> --Dr. Joyce Brothers

> Or he could be going deer hunting.

The order of events is of concern to all sciences;
linguists are especially conscious of linguistic order. Lashley pointed out the usefulness of studying mistakes and slips
in ordering. More recently Fromkin made a study of linguistic slips and lapses--mistakes in ordering of events, as
well as substitution items and so on. [24] This was useful for
linguistic theory. I propose that a study of slips and lapses
in nonverbal behavior would also be useful in understanding
human communication.

L. Universality and Future of Nonverbal Studies

What are the basic characteristics and properties of
the human being and what are the basic characteristics of
human communication and interaction? These questions are
still before us--to stimulate research and urge us out to
other frontiers. As is evident from the bibliography, most
of the studies have been done in Western societies by
Western investigators. We are on the fringes of hearing
from scholars in Asia and Africa, and from native American
Indians who have entered academia and are interested in
these questions. It seems patently obvious that all people
in all parts of the world have the same basic emotions and
needs, but until we hear from other voices, speaking in
their own terms, and in the language of academia, we cannot be sure even of the basic inventory of universal aspects
of communication.

In addition to cross-cultural studies, it is necessary to move forward in cross-disciplinary studies. All the perspectives from all the disciplines that study human behavior and human communication will be necessary in order to fit in all the parts, as a general systems theory would have it. Research strategies of many kinds are needed, as well as replication in different countries and in different milieu to confirm the hypotheses set forth.

The idea of a gesture sign language as a universal language has been advocated from time to time. Knowlson reviews the discussion of the seventeenth and eighteenth centuries. Two centuries later we still don't have such a convenience, though recently Margaret Mead again suggested that it might be a worthwhile goal to consider. In addition to that universal goal, there is the day-by-day need to communicate, and nonverbal studies have added to the understanding of human interaction. Indeed, the recent focus on nonverbal behavior has been overwhelming, which surely speaks to the real needs of human beings. The important advances in communication technology in the last centuries have bypassed paralanguage and kinesics--the most important means we have in relating to each other emotionally. The telegraph could not convey the warmth of tone of voice; a handwritten note could not communicate the twinkle in an eye; the telephone could not show a hand reaching out. Even the wheel took people away from their centers. The steamship and the airplane took people so far away from their intimate circles that they no longer had the daily reinforcement of relating to others and thereby maintaining their identity. They had to forget their former close relationships. Now, in isolation and alienation, people are turning back to "sensory awareness," "touching sessions" and "nonverbal techniques." All of the senses that nontechnological people use are again subjects of experimentation in technological societies--awkwardly and self-consciously perhaps, but honestly. People are attempting to close the space between themselves and others--to touch and feel again.

3.

REVIEW OF THE LITERATURE

All of us who have studied and written about nonverbal communication think that we ourselves have discovered it. A review of the literature shows that scholars have recognized aspects of nonverbal communicative behavior since the earliest writings of any kind. The bibliography contains references which are found, literally, in every part of the library which has to do with any kind of human behavior. Many of the earlier writings display a certain naïveté; recent studies indicate that the interaction between human beings is an immensely complex network of systems that we are only beginning to fathom. To get a feel of how distorted and limited our perception of the phenomena is, one can look at the early maps made before the discovery that the world is round, and contemplate the state of mind of the early explorers. If we are embarrassed now at our lack of theory and confused situation, we might remind ourselves that the precise maps of today would not have been made without the first rough steps taken in cartography.

Interestingly enough, the recent surge of discussions on nonverbal communication has not come predominantly from linguists who are concerned with language, but rather from other humanists and social scientists concerned with the communicative and interactional behavior between human beings; for example Allport and Vernon; Chapple; Krout; LaPiere and Farnsworth; Malinowski; and George Mead. Some linguists nevertheless have made strong statements recognizing the indissoluble relationship. In fact, the terms paralanguage and kinesics came out of conferences where linguists were very much in prominence. A few linguists are listed in the bibliography: Abercrombie; Bloomfield; Bloomfield and Newmark; Bolinger; Brooks; Chao; Crystal; Fónagy; Grimes; Hamp; A. A. Hill; Hockett; Hymes; Jakobson; Jespersen; Key; Krapp; Lado; Laver; Lloyd and Warfel;

Lyons; McDavid; McQuown; Martinet; Newman; Passy; Peng; Pike; Poyatos; Samarin; Sapir; Sebeok; H. L. Smith; Stokoe; Strang; Trager; Uldall; Vendryes; Whitehall; Zwicky, among others.

A surprising observation that has come to my attention during the years of collecting the bibliography is that many communicative acts and transactions are only reported by journalists in popular articles, or are only slightly referred to in serious academia. Examples include: railroad signals (Anon, "Cross country... "); auctions (Anon, "Ear-wiggling... "); radio signals (Anon, "Strange radio sign... "); television signals (Anon, "Video... "); audience behavior (Cobb); secret signals in prison (Harold Fischer); animal mimicry and noises (Koht; Perrin); sneeze mimicry (Rice).

For bibliographies and reviews of the literature on specific topics see: T. G. Andrews (research equipment); Gilbert Austin; Beaumont (dance); William Blake; Bruneau (silence); Ciolek; Cratty (physical education); Crystal (paralanguage); Martha Davis; Eco, 1974; Efron; Ekman (facial expression); Eschbach; Sandor Feldman; Foley (facial expression); Harrison, Cohen, Crouch, Genova, and Steinberg; Francis Hayes (gestures); Hinde; Huber (facial expression); Key (1975); Landis (facial expression); Mahl and Schulze (psychological research); Mallery (1879-80); Millum; Ostwald (1963); Pike (1943, 1945, 1960); Pittinger; Pollnow; Sarles; Schmidt; Sebeok, Hayes, and Bateson; Stokoe (deaf sign language); Wespi. For a bibliography of Notation Systems, see the next chapter.

A chronological survey of the writings on aspects of nonverbal communication starts with classical writings in the Western world and ancient studies of India. See Francis Hayes' bibliography on gestures for other references on Classical Gestures. See also: John Allen; Anthriotis; Apuleius; Gilbert Austin; Mary Austin; Bede; Brilliant; Macdonald Critchley; Darwin; Elworthy; Giner de los Rios; Grajew; Hoppe; H. P. Jones; Jorio; Jucker; Lasaulx; Lucretius; Lutz; Mallery (1879-80); Montaigne; Neumann; Oesterley; Ovid; Penzer; Fred Peterson; Praetorius; Ptolomey; Quintilian; Seneca; Sittl; Sorell; Wandruszka. For studies of ancient India see: Bharata Muni; Naidu; Nadikesvara.

After the classical period the first bibliographical references are dated soon after the printing press was invented. Montenovesi wrote on the language of the deaf in

1472. Books on manners and courtly behavior printed in the
next century discuss body movement (Casa; Castiglione, for
example). Sign language of religious orders was also documented in the sixteenth century (Rossellius), as well as physiognomy (Porta) and dance (Arbeau; see Notation Systems for
other early references on dance). Many references from the
seventeenth century indicate scholarly interest in gesture
(chirologia) and facial expression: Amman; Anon, Digiti
Lingua; Arnason; Francis Bacon; Bartoli; Bonet; Bonifacio;
Boyvin; Bulwer; Dalgarno; Descartes; Hartmann; Holder;
Kortholt; La Fin; Le Brun; Locke; Praetorius; Testelin;
Thomasius; Wilkins; Zeidler.   See Francis Hayes for other
early references.

The Fine Arts are generously represented in the
eighteenth century. Additional studies on facial expression
and religious gestures were produced: Anon, Kurze Abhandlung...; Beauchamp; Boguslawski; Callotto; Cavendish; Eder;
J. J. Engel; Feüillet; Gallini; Groschuf; Hemsterhuis; Herrgot; Kirchner; Lavater; Leibnitz; L'Epée; Lichtenberg; Monde;
Paschius; Pécourt; Requeno y Vives; Shaftesbury; Sheridan;
Walker; Weaver.

American Indian sign language was first documented
in 1801 (Dunbar). The nineteenth century produced several
extensive studies from the point of view of oratory (Gilbert
Austin; Barber; Delsarte; Knowles, etc.). Scientific studies
on facial expression started with Charles Bell in 1806. Major anthropological and cross-cultural studies were published
(Darwin; Tylor).

4.

NOTATION SYSTEMS

The difficulties of describing paralanguage and body movement are a commonplace. The task of devising notation systems for these human behaviors defies even the most ingenious person and groups of persons. Nevertheless there have been some valiant attempts, and notation systems are being refined and improved upon by dedicated researchers. The notation systems referred to in this chapter and listed in the bibliography come from several disciplines: dance, drama, oratory, anthropology, psychology, linguistics, language teaching, medicine, psychiatry, and studies of the deaf. In these various systems, choices were made depending upon the needs; thus, dance notation systems highlight the feet, sign language systems highlight the hands, intonation systems highlight the pitch of vocalizations. Systems overlap in their needs; for example, dance systems from India take account of the hands as in hand gesture systems, because the hands are important in dancing in India. Facial expression is hardly noted in Western dance notation systems, but is the focus in studies of emotion.

No system of notation for either paralinguistic or kinesic acts is adequate in itself to enable the reader to reproduce the acts as the writer desired or envisioned them. For example, dancers have been given a script ahead of time to study, and each dancer came up with a slightly different dance. It should be noted that the same can be said for orchestral notations. Instructions for paralanguage and kinesics seem incredibly difficult to formulate. Written instructions without accompanying demonstration seem impossible. Try writing instructions on how to ride a bicycle or how to whistle.

In discussing notation systems one must be aware of the difference between recording and analyzing behavior. Gypsy music in its pristine state had no notation system.

However, it could have been recorded, either by a tape recorder or by pencil and paper using a musical staff. Analyzing it is another step, but not altogether separable from
the process of transcribing with pencil and paper. This has
been illustrated in language in the invention of alphabets.
Languages were recorded on paper, or papyrus, long before
linguistic theory explicated the phonological systems underlying the chosen alphabets; nevertheless the alphabets are
phonemic, in general. Human beings have this ability to
analyze along with describing--is it an innate quality? In
very keen observation one notes infinite variety in paralinguistic and kinesic acts--the better the training, the more
varieties one is able to detect, audibly or visually. The
use of instruments augments the observations of varieties
even more. Voiceprints, spectrograms and film provide
enormous amounts of information. For some purposes this
may be desirable, but for our purposes in understanding
communicative behavior, the fine detail gives too much information. Fine differences should be filtered out so that
manageable kinds of data are available to analyze. Thus,
researchers working with film make graphs of every tenth
frame, or in some other way choose peaks of movement to
work with. Phoneticians deal with directions of pitch, or
beginnings and endings, rather than with all degrees of pitch
in the utterance.

        The choice of how much detail to work with moves
into the area of emic and etic behavior. See Pike (1966)
for clarification of these views which he discussed in the
1950s. To understand these concepts, one has to think
cross-culturally and grasp the meaning of human events from
the points of view of an outsider and an insider. A useful
notation system will reflect the emic point of view of an insider of the system. It is also useful to think of the relationship of morphemes (meaningful units) and notational systems. It is this relationship that makes the spelling system
of English an unusually good and workable system. It is
very useful to have morphemes recorded in a like matter,
with less regard for how they sound. For example, while
reading, meaning is enhanced when the morpheme "flame"
is spelled the same in "inflamation" and "inflammable,"
even though the morpheme is pronounced in three different
ways. Likewise, a notation system that captures essential
meanings is eminently more useful than one that flounders
in detail. Nevertheless, scholars have made significantly
more progress in devising notation systems for language
(alphabets) and for dance (see those following) than they have

for paralinguistic and kinesic behavior beyond language and beyond the formalized movement of dance. For more pene- trating discussions of notation systems for gesture communi- cation see Voegelin, and West, who show important insights from linguistics.

The study and invention of notation systems is a field in itself, and since it involves expertise in both the ability to make representations (devising alphabets, for example), and thorough knowledge of the communicative behavior to be represented (for example, sign language, dance, or intona- tion), it requires the qualifications of an expert. Criticisms have been made of elaborate systems of notation such as Birdwhistell's and Labanotation, in that they are said to be too difficult to learn or that it takes a long time to learn them. These criticisms seem shallow; it also takes a long time and is difficult to become a doctor, or a dancer, or a physicist.

A.   Paralinguistic Notation

The first conscious effort to devise a system of nota- tion for paralanguage was worked out during the 1950s by George L. Trager, Henry Lee Smith, Jr. , Norman A. McQuown, and Ray L. Birdwhistell, along with Gregory Bateson, Henry W. Brosin, and Charles F. Hockett at the Center for Advanced Study in the Behavioral Sciences (Tra- ger, 1958, p. 275). Trager summarized the work and out- lined paralinguistic features such as voice set, voice quali- ties, and vocalizations, which comprise vocal characterizers, vocal qualifiers, and vocal segregates. Two studies-- McQuown (1957); and Pittenger, Hockett, and Danehy (1960) --applied this and modified notations to actual data. These transcriptions deal with such features as hesitation, rasp, whine, click, inspirated noise, silence, throaty sigh, gasp, pharyngeal constriction, buzz, and breaking.

Sometime earlier Pike had recognized paralinguistic effects in language and devised a simple notation for these "qualitative gradations, " which he noted were "socially sig- nificant. " In his work on the intonation of American English he listed the following symbolism for these features (1945, p. 101):

Personal Characteristics:

Y^{1-100} Age, in years

X^{M-F} Sex

Basic Type of Utterance

M, S, W, F   Song, Speech aloud, Whisper, Falsetto

Articulatory Characteristics

V^{1-5} Vocal cords, tense to lax

Th^{1-5} Throat, closed to open

B^{1-5} Breath, breathy to clear

L^{1-5} Lips, rounded to spread

T^{1-5} Tongue position, front to back

A^{1-5} Articulation, precise to lax

Pitch, Rate, Strength

K^{1-5} Key, generally high to generally low

P^{1-5} Pitch Gap or Interval (between the four contrastive levels of intonation contours), wide to narrow

R^{1-5} Rate, fast to slow

St^{1-5} Strength, loud to quiet

I^{1-5} Intensity, strong to weak

Crystal and Quirk treated voice qualities and qualifications with a few suggestions for notation. Subsequently Crystal discussed paralinguistic features in an encyclopedic study (with an impressive bibliography) and dealt with notation systems under "transcriptions." Abercrombie (1967) outlined the history of notation systems, including phonetic and intonational systems.

Though many linguists have been sensitive to voice qualities, intonation features (pitch, stress, and length) have been dealt with more extensively by linguists, since these features seem more closely allied to linguistic structures. Bolinger, for example, has made extensive contributions to

the understanding of paralinguistic features of meaning.   The
following illustrates the notation system he uses to show
three different meanings to the phrase, "Don't be angry"
(Bolinger, 1972, p. 12):

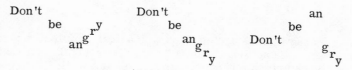

Other examples of intonation notations derived from
major studies in suprasegmentals are shown below.   For
studies on intonation see: Bolinger; Croft; Crystal; Fonagy
and Magdics; Halliday; Hill; Lefevre; Lieberman; Pike; Prator; Schubiger; Tompa; Trager and Smith.

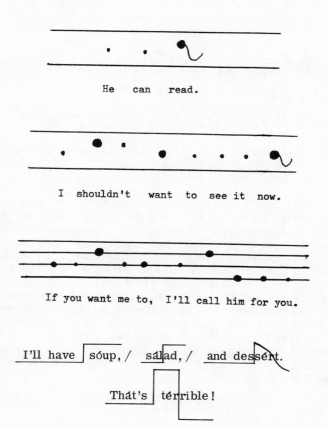

[2]He went to the [3-1] store #

[2]Will he [3]go ? ||

Fónagy and Magdics used a musical notation, and contrasted each "emotional pattern" with the neutral forms of the sentence intonation under discussion (p. 294):

> Tenderness is also expressed on a higher pitch
> level. The level does not fluctuate in this case.
> The stressed syllable keeps the phrase in a
> 'legato-arc,' enclosing it so to speak; the melody
> of the phrase is very slightly descending and ends
> far above the basic level. Sentences consisting of
> more phrases show a gentle undulation of the pitch-
> level. The tempo is restrained, the loudness

> reduced. The articulation is extremely soft, often
> labialized and a little nasal. The voice sounds
> 'full.'

Pike has compared four languages in the sketches following (Pike, 1957, p. 32). Figure 1 represents the dynamics of Arabela (Zaparoan) with two contrastive patterns. Figure 2 represents Culina (Arawakan) with a syllable-timed rhythm. Figure 3 is also Culina, this time from a story-telling text, where a final syllable of some of the utterances ends in a sudden, sharp, loud crescendo, breaking away with great suddenness into a very sharp, rapid decrescendo. Figure 4 represents Aguaruna (Jivaroan) in a not unusual text. Figure 5 is a special antiphonal greeting pattern. It may be carried on for an hour or two with a regular, sharp rhythmic beat. Figure 6 is a singing or chanting pattern of Aguaruna witch doctors. Figure 7 illustrates three word patterns of Campa (Arawakan).

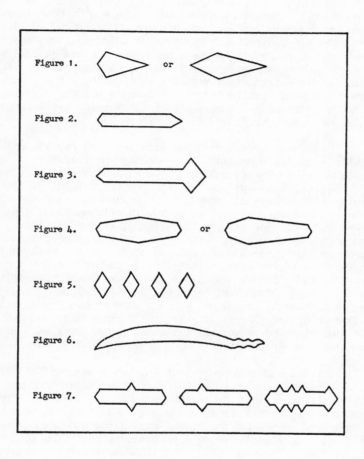

Figure 1.   or

Figure 2.

Figure 3.

Figure 4.   or

Figure 5.

Figure 6.

Figure 7.

B.   Kinesic Notation

Birdwhistell, of course, is a classic study which provides a notation system for body movement.   As with the
Trager study on paralanguage, I will not quote extensively
from Birdwhistell's study because I consider it to be of such
major importance that a serious student of nonverbal communication will go directly to these studies.   Instead I refer in
this volume to complementary or additional contributions.

Notation systems necessarily are two-dimensional and
the problems inherent in representing more than two dimensions are legion.   Spatial and temporal characteristics of
movement are difficult to represent on paper and in many
respects are analogous to the suprasegmental and qualitative
features of vocalizations.   Previously I have noted that the
intonational components of paralanguage (pitch, stress, and
length) are also seen in body movement in the way of range
or extent of movement, intensity of the action, and duration
of the movement (Key, 1975b, p. 77).

Recording body movement also involves rhythm and
regularity of the movement; phrasing (or the hierarchies) of
the units of movement; quality of movement, the interactional responses, voluntary and involuntary movement, and the
floor pattern of the movement of the participant(s).   Notation
systems must also be able to deal with relationships of parts
of the body--to self and to others, such as hand to arm,
hand to forehead, kicking actions, as well as direction of the
movement, or direction of eyes during the movement.   In
dance, do the eyes look to the self, or to the partner, or to
the audience?   Scholars in kinesiology use the terms: flex-
ion, extension, abduction, adduction, and rotation.   Some
studies have been concerned with measuring movement, such
as Bouissac, and Oseretzky.   Others have been concerned
with analyzing the movement for medical purposes, and have
done intricate graphing (Dierssen, Lorenc, and Spitaleri).

Analysis of movement and a notation system for communicative behavior was dealt with in a scientific way by
Gilbert Austin in 1806.   He believed that his work was the
first to describe gesture by symbol (p. iii).   His comprehensive study provided the basis, during the following century, for countless statements on gestural and vocal behavior, particularly in oratory.   His illustrations begin with
foot patterns and he noted weight distribution by degrees of
shading (Plate 1).

Austin's next Plate shows the human figure in an
imaginary circle, showing degrees of movement of the arm
around the body.   Note that he also shows the body from a
bird's eye view--a perspective not often used.

Austin (p. 366) summarized his letter abbreviations
in the chart on the following page.   These abbreviations and
modified forms were to show up again and again in the notation systems of oratorical behavior.

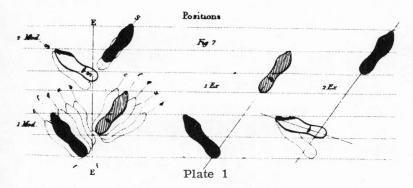

Plate 1

Alphabetical Arrangement of Symbolic Letters.

		Above the Line. Hands, Arms, Body and Head.						Below the Line Feet.		
	Small Letters relating to the Hand and Arm.				Capital B and double small Letters. Both Arms and both Hands.	Capitals for particular Parts.	Capitals for Head and Eyes.	Small Letters Steps.	Capitals Positions.	Capitals and small; significant Gestures.
	1. Hand.	2. Elevation of the Arm.	3. Transverse Position of the Arm.	4 and 5. Motion and Force.						
A	- - -	- - -	- - -	ascending alternate	applied	- - -	⟨ assenting ⟨ averted	advance	- - -	appealing attention admiration aversion
B	backwards	- - -	backwards	backwards beckoning	both	breast	- - -	- - -	both	
C	clinched	- - -	across	collecting contracted clinching	crossed clasped	Chin	- - -	cross	- - -	commanding
D	- - -	downwards	- - -	descending	- - -	- - -	⟨ down- wards ⟨ denying	- - -	- - -	deprecation declaration
E	- - -	elevated	- - -	- - -	encumbered	Eyes	erect	- - -	- - -	encourage- ment.
F	forwards	- - -	forwards	forwards flourish	folded	Forehead	Forward	- - -	front	fear
G	grasping	- - -	- - -	grasping	- - -	- - -	- - -	- - -	- - -	Grief
H	holding	horizontal	- - -	- - -	- - -	- - -	- - -	- - -	- - -	Horror
I	index	- - -	- - -	inwards	inclosed	- - -	inclined	- - -	- - -	
K	- - -	- - -	- - -	- - -	a kimbo	- - -	- - -	- - -	kneeling	⟨ Lamenta- ⟨ tion ⟨ Listening
L	collected	- - -	- - -	left	- - -	Lips	- - -	- - -	left	
M	thumb	- - -	- - -	moderate						
N	natural inwards	- - -	- - -	noting	enumerating	Nose				
O	outwards	- - -	- - -	outwards						
P	prone	- - -	- - -	⟨ pushing ⟨ pressing	- - -		- - -	- - -	- - -	Pride
Q	- - -	- - -	oblique	- - -	- - -		- - -	- - -	oblique	
R	- - -	Rest	- - -	⟨ right re- ⟨ coiling re- ⟨ pressing ⟨ rejecting	reposed	- - -	round	retire	right	
S	supine	- - -	- - -	⟨ sweep ⟨ springing, ⟨ striking ⟨ shaking	- - -		⟨ shaking ⟨ aside	⟨ start ⟨ stamp ⟨ shock	side	shame
T	- - -	- - -	- - -	⟨ touching ⟨ throwing	- - -		Tossing	traverse	- - -	threatning
U	- - -	- - -	- - -	- - -	- - -		Upwards	- - -	- - -	
V	Vertical	- - -	- - -	revolving	- - -		Vacancy	- - -	- - -	Veneration
W	hollow	- - -	- - -	waving	wringing					
X	extended	- - -	extended	extreme						
Z	- - -	Zenith								

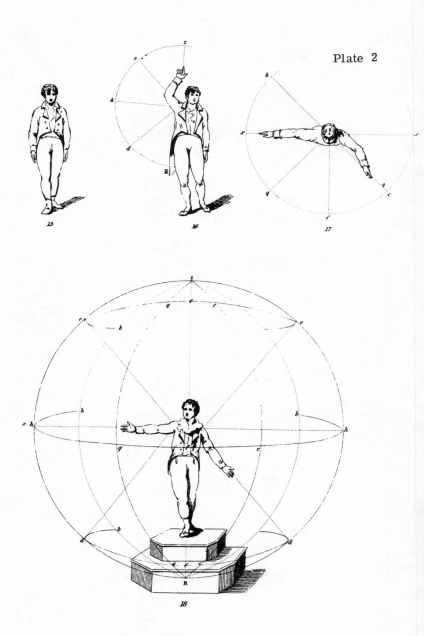

Plate 2

Symbols for Noting the Force and Rapidity or Interruption of the Voice in Delivery.

The symbols are to be marked in the margin near the commencement of the passage which they are to influence.

	Symbols.
Piano . - - . - .	☰
Uniform loudness, or forte - - -	⋀⋀
Crescendo (as in music) - - -	⟨
Diminuendo (as in music) - - -	⟩
Rapid - . - - - -	○ ○ ○
Slow - - - - - -	− − −
Suspension of the voice, the break or dash after a word - - - }	- —
Long pause, or new paragraph - - -	◖
Whisper or monotone - - - .	___

Compound Symbols.

Piano and slow - - - - -	☰
Piano and quick - - - - -	○ ○ ○
Loud and slow - - - - -	⋀⋀
Loud and quick - - - - -	○ ○ ○ ⋀⋀
Monotonous or whisper slow - - -	≡≡
Monotone or whisper quick - - -	○ ○ ○

Delsarte was another great influence during the 19th century. Shawn; Warman; and John Zorn give sketches and diagrams of Delsarte's system of analysis. For other discussions of his method see: Delaumosne; Douailler; LeMee; Parrish; and Stebbins. Notation of hand gestures by sketches is of very long standing. Sketches of hand gestures indicating counting and multiplying by the fingers occurred in a document by Luca Pacioli in 1494. Dantzig (p. 2) shows illustrations from a manual published in 1520.

Notations of deaf sign language have also made use of sketches. Bonet, in 1620, published an alphabet for the deaf, with sketches of the hand. More recently David Watson used sketches in his topical dictionary of deaf sign language. He included facial expressions to reinforce meaning. Arrows and dotted lines indicate direction and movement of the hands. For clarity, he adopted a bird's eye view perspective (pp. 4, 51, 84):

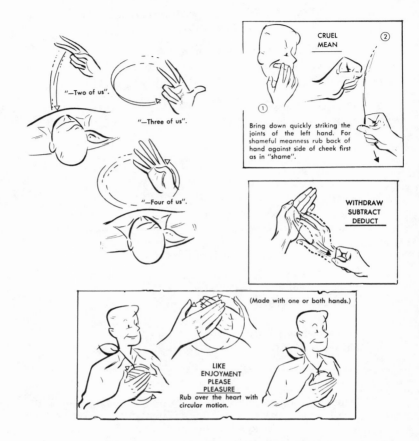

Indian sign language has been successfully notated by sketches of hand gestures (see references under Indian and other sign languages from Australia, for example). Lexical gestures from other cultures and languages, for example Spanish and Italian, have been annotated with sketches (De-Jorio; Efron; Jerald Green; Kany; Saitz and Cervenka). These have been useful in teaching languages. The following sketches are from Jerald Green (pp. 47, 59) and Kany (p. 207):

COLLISION AND CONFRONTATION   COLLISION AND CONFRONTATION

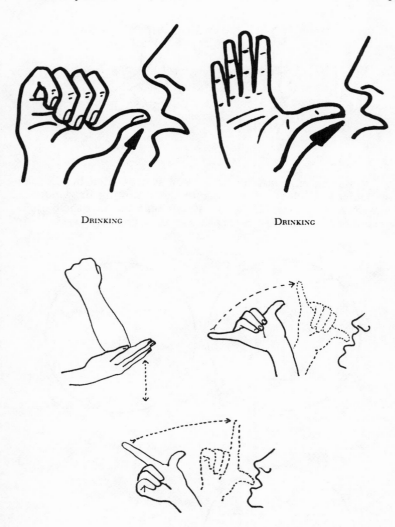

DRINKING   DRINKING

Posture and facial expression have also been annotated by sketches.   Postures of standing and bent knee positions were sketched in Hewes' analysis of postural behavior.
Salient examples of these were published in his 1955 and
1957 articles, which should be studied for the various types.
The following are from his field notes (by correspondence):

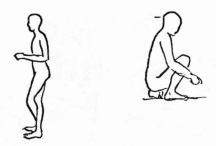

Facial expressions have been represented by the barest number of clues, for example the following drawings from Francis Irwin (1932, p. 4), to test the threshold for perception in smiling, neutral, and frowning.

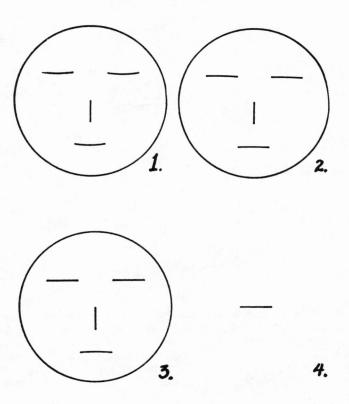

Gibson and Pick (1963, p. 388) used the following scheme to study direction of gaze:

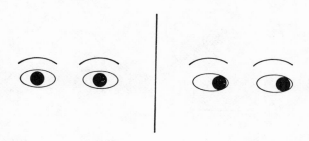

Schematic Centering or Off-Centering of the Pupil
in the Sclera as the Stimulus for the Impression of Being
or Not Being Looked At

More elaborate sketches and photographs were used to test Piderit's theories, put forth in 1867, suggesting models to test facial expression. The following are from Boring and Titchener, but see also Frois-Wittmann; Guilford and Wilke; Hulin and Katz; and Landis.

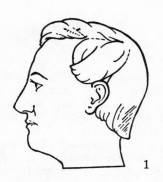
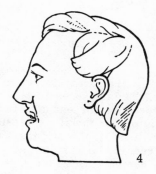

Passive   Very displeased

7

Quizzical

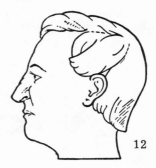

12

Unpleasant olfactory attention

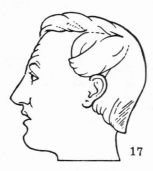

17

Bewildered

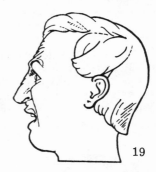

19

Horrified

Margaret Morris (p. 95) suggests that in dance notation, facial expressions should be noted when they are
needed, as for example in comic dance.   Another type of
notation for facial expression was devised by Washburn in
her study of the smiling and laughing of infants.   In order
to record the various movements, a chart which listed all
the components of the face was devised to check while observing.   Brannigan and Humphries abstracted three smiles
in their research: the simple, the upper, and the broad
smile (1969, p. 406):

Simple smile

Upper smile

Broad smile

C. Dance Notation Systems

Dance notation systems have been variously known as:
dance-script, chorography, choreography, choregraphy,
choroscript, kinetography, and kineseography. For references other than those I refer to, see the bibliographies of
Beaumont; M. Davis; and Kamin. Older systems which have
been much discussed in dance literature are: Arbeau; Beauchamp; Feüillet; Pécourt; Playford; Saint-León; Stepanov;
Toulouze; and F. A. Zorn. Some dance notation systems
are relatively unknown, since they were theses which remain
unpublished, for example, Craighead; and Dyke. Others,
such as Bjørn; Cross; Letitia Jay; Kool; Nikolais (in Nadel
and Nadel, pp. 145-150); Priest; and Sutton are simply not
well-known. I include an illustration of Jay's stick man notation system below in the section on "Kinds of Notation Systems"; Sorell (p. 289) also offers an example of her system.
Canna and Loring (see Maynard for Loring's Kineseography,
pp. 296-304); Conté (in Bouissac); McCraw; and Morris are
often referred to, but these works are difficult to obtain.
Morris provides notations for breathing (p. 80); touching
(p. 88); and facial expressions (pp. 95-97)--aspects not often

taken into account in dance notation.   Kurath should be recognized for her contributions to ethnomusicology and ethnic
dance.   Though the Eshkol and Wachmann system is intended
for movement notation, not solely for dance notation, it should
be mentioned here as an important contribution to dance,
since it was also applied to ballet.   See the M. Davis bibliography for further comments on Eshkol and Wachmann notation.

        The Benesh notation system is used at the Royal Bal-
let.   Causley gives several illustrations of its application to
other movement in gymnastics and athletics.   For other explanations and applications of the Benesh system, see: Anon,
"Notation, choreology... "; Benesh; Causley; Curl; Fernau
Hall; Morrice; Mossford; Nadel and Nadel.

        Curl recently made a comparative study of Benesh no-
tation and Laban notation (Labanotation or Kinetography).
His inquiry consisted of a questionnaire with twenty-four
questions which were answered by Ann Hutchinson for Labanotation and Rudolf Benesh for his own system.

        Laban notation is the basis of "effort notation" pre-
sented by Bartenieff (in Nadel and Nadel); and Bartenieff and
Davis.   Other references for Labanotation are: Curl; Dell;
Hutchinson; Knust; Kurath (1960); Laban; Lamb; Nadel and
Nadel; North; Preston; Preston-Dunlop; Redfern; Thornton;
and Topaz.

        D.   Annotating Both Paralanguage and Kinesics

        Few of the notation systems used for research pro-
vide a means of recording both paralinguistic and kinesic behaviors.   Gilbert Austin's study is noteworthy again for this
reason; he treated both body movement and vocalizations in
his notation.   The reasons for not dealing with both systems
are apparent.   One is that the focus may preclude one or
the other; for example, dance notation seldom needs to note
vocalizations; deaf sign language needn't be concerned with
paralanguage.   Another is that recording both kinds of behavior is a complex procedure, and most of the studies concern themselves with a limited part of communicative behavior.

        Kendon made observations on both vocalizations and
body movement (1967, p. 32):

	NL SPEECH	EYES	BROWS	MOUTH	HEAD	GAZE	GAZE	HEAD	MOUTH	BROWS	EYES	JH SPEECH
352	and um	O	⊓r	O	□			□◄T	–	W	≍	
3	sometimes	O	⊓r	O	□◄	■		○►	–	W	⤫	
4	of course it's	≍	⊓r	O	□◄⊥			○►T	⸴	⊓r	⤫	
355	only one of	≍	m	O	□◄⊥			□►	=	⊓r	O	
6	parents in which	≍	m	O	□ ⊥			□►	=	W	⤫	
7	case you can	≍	m	O	□◄⊥	■		□►	=	W	⤫	
8	take it	≍	⊓r	O	□◄			□►	=	W	⤫	
9	away and	O	⊓r	O	□►			□►	=	W	O	
360		O	⊓r	O	□►			□►	=	W	O	
1	let the	O	⊓r	O	□►			□►	=	W	⤫	
2	other one feed them	≍	⊓r	O	□ ⊥			□►	=	W	≍	
3		O	⊓r	O	□►			□►T	=	W	≍	
4	itself	O	⊓r	O	□			□►T	=	W	≍	
5		O	⊓r	–	□			□T	◎	W	≍	
6		O	⊓r	–	□			□T►	◎	W	≍	some breed-
7		O	⊓r	–	□			○►T	◎	⊓r	≍	ers
8		O	⊓r	–	□			○►T	◎	⊓r	≍	um
9		O	⊓r	–	□			○ T	◎	⊓r	≍	pair
370		O	⊓r	–	□			○ T	⊖	m	≍	with
1		O	⊓r	–	□			○ T	⊖	m	≍	infer-
2		O	⊓r	–	□			○ T	⊖	m	≍	ior
3		O	⊓r	–	□			○ ◄T	⊖	m	≍	birds for
4		O	⊓r	–	□		■	□ ◄	⊖	m	O	this purp-
5		O	⊓r	–	□			□ ◄T	=	m	≍	ose
6		O	⊓r	–	□			□ ◄T	–	⊓r	O	
7		O	⊓r	–	□		■	□ ◄T	⊖	⊓r	⤫	em I mean
8		O	⊓r	–	□			□► T	⊖	W	≍	
9		O	⊓r	–	□			□► T	⊖	W	≍	
380		O	⊓r	–	□			□►	⊘	W	≍	those that don't

Key:
- **Head**: □ Head erect, face pointing forward; -○ Head turned left; ○- Head turned right; ◄ Head tilted left; ► Head tilted right; ⊥ Head tilted back; T Head tilted forward
- **Brows**: ⊓r Normal; m Raised brows; W Puckered or "frowning" brows
- **Mouth**: – Closed, lips relaxed; ⊖ Lips relaxed, mouth open; ◎ Lips pouting; = Lips drawn tight at corners; ⊘ Lips pressed forward, "pursed"
- **Eyes**: O Fully open; ⤫ Narrowed eyes; ≍ Closed eyes
- **Gaze**: ■ p looking at q

Partial extract from the film-transcript showing a long utterance exchange.

Condon also treated speech and movement in his studies with other colleagues. Condon and Ogston (1966, p. 338) concluded that their intensive analysis "revealed harmonious or synchronous organizations of change between body motion and speech in <u>both</u> intra-individual and interactional behavior. Thus the body <u>of</u> the speaker dances in time with his speech. Further, the body of the listener dances in rhythm with that of the speaker!" The following illustrates their recording (p. 340):

Subject B saying "I" while Subject A listens

E.   Annotating Interactional, Tactile,
     and Proxemic Behavior

Spiegel devised a simple notation to record the position of the participants in the interaction (1967, pp. 299-300):

1.   [ ]   Maximum confrontation and interpersonal ex-
           change, for affectionate, aggressive, or
           more neutral goals.

2. [[A queue or a chase.

3.] [Two angry people conspicuously not speaking to each other, or two collaborators searching the horizons for a missing friend or approaching enemy.

Also: [[⌐   [⌐⌐   [↘
        [↘]

See Jourard for diagrams to study <u>tactile behavior</u>. William Austin devised the following system for recording tactile behavior, which he called a <u>haptic notation</u> (1972, pp. 151-152):

> The following is a sample attempt at a haptic notation. The left side of the arrow is the source of haptic signaling; on the right is the receptor. The physical areas of both are then indicated. Lines arranged vertically indicate degree of pressure with − for slight, = for medium, and ≡ for heavy. The number of lines arranged horizontally gives the number of repetitions.

p = = > 1 sh	two rather heavy pats by the palm on the left shoulder
p − > r k	one light touch of the palm on the right knee (left versus right is probably nonemic or nonsignificant)
f ≡ > j	a punch in the jaw
fn − > lo a	a fingertip touch on the lower arm (a "woman's touch")
el − − > el	two slight nudges of one elbow against someone else's
ft − > ft	a foot nudge (generally under the table—"discontinue that line of talk" or "watch the card you're about to play" or the like)
kn = > st	a fairly heavy knuckle touch (mock fist) in the stomach ("you old so-and-so")
k − > k	a knee nudge, for people sitting side by side
pp = > ha	both palms covering another's hand with some pressure
kn − − − > up 1 a	repeated light taps of the knuckle on the upper left arm; a warning
lp − > ck	a light kiss on the cheek

Proxemics is the term devised by Edward Hall to refer to spatial behaviors. He has published a comprehensive
guide to proxemic research and anyone concerned with proxemic behavior will want to go directly to the original (Hall,
1963, 1974), so I will not duplicate it here. Hall treats
other behaviors that have to do with distance and space, for
example, body orientation, change of distance, gestures, eye
behavior, auditory, olfaction, thermal, and touching behaviors.

F.   Kinds of Notation Systems and Recording Devices

Notation systems comprise symbols, sketches, instru-
ment/equipment recording, and combinations of these.   Symbol notation may be abstract and arbitrarily chosen.   A good
example of this is shown in Stokoe's symbols for writing the
signs of the American Sign Language for the deaf (Stokoe,
Casterline, and Croneberg, 1965, pp. x-xii, 28).   A sample
from the dictionary follows their symbols.   They also include photographs in their dictionary to illustrate their entries.

**Table of symbols used for writing the signs of the
American sign language**

Tab symbols

1. Ø   zero, the neutral place where the hands move, in contrast
   with all places below
2. ◠   face or whole head
3. ⌒   forehead or brow, upper face
4. ⊔   mid-face, the eye and nose region
5. ∪   chin, lower face
6.)   cheek, temple, ear, side-face
7. π   neck
8. []   trunk, body from shoulders to hips
9. \   upper arm
10. /   elbow, forearm
11. α   wrist, arm in supinated position (on its back)
12. D   wrist, arm in pronated position (face down)

Dez symbols, some also used as tab

13. A compact hand, fist; may be like 'a', 's', or 't' of manual
     alphabet

14. B flat hand

15. 5 spread hand; fingers and thumb spread like '5' of manual
     numeration

16. C curved hand; may be like 'c' or more open

17. E contracted hand; like 'e' or more clawlike

18. F "three-ring" hand; from spread hand, thumb and index
     finger touch or cross

19. G index hand; like 'g' or sometimes like 'd'; index finger
     points from fist

20. H index and second finger, side by side, extended

21. I "pinkie" hand; little finger extended from compact hand

22. K like G except that thumb touches middle phalanx of
     second finger; like 'k' and 'p' of manual alphabet

23. L angle hand; thumb, index finger in right angle, other
     fingers usually bent into palm

24. 3 "cock" hand; thumb and first two fingers spread, like
     '3' of manual numeration

25. O tapered hand; fingers curved and squeezed together over
     thumb; may be like 'o' of manual alphabet

26. R "warding off" hand; second finger crossed over index
     finger, like 'r' of manual alphabet

27. V "victory" hand; index and second fingers extended and
     spread apart

28. W three-finger hand; thumb and little finger touch, others
     extended spread

29. X hook hand; index finger bent in hook from fist, thumb tip
     may touch fingertip

30. Y "horns" hand; thumb and little finger spread out extended
     from fist; or index finger and little finger extended,
     parallel

31. 8 (allocheric variant of Y); second finger bent in from
     spread hand, thumb may touch fingertip

Sig symbols

32. ^ upward movement
33. ˅ downward movement   } vertical action
34. ᴎ up-and-down movement   ⌡

35. `>`   rightward movement }
36. `<`   leftward movement   } sideways action
37. `ᶻ`   side to side movement }

38. `T`   movement toward signer   }
39. `⊥`   movement away from signer } horizontal action
40. `ᴵ`   to-and-fro movement   }

41. `ɑ`   supinating rotation (palm up)   }
42. `ᴅ`   pronating rotation (palm down) } rotary action
43. `ω`   twisting movement   }

44. `ŋ`   nodding or bending action
45. `▢`   opening action (final dez configuration shown in brackets)
46. `⁑`   closing action (final dez configuration shown in brackets)
47. `ᴧ`   wiggling action of fingers
48. `ⓐ`   circular action

49. `ᵡ`   convergent action, approach }
50. `ˣ`   contactual action, touch   }
51. `ᴵ`   linking action, grasp   }
52. `✦`   crossing action   } interaction
53. `⊙`   entering action   }
54. `⁺`   divergent action, separate   }
55. `⟨⟩` interchanging action

$BB^\perp$
N *street, way, method.* 'Street' will have a straight outward sig, but 'road' or 'path', especially in poetic context, will call for the hands, parallel, to follow a winding course.

$B_\wedge B_\wedge{}^\perp$
N *hall, corridor.*

$\overset{...}{B}_{>}\overset{...}{B}_{<}{}^\perp$
v *go ahead; get along; make out.*

$B_< B_>{}^{\perp\,..}$
v *encourage.*

$B_\perp B_\perp{}^\perp$
(imit., variants below) v *push.*
— `^` v *push up* (heel of palms prominent).
— `>` v *push aside, push out of the way.*
— `⊥` v *shove.*

——˅ ᵥ *depress, push down* (palms down).

√B⊥√B⊥ ⁱ

(dez may be spread in 5-allocher; sig may be repeated, or for emphasis may be inward then outward in sharp, checked motions--
ᵀⁱ) ₓ *wonderful.*

B⊥B⊥ ⊥···

ᵥ *calm down, take it easy.* As much a gesture in standard
American kinesics as a sign.

BᴵᴵB ⊥   BᴵᴵC ⊥

(right hand grasps tips of left and pulls outward) ᵥ *lead.*

—— ⁞[] BBᵛ

ɴ *leader, guide.*

BₐBₐ ⊥⌃

ᵥ *offer, suggest,* in ordinary situations; *move, nominate,
propose,* in meetings under formal rules of order.

√B⊥√B⊥ ⊥⌃˙

(panto.) ɴ *volley ball;* ᵥ *play volley ball.*

West also used abstract symbols in his flabbergast-
ingly intricate study of Indian sign language. I noted above
that West (who worked with Voegelin) has a valuable discussion on the relationship of morpheme and meaning to the notation system--a perspective which makes his work well
worth the effort of understanding it. Following are some
examples from his dissertation (p. 66):

hard   h∳éʔɛń́ɛə̖   (Left flat hand is held palm up.
                            Right fist, palm active, strikes
                            hard and direct down upon left
                            palm.) Note that two packages
                            are combined in the sign for
                            HARD:

                            h∳e-   and   -ʔɛń́ɛə̖

tree   ɫene   (Either hand, fingers basket-
                            shaped and pointing up, moves
                            slowly upwards before same
                            shoulder.)

Note that the "letters" used in the glosses are not phonemes
of a language, but represent shapes and positions of the hand
which is making the gesture for "hard" and "tree."

Another use of letters in notation systems is a letter-
abbreviation of a word that designates the gesture or the
paralinguistic effect. Trager uses Lf for laugh; Wh for
whisper; PH- for pitch height. Pitches may be represented
by letters: l, m, h, hh, meaning lo, mid, high, and very
high. Birdwhistell combined letter abbreviation with abstract
symbol: H meaning "head"; Ħ meaning "cocked head."

Dance notation systems have used letters to designate
a step or movement which is already known to the reader.
Pollenz (p. 429) gives an example from Arbeau, done in
1588.   Reverence was the term for a low sweeping bow;
Volta was a quick turn; Simple was a step forward.   The notation 6s, v, r meant for the dancer to take six steps forward, a turn, and a bow.   The great disadvantage of the
letter-abbreviation, of course, is that researchers are not
all of the same language and abbreviations reflect only the
language of the inventor of the system.

Symbols may be iconic or illustrative in nature, or
they may be suggestive of a position or a movement.   Edward Hall's Handbook makes some use of this kind of symbol (1974, p. 58):

Body Distance   0 - ⌒ ⌒
                           (two persons leaning—
                           out of reach of each
                           other)
                       1 - ⌒
                           (two persons leaning—
                           can barely touch)
                       2 - ⌐ ⌐
                           (two arms extended)
                       3 - ⌐ |
                           (arm extended—plus)
                       4 - ⋈   ⌐|
                           (two forearms or elbows
                           extended or arm ex-
                           tended)

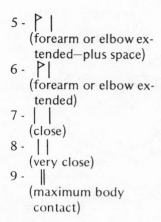

5 - ⳁ |
(forearm or elbow ex-
tended—plus space)

6 - ⳁ|
(forearm or elbow ex-
tended)

7 - | |
(close)

8 - ||
(very close)

9 - ‖
(maximum body
contact)

Birdwhistell also makes use of suggestive devices (1970, p. 260):

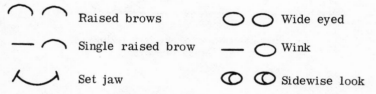

⌒ ⌒ Raised brows

— ⌒ Single raised brow

‿ Set jaw

◯ ◯ Wide eyed

— ◯ Wink

◍ ◍ Sidewise look

Symbols for paralanguage may reflect linguistic con-
ventions already known to linguists. Trager uses M for a
closed-lip nasal, or the sound murmured for pleasantries,
"Mmmmmm, good." R is used for a trill. Bullowa, Jones,
and Bever use B for labial and G for velar sounds in their
infant studies. It is useful to take into account the mechanical problems of using symbols in publishing, thereby making
use of symbols already on the typewriter or in the printer's
font. Special phonetic typewriters have an array of symbols
that can be modified for paralinguistic effects. Labanotation
now has an accessory that IBM has produced to record
choreography. It is a ball-shaped element containing eighty-
eight symbols used in Labanotation.

Sketches are one of the oldest forms of notating hand
gesture and body movement. Several of these were illustrated above. Sketches may be symbolic, as in the case of
the facial expressions represented by Irwin. Stick figures
are also a symbolic representation of meaningful movement.

Leticia Jay devised a stick man notation for dance.   It has
instantaneous effect (Jay, p. 7):

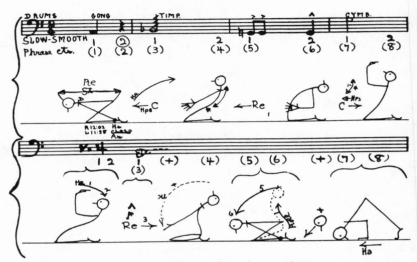

**An eight-bar phrase of modern technique
in Jay Dance Notation**

        Lawson and Mason also used stick figures in their
studies of ethnic dances.   The European illustrations are
from Lawson (pp. 53, 153, and 185).   The American Indian
illustrations are from Mason (pp. 36, 126).

KEY TO THE ILLUSTRATIONS

R. side of body is drawn thickly.   L. side is drawn finely.
Direction of movement is indicated by arrows.

Back to audience	Facing audience	Moving to R. with R. ft.	Moving to L. with L. ft.

Gavotte (an old Breton dance)

1. Step obliquely forwards on to L. ft.

2. Bring R. ft. to side of L.

3. Step obliquely forwards on to L ft.

4. Hop on L. ft raising R. knee straight upwards, R. heel roughly at level of L. knee.

1. Carry R. leg round in a circle and place R. ft. on ground just behind L. ft. (These 2 movements are known as the *Paz Dreo*.)

2. Step obliquely on to L. ft.

3. Bring R. ft. to side of L.

4. Hop on R. ft. raising L. knee upwards and slightly sideways, roughly L. toe is on level with R. knee.

Repeat, always starting with L. ft. Dance gets a little faster.

HIGHLAND SCHOTTISCHE

Step No. 1 in the Strathspey

1. Hop off L. ft., pointing R. ft. to side in air.

2. Hop off L. ft. bringing R. toe behind L. calf.

3. Hop off L. ft., pointing R. ft. to side in air.

4. Hop off L. ft., bringing R. toe in front of L. calf.

1. Glide sideways on R. ft.

2. Bring L. ft. behind R. ft.

3. Glide sideways on R. ft.

4. Hop lightly off R. ft., bringing L. ft. behind R. ankle.

Dances and Stories of the American Indian

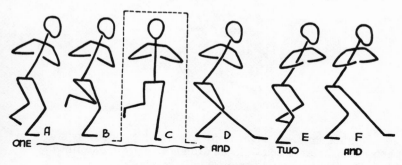

The Sti-yu Step

This step appears often in the powwow dancing of the Chippewas and the Sioux.

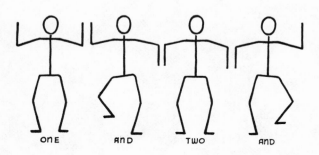

These are his basic movements. Near the end of his dance he performs a movement shown on the next page, with one leg extended far out and twisted around so that the sole of the foot is up. He does this in the following routine:

1 Jump on both feet
& Jump on left extending right out
2 Jump on both feet
& Jump on right foot extending left out

Stick figures have also been used to study posture and gesture in communication, as illustrated by the following from Rosenberg and Langer (1965, p. 594):

Stick Figure Test.

Sketches which indicate movement and direction have long been in use in music studies to illustrate the conductor's beat.

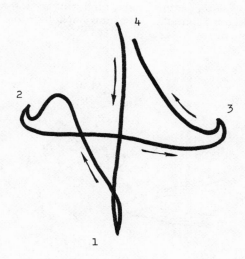

Efron capitalized on this type of symbol and gives
some very effective illustrations of the gestures he documented. I have selected a few from pages 100, 101, 127,
141 of the 1972 reprint:

Words Uttered	Accompanying Movements
hit him on the head	
a tremendous explosion	
too low	
going from one extreme to the other	
"Just another of those flag-waving speeches"	

Artists have captured the feeling of movement that
carries one beyond the static representation of it. Kepes

has published on the nature, art, and science of motion and includes a sketch from the 1895 chronophotographic work of Etienne Jules Marey (Marey, p. 143):

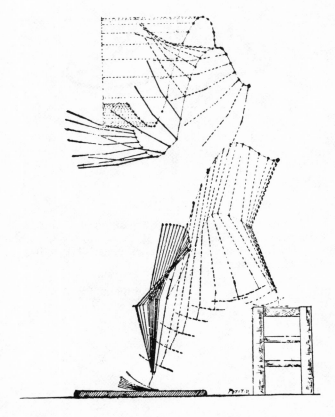

Jump from a height with stiffened legs

Filming and photography have added immeasurably to the advancements in research. Some very sophisticated studies have resulted from the benefits of being able to slow down, play back, and stop at certain points. Scholars such as Condon, Ekman, Kendon, Worth, and many others have spent years perfecting their techniques. Paralinguistic studies have benefitted from the spectrograph and the tape recorder. The electromyograph (E.M.G.) has added to our

knowledge of movement.   For studies using these instru-
ments and equipment see: Balazs; Birdwhistell; Brody, New-
man, and Redlich; Byers; Carmichael, Roberts, and Wessell;
Collier; Condon (1970); Condon and Brosin; Condon and Ogs-
ton; Condon and Sander; Deutsch; Dierssen, Lorenc, and
Spitaleri; Dittmann, Stein, and Shakow; Efron; Ekman and
Friesen (1969); Haith; Harrison; Hogan and Alger; Island;
Jablonko; William T. James; Leonard; Osgood; Sainsbury;
Silverstein; Sorenson; Van Vlack; Worth.

G.   History of Notation Systems

        One of the first great linguistic studies was done by
Panini, in the Sanskrit language.   It is interesting that notation systems of body movement also go back to this time
and area of the world--back to the great temples where
dance poses were sculpted on the walls.   Later these were
sketched for printed publications which are now available for
study.   See Bharata-Muni; Chatterji; Devi; Naidu, and Nadikesvara, and other references given in the section on dance.
The following illustrations show several fundamental hand
movements discussed by Bharata Muni, sometime between
the fourth and the first century B. C.   (Naidu, Naidu, and
Pantulu, pp. 85-88):

Fig. 125.
Catura

Fig. 130.
Padmakōśa

Fig. 134.
Sūcyāsya

Fig. 127.
Kapiddha

Fig. 131.
Patāka

Fig. 136.
Tripatāka

Notation systems for body movement were done almost entirely in the area of dance up until the last two centuries. Several scholars have treated the history of these
systems successfully and I will not do more than give references for these. For the history of dance notation, see:
Bartenieff; Beaumont; Brock; Cross; De Mille; Feves; Hutchinson; Kurath (1960); Michel; Nadel and Nadel; Pollenz;
Sorell; and West. The history goes back to the mid-fifteenth
century. Kamin's bibliography on dance notations gives
about twenty references for works done before the 1700s.
Noverre (p. 140) and De Mille (pp. 204-205) reproduce
pages from Diderot and D'Alembert's Encyclopédie (1751-
1772) which illustrate signs used in dance notation for the
18th century. During that century, there was even a system of recording the steps of horses in the art of dressage
(according to R. Lister, in Stepanov, pp. 1, 41; see also
Sorell, pp. 102-103). More recently a movement notation
was applied to the behavior of a pair of jackals, which was
recorded with the Eshkol-Washmann notation by Golani and
Zeidel (Martha Davis, 1972, p. 80). Burtner (in Nadel and
Nadel, p. 129) reports that a notator on the dance faculty
has notated the movements of the jumping spider mating
dance as a part of a research project in biological sciences.

Gilbert Austin (1806), as I have already mentioned,
is thought to have provided the first system for notating gestures in a field other than dance. Kurath pioneered the application of notation systems to ethnic dance. For notation
of ethnic dance see also Evans and Evans; Jablonko; Lawson; and Mason. Laban and Lawrence investigated the use of
Labanotation in industry. Curl's study was done for the purposes of physical education. North was concerned with personality development through movement. Causley; North;
Preston-Dunlop; and Thornton discuss the use of movement
notation in education. For older studies relating to oratory
see G. Austin; Bacon; Alexander Bell; Delsarte; Mosher;
Ott; Ross; and Warman.

The history of notation systems for paralanguage is
much briefer. It involves studies which were precursors
of linguistic statements, mainly in the area of intonation.
Abercrombie (1965, 1967) reviews some of these older
studies and gives examples of their notation systems. Lieberman's book on intonation (1968) surveys studies done in
this century and gives several examples of notation systems
used for intonation. I have already mentioned Crystal's
careful recounting of past studies. Perhaps the International

Phonetic Alphabet (IPA) and its development should also be
mentioned here (Albright).

For all this, and in spite of the seemingly large number of works that I have mentioned in this chapter, we can
still say that we are in the beginning stages of devising notation systems for paralanguage and kinesics. Investigators
worldwide should eventually come to some agreement as to
systems in order to exchange information more efficiently
and to understand each other's statements more clearly.
That day is yet to come.

For notation systems, in addition to the references I
have mentioned above, see Bouissac; Duncan (1969, pp. 119-
120); Ex and Kendon; Nelson Goodman; Halprin; Koechlin;
LaCuisse; Leventhal and Sharp; Lieth; Lifar; Ljung; Lynge;
Machotka; Marshack; Maynard; Meunier; Peng; Penrod; Polti;
Reuschert; Spreen; Sutton; Tetley.

5.

THE ELEMENTS OF NONVERBAL BEHAVIOR

All the sensory phenomena known to man can serve
as channels of communication in informative and expressive
behavior. Generally recognized are: acoustical, optical,
tactual, chemical, and electrical. All of these work together, of course, but for purposes of references I will outline various topics.

A.   Paralanguage

Paralanguage is some kind of articulation of the vocal apparatus, or significant lack of it; i.e., hesitation, between segments of vocal articulation. This includes all
noises and sounds which are extra-speech sounds, such as
hissing, shushing, whistling, and imitation sounds, as well
as a large variety of speech modifications, such as quality
of voice (sepulchral, whiney, giggling), extra high-pitched
utterances, or hesitations, and speed in talking (Key, 1975b,
p. 10). A good foundation in phonetics is requisite to understanding paralinguistics. This bibliography does not attempt
to cover the field of phonetics, though some items are basically phonetic in nature. Many scholars, including Abercrombie, Bolinger, Crystal, Fonagy, A. A. Hill, Lieberman, Pike, Trager, and Uldall, have expressed a vital interest in both.

The following suggests an outline for convenience in
discussing the various elements used in paralanguage.

Elements Used in Paralanguage

Language Sounds

Segmental
Specific Language Sounds: stops, fricatives, nasals,

92

trills, clicks, vowels ...
Language Element Modifications: labialization, palatalization, nasalization, pharyngealization, muscle
constriction, sound placement, laryngealization,
unvoicing (whisper) ...

Suprasegmental--Prosodic--Intonational

Pitch

Stress Length, Quantity, Timing Pause, Juncture, Hesitation	Rhythm/Speed (rate of speech)

Non-Language Sounds

Segmental
Non-speech Sounds: whistle, bilabial click (kiss),
yell ...

Suprasegmental
Non-language Modifications, Voice Quality: faucali-
zation, raspy, shrill, robust, resonant, sweet,
smooth ...
Voice Disguisers: ventriloquism, falsetto, humming ...
Modification Made With By-Element: membrane,
grass blade, paper on comb, electronics ...
Laugh--Giggle--Tremulousness--Sob--Cry

Control of Air Movement

Direction, Source, Amount

For studies on Nasalization see: Dickson; Essen;
Glasgow; Kelly. For studies on Unvoicing of sounds, or
Whisper, see: Bruneau (1973, p. 31); Catford (1968, p. 319);
Das Jain and Jones; Dieth; Giet; Helmholtz (pp. 108, 112);
Martin K. Jensen; Meyer-Eppler; C. B. Miller; John D.
Miller; Panconcelli-Calzia; Rigault and Gillis; Trim; Vygot-
sky (1934, pp. 44-46); Wise.

Suprasegmental, or intonational features comprise
pitch, stress, and length. These features, along with juncture, make up the rhythm of a language. It is not yet clear,
in linguistic studies, where linguistic intonation ends and
paralinguistic intonation begins. Perhaps they are inseparable

and should be discussed as one system, or perhaps they are
two systems that exist simultaneously and independently, and
intertwine in an interdependent way (Key, 1975b, pp. 48-53).
Studies of emotion should consider the intonational patterns
which signal emotive expression, along with facial expression
and other nonverbal indicators. Compare, for example, Ekman, Sorenson, and Friesen's list of facial displays: "happiness, anger, fear, disgust, surprise, and sadness," with
Fónagy and Magdics' emotional patterns in intonation: joy,
tenderness, longing, coquettish, surprise, fright/anguish,
complaint, scorn, anger, sarcasm. Dance studies also
categorize emotions in terms of range and kind of movement.
Compare the emotional states listed in the Natya Shastra:
love, humour, pathos (grief), anger, heroism, terror, disgust, wonder, and serenity (Singha and Massey, p. 26). In
music, composers sometimes change the key to change the
mood for a song; in conversation, people "change" the key
as they change mood and attitude in an interaction.

     See Chapter 4 for notation of Suprasegmentals. For
other studies see: Abe [Japanese]; Abercrombie; George Allen; Bolinger; Bowen [Spanish]; Buning and Schooneveld [Rus-
sian]; Nien- T. Chang [Chinese]; Covington; Delattre [French,
German, Spanish]; Delattre, Olsen, and Poenack [Spanish];
Essen [German]; Flint; Fónagy and Fónagy; Fónagy and Magdics [Hungarian]; Grimes [Huichol]; Gunter; Halliday; A. A.
Hill; Isačenko and Schädlich [German]; Ladefoged [West African languages]; Landar [Navaho]; Lefevre; Lieberman; Magdics [Hungarian]; Olsen [Spanish]; Painter; Pederson; Evelyn
Pike; K. L. Pike; Prator; Schubiger; Shen; Snell; Tompa
[Hungarian]; Trager; Trager and Smith; Uldall; Urbain.

     Hesitation phenomena must be distinguished from
linguistic juncture or pause, which correlates with grammatical structures. Hesitation phenomena include "unfilled"
pauses (or silence) and "filled" pauses. The fillers consist
of any number and variety of vocal dawdling: er, ah, uh,
mmmm, um. Modifications such as laryngealization, nasalization, rough breathing, and certain physiological acts--a
sigh, a sniff--also occur as fillers of hesitation pauses (Key,
1975b, pp. 50-51). These modifiers have been noted in
scholarly studies since early in this century. See Mahl and
Schulze for a bibliography of the psychological research in
this area. Observations of hesitation patterns should also
take into account the eye shift, facial expression of concentration, and hand gestures which are peculiar to hesitation.
They are also related to slips of the tongue or lapses which

were referred to previously in chapter 2. Some researchers,
for example Boomer and Dittmann, were especially concerned
with their relationship to linguistic structures.

Cross-cultural studies show a slightly different vowel
quality in the relaxed, neutral vowel (the sound often referred
to as schwa, as in up or uh) in the hesitation in various
languages. Robert Hall notes that Italian speakers express
hesitation with [ɛ... ɛ...]. [25] Delattre (1964, p. 93) com-
pares English, German, Spanish, and French:

> At present, the point of articulation of the neu-
> tral vowel appears to be most fronted in Spanish
> and most backed in English; its lip rounding most
> pronounced in French and least pronounced in Span-
> ish; its degree of opening greatest in English and
> smallest in Spanish. We might tentatively say that
> the English neutral vowel is somewhat back, lower
> than mid, and rather unrounded. The German
> neutral vowel is fairly fronted, mid-open, and be-
> tween rounded and spread, a little closer to the
> former. The French neutral vowel is fairly
> fronted, somewhat higher than mid-open, and
> rounded. The Spanish neutral vowel is fairly
> fronted, fairly spread, and between mid-open and
> mid-close.

Comedians and politicians use hesitation pauses to
create an effect or to indicate that what is being said is important! Writers have struggled with the problem on putting
down on paper this phenomena which occurs in spoken language. Thomas Hardy wrote in "The Man He Killed,"[26]

> I killed him, because .....
> Because

Heinrich Böll became absorbed in these phenomena when he
wrote "Murke's collected silences." The protagonist Murke
was a tape editor in a broadcasting studio. His hobby was
to collect the bits of tapes with silences from the speech of
various speakers!

For studies on Hesitation see: Gilbert Austin (pp. 50-
55); Sidney Baker; Bernstein; Blankenship and Kay; Bödtker;
Böll; Boomer; Boomer and Dittmann; Cook; Cowan and Bloch;
Crystal (1969, pp. 166-172); Delattre (1964); Duncan (1969,
pp. 127-129); Goldman-Eisler; Hawkins; Hegedüs; Henderson,

Goldman-Eisler, and Skarbek; Howell and Vetter; Kanfer;
Kasl and Mahl; Lallgee and Cook; Lay and Paivio; Levin and
Silverman; Levin, Silverman, and Ford; L. Little; Livant;
Lounsbury; Maclay and Osgood; McKay; Mahl; Mahl and
Schulze; James Martin; Matarazzo, Wiens, Matarazzo, and
Saslow; Panek and Martin; Quinting; Mary Rowe; Fillmore
Sandford (1942); W. Clifford Scott; Siegman, Pope, and
Blass; Simkins; Suci.

Rate of speech or speed in talking is a paralinguistic
feature dependent upon the style and mood of the speaker,
as well as cultural differences. Wescott (1962a) describes
seven tempos of speech in the Bini language: ceremonious,
deliberate, slow, ordinary, rapid, hurried, and slurred.

For studies on Rate of Speech see: John Black; Cook;
Fairbanks and Hoaglin; Fónagy and Magdics; Goldman-Eisler;
Karlgren; Levin and Stigall; Osser and Peng; James Webb;
Wescott (1962a); Wigdorsky.

Non-language sounds include all vocalizations which
do not occur as speech sounds in any language of the world,
as far as is known. These comprise various kinds of whis-
tles, the kiss, and various yells, hollers, and shouts.

The whistle is used as a language substitute in a
codified system; this use will be dealt with in Chapter 7.
Beyond these well-documented studies of whistle language,
little has been written about whistling, though it occurs
worldwide in many communication situations. Where once
the whistle was used for hunting, now it is used to direct
the man who manipulates the equipment for pouring cement.
An interesting perspective is the use of the word "whistle"
in language expressions: "whistle for his money, whistling
up the law, whistle me off, cannot be whistled away..."
(see Webster's Third New International Dictionary, for example). During the T'ang Dynasty (618-907 A.D.) it was
thought that "whistling can move supernatural beings and is
everlasting," and a scholarly work called Principles of
Whistling described twelve methods of whistling, a communication necessary to command the attention of the whole
world of spirits (E. D. Edwards, pp. 217-220).

For studies on Whistle see: E. D. Edwards; Feld-
man (1959); Hurley; Dave Larsen; Ostwald (1959); K. L.
Pike (1943, pp. 146-147); Ritzenthaler and Peterson; C.
Scott and Goldney; Voorhis.

For studies on the Kiss see: Apuleius; Eibl-Eibes-feldt; Fielding; Raymond Firth; Goffman (1963, pp. 166-167); Hopkins; Löw; Mallery (1891); Nyrop; Perella.

For studies on Yells and Hollers see: Bales; Botkin; Browne; Marshall; A. W. Read; Stearns.

Non-language modifications involve such features as voice quality. These qualities are usually stated in impressionistic terms: harsh, gruff, squeaky, shrill, and so on. For studies on Voice Quality see: Abercrombie; Gilbert Austin; Crystal; Crystal and Quirk; Dickens and Sawyer; Ladefoged; Laver; Trager.

Non-language modifications include other variations on speech such as ventriloquism and falsetto. For studies on Falsetto see: Sandor Ferenczi (1915); Lieberman (1967, pp. 20-22); Zerffi.

Laughing and crying are undoubtedly universals in the repertoire of expressive behavior of human beings. The similarities between laugh and cry are extraordinary, and indeed, Crystal and Quirk have analyzed them as a spectrum: Laugh--giggle--tremulousness-sob-cry. The following chart is the result of their tabulating some of the more important articulatory components (Crystal, 1969, p. 135).

Laughing and crying are physical releases to maintain psychological homeostasis--expressions to alleviate pain, physical or emotional. They are social phenomena and can be used to control social behavior. The reasons for laughter must be shared; one cannot laugh individually without telling the immediate listeners what was funny. Laughter has long intrigued scholars, and throughout the ages writers have made their comments. Catherine the Great discussed several kinds of laughter in one of her scientific essays. [27]

For studies on Laughing see: Ambrose; Bergler; Bergson; Blatz, Allin, and Millichamp; Buytendijk; Rose Coser; Crystal and Quirk; Darwin; Martha Davis (1972, see index); Davitz (1969, pp. 172-192); Dearborn; Ding and Jersild; Dries; Enders; Feldman (1959, pp. 246-248); Gregory; G. Stanley Hall and Allin; Hayworth; Hinde (see index); Jacobson; Justine; Kenderdine; Klineberg (1935, pp. 285-289); Kris; LaBarre (1947 and 1964); Leuba; Lorenz (1963, pp. 171-172, 284-287); McComas; Montagu (1960); Fred Peterson; Petö; Piddington; Plessner; Lawrence Sherman; Herbert

TABLE 1. *Parametric analysis of voice qualifiers and voice qualifications*

	VOICE QUALIFIERS						VOICE QUALIFICATIONS				
	whisper[1]	breathy	husky[2]	creak	falsetto[3]	resonant	laugh[4]	giggle	tremulousness[6]	sob[6]	cry
Air pressure	usually weak	relatively strong	variable[2]	weak	weak	strong	usually very strong	usually strong	very weak	usually strong	usually very strong
Oral aspiration	usually strong	excessive	usually weak	weak	usually weak	strong	usually strong	usually strong	usually inaudible	usually strong	excessive
Nasal friction	inaudible	variable	inaudible	inaudible	inaudible	inaudible	variable	variable	inaudible	usually audible	strongly audible
Pulsation type	neutral	neutral	neutral	neutral	may be aperiodic	neutral	periodic	periodic	aperiodic	aperiodic	aperiodic
Pulsation speed	neutral	neutral	neutral	neutral	neutral	neutral	slow	fast	fast	slow	slow
Phase with syllable	in phase	in phase	in phase	in phase	variable	in phase	usually out of phase	out of phase	usually out of phase	variable	variable
Vocal cord amplitude	usually small[1]	usually small	usually small	usually small	small	great	usually very great	variable	usually small	variable	usually very great
Vocal cord vibration	never vibrating	irregular	irregular	vibrating	variable	vibrating	usually vibrating	usually vibrating	vibrating	usually vibrating	usually vibrating
Volume of supraglottals	usually small	usually large	variable	variable	variable	large	usually large	variable	usually small	variable	usually large
Tension of supraglottals	lax[1]	usually lax	usually tense[1]	variable	tense	variable	usually lax	usually tense	usually lax	usually tense	usually tense
Extent of horizontal glottal movement	relatively narrow (slight friction usual)	relatively wide	narrow (fairly strong friction)	narrow (trill)	narrow (often slight friction)	wide	relatively wide	relatively narrow	narrow	relatively wide	relatively wide
Ingressive airflow	inaudible	variable	inaudible	inaudible	inaudible	inaudible	usually inaudible[5]	inaudible	inaudible	usually audible	usually audible

1 Unless 'stage' whisper.
2 A weak and lax kind of *husky* voice is common as part of voice-quality in females.
3 Generally an adult male feature, involving a change in register.
4 The continuum between features is particularly noticeable with *laugh–giggle* and *sob–cry*.
5 The important point is inaudibility: inspiration does occur with normal laughter (cf. Luchsinger & Arnold, 1965, p. 84), but it is rarely audible.
6 Cf. Pittenger *et al.*'s 'breaking' effect (1960). As with *falsetto*, a change of register is involved.

Spencer (1860); Stanley; Paul Turner; Vasey; R. W. Washburn; Zuk.

Crying is a human expression associated with many different emotions, as well as a component of certain acts or rituals; for example, mourning and greeting patterns (Frazer; Friederici; Lubbock). When weeping occurs as a symbolic gesture, it is the vocalization which is important --not the tears. American Indians are known to cry in situations startlingly unlike those of Westerners. The Aymaras may cry when they ask for a favor. Both crying and sexual expression are releases of different kinds--climaxes of extreme emotionality. At a point of sexual climax a lover may shed tears in a relationship that is poignant, unsatisfactory, or when the encounter is a "Goodbye."

For studies on the cry behavior of infants see section on infant development (see index). For studies on Cry see: Crystal and Quirk; Darwin; Etzel and Gewirtz; Sandor Feldman (1956); Frazer (1919); Friederici; Klineberg (1935); LaBarre (1947, pp. 54-55); LaBarre (1964, pp. 196-197); Landreth; Lubbock; Mauss (1921); Montagu (1959); Petö; Joseph Weiss.

The control of air movement (with reference to air mechanisms, see Pike, 1943), is of special significance in paralinguistic articulations, with concern for direction, source, and amount. Ingressive (or inspirated) speech may be a symptom of a psychosomatic illness (Moses). In normal speech ingressive air movement is often used as a voice disguise in courting behavior. It has been reported in the Philippines (Conklin), among the Swiss-German, in Newfoundland in "Mummer-talk" (W. K.), and according to Abercrombie (personal communication) it also occurs in the Outer Hebrides. In a performance of "The Mikado" a seasoned performer conveyed the character of this infamous ruler who "let the punishment fit the crime" by ghastly noises produced by changing the direction of the air stream during his singing. The matter of breath control is of major importance in the dance technique developed by Martha Graham. "Her technique is built on the breathing cycle of the body and its principles of 'contraction and release' ... " (Penrod and Plastino, p. 44).

For studies on the Control of Air Movement see: Abercrombie (1967); Altschule; Bosma; Catford; Conklin; Martha Davis (1972, see index); Goldman-Eisler; W. K.;

Ladefoged; Lieberman; Moses; Gordon Peterson; Kenneth
Pike (1943, 1957); Stetson; Stetson and Hudgins; Werner
Wolff (1943).

During the last few years much attention has been
given to voiceprints and other means of speech analysis by
intricate instrumentation, such as the Psychological Stress
Evaluator. The voiceprint is the "fingerprint" of vocalization. It preserves the individual characteristics of the human voice. At the same time, reputable scholars recognize
that the variables are so numerous and so complex that an
accurate interpretation of the speech event is yet to be per-
fected.

For studies on Voiceprint and Speaker Identification
see: Bolt, et al.; Hazen; Lummis; Vanderslice.

B.   Kinesics

"Action is a sort of language which perhaps one time or other, may come to be
taught by a kind of grammar-rules. "
--William Hogarth (1753),
Analysis of Beauty

Kinesic behavior incorporates all movement resulting
from muscular and skeletal shift. This includes physical or
physiological actions, automatic reflexes, gestures, and facial expressions. Various terms have been used down
through the ages to ascribe communicative value to body
movement. Gilbert Austin (1806, p. 1) credits Cicero with
saying that action is the language of the body. Not all movement is communicative in a linguistic sense; it may result
from one's relationship to the physical environment. Some
kinesic action is related to the technique required in performing an act or to excellence of movement. There are
embellishing features that evade description in precise terms,
and that do not accommodate lexical translations, though they
have meaning in their own way.

Kinesic behavior has a close relationship to vocali-
zations--in ways that are not yet satisfactorily defined. One
area of relationship is seen in the comparison of intonational
components of paralanguage--pitch, stress, and length--and
the "intonational" components of movement, that is, the
range or extent of movement, intensity of the action, and

duration of the movement (Key, 1975b, p. 77). Paralinguistic hesitation is kinesic immobility. Movement and intonation are not just linear or binary and it is these other dimensions that make analysis incredibly difficult.

The technological aids available today will contribute to the analysis of movement and vocalizations in ways not possible before this century. Replays permit observations not possible when the unrecorded act was lost forever. Videotape makes it possible to view side and front simultaneously by splitting the screen with two cameras. There is apparently no end to the possibilities of research in the future. There are enough analyses available now to do comparative studies. For example, the classification of body movements made for dance in India could be compared with the categories abstracted by Birdwhistell. Important discoveries are yet to come.

The following suggests an outline for convenience in discussing the various elements used in kinesics.

Elements Used in Kinesics

Posture

Facial Expression
Eye
Mouth
Nose

Other Body Movement
Hand

Physiology
Regular Physiological Functions
Spontaneous Physiological Acts
Automatic Reflex, Instinctive

Combinatory--Body Movement and Noise

Posture falls into three basic categories: Bent Knees, Lying Down, and Standing. The functioning of the larynx in vocalizations with relationship to posture has been discussed by phoneticians (Bolinger, 1968, pp. 311-316; Kantner and West, p. 30; Lieberman, 1967, pp. 36-37). Lashley (1951, pp. 517-518) discussed posture and spatial integration in terms of neural mechanisms. Ekman and Friesen (1969,

p. 76) discussed postures which coincided with and followed
a facial affect display.

The three basic positions, Bent Knees, Lying Down,
and Standing, are manifested in linguistic structures in several languages of the world. Humboldt observed this grammatical feature in the Abipon language of Argentina. [28] It
has been noted in other American Indian languages: Chama,
Tacana, Caingang, Toba, [29] and Totonac (McQuown, 1954,
p. 29). Haas shows that the Tunica language observes positional agreement:[30]

   ta'săku, ?urá   There is the dog (in a lying posi-
                         tion).

   ta'săku, ?uná   There is the dog (in a sitting po-
                         sition).

   ta'săku, ka'l?urá   There is the dog (in a standing
                         position).

The Tacana language of the Amazon area and Russian
have, in addition, a fourth category, one meaning to hang,
or hanging. Donald Johnson describes the Russian "verbs
of body position" which have other unique characteristics.
They are based on the Slavic roots sed-/sad- 'sit/set',
leg-/log- 'lie/lay', sto-/sta- 'stand', and vis-/ves- 'hang'.
Beigel did a study of the influence of body position on mental processes, measuring the responses of subjects as they
stood, sat, and reclined.

Sleeping posture is not always in a horizontal position. In medieval times people slept in cupboard-like beds
which were about four feet long. They slept in a half-
sitting position with weapons at hand, for the protection of
their households (Robert Franklin, in correspondence).
Standing position does not always involve both feet. The
one-legged resting position has been documented in several
parts of the world: in Iran, India, Ceylon, Melanesia,
South America, and among North American Indians (Hewes,
1953). See also Dupouy; Elkin; Fischer (1963, p. 70); Hutton; Lindblom.

The chart on page 103 was formulated by Hewes from
his extensive studies of posture (1966, p. 110).

POSTURES

Category	Subcategory	Details
FACIAL EXPRESSION, GESTURE		
QUADRU-PEDAL		position / crawling; on all fours
LYING DOWN		on stomach (prone); on back (supine); on side; reclining – partly supported
SQUATTING	Squatting	on toes; on soles of feet
SITTING, KNEELING, SQUATTING	Sitting — on chair, stool, bench, etc.	legs apart; legs together; knee, leg, or ankle crossed
	Sitting — on floor, on ground, legs out	tightly flexed; semi-flexed; extended; to left; to right; legs crossed; on heels
	Kneeling	on both knees; on one knee; bent or crouching
STANCES	Upright, Erect	with support; other; at attention; on head, shoulders, or hands
BODY MOVEMENT		symmetrical / asymmetrical

For studies on Posture see: William Austin (1972);
Bailey; Basmajian; Beigel; Blazer; Boynton and Goodenough;
Brilliant; Chance; Charney; Christiansen; Cossetta; Deutsch;
Dupouy; Ekman (1964); Elkin; Feldenkrais; Raymond Firth;
Herbert Fischer (1963); Fretz; Goldring; Haith; Hewes; Hut-
ton; Irizawa; C. V. Jackson; William T. James; Jarcho;
Jelliffe; Donald Johnson; Kempf; Robert Knapp; Kretsinger;
Kuepper; Lamb; Eleanor Larsen; Lindblom; Marquis; Mauss;
Mehrabian (1969); Mezey and Melville; Murdock; Nakajima;
Nilsson; Prince Peter; Prost; Quackenbos; Rand and Wapner;
Rosenberg and Langer; Rothschild; Scheflen (1964); Schulman
and Shontz; Sheldon; Silver; Edward Smith; Steig; Zeligs.

Facial expression has been "scientifically" studied in
great detail since the early 1800s (for example, Gilbert Austin, 1806; Charles Bell, 1806; Lavater). See Landis (1924,
pp. 448-453) for historical perspective. Artists have always
been among the keenest observers of human behavior.
Michelangelo carved several faces of women in childbirth.
Later Theodore Gericault (French, 1791-1824) was commis-
sioned by a doctor at the Salpêtrière Hospital to do facial
studies of the insane. [31] Many attempts have been made to
correlate intelligence with facial features, for example,
William Blake, p. 17; Gurnee; Levitt, p. 100; Michael and
Crawford; and Weisgerber.

The mask is a commonplace which is ritualized in
the art of Mime. In everyday life cosmetics provide a
cover which is more exaggerated on the stage. Studies by
Haggard and Isaacs focus on what may be the transitional
stages between mask expressions and real expressions.
They report the discovery of "micromomentary expression"
--MME--by running motion picture films at about one-sixth
of their normal speed. These are facial expressions which
are so short-lived that they seem to be quicker-than-the-eye.
Findings suggest that MMEs tend to occur in a context of
conflict (p. 161). They are associated with denial statements and instances of verbal blocking; they are incongru-
ent with the verbal message and the adjacent facial expression. Haggard and Isaacs believe that MMEs occur so rapid-
ly that they are subliminal. See also Garwood, et al., for
micromomentary expression. Cross-cultural studies are
prerequisite to finding universals in facial expressions. To
what extent are facial displays expressions of emotions?
To what extent is facial behavior a control mechanism in
the interaction? An example of the usefulness of cross-
cultural studies is illustrated by the experiment described

by Dickey and Knower, using subjects in Mexico City. Among their list of emotions tested is religious love or reverence, an expression observed often in Mexico, even on the streets when people pass a church. Few other studies include this expression in the inventory.

For studies on Facial Expression see the following. Several cross-cultural studies can be identified by the name of the language following the author. Abelson and Sermat; J. A. Ambrose; R. J. Andrew; Asano (Japanese); Balázs (pp. 39 ff., 111); Barnlund; Beier, Izard, Smock, and Tougas; Charles Bell; Birdwhistell; William Blake; Bokander; Bolwig; Boring and Titchener; Boucher; Brannigan and Humphries; Brophy; Bruner and Tagiuri; Buck, Savin, Miller, and Caul; Buzby; Cline; James Coleman; Cuceloglu (cross-cultural); Darwin; Dashiell; R. C. Davis; Davitz (Uganda); Dearborn; De Silva and Simson; Dickey and Knower (Spanish); Dittmann, Parloff, and Boomer; Drag and Shaw; Dunlap; Dusenbury and Knower; Ekman; Ekman and Friesen (1971, cross-cultural); Ekman, Friesen, and Ellsworth; Ekman, Friesen, and Tomkins; Ekman, Liebert, et al.; Ekman, Sorenson, and Friesen (cross-cultural); Engen and Levy; Engen, Levy, and Schlosberg; Engen, Levy, Schlosberg, and Woodworth; Ex and Kendon; Feleky; Fernberger; Fields; Foley; Frijda; Frois-Wittmann; Fulcher; Galper; Garwood, Guirora, and Kalter; Georgina Gates; Gladstones; A. G. Goldstein and Chance; Goldstein and Mackenberg; Kurt Goldstein; Goodenough and Tinker; Grant; Gratiolet; Greenbaum; Gubar; Guilford; Guilford and Wilke; Gurnee; Haggard and Isaacs; Hammes; Hanawalt; Harmon; Harrison (1964); Harrison and MacLean; Hastorf, Osgood, and Ono; Hochberg and Galper; Honkavaara; Huber; Hulin and Katz; Inui; Francis Irwin; Izard (cross-cultural); Jarden and Fernberger; Jenness; Blurton Jones; Kagan, Henker, et al.; Kanner; Kauranne; Kline and Johannsen; Kris and Gombrich; Kwint; Lambert and Lambert; Landis; Lange (German); Langfeld; M. Lemoine; Leventhal and Sharp; Levitt; Levy, Orr, and Rosenweig; Levy and Schlosberg; M. Lewis; Lynn; Mantegazza; Helen May (Chinese); Modiliani; Mordkoff; Harris Mosher; Munn; Nummenmaa; Nummenmaa and Kauranne; Odom and Lemond; Ono, Hastorf, and Osgood; Osgood; Osgood and Heyer; Piderit; Pittman, Parloff and Boomer; Polak, Emde, and Spitz; Rosenberg and Gordon; Rosenfeld; Royal; Ruckmick; Rudolf; Rump; Sarles; Schlosberg; Schuhl; Seaford (southern American); Secord; Secord, Dukes, and Bevan; Anna Shannon; Shapiro; Sherman; Simmel; G. H. Smith; Spitz and Wolf (American Indian, Negro); Stenvenson and Ferguson (Negro);

Straus; Stritch and Secord; Swan; Stephen Thayer; Thayer
and Schiff; Diana Thompson and Meltzer; Jane Thompson;
Thorek; G. R. Thornton; Tickell; Silvan Tomkins (cross-
cultural); Triandis and Lambert (Greece); Turhan; Tykulsker
(French); Van Hooff; Vinacke (Japanese, Chinese, and Caucasian); Vinacke and Fong; Vine; Ruth Washburn; J. S. Watson; Weisgerber; F. Williams and Sundene; Williams and
Tolch; Winick and Holt; Peter Wolff; Woodworth; Woodworth
and Schlosberg.

        For facial expression see also the following sections
on eye, mouth, and nose.

        Other animals have eyebrows, but only man's ex-
        press grief and joy, mercy and severity, by mov-
        ing together or singly to signal from his soul.
        They show our agreement and disagreement, and
        supremely our contempt. Haughtiness enthrones
        herself in them, and though conceived in the heart,
        rises to the eyebrows and there hangs in the lofti-
        est and steepest part of the body which it can oc-
        cupy alone.
                                        --Pliny (A.D. 23-79)
                                        Natural History[32]

        For studies on the Eye see: Appel, McCarron, and
Manning; Argyle; Argyle and Dean; Argyle and Exline; Ar-
gyle and Ingham; Argyle, Ingham, Alkema, and McCallin;
Argyle, Lalljee, and Cook; Bakan; Barlow; Charles Bell;
Blount; Brannigan and Humphries; Cason; Chance; Daniell
and Lewis; Davey and Taylor; Bill Davidson; Day; Devereux;
Doehring; Eibl-Eibesfeldt; Ellsworth and Carlsmith; Ells-
worth and Ludwig; Etzel and Gewirtz; Exline; Exline and
Absalom; Exline and Clark; Exline, Gray, and Schuette; Ex-
line and Messick; Exline, Thibaut, Brannon, and Gumpert;
Exline and Winters; Fugita; Gibson; Gibson and Pick; Goff-
man (1963); Hess; Hess and Polt; Hess, Seltzer, and Shlien;
Hinde (see index); Hindmarch; Hobson, et al.; Hutt and
Ounsted; Kanfer; Kendon; Kennard and Glaser; Kepes; Kleck
and Nuessle; Lambert and Lambert; Llewellyn and Stasiak;
McConnell; Mackworth and Bagshaw; Marks; Meyer, Bahrick,
and Fitts; Miles; Mobbs; Modiliani; Robert Murphy; Nachson
and Wapner; Ortega y Gasset; Ponder and Kennedy; Rands;
Riemer; Robson; Sanford and Wrightman; Sartre; Schuhl;
Simmel; Simms; Stass and Willis; Strongman and Champness;
Tankard; Telford and Storlie; Stephen Thayer; Silvan Tom-
kins; Wapner and Nachson; Webb, Matheny, and Larson;

White, Hegarty, and Beasley; Wood and Saunders; Woodman-see.

For studies on the Mouth, including smiling behavior, see: J. A. Ambrose; Louise Ames; Brackbill; Brannigan and Humphries; Courogyer; Dearborn; Dennis; Ding and Jersild; Etzel and Gewirtz; Daniel Freedman; Gewirtz; Kurt Goldstein; Gottschalk (1974); Hinde (see index); Kendon; Fred Peterson; Polak, Emde, and Spitz; Simpson and Capetanopoulos; Spitz and Wolf; Ruth Washburn; Peter Wolff.

For references and studies on the Tongue see: Barakat (1973, pp. 769, 784); Harold Bayley; Courten; David-Neel; Eibl-Eibesfeldt (1969, p. 13); Feldman (1959, pp. 244-246); Hinde (see index); Houde; Kendon and Ferber; LaBarre (1947, pp. 56-57); Mallery (1891, pp. 478, 489); Montagu (1971, see index); Scheck; W. John Smith, Chase, and Lieblich; Thorson.

For references to the Nose see: Barakat (1973, pp. 761 ff., 780); Sandor Feldman (1941, p. 257); Feldman (1959, p. 265); Klineberg (1935, pp. 286-287); Mantegazza (1885, p. 12); Montagu (1971, see index).

Other Body Movement is only now beginning to be treated in terms of communicative value or utilitarian purposes. The Movima Indians of the Amazon rainforest spin with their toes. Courtship behavior is abetted by toe gestures and/or foot movement. A few references focus on other body movement such as head and arm gestures and shoulder movement: Allport and Vernon (especially pp. 24-35); Efron (pp. 81-86, 115-118); Feldman (1959, pp. 198-199, 270-271); Winick and Holt (1962, pp. 77-78).

Hand movement occurs along a continuum, with slight, incidental, or embellishment movement at one end, and precise, meaningful, ritualized gestures at the other end. The matter of left-handedness and right-handedness is of special concern in hand movement. The relation of thought and hand movement has often been referred to, but without a clear understanding of the processes involved. Kimura commented on hand gestures in her studies of the brain. The entries on gestures are so numerous in this bibliography that I will not try to list them here. For other studies on hand movement see: Frank Baker; Cabrol; Carmichael, Roberts, and Wessell; Carus; Courogyer; Cushing; Ekman and Friesen (1968, pp. 201-212); Ekman and Friesen (1972); Eldernbosch;

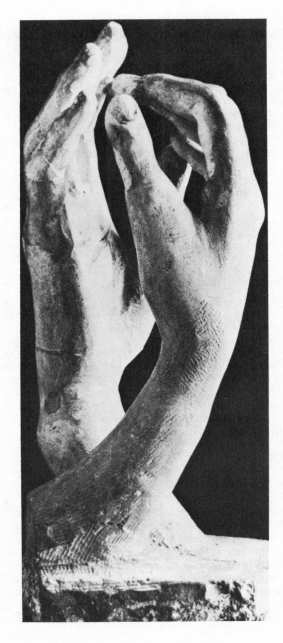

Rodin's "La Cathédrale"

Enjoy; Eshkol; Sandor Ferenczi (1926); Gitin; Gottschalk;
Francis Hayes (1957, pp. 257-258); Krout (1954); Frank Lutz;
Mallery (1891, p. 481 ff.); Misiak and Franghiadi; Pengniez;
Revesz; B. Shannon; Tikkanen; Vaschide; Charlotte Wolff.

Physiology and behavior, particularly communicative
behavior, are recognized as interdependent, but their interaction is not well understood. Interpersonal behavior between
human beings is very much in evidence in physiological events
and to a great extent determines their style and when and
where they will be performed.

Regular Physiological Functions include the necessary
acts of locomotion, breathing, eating, drinking, and sleeping,
and the functions involved in body elimination, sexual behavior, and reproduction. See Murdock for examples in other
cultures.

Locomotion includes all the varieties of getting from
one place to another, such as walking, running, skipping,
hopping, jumping, and crawling. The only study on jumping
that has come to my attention was made by a French photog-
rapher, Halsman, who, in a hilarious mood, put together a
collection of famous people jumping. However, it was not
beneath the dignity of Leonardo da Vinci to study this form
of locomotion (Lifar, 1951, p. 102):

> Nature instructs and acts by herself, without
> the aid of reason. When a person wishes to jump,
> he swiftly raises his arms and shoulders which
> are then propelled simultaneously with the upper
> part of his body; they remain lifted as long as
> support is provided by this movement of the body
> (the back being bent) and by the impulse of the
> joints or springs of thighs, knees and feet. This
> tension develops in two directions, upwards and
> forwards; the movement intended to throw the body
> forward acts in that way at the moment the jump
> is made and, together with the movement that lifts
> the body, makes it describe a large arc of a circle,
> rendering the jump still more rapid.
>
> --Leonardo da Vinci,
> Treatise on Painting

Lifar goes on to comment on the difference between
jumps in dancing and jumping in sports. "The final aim and
object of the athletic jumper is the jump; each of his springs

is complete, absolute, constitutes an end in itself ... what
distinguishes the dancer's jump from the athlete's is the famous 'pause in the air,' the act of 'touching the sky and re-
maining there,' which is obviously an optical effect obtained
by a few movements of the torso or feet."

For studies on Locomotion see: Allport and Vernon
(pp. 10-13, 67-69); Bailey; Balázs (pp. 134-135); Birdwhistell (1952); Hellmuth Bogen and Lippmann; Philip Eisenberg
and Reichline; Halsman; LaBarre (1947); Prost (1965); Werner Wolff.

For references on Breathing see: Balázs (p. 277);
Goldman-Eisler (especially 1955); Heim, Knapp, Vachon,
Globus, and Nemetz; Hopkins; Montagu (1971, pp. 98-99);
Gordon Peterson.

For references on Sleeping and Snoring see: Boulware; Boynton and Goodenough; Hinde (p. 357); Marquis;
Sheldon (p. 262).

Body elimination has been well established as having
communicative power (Key, 1975b, pp. 94-96). Social work-
ers can relate experiences about people who are misfits or
rebellious against society who have defecated in unusual
places to show their hostility. This form of aggression is
also done in times of war. The matter of "digestive winds"
(a quaint expression from past times) can also be considered
as communicative behavior. A well-known medical school
in the Southwest has a student paper called The Weekly Flatus.

For references on Body Elimination see: Barakat
(1973, p. 759); Sandor Ferenczi (1926); Hewes (1955, p. 238);
Kristeva (pp. 301-302); Lorand; Merrill.

Sexual behavior can be seen to have many variants in
different cultures of the world. MacDougald includes sections on erotic sounds and articulations, with examples from
various cultures, particularly from India.

Reproduction. The posture for childbirth is not always in a lying-down position. South American Indians give
birth in a half-sitting position. For childbirth see Jaracho.
The illustration on page 111 depicts a specially designed ob-
stetrical stool used in the sixteenth century.[33]

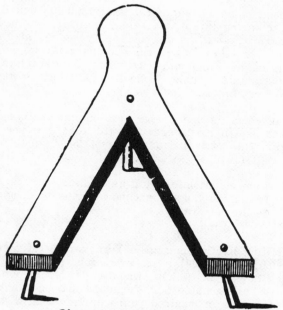

Obstetric stool of de Savonarola, 1547.

De Savonarola's stool in use.

Spontaneous Physiological Acts include such things as:
coughing, clearing throat, sneezing, spitting, belching, sucking, hiccupping, swallowing, choking, yawning, sighing,
scratching, stretching. Several authors refer to these phenomena as having communicative value in interaction situations; for example: Sidney Baker; W. Clifford Scott; Karl
Stern, Boulanger, and Cleghorn; Tylor.

The cough is one of the first communicative devices
that infants use in the interaction with others in the surroundings. This is included as one of the "games babies
play" by Call (1970).

Silence, attention, for as if about
To talk at length, she now begins to cough,
As do the orators.
                          --Aristophanes[34]

Spitting has an unusually large variety of meanings
(Key, 1975b, pp. 98-99). Catherine the Great related an
experience during an illness, when a girl would come to
minister to her--rubbing her shoulders and back with her
saliva. A couple of hundred years earlier than that Mary,
Queen of Scots, at the baptism of James, refused to let the
priest spit in her babe's mouth, as was the custom.

The sigh is a particular kind of breathing, more com-
mitted to expressive behavior than to breathing processes.
Straus has done a serious study on the sigh.

C.   Tactile Behavior

Tactile behavior is manifested in several categories:
1) Greetings and congratulations; 2) Conversation and communication; 3) Ritual and Rites of Passage; 4) Affection;
5) Play and recreation; 6) Occupation; 7) Learning or evaluation activity; 8) Manipulation in interpersonal relationships;
9) Warfare and aggression (Key 1975b, pp. 102-104).

For studies on Tactile Behavior see: Alrutz; William
Austin (1972); Basler; R. Q. Bell and Costello; Buch; A.
Burton and Kantor; Call; Clay; Martha Davis (see index);
Sandor Feldman (1959, see bibliography for tickling); Fisher;
Frank; Geldard; Genot; Gibson; Goldberg and Lewis; Felicitas
Goodman (1969); Gregory (tickling, pp. 41-51); Gunther; Ed-
ward Hall (1966); Stanley Hall and Allin; Henley; Hopkins;

Howard; Jourard; Jourard and Rubin; Kauffman; Leuba; Lister; Margaret Mead (1954); Montagu (1971); Desmond Morris (1971); Murray; Ostrander and Schroeder; Charlotte Read; Robinson; Schaffer and Emerson; Sparks; Stanley; Sternberg; Pearl Turner; Thomas Williams.

D. Sensory Communication

All the sensory phenomena known to man can serve as channels of communication in informative and expressive behavior. Olfactory interaction is especially vital to interpersonal relationships. Napoleon is said to have been in the habit of writing to his mistress a few days before he was to visit her. His message was, "Don't wash; I'm on my way!"

For studies on Sensory Communication see: William Austin (1972); Geldard; Edward Hall (1966, 1972, 1972); Jakobson (1964, 1967); Moles; Johannes Müller; Max Müller; Reik; Rosenblith; Scovel; Sebeok (1967); Kathleen Smith and Sines; Vendryes (1921); Wathen-Dunn; Wescott (1967); Harry Wiener; Wyburn, Pickford, and Hirst.

For studies on Cutaneous Response see: Altschule; Bowling Barnes; Ellen Brown; Burgess; Darwin (on blushing); Sandor Feldman (1922, 1941); Geldard; Edward Hall (1966, pp. 52-57); Harold Jones; Kuno; Lister; McBride, King, and James; McCray; Mantegazza; Mitchell; Moles; Montagna; Montagu (1953); Panek and Martin; Rosenblith; Sattler; Thiselton-Dyer; Wescott (1969). See also references under tactile.

For studies on Olfactory Communication see: Bedichek; Bedini; Chalke and Dewhurst; Comfort; Coon (1966); Erb; Erhardt-Siebold; Fabricant; Freud (1953); Glaze; Hald; Haldane; Edward Hall (1966); Hicks; Hoffer and Osmond; Holmes, et al.; Hopkins; Kalmus; Kalmus and Hubbard; Kalogerakis; Helen Keller; Kinross; Kloek; Kniep, Morgan, and Young; Krebs; Langey and Watson; McCartney; Meerloo (1964); Moncrieff; Montagu (1966); Ostwald (1963); G. H. Parker; Parkes; Pfaffmann; Kathleen Smith and Sines; Stein, Ottenberg, and Roulet; Harry Wiener; Wright.

E. Proxemics (Space)

You were born together, and together you shall be forevermore.... But let there be spaces in

your togetherness, And let the winds of the
heavens dance between you.

--Kahlil Gibran, On Marriage[35]

The consideration of space would include not only distance, but location and position--at the head of the table or
the middle, to the right or to the left of a person. The
avoidance behavior in societies can be described in terms
of physical spacing and location, but may also be psychological spacing.

For studies on Proxemics see: Aiello and Jones; Albert; Irwin Altman; Altman and Haythorn; Altman, Taylor,
and Wheeler; Balint; Ball; Batchelor and Goethals; Ernest
Bauer; Baxter; Beistle; Bennet; Bertalanffy; Beym; Blakely;
Bogardus; Brodey; Donald Campbell, Kruskal, and Wallace;
C. R. Carpenter; Cheyne and Efran; Virginia Clark, Esch-
holz, and Rosa; Cratty; Daniell and Lewis; Martha Davis
(see index); DeVita; Dinges and Oetting; Engebretson and
Fullmer; Ervin; Esser; Esser, et al.; Gary Evans and How-
ard; Fabbri; Felipe and Sommers; Forston and Larson; Lynn
Friedman; Friedrich; Goldberg, Kiesler, and Collins; Gold-
finger; Goldring; Gordon Greene; Edward Hall; Hallowell; G.
Hearn; Hiat; Horowitz; Horowitz, Duff, and Stratton; F. P.
Jones and Hanson; Stanley Jones; Stanley Jones and Aiello;
Kishimoto; Kleck; Klopfer; Koneya; Kummer; Kurylowicz; La
Barre (1970); Lassen; Laurendeau and Pinard; Lehrer; Leib-
man; Kenneth Little; McBride, King, and James; Matoré;
Moles and Rohmer; Nachson and Wapner; Norum, Russo,
and Sommer; Ohnuki-Tierney; Patterson, Mullens, and Ro-
mano; Patterson and Sechrest; Peng; Porter, Argyle, and
Salter; Proshandky, Ittelson, and Rivlin; Rawls; Rosenfeld
(1965); Mary Rowe; Scheflen (1970); McFarlane Smith; Sommer; Sommer and Becker; Stea; Steinzor; Stephenson and
Rutter; Tesch, Huston, and Indenbaum; Triandis, Davis, and
Takezawa; Tringham; Vine; Michael Watson; Willis; Winick
and Holt; Zlutnick and Altman.

F.   Chronemics (Time)

Time measured by the year is no measure
of our days. --Perse[36]

People in different cultures have different ways of di-
viding time. The following illustrations are from the Amazon

rainforest of South America, where time is conceptualized according to the position of the sun or seasonal cycles. Two languages--Candoshi and Aguaruna--belong to the Jivaroan language family. The Candoshi people divide the 24 hours as follows:[37]

pótórita, morning

zaar pótoriita	in the early morning	6 a. m.
zaar magina káchigárato	past the trees	7 a. m.
zaar magínamon yóovári	above the jungle trees	9 a. m.
zaar vacháamoríats totónkáacho	toward midday	10 a. m.
zaar vacháamoría kayómárato	nearing the middle of the day	11 a. m.
zaar vacháamoríatsi	midday	12 m.

pókamcho, afternoon

zaar isírogótarato	turning around	1 p. m.
zaar ksomis isírogótarato	well turned	2:30 p. m.
zaar xamíakamcho	hanging in suspension	3:30 p. m.
zaar magínamon yovaazi	above the trees	4 p. m.
zaar maginosh pshtóyallo	entered into the jungle	4:30 p. m.
zaar magínosh iróyirórtarallo	filtering through the trees	5 p. m.
zaar pópótoniya	covering itself	5:30 p. m.
zaar pókamcho	covered	6 p. m.

psáná, night

tápíyakcho	getting dark	7 p. m.
schirsa	midnight	12 m.
tarás motátákcho	toward dawn	2 a. m.
ktash tadáníikaa ato	song of the rooster	3 a. m.

mallirsa kamanko, o pchíchiriats chiríii tarás taráaas átarasha	song of the cricket	4 a. m.
sítkacho	first appearance of dawn	4:30 a. m.
kanîz kooh kooh ato	song of the talkative ones	5 a. m.
ánnish tarásiakcha yosáako	song of the heron	5:15 a. m.
tarásíakaacho	dawning	5:30 a. m.

The related Aguarunas divide the year into several seasons:[38]

wampuštin	'time of the kapok'
wačitín	'the flowering of the bamboo'
šinutín	'time of the noises' (when the parrots and the monkeys fill the air with their trills and screams, inviting the hunt)
kuntútin	'time of the fat' (when the animals are fat)
sakamtín	'time of the lean' (when the animals are lean)
kuyutín	'dry season' (when the river is low)
kucatín	'time of the downpours'
esát	'time of the burned out' (when the sun is very hot)

For studies and references to Time see: Bedini; Bruneau; Doob; Fraser; Lynn Friedman; Edward Hall (1964); Hallowell; Jefferson; F. P. Jones and Hanson; Klineberg (1927); Lenneberg (1971). See also rhythm, rate of speech, and features of intonation.

G. By-Elements: Artifacts, Clothing, Hair

Movement and vocalizations may be modified by other elements. These objects may be extensions of a limb, such as the arm--an umbrella is used to push elevator buttons or knock on doors. A cigarette can be thrust into the air as though to attack whatever is the subject of the discussion. Clothing can modify movement and walking. Dancers are especially conscious of this "outer skin." Penrod and Plastino say that "Any clothing that does not conform to the outline of his body will alter the designs created in that space."

Styles will change across cultures and across time. In the
last decade long hair has taken on a "radically" different
meaning.

For studies and references to By-Elements or objects
see: Balfour; Barahal; Berg; Boehn; Carlyle; Chisman and
Raven-Hart; Dali; Douty; Firth (1973); Flugel; Frazer; Daniel
Freedman (1969); Green; Hallpike; Hamid; Hildebrand; Hinde
(see index); Leach; Messing; Pear; Rawson; Roach and Eicher;
Schurtz; Sperling; Thiselton-Dyer; E. S. Turner.

The illustrations of the famous dancer, Loie Fuller
(see page 118), show the close integration of clothing and
movement.[39]

H. Silence

Silence can be a powerful communicative element. It
can be dominant in the interaction, controlling and intimidat-
ing or soothing and encouraging.

For studies on Silence see: Anon, "Regulations of the
Order of Cistercians..."; Arlow; Balázs (pp. 62, 68-73, 132,
205-207, 225-227); Basso; Bauman; Beier; Blackmur; Böll;
Bruneau; Chaitanya; Dumont; Fabun; Sandor Feldman (1959,
p. 226); Fliess; Frazer; Ganguly; Guillén; Hastings; Huxley;
J. Vernon Jensen; Key (1975a); Khan; Kata Levy; Mahl (1956);
Matarazzo and Wiens; Matarazzo, Wiens, and Matarazzo;
Meerloo (1960, 1964); Mowrer; Tillie Olsen; Ostwald (1970);
Reik; Rijnbeck; Samarin (1965); Seigel; Shopen; Susan Sontag;
Steiner; Tedlock (1971, 1972); Tindall and Robinson; Witzle-
ben; Zeligs; Zubek, Sansom, and Goving; Zubek, Sansom,
and Prysiaznuik. See also Hesitation.

La danse serpentine

6.

SPECIFIC NONVERBAL ACTS

A. Outcries

Outcries include interjections and exclamations, syntactically detached utterances which grammarians are loath to consider in the grammatical scheme. Note that these are not expressed in indirect speech, "John says that Wow, this shirt is fantastic!" Herbert Spencer (pp. 164-165) called these the "lowest form of language" and compared them to sounds made among the lower animals.

B. Mimicry--Baby Talk

Mimicry involves human sounds, or speech mimicry; natural sounds, or noise mimicry; and animal noises, such as animal mimicry and animal calls. R. K. Sprigg (in correspondence) has made sociolinguistic observations on animal calling in Tibet and notes status values in the various calls. For studies on Mimicry and Animal Calls see: Beinhauer, 1930; Bolton; Carruth; Chandola; Koht; Carlyle May; Perrin; Rice; Tylor.

For studies on Baby Talk see: Austerlitz; William Austin, 1972; Casagrande; Chamberlain; Crawford; Ferguson; Frachtenberg; Haas; Haugen; Heraeus; Hymes, 1961; Jakobson, 1962; Kelkar; Kay Larsen; Evelyn Pike; Sapir, 1915; Scheflen, 1964; Frank Smith and Miller; Voegelin and Robinett.

C. Descriptive and Symbolic Gestures

Descriptive gestures include quantitative or measurement, and pictorial descriptions, such as "drawing in the

119

air. " Symbolic gestures include crossing the fingers for
Good Luck, the old Roman thumbs down for Kill Him, and
the two fingers held up in V for Victory. For references
on the sign for V for Victory see: Anon, "Frivolous V";
Antrim; Beard, pp. 102-106; Hinde, p. 323; Jaeger; Schuler.

D.   Greetings and Leave Takings

Love affairs and wars are easier to get into than to
get out of. How does one end a boring conversation, a business relationship, a casual conversation with a stranger on
a plane, an office appointment? How does one say Goodbye
to an in-law you hope not to see again, a child on his or her
first day of school, or a friend who is terminally ill? At
the beginnings and endings of human interactions, human emotions are often at their peak level. Greetings and Leave
Takings comprise a wide range of behavior from the informal, casual dismissal to someone that will be seen again in
the hall or in the afternoon, to highly ritualized ceremonies,
complete with red carpet and accompanying music. In the
acquisition of communication, Engel (1974, p. 1) notes that
most children say bye-bye before they say Hello. For studies
on Greetings and Leave Takings see: Callan; Eibl-Eibesfeldt,
1969; Walburga Engel, 1974; Raymond Firth; Frazer, 1919;
Friederici; Geiger and Weiss; Goffman; Goody; Grohne; Heslin and Boss; Hopkins; Kendon and Ferber; Knapp, Hart,
Friedrich, and Shulman; Mallery, 1891; Mehrotra; Mehta;
Modi; H. Roth; Ruesch and Kees; Sherzer; Tegg; Tylor.

E.   Deictic Gestures

Pointing or directional gestures may be articulated
with the hand or fingers, or they may be articulated with
parts of the face such as the lower lip or the jaw thrust
forward. Pointing with the fingers may be associated with
supernatural elements and is taboo in some societies. For
references to Deictic Gestures see: Key, 1962; Kurylowicz;
Sherzer.

F.   Affirmation and Negation

Darwin discusses the "firm closure of the mouth"
under "Decision or determination" (p. 233). Bolinger (1946)
refers to the nonphonemic status of "p" in Nope/Yep--a

gestural lip-closure, a gesture of finality. He also reminds us of expressions such as "She preserved a tight-lipped silence. " 'His mouth was a thin line of determination. " "... clamping his mouth shut when he had finished. " For studies on Affirmation and Negation see: Bolinger, 1946; Dolores Brown; Call; Darwin; Frink; George; Jakobson, 1972; Kulovesi; McDavid; Painter; Spitz; Sugar; Uldall.

DIALECTS AND VARIETIES OF
NONVERBAL BEHAVIOR

The following outline can be used for discussing the various articulations of nonverbal behavior. This includes all dialects and special message systems which are interrelated and intricately involved. It is impossible to observe only one facet without regard for other dimensions.

A. Patterned Individual Behavior--Personality, Autism

B. Patterned Group Behavior (Non-coded Systems)
    Geographic Varieties
    Temporal Varieties
    State-of-Being Dimensions
        Age--Child/Adult Behavior
        Sex--Male/Female Behavior
        Status--Socioeconomic Behavior

C. Cultural Dialects (Coded Systems)
    Rites of Passage
    Occupation
    Education
    Athletics
    Societies and Clubs
    Warfare
    Religious Ritual
    Folk Gestures
    The Arts and Performance

D. Language Substitutes/Surrogates
    Lingua Franca
    Circumstantial
    Non-Normal

E. Cross-Cultural

A. Patterned Individual Behavior

The individuality of human behavior is exhibited from the day of birth, according to maternity nurses who can identify their charges by their cries. Birdwhistell speaks of idiomovement with regard to individual kinesic behavior. Personality is implicit in individual patterns.

For studies on Individual Behavior see: Allport and Cantril; Allport and Vernon; Barbara (1960); Chao; D'Arcais; Diehl; Melba Duncan; Estes; J. R. Firth; Fretz; Herzog; Hymes; Izard (1968); Kramer; Krout (1937); Ladefoged and Broadbent; McGehee; McKelvey; Mahl, Danet and Norton; Markel, Eisler, and Reese; Markel, Meisels, and Houck; Markel and Roblin; Matarazzo; W. E. Moore; Murphy; North; Pear; Ramsay; Roback; Sanford; Sapir; Scherer; Stagner; Starkweather; Taboureau; H. C. Taylor; Janet Taylor; J. G. Vance; Werner Wolff.

Autistic behavior, which at times is related to day dreaming, is normal activity and occurs in the repertoire of behavior as a means of adjustment and creative production. Goffman (1963, p. 69) refers to "creative releases. " For studies on Autism see: Susan Barnes; Currie and Brannigan; DeMyer, et al.; Ekman and Friesen, 1969; N. Freedman and Hoffman; Goffman, 1963; Hinde; Corrine Hutt and Ounsted; Marshall Jones; Kendon and Ferber; Krout; McConnell; Maginnis; Mahl, 1968; Mantegazza; Melbin; Montagu, 1971; Rosenfeld, 1966; Tinbergen; S. Wolff and Chess.

B. Patterned Group Behavior

For studies on Geographic Varieties of nonverbal behavior see: T. Z. Lawrence; McDavid; Seaford.

For studies on Infant Prelinguistic Behavior see the section on Acquisition of Communication in Chapter 2. For other studies and studies on Children's Nonverbal Behavior see: Allport and Vernon; J. A. Ambrose; Louise Ames; J. W. Anderson; Beard; Blatz, Allin, and Millichamp; Bosma; Brackbill; Brannigan and Humphries; Bugental, Love, and Kaswan; Bugental, Love, Kaswan, and April; Charlotte Bühler; Bühler and Hetzer; Bullowa; Byers and Byers; Call; Cameron, Livson, and Bayley; Clay; Condon and Sander; Currie and Brannigan; Dennis; Dewey; Dimitrovsky; Ding and Jersild; Enders; Walburga Engel; Etzel and Gewirtz;

Fairbanks; Fairbanks, Herbert, and Hammond; Fairbanks,
Wiley, and Lassman; Liselotte Fischer; Susan Fischer; Fisi-
chelli, Karelitz, Eichbauer, and Rosenfeld; Foss; Daniel
Freedman; Georgina Gates; Gleason; A. G. Goldstein and
Chance; Kurt Goldstein; Gomme; Goodenough; Philip Gray;
Gulick; Guillaume; Haiding; Hansen; Hattwick; Hinde; Irwin;
Irwin and Chen; N. G. Blurton Jones; Justine; Karelitz;
Karelitz and Fisichelli; Kashinsky; Kenderdine; Helen Koch;
Kumin and Razar; Kurtz; Landreth; Lane and Sheppard;
Lenneberg; Levin and Silverman; Levin, Silverman, and
Ford; M. M. Lewis; Lieberman; R. S. Lourie; McConnell;
McGrew; Maginnis; Marquis; Meerloo; Mehrabian and Wil-
liams; Milmoe, Novey, Kagan, and Rosenthal; Minkowski;
Mittelmann; Moss; Murai; William Newell; North; W. C. Ol-
son; Opie and Opie; Oseretzky; Ostwald; Ostwald, Freedman,
and Kurtz; Ostwald and Peltzman; Ostwald, Phibbs, and Fox;
Petö; Petrov; Phillis; Poon and Butler; Potter; Poulsson;
Prechtl; Ptacek and Sander; Rheingold, Gewirtz, and Ross;
Rheingold and Keene; Ringel and Kluppel; Ringwall, Reese,
and Markel; Robson; Roderick and Moyer; Rosenfeld; Schäfer;
Schaffer and Emerson; Schlesinger and Meadow; Schmidt and
Hore; Schreiber; Seton; Seuss; Sheppard; Sheppard and Lane;
Sherman; Shiver; Slobin; Frank Smith and Miller; P. Smith
and Connolly; Lester Sontag and Wallace; Stanistreet; Sutton-
Smith; Todd and Palmer; Truby; Truby and Lind; Turkewitz;
Uklonskaya; Wagoner and Armstrong; R. W. Washburn;
Wasz-Höckert, et al.; J. S. Watson; Weeks; Weir; Weisberg;
Werner and Kaplan; Peter Wolff.

Studies on the dimensions of age above the childhood
period are far fewer. For studies on Adult Behavior see:
Donovan Greene; Heshka and Nelson; Lakin and Eisdorfer;
W. R. Miles; Mittelmann; O'Connell and Kowal; Shipp and
Hollien; Singleton.

Male/female differences show other dimensions of
patterned group behavior. When one considers the hierarchy
of importance that sex differences have in human interaction,
whatever the sexual orientation, it is amazing that so few
scientifically based studies are available on male/female
differences. Though the following list looks quite long,
most of the references are not full studies on sex differences, but all make some comment or refer to some aspect of study which reflect sex differences. For studies on
Male/Female Behavior see: Argyle, Lalljee, and Cook; Edward Armstrong; William Austin (1965); Balfour; Nancy Bayley; Bedichek; Beekman; Beinhauer (1934); Bell and Costello;

Birdwhistell (1970); Harvey Black; Brend; Brilliant; Bugental,
Love, and Gianetto; Call (1965); Cammack and van Buren;
Castiglione; Chapman (1943); Cosper; Martha Davis (see index); R. C. Davis and Buchwald; Davitz (1964); Devereux
(1949); Doob (pp. 209-210); Harold Edwards; Philip Eisenberg;
Ekman, Liebert, Friesen, Harrison, Zlatchin, Malmstrom,
and Baron; Ellsworth and Ludwig; Epstein and Ulrich; Exline
(1960, 1963); Firestone; Susan Goldberg and Lewis; Goodland;
Gottschalk (1972); Donovan Greene; Guilford (1929-30);
Hammes; Henley; Heshka and Nelson; Hewes (1973); Hind-
march; Honkavaara; Jourard and Rubin; Kahn; Kelkar; Ken-
don and Ferber; Key (1975a); Kimura; Robert Knapp; Kozel;
Kurath (1960); LaBarre (1947); Lefcourt, Rotenberg, Buck-
span, and Steffy; Liebman; Machotka; Markel, Prebor, and
Brandt; Markel and Roblin; Mattingly (1966); Margaret Mead;
Mehrotra; Geraldine Michael and Willis; Montagu (1971);
Moss; Lynn O'Connor; Carroll Olsen; Rosenfeld (1966);
Scheflen (1965); Martin Schwartz; Schwartz and Rine; Simms;
Sommer (1959, 1967); Steig; Terango; Tesch, Huston, and
Indenbaum; Thiselton-Dyer; Trager (1962); Vaughan; Weitz;
Willis; Zerffi.

For studies on Homosexual Behavior see: Hess
(1968); Lerman and Damsté; Sanford and Wrightman.

Status and socioeconomic behavior is signaled by non-
verbal means. Some of the behavior is ritualized or forma-
lized, as is noted in etiquette books. See Murdock's listing
of etiquette for several topics that treat status differences.
For studies on Status and Socioeconomic Behavior see:
Bailey; Gregory Bateson (1972); Bond and Shiraishi; Brilliant;
Brooks, Brandt, and Wiener; Cronin; Crystal (1971); Martha
Davis (see index); Efran; Efron; Exline (1971); Ferdon; Ray-
mond Firth; Flack (1967); Foa; Lawrence Freedman and
Hollingshead; Geertz; Goffman; Edward Hall (1955); Harms;
Henley; Hildebrand; Hinde (see index); Hore; Kashinsky and
Wiener; Keesing and Keesing; Klineberg; Lott and Sommer;
Lozier; McDermott; E. B. McNeil; Maginnis; Mehrabian
(1969); Melly; Geraldine Michael and Willis; Moe; Rashevsky;
Schurtz; Sibree; Starkweather (1967); Sulzberger; Vanderbilt.

C. Cultural Dialects

Rites of Passage include the ceremonial and ritual
movements and gestures of birth and christening ceremonies,
weddings, and funerals. For marriage customs see Lodge.

See Francis Hayes' bibliography for other references. Customs and ceremonies constitute a large area of human behavior which is studied by anthropologists and folklorists,
and I have not included such references in this bibliography.

Dialects in Occupation should be cross-referenced
throughout the research. Gestures controlling the economy
and market transactions may also be secret dialects. Some
may be public, such as the policeman's gestures: others
are known to an exclusive group, such as the surgeon's gestures. Hunting communication may be found under whistle
languages.

For Occupational Dialects see: Anon, "Cross country hot shots..."; Beard; Broeg; Charles Carpenter; Macdonald Critchley (1939); Loomis; Mehrotra; Meijer; Moulton;
Phillott; Ribsskog; Seton; Shor; Verplanck.

Dialects in Education comprise coded systems such
as gestures used in language teaching and other forms of
nonverbal communication in the interaction between student
and teacher. Rosenthal and Jacobson found that the teacher
communicated to the students by facial expresssions, postures, and touch, that she expected improved intellectual
performance. For implications in education, see the index
for Written/Spoken language. For studies concerned with
Education see: Asher, Kusudo, and de la Torre; William
Austin (1972); Banks; Brault; Byers and Byers; Conn; Cosper; Cratty; Crutchfield; Galas; Galloway; Giles Gray; Jerald
Green; Harwood; Alfred Hayes; Hong; Jecker, Maccoby, and
Breitrose; David Johnson; Kalish; Lefevre; Liphan, and
Francke; Maccoby, Jecker, Breitrose, and Rose; Mathieu;
Mehegan and Dreifuss; Donald Moores; North; Pardoe; Pol-
gar; Rosenthal; Harvey Taylor; Whitmire; Worth (1974).

Nonverbal behavior in Athletic activities gives special
opportunities for observing human beings in relationship to
the elements and other aspects of the environment. Note the
movement of horse and accomplished rider, when the horse
and rider are one. Perhaps we have gotten too far away
from the pristine behavior of human beings when survival
was dependent upon people moving in rhythm with the environment. An interesting example of coded gestures was
seen at the basketball games between the Soviet Union and
the United States which took place in 1973. The referees
were from Brazil and Finland and the only common language
was sign language. For references to Athletics see: Broeg;
Cratty; Curl; Gates; North.

Societies and Clubs range from the juvenile through college fraternities and sororities to lodges and professional societies. Secret societies have a special inventory of gestures which may change from time to time when they are no longer secret. The elements of communication in secret transactions vary from a single greeting to elaborate rituals and ceremonials. Counting under the cloth is a secret system used for counting for marketing purposes. For references to special communication in Societies and Clubs see: Balfour; Macdonald Critchley (1939, chapter 8); Harold Fischer; Kesson; Jean-Gabriel Lemoine; Lepper; Phillott; Ribsskog; Voorhees; Walpole; Ward.

The nonverbal communication which occurs in Warfare binds and incites communities to cohesive behavior. Military salutes symbolize profound beliefs and values. It was said during World War II that, "When you salute an officer of the U. S. Army, in a very real sense you're saluting God..." (Francis Hayes, 1957, p. 298). Warfare and aggressive action is spurred on by yells and noisy behavior. The Walls of Jericho fell after much shouting and clanging noise. Yells are an important part of the art in karate. For references to Warfare see: Bales; Field; Herbert Fischer; Hobbs; Allen Walker Read; Schuler; Sebeok (1967, p. 1780); Stead.

Religious Ritual has a wide range of gestural behavior and paralinguistic modifications on the verbal act. For other references see Silence and Sign Language in the index. See Francis Hayes (1957) for references to many religious gestures. For Religious Ritual see: Anon, "Regulations of the order of Cistercians..."; Anon, "La Trappe in England"; Edward Andrews; Barakat; Bauman; E. Brandt; J. Burgess; Macdonald Critchley (1939); Daniel-Rops; Dubois; Herbert Fischer; Frazer; Felicitas Goodman; Hackett; Francis Hayes (1957); Hertz; Jaquith; Jaspan; Jucker; Kiener; Kleen; Ladner; S. Langdon; Laufer; Lubienska; Carlyle May; Mencken; Th. Michels; Ohm; Ostwald (1965); Pattison; Gerard Rijnbeck; Susie Rijnhart; Samarin; Satow; Si-Do-In-Dzou; T. C. Smith; Blanche Speer; Stählin; Tylor; Vorwahl; Wolfram.

Folk Gestures are given special attention in the Francis Hayes bibliography. For studies on Folk Gestures see: Bäuml and Bäuml; Brunvand; Jean Cooke; Levette Davidson; Devereux; Dorson; Herbert Fischer; Frazer; Geiger and Weiss; Haiding; Francis Hayes; King; Kleinpaul; Klitgaard; Robert Lawrence; Löw; Moser; Phillips; Potter;

Röhrich; Rolland; Schücking; Schuler; Robert Scott; Stead; Archer Taylor; Stith Thompson; Wundt.

A large number of folk gestures fall in the range of insulting, offensive, and obscene gestures.   Often they are used in a euphemistic way in place of speech.   Body waste materials (or referent, for example the nose) may be used in accompaniment with the insulting gesture.   See Francis Hayes' bibliography for many references and explanations of insulting gestures.   For references to Obscene, Insulting, Offensive Gestures see: Barakat (1973); Macdonald Critchley (1939); Devereux (1951); Elworthy; Sandor Feldman (1941, 1959); Goodland; DeJorio; Kany; King; Kleinpaul; Klitgaard; Knight; Mallery; Moser; Róheim; Walter Roth; Saitz and Cervenka; Sittl; Archer Taylor; Twain; Tylor.

Quantitative and measurement gestures are included in folk gestures in this volume.   The relationship between verbal and nonverbal behavior can be seen in gestures of measurement in Spanish.   A major division is made between nouns with a soul (humans) and those without a soul (animals and inanimate objects). [40]

To indicate the height of a child one holds the hand with palm toward the speaker and index finger pointing upward at the height of the person.   To indicate the height of an animal the hand is held horizontally--either sideways or flat. In English, the division is between animate (humans and animals) and inanimate objects.

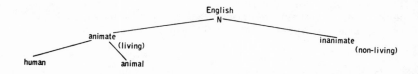

This dichotomy is corroborated in some terms for body parts:

human		animal	
English	Spanish	English	Spanish
leg	pierna	leg	pata (also table,
lung	pulmon	lung	bofe chair, etc.)
back	espalda	back	lomo
neck	cuello	neck	pescuezo

For studies on Quantitative and Measurement gestures see:
Bede; Cajori; Cheng-ming Chang; Macdonald Critchley (1939);
Cushing; Dantzig; Farquhar; Martin Gardner; Gulliver; E. E.
Kramer; Lee; Jean-G. Lemoine; Roger Pack; Wilfred Powell
(1884); Ruska; N. W. Thomas; Tylor.

The Arts and Performance comprise all forms of
Written Language; Art; Drama; Dance; Music; and Solo Performance, which includes Concert Artists, Comedians, Orators.   Media such as Radio, Television, and Film are also
considered here.   In the Arts and Performance nonverbal
behavior is seen in constructed or contrived situations, but
always reflecting real life.   Edward Hall has observed that
the artist and author are both sensitive observers and com-
municators.   Trager (1966) has stated that dancing and music are refinements of kinesics and paralanguage--highly developed and patterned control of body movement and pitch.
Robert Hall[41] further suggests that the melodic line in music is closely related to intonation.   Bolinger (1972) devotes
a section to "Intonation and Music. "

For general studies on the Arts and Performance see:
Birdwhistell; Nelson Goodman; Edward Hall (1966, 1968,
1972); Francis Hayes; Hinde; Kepes; Susanne Langer; Ruesch;
Trager (1966).

Written Language includes all forms of literature,
popular writing, advertising language, comic strips, and
personal communications.   Attempts to transcribe paralanguage have resulted in various spellings and representations.
The alveolar click used in English for commiseration (Key,
1975b, p. 44) has been variously spelled "tsk-tsk; tut-tut;
tch-tch; tusk-tusk. "   An interruptive cough becomes "Ahem!"
A sneer becomes "Hmmm!"   The communicative laugh has
many forms of representation: "tee-hee; heh-heh; har-har;
ho-ho; yuk-yuk; awk-awk. "   Advertising has produced the
following paralinguistic effects in print: Shhhh [for a library

advertisement]; Psssst; Grrrr-Purrrr [a fragrance for men];
the soffft dress; boxxxesss [sterling silver artifacts].

The outstanding difference between oral literature and
written literature is the matter of conveying paralinguistic
and kinesic information. In fact, one might maintain that
an author who couldn't convey nonverbal communication
would be an unsuccessful author. The following examples
illustrate how some authors reduce a three-dimensional message to the two-dimensional written page.

> Rage was in his voice.... Rage came first and
> then a coldness, a possession; noncommittal eyes
> and a pleased smile and no voice at all, only a
> whisper.
>   --John Steinbeck, East of Eden[42]

> Before, when she was well, she shrugged her
> shoulders. But since sickness had weighted down
> her body, she replaced the gestures which would
> have tired her by plays of emotion in the face:
> she said yes with her eyes, no with the corners
> of her mouth: she raised her eyebrows instead of
> her shoulders.
>   --Jean-Paul Sartre, "The Room"[43]

> in your most frail gesture are things which en-
> close me, or which i cannot touch because they
> are too near
>   --e. e. cummings,
>   "somewhere i have never travelled"[44]

For studies on Written Language see: Allport and Vernon;
Beinhauer; Blackmur; Boggs; Bonifacio; Brault; Brunvand;
Candido; Chatman; Macdonald Critchley; Escholz; Forrest;
Fussell; Gerstner-Hirzel; Habicht; Haiding; Hald; Edward
Hall, 1966; G. Stanley Hall and Allin; Hamayon; Hansen;
Hayman; Hinde; Hoppe; Herbert Josephs; Kapsalis; Kaulfers;
Key, 1974; Klineberg; Knowles; Kuepper; Löw; Maresca;
Montagu, 1971, pp. 4-5, 110 ff., 218, 270; Oldfield; Ost-
wald, 1960; Schrero; Suess; Ella Sharpe; Sloan; David Smith;
Snell; Karl Stern, et al.; Archer Taylor; Twain; Tykulsker;
Vogel; Zons.

For studies on Art see: Baxandall; Charles Bell;
Birdwhistell; E. Brandt; Brophy; Coss; Darwin; Deonna;
Efron; Gombrich; Gombrich, Hochberg, and Black; Edward

Hall, 1966; Hanawalt; Henser; Hinde; Kapsalis; Knight; Kris
and Gombrich; Susanne Langer; Le Brun Marshack; J. Montagu; Neumann; Rawson; Riemschneider-Hörner; Roth; Saunders;
Saxl; Testelin; Tikkanen.

Drama includes Mime and all theatrical productions.
Paralanguage and kinesics are the vehicles of mood that
make it possible for Maurice Evans and Helen Hayes, in the
autumn of their careers, to play the springtime Romeo and
Juliet, and successfully portray the lilt of young voices and
youthful movements.

Some of the most successful "lines" in drama are
gestural or paralinguistic acts. It is not unusual in the
theater to witness a nonverbal act eliciting the most abound-
ing audience response.

For studies on Drama see: Florence Adams; Aldrich;
Alfau; Armfield; Arnals; Aubert; Mary Austin; Balázs; Bau-
din; Birdwhistell; Boguslawski; Robert Bowers; Bruford;
Chaitanya; Checkov; Chisman and Raven-Hart; Clevenger and
King; Coger; Coger and Pelham; Milton Cowan; Macdonald
Critchley; Decroux; Delsarte; Dorcy; Douailler; Efron; Jo-
hann Engel; Fine; Frijda, 1965; Gerstner-Hirzel; Grotowski;
Gunkle; Hallar; Hinde; Hobbs; Jelgerhuis; Joseph; Kelley;
Kingson and Cowgill; Kirchhoff; Kleen; Peter Kline; Knowles;
LaBarre, 1947; Lawson; Le Bidois; Le Mee; Mawer; Men-
doza; Montagu, 1971, p. 210; Mowat; Pearn; Pickersgill;
Rawson; Rich; Ruesch and Kees; Salisbury; Selden; Shaftes-
bury; Shea; Siddons; Skraup; Speck; Stanislavski; Stanistreet;
Stebbins; Tylor; Kathrine Walker; Warman; White and Battye;
Whitmire; Zung.

Dance exemplifies the flow of body movement analogous to the melodic line of music. For studies on Dance
see: Anon, "Notation, choreology..."; Aeppli; Arbeau; Ashihara; Auboyer; Bartenieff; Bartenieff and Davis; Beauchamp;
Beaumont; Beaumont and Serge; Benesh; Bhadbury; Bharata
Muni; Bjørn; Blasis; Franziska Boas; Bouissac; Faubion
Bowers; Brock; Canna and Loring; Causley; Chatterji; Craighead; Macdonald Critchley; Cross; Cuisinier; Curl; Martha
Davis, 1972; Dell; De Mille; Devi; De Zoete; Isadora Duncan; Dyke; Eshkol and Nul; Bessie Evans and Evans; Feüillet;
Feves; Fuller; Gallini; Alice Gates; Manomohan Ghosh; Glas-
sow; Groslier; Fernau Hall; Haskell; Russell Hughes; Hum-
phrey; Hutchinson; Ikegami; Jablonko; Leticia Jay; Kaeppler;
Kamin; Keallinohomoku; Kirstein; Kleen; Knust; Kool; Kurath;

Kuttikrishna; LaCuisse; Laban; Lawson; Lekis; Lifar; Mc-
Craw; Bernard Mason; Meerloo, 1961; Meunier; Arthur Mi-
chel; Morrice; Margaret Morris; Mossford; Nadel and Nadel;
Naidu; Naidu, Naidu, and Pantulu; Nandikesvara; Noverre;
Oesterley; Pandeya; Pécourt; Penrod; Playford; Pollenz; Pre-
makumar; Preston; Preston-Dunlop; Priest; Redfern; Rodrí-
quez; Sachs; Saint-León; Shawn; Singha and Massey; Sorell;
Speck; Spreen; Stepanov; Edith Stern; Sutton; Tetley; Samuel
Thornton; Topaz; Toulouze; Venkatachalam; Vuillier; Kathrine
Walker; West; Whiffen, Chapter 15; Wigman; Wooten; Fried-
rich Zorn.

For studies on Music see: Arnals; Lomax; Markel,
1968; Moses, 1961; Ostwald, 1961, 1962; Otterstein; Roberts
and Ridgeway; Rochas; Rogge; Scotto di Carlo; Shea.

Solo Performance includes Concert Artists, Comedians, and Orators. Story Tellers (Oral Literature) are also
included here. Ruth Slenczynska, former child prodigy, who
has performed over two generations, has noted the change of
style between the generations:[45]

> Avoid mannerisms. Theatricals went out of fash-
> ion with the silent movies, in which gestures had
> to tell the whole story without the spoken word.
> At the piano mannerisms are not only in bad taste
> but physically impossible except for artists who
> are not really engrossed in the music. Besides,
> the natural, effortless abandon that comes with
> good, relaxed piano technique is sufficiently spec-
> tacular in itself.

Television has made possible the visual approach to humor
to a much larger audience than the story-teller was able to
reach. Performers add to their own fun by throwing in a
gesture or facial expression, producing a double entendre.
Paralinguistic and kinesic features make it possible for
comedians to impersonate. They capture the sounds and
movement of the subject.

For studies on Solo Performance see: Gilbert Aus-
tin; Albert Bacon; Alexander Bell; David Bell; Moses Brown;
Comstock; Macdonald Critchley; Delsarte; Doat; Efron; Emer-
son; Glasgow; Giles Gray; Grover; Harshbarger; Kightlinger;
Knowles; Joseph Mosher; Ott; Parrish; Quintilian; Ross;
Russell; Sheridan; Siddons; Tedlock; Thwing; John Walker;
Warman.

Radio, Television, and Film brought back an awareness of paralinguistic and kinesic components in communication. The careful attention to gestures in public speaking
which was given much attention in the last century is once
again a priority to people in public relations. It seems as
though styles come and go, and that if one waits around long
enough, things will be back in style eventually. Drama, too,
has to be scaled down and modified for the television camera
where spacing necessitates smaller gestures and shorter
movements.

For studies on Radio, Television, and Film see:
Anon, "Strange radio sign talk... "; Anon, "Video director";
Balázs; Carlile; Carmichael, Roberts, and Wessell; Ekman
and Friesen, 1969; Gaines; Gilmore and Middleton; Hanna;
Kingson and Cowgill; Christian Koch; Metz; Strowski; Worth.

D. Language Substitutes/Surrogates

Coded systems which substitute for the verbal act
have been created for various practical and circumstantial
reasons, or have been forced into existence by non-normal
conditions.

Lingua Franca comprise hand signals developed by
North American Indians and some Australian tribes. Deaf
Sign Language (which see below) should also be considered
along with sign languages. For studies on American Indian
Sign Language see: Beard; William Clark; Cody; De Haerne;
Dodge; Dunbar; Eder; Gerland; Grinde; Hadley; Harrington;
Walter Hoffman; Hofsinde; Robinson Johnson; Kakumasu;
Kroeber; Krout, 1942; Lance; Lévy-Bruhl; Ljung; Stephen
Long; MacGowan; Mallery; Mas-Latrie; Nordenskiold; Hugh
Scott; Seton; Starr; Stokoe, 1966; Teit; William Tomkins;
Tylor; Voegelin; Voegelin and Kroeber; Vuillemey; Jerell
Walker; Walter Webb; Weil; West; Wied-Neuwied.

For studies on Other Sign Language see: Anon,
"Regulations of the order... "; Anon, La Trappe in England;
J. D. Anderson; Barakat; Berndt; Macdonald Critchley; Ga-
son; Grolleau; Haddon; Howitt; Hutt; Kuschel; Leibniz; Meg-
gitt; Mountford; Rijnbeck; Rossellius; Walter Roth; Seligmann;
Spencer and Gillen; Stirling; W. L. Warner; Wundt.

Circumstantial reasons such as distance and silence
underlie the use of both Gestural and Paralinguistic substitutes for language. Drum, Whistle, and Gong languages,

134 Nonverbal Communication

Australian sign language, and American Indian sign languages
are reported in use over great distances. When silence is
desired for religious reasons sign languages may be used.

For studies on Whistle, Gong, and Drum languages
see: Anon, "Gomera..."; Alexandre; D. W. Ames, Greger-
sen, and Neugebauer; Robert Armstrong; Betz; Brusis; Burs-
sens; Busnel; Busnel, Moles, and Gilbert; Busnel, Moles,
and Vallancien; Carrington; Chandola; Clarke; Classe; George
Cowan; Eberlein; Eboué; E. D. Edwards; Hasler; Heepe;
Heine-Goldern; Heinitz; Herzog; Hooton; Hulstaert; Hurley;
Kirby; Labouret; Lajard; Lenneberg; Leroy; Meijer; Moles;
Moles and Busnel; Nekes; Niggemeyer; Nketia; Quedenfeldt;
Rattray; Ritzenthaler and Peterson; Schefold; Schneider;
Simmons; Snyders; Steinmann; Theodore Stern; Thiesen;
Thilenius; Valen; Verneau; Very; A. Witte; Zemp and Kauf-
mann.

Non-normal varieties of nonverbal behavior comprise
a wide range of articulations, from the deaf sign language,
which may be a complete substitution for the verbal act, to
slight modifications of nonverbal behavior by blind people or
people who have physical differences. For studies on Deaf
Sign Language see: Sign Language Studies [semi-annual
journal, ed. by William C. Stokoe, Jr.]; Anon, Digiti Lingua;
Abraham; Amman; Anthony; Carlotte Baker; Barrois; Battison; Alexander Bell; Bellugi; Bellugi and Fischer; Bellugi
and Klima; Bellugi and Siple; Bergman; Best; Boese; Bonet;
Bornstein; Bornstein and Hamilton; Breger; Callow; Charlip
and Ancona; Chen; Cicourel; Cicourel and Boese; Cohen,
Namir, and Schlesinger; Covington; Macdonald Critchley,
1938; Crutchfield; Dalgarno; Anne Davis; De Haerne; Eibl-
Eibesfeldt, 1973; L'Epée; Fant; Susan Fischer; Fletcher;
Lynn Friedman; Goodenough; B. P. Green; Gustason, Pfetzing, and Zawolkow; Higgins; Hodgson; Holder; Holm;
Hutcheson; Robert Ingram; Harry Jones; Kakumasu; Klim
and Bellugi; Knowlson; Kruse; Kuschel; La Fin; Lieth; Jo-
seph Long; Lynge; McCall; Macleod; Mallery; Markowicz;
Mas-Latrie; Mendelson, et al.; Michaels; Montenovesi;
Moores; Moores, McIntyre, and Weiss; Nash; Nordenskiold;
Peale; Peled; Peng; Pesonen; Reuschert; Rich; Rowe, Brooks,
and Watson; Sallop; Hilde Schlesinger; Schlesinger and Meadow; I. M. Schlesinger; Schlesinger, Cohen, and Namir;
Schlesinger and Presser; Schmalz; W. R. Scott; Jules Seigel;
Sella; Sharoff; Shunary; Shunary and Miransky; Sicard; Silverman; Siple; Steinthal; Stokoe; Stokoe, Casterline, and Crone-
berg; Tervoort; Tweney and Hoemann; Tylor; Van Son; Vetter;

David Watson; Wilkins; Judy Williams; J. G. Wolff; James
Woodward; Mary Woodward.

For studies on the Blind and their relationship to non-
verbal behavior: Apple; Blau; Brodey; Leslie Clark; Darwin;
Eibl-Eibesfeldt, 1970; D. G. Freedman; Fulcher; Goodenough;
Griffin; Jane Thompson; Yahraes; Zahl.

Non-normal behavior may also be exhibited in emotionally disturbed or mentally ill behavior. Darwin believed
that we could understand normal behavior by studying the
aberrations of mental disorders, as well as other physically
handicapped persons. In normal behavior, language and nonverbal components are successfully integrated. In the communicative behavior of the mentally ill, the person fails to
integrate expressions, gestures, and speech with the actual
situation. In normal behavior, the communicative aspects
are relevant, appropriate, and predictable in the context of
situation (Key, 1975b, chapter 7).

Emotional states are represented in metaphors: can't
swallow it, can't stomach it, pain in the neck, to burn up,
load on the chest (Stern, Boulanger, and Cleghorn). A
summary of the psychological research and a large bibliography are found in Mahl and Schulze, 1964. For studies on
Emotionally Disturbed or Mentally Ill see: Barahal; Barbara;
Baxter, Winters, and Hammer; Beier; Bender and Mahl;
Berger; Berkson; Berkson and Davenport; Berkson and Mason; Birdwhistell; Brody, Newman, and Redlich; Corbin;
Davenport and Berkson; Deutsch; E. Duffy; Duffy and Moore;
Ekman; Ekman and Friesen; Ekman, Liebert, Friesen, Har-
rison, Zlatchin, Malmstrom, and Baron; Eldred and Price;
Sandor Feldman; Sandor Ferenczi; Fine; Fliess; Gostynski;
Gottschalk; Gottschalk and Auerbach; Gratiolet; Hagen, Port-
er, and Brink; Hargreaves and Starkweather; Herbert Harris;
Hinchliffe, Lancashire, and Roberts; Hinde; Jelliffe; Kasl
and Mahl; Krim; Krout; Laffal; Lefcourt, Rotenberg, Buck-
span, and Steffy; Luchsinger; McQuown; Mahl; Mahl and
Schulze; Stella Mason; Matarazzo; Matarazzo, Wiens, Matarazzo, and Saslow; Mehegan and Dreifuss; Mendelson, Siger,
and Solomon; Meyer, Bahrick, and Fitts; Moses; Needles;
Ombredane; Ostwald; Perrot; Pittenger; Pittenger, Hockett,
and Danehy; Pittenger and Smith; Reece and Whitman; Riemer; Rioch; Rosenberg and Langer; Rosenberg and Gordon;
Ruesch; Sainsbury; Scheflen; Shands; Starkweather; Edith
Stern; Stern, Loulanger, and Cleghorn; Sullivan; Szasz; Taylor, Pottash, and Head; Thorek; Tredgold; Harry Wiener;

Charlotte Wolff; S. Wolff and Chess; Werner Wolff; Zimbardo, Mahl, and Barnard.

E. Cross-Cultural Varieties

Nothing in nature is isolated; nothing is
without connection to the whole... --Goethe[46]

Cross-cultural means across sub-cultures within a
language group, as well as across language groups. The
most extensive study on body movement comparing cultural
differences in time and space was inspired by Boas and done
by his student David Efron. In this study Efron compared
the changes in body movement from Eastern European Jews
and Southern Italians, and their counterparts in America
who had become Americanized.

For studies on African cultures see: John Adams;
Ames, Gregersen, and Neugebauer; Doob; Goody; Keallinohomoku; Kirk; Ladefoged; Mahgoub; Marshall; Mathon; Messing; Nketia; Olofson; Revill; Samarin; Tremearne; Wescott.

For studies on American Indian see: Bailey; Basso;
Braun and Crofts; Cole; Devereux; Eder; Grimes; Hamp;
Kakumasu; Key, 1962; Landar; Ransom, Trager.

For studies on Arabic see: Barakat; Bauer; Berque;
Brewer; George; Goldziher; Hall; Hamalian; Khatchadourian;
Van Ess; Yousef; Yousef and Briggs.

For studies on Asia see: Bateson and Mead; Harold
Bayley; Blakely; Bouillard; Chang; Christian; Conklin; David-
Neel; DeVita; Geertz; Hamayon; Hockett; Hopkins; Irizawa;
Jepson; Keesing and Keesing; Kelkar; Klineberg; Lodge;
Kenneth Love; Helen May; Margaret Mead; Mead and Mac-
Gregor; Mehrotra; Mehta; C. B. Miller; John Miller; Roy
Miller; Modi; Neumann; Phillott; Powell; Rijnhart; Róheim;
Roth; Saunders; Sorenson and Gajdusek; Vinacke; Vinacke and
Fong; Yutang.

For studies on Black English see: Anon, Black girls
at play; Ames, Gregersen, and Neugebauer; Aiello and
Jones; Ernest Bauer; Nancy Bayley; Byers and Byers; Dickens and Sawyer; Dorson; Dubner; Walburga Engel; Frankel
and Frankel; French; French and Engel; Fugita, Wexley, and

Hillery; Guttentag; Henry; John Horton; Kenneth Johnson; Stanley Jones; Jones and Aiello; Keallinohomoku; Kochman; LaFrance and Mayo; Markel and Sharpless; Rhodes; Roland Scott, et al.; Secord, Bevan, and Katz; Stevenson and Ferguson; Tremearne.

For studies on French see: Banks; Brault; Delattre; Goude; Le Mée; Malecot; Margaret Mead, 1961; Tykulsker.

For studies on German see: Delattre; Essen; Hoffman-Krayer and Bächtold-Stäubli; Isačenko and Schädlich; Triandis, Davis, and Takezawa; Troyanovich.

For studies on Greek see: Anthriotis; Blasis; Deonna; Kapsalis; Mawer; Neumann; Sittl; Triandis and Lambert.

For studies on Hungarian see: Fónagy and Magdics; Magdics; Tompa.

For studies on India see: J. D. Anderson; Richard Burton; Hopkins; Margaret Mead, 1961; Uklonskaya.

For studies on Italian see: D'Angelo; Efron; Graham and Argyle; Graham, Bitti, and Argyle; de Jorio; Lyall; Mallery; Pitre; Rosa; Wandruszka; Wiseman.

For studies on Japanese see: Abe; Akiyama and Yumoto; Asano; Bond and Iwata; Bond and Shiraishi; Cammack and Van Buren; Hearn; Hinds; Ishii; Kishimoto; Margaret Mead, 1961; Roy Miller; Morsbach; Nakajima; Peng; Saint-Jacques; Satow; Si-Do-In-Dzou; Harvey Taylor; Triandis, Davis, and Takezawa.

For studies on Portuguese see: Basto; Merryman; Pierson.

For studies on Russian see: Buning and Schooneveld; Donald Johnson; Neumann.

For studies on Spanish see: Beinhauer; Beym; Bowen; Dolores Brown; Caballero; Canfield; Cardona; Daniels; Delattre; Delattre, Olsen, and Poenack; Dickey and Knower; Fernandez Mines; Flachskampf; Fridman; Giner; Jerald Green; Francis Hayes; Pam Johnson; Kany; Kaulfers; Lado; Lekis; Marañón; Marden; Martí; Matluck; Meo Zilio; Moreno Villa; Nine-Curt; Olsen; Poyatos; Rabanales; Saitz and Cervenka; Sorenson and Gajdusek; Stockwell, Bowen, and Silva-Fuenzalida; Van Deusen and Gunn; Wainerman; Wigdorsky.

138   Nonverbal Communication

For studies on Cross-Cultural Varieties see: Anon,
Black girls at play; Abe; John Adams; Aiello and Jones;
Akiyama and Yumoto; Ames, Gregersen, and Neugebauer;
J. D. Anderson; Anthriotis; Argyle; Arnason; Asano; Bailey;
Banks; Barakat; Basso; Basto; Bateson and Mead; Ernest
Bauer; Leonhard Bauer; Harold Bayley; Nancy Bayley; Bein-
hauer; Berque; Harvey Black; Blakely; Blasis; Franz Boas;
Bond and Iwata; Bond and Shiraishi; Bouillard; Bowen; Brault;
Braun and Crofts; Brewer; Brilliant; Brooks, Brandt, and
Wiener; Buning and Schooneveld; Bursack; Richard Burton;
Byers and Byers; Caballero; Cammack and van Buren; Can-
field; Cardona; Cheng-ming Chang; Nien-Chuang Chang;
Christian; Cole; Condon and Yousef; Conklin; Cuceloglu;
D'Angelo; Daniels; David-Neel; Davitz; Delattre; Delattre,
Olsen, and Poenack; Deonna; Devereux; DeVita; Dickens and
Sawyer; Dickey and Knower; Doob; Dorson; Drechsler; Dubin;
Dubner; Eder; Efron; Efron and Foley; Ekman and Friesen;
Ekman, Sorenson, and Friesen; Walburga Engel; Essen; Fer-
don; Flachskampf; Foa; Fónagy and Magdics; Frankel and
Frankel; Frazer; French; French and Engel; From; Geertz;
Geiger and Weiss; George; Germanović; Giner; Goldziher;
Goody; Goude; Graham and Argyle; Graham, Bitti, and Ar-
gyle; Jerald Green; Grimes; Guttentag; Edward Hall; Hamali-
an; Hamayon; Hamp; Alfred Hayes; Hearn; Henry; Hinde;
Hinds; Hockett; Hoffman-Krayer and Bächtold-Stäubli; Holm;
Hong; Hopkins; John Horton; Irizawa; Isačenko and Schädlich;
Ishii; Izard; Jepson; Donald Johnson; Kenneth Johnson; H. P.
Jones; Stanley Jones; Jones and Aiello; de Jorio; Kakumasu;
Kany; Kapsalis; Kashinsky; Kaulfers; Keallinohomoku; Kee-
sing and Keesing; Kelkar; Key, 1962; Khatchadourian; Kirk;
Kishimoto; Klineberg; Kochman; Kozel; LaBarre; Ladefoged;
Lado; LaFrance and Mayo; Landar; Leibman; Le Mée; Lodge;
Kenneth Love; Lyall; Magdics; Mahgoub; Malecot; Marañón;
Marden; Markel and Sharpless; Marshall; Mathon; Mawer;
Helen May; Margaret Mead; Mead and MacGregor; Mehrotra;
Mehta; Meo Zilio; Merryman; Messing; Michael and Willis;
C. B. Miller; John Miller; Roy Miller; Modi; Moreno;
Morsbach; Nakajima; Neumann; Nine-Curt; Nketia; Olofson;
Carroll Olsen; Osser and Peng; Peng; Phillott; Pierson;
Pitre; Powell; Poyatos; Rabanales; Radlovic; Rands; Ransom;
Revill; Rhodes; Rijnhart; Róheim; Rolland; Rosa; H. A. Rose;
Roth; Ruesch; Saint-Jacques; Saitz and Cervenka; Salisbury;
Samarin; Samovar and Porter; Satow; Saunders; Scherer;
Robert Scott; Roland Scott, et al.; Sechrest and Flores;
Sechrest, Flores, and Arellano; Secord, Bevan, and Katz;
Seelye; Si-Do-In-Dzou; Sittl; Alfred Smith; Sorenson and
Gajdusek; Stenvenson and Ferguson; Stockwell, Bowen, and

Silva-Fuenzalida; Harvey Taylor; Silvan Tomkins; Tomkins
and McCarter; Tompa; Trager, 1960; Tremearne; Triandis,
Davis, and Takezawa; Triandis and Lambert; Troyanovich;
Tykulsker; Tylor; Uklonskaya, et al.; Upshur; Van Ess;
Vinacke; Vinacke and Fong; Wainerman; Wandruszka; Weitz;
Wescott; Wiseman; Yousef; Yousef and Briggs; Yutang.

8.

BIBLIOGRAPHY

> The correction of Textual Errors (Courte-
> ous Reader) is a work of Time, and that
> hath taken wing. The more faults thou find-
> est, the larger field is presented to thy hu-
> manity to practice in. Be indulgent in thy
> censure, and remember that Error, whether
> Manual or Mental, is an inheritance, descend-
> ing upon us, from the first of our Race.
> --Errata leaf in Francis Bacon's
> Of the Advancement and Proficience
> of Learning, Oxford, 1640. 47

This bibliography is fairly complete in its focus on the
communicative aspects of paralanguage and kinesics, together
with contributing features in proxemics, tactile behavior, silence, and so forth. It is not complete in areas which are disciplines in themselves--for example in dance, psychology, and
education. I have freely used other bibliographies and even included some of their comments (for example from M. Davis,
and F. Hayes), but in no case have I copied their every item;
therefore the reader should use them for further references
along the lines that interest them. I have also gleaned references from unpublished bibliographies, such as one by Robert
Kleck, and various course outlines that I have exchanged with
other instructors. Through the kindness of David Efron (whose
classic work was recently translated into Spanish and Italian), I
had access to the unpublished bibliography which he collected
many years ago. In a few cases I have not included every reference which a scholar has to his or her credit, particularly if
the items are numerous and repetitive. I have included manuscripts (and the author's institution) so that we may all be aware
of what research is in progress. I have not always itemized all
of the articles and chapters in journals and books which are devoted to nonverbal studies; for example, the journals Sign Language Studies and Semiotica.

A bibliography does not always reflect the influences in the field. Some scholars, such as Bolinger, Archibald Hill, and Margaret Mead, have not published much in these aspects per se, but their influence has been felt widely, in pointing to and encouraging research in these matters. I have usually followed the Library of Congress' listing of names if there is a problem of double names, such as Blurton Jones (located under Jones), or names with prefixes, such as von Cranach (located under C). Marriage creates a dilemma for women scholars, who become lost in the naming system. Therefore Jane Goodall is cross-referenced to Lawick-Goodall. I hope that in the future something will be devised so that bibliographies won't have to cross-reference every marriage! I have added birth and death statistics for older authors, because it is important to evaluate these works in relationship to their times.

I have tried to make the Table of Contents and Index ample as well as lucid, so that the book will be useful as a reference guide. In referring to items I have not always specified which entry when an author has more than one. It is usually obvious from the title, and it seems "cluttery" to add information which is apparent. Getting the correct or the most useful information is increasingly arduous, in view of the proliferation of publishing, reprinting, revising, and excerpting.

I feel it is necessary to enter the earliest date of publication, so that one can measure the impact of the material in the context of its times. This stance, however, sometimes runs into conflict with sound bibliographical procedures; for example, Darwin has been reprinted without its original date! Furthermore, I find it increasingly difficult to cite references for statements made. So much of knowledge is becoming commonplace and in the public domain-- and we may easily forget where, how or when we first encountered the material.

There may be some "ghosts" in these pages ... I have been collecting for about fifteen years. Inevitably my slips and lapses rear their heads to remind me that some of the references are incomplete. I have two choices: to pull out all except the immaculately perfect entries, or to publish the most accurate information possible. In the interest of future research there is little question as to which alternative is more profitable. Sometimes ghosts lead us to unexpected and worthwhile surprises. If readers have further information and corrections, I would welcome such contributions.

BIBLIOGRAPHY

The following journals are of special interest in the study of nonverbal communication: Semiotica: Journal of the International Association for Semiotic Studies, Thomas A. Sebeok, editor-in-chief (The Hague: Mouton). Sign Language Studies, William C. Stokoe, Jr., editor (Silver Spring, Maryland: Linstok Press). Journal of Human Movement Studies, H. T. A. Whiting, ed. (University of Leeds, England). VS: Quaderni di Studi Semiotici, Umberto Eco, ed. (Milan, Italy: Valentino Bompiani).

The following journals published special issues on nonverbal communication: Comparative Group Studies, William Fawcett Hill, editor, "Nonverbal Communication" (special issue) 3. 4 (November 1972), (Beverly Hills, California: Sage Publications). The Journal of Communication, Randall P. Harrison and Mark L. Knapp, special issue editors, "A special issue on nonverbal communication," 22. 4 (December 1972). Langages, A. J. Greimas, editor, "Pratiques et langages gestuels," 10 (June 1968). Scientific American 227. 3 (September 1972).

See also the encyclopedias for various topics.

Anon
1975 Black Girls at Play: Folkloric Perspectives on Child Development. Austin, Tex. : Southwest Educational Development Laboratory.

Anon
1969 "The body: man's silent signals," Time (June 13), p. 86.

Anon
1967 "Choreology: Benesh movement notation today," Ballet Today 1:17 (January-February), pp. 12-13.

Anon
1972 "Communication" (Special issue), Scientific American (September).

Anon
1941 "Cross country hot shots: story of a freight train's crew," Pic Magazine (December 23), pp. 37-41.

Anon
1698 Digiti Lingua: or, the most compendious, copious, facile, and secret way of silent converse ever yet discovered ... By a person who has conversed no otherwise in above nine years. London.

Anon
1969 "Do gestures tell your secret thoughts?" Good Housekeep-
ing (February), p. 163.

Anon
1956 "Ear-wiggling philatelists," an Associated Press story
(September 8), which appeared in U. S. newspapers. [A stamp
auction--wiggling ears, tapping chest with pencil, moving an
ankle, Hayes.]

Anon
1975 "Eléments verbaux et non verbaux dans l'analyse discursive
du séminaire," University of Nancy: Centre de Recherches et
d'Applications Pédagogiques en Langues, 12 pp.

Anon
1950 "Every little movement: gesture 'art' south of border,"
New Orleans Item (April 23), p. 5A.

Anon
1941 "Frivolous V," Time (July 28), p. 20.

Anon
1968 "Gebärde," Brockhaus Enzyklopädie, Vol. 6. Wiesbaden:
F. A. Brockhaus.

Anon
1946 "Gestural language discussed," New York Times (December 22), Section VI, 49:2.

Anon
1950 "Gesture language," Life 28 (January 9), pp. 79-82.

Anon
1948 "Gestures betray you," Science Digest (December), p. 42.

Anon
1941 "Gestures not inherited," Science News Letter 40, p. 243.

Anon
1951 "Give-away gestures," Coronet Magazine 30 (May), pp.
116-119.

Anon
1750 Kurze Abhandlung von der Händesprache, insoweit deren
Merkmaale bei den alten Schriftstellern sich äussern, mit deren
eigenen Beweistümern bestätiget. Cassel.

Anon
1941 "Mexico says it with gestures," Pemex Travel Club Bulletin III (November-December), pp. 5-6.

Anon
      1715   Monde (Le) Plein de fols, Amsterdam.   [Published later
      as I Calotto Resucitato, q. v.   Gesticulation portrayed in engrav-
      ings of grotesque figures.]

Anon
      1965   "Notation, choreology and the B. Ed. ," Progress Reports
      of the Institute of Choreology (June 1965, July 1966, December
      1966).

Anon
      1914   "The rambler," Travel 22 (February), p. 35.

Anon
      1926   Regulations of the order of Cistercians of the strict ob-
      servance, published by the General Chapter.   Dublin: M. H.
      Gill and Son, 357 pages.

Anon
      1946   "Speaking of pictures," Life 21 (September 16), pp. 12-15.

Anon
      1932   "Strange radio sign talk directs radio broadcasts," Popu-
      lar Mechanics 58 (July), p. 25.

Anon
      1937   La Trappe in England.   London.

Anon
      1952   "Urges sign language to promote world peace," Hobbies
      57 (August), p. 137.

Anon
      1948   "Video director," New York Times Magazine (October 24),
      p. 58.

Anon
      1973   "What are the politicians really saying?   Body language
      tells you," Life, "Parting Shots," pp. 82-84.

Anon
      1940   "Words, words, words," American Speech 15:2 (April),
      p. 131.

Anon
      1955   "Your gestures give you away," Science Digest (October),
      p. 30.

Aaronson, Doris, and Robert W. Rieber, eds.
         Developmental Psycholinguistics and Communication Dis-
      orders, "The influence of verbal and nonverbal factors in the
      acquisition and development of language," New York: New York
      Academy of Sciences.

Abbey, David S.
1973   Now See Hear! Applying Communications to Teaching.
Toronto, Ontario, Canada: Ontario Institute for Studies in
Education, 74 pages.

Abe, Isamu
1955   "Intonational patterns of English and Japanese," Word
11:3, pp. 386-398.

Abecassis, Janine
1972-1973 "A propos de la communication non-verbale chez
l'enfant d'age préscolaire: etude de certains aspects de la
communication gestuelle," Bulletin de Psychologie 26, pp. 506-
512.

Abelson, Robert P., and Vello Sermat
1962   "Multidimensional scaling of facial expressions," Journal of Experimental Psychology 63:6, pp. 546-554.

Abercrombie, David
1956   "Gesture," chapter 6 in Problems and Principles in
Language Study. London: Longman, pp. 70-83.

1964   "A phonetician's view of verse structure," Linguistics
6 (June), pp. 5-13.

1965   "Conversation and spoken prose," chapter 1 in Studies
in Phonetics and Linguistics. Oxford University Press, pp. 1-
9.

1967   "Voice quality and voice dynamics," chapter 6 in Elements of General Phonetics. Chicago: Aldine Publishing
Company, pp. 89-110. Partially reprinted as "Voice qualities,"
in Norman N. Markel, Psycholinguistics. Homewood, Illinois:
Dorsey Press, 1969, pp. 109-134.

1968   "Paralanguage," British Journal of Disorders of Communication 3:1, pp. 55-59.

1971   "Some functions of silent stress," Edinburgh Studies in
English and Scots, A. J. Aitken, Angus McIntosh, and Hermann Pálsson, eds. Longman, pp. 147-156.

Abraham, E. J. D.
[Pre-1939] The Story of the Deaf and Dumb, and the Language
of Gesture. Melbourne.

Adair, John, and Sol Worth
1967   "The Navaho as filmmaker," American Anthropologist
69:1 (February), pp. 76-78.

Adams, Florence Adelaide
1891   Gesture and Pantomimic Action. New York, 221 pages.

Adams, John Boman
    1957   "Culture and conflict in an Egyptian village," American
    Anthropologist 59, pp. 225-235. Reprinted as, "On expressive
    communication in an Egyptian village," in Dell Hymes, Lan-
    guage in Culture and Society. New York: Harper and Row,
    1964, pp. 272-273.

Adamson, Lauren, Heidelise Als, Edward Tronick, and T. Berry
    Brazelton [Children's Hospital Medical Center]
    1975   "Social interaction between a sighted infant and her
    blind parents." Read at the Society for Research in Child De-
    velopment, Denver.

Addington, David W.
    1968   "The relationship of selected vocal characteristics to
    personality perception," Speech Monographs 35:4, pp. 492-503.

Aeppli, F.
    1925   'Die wichtigsten Ausdrücke für das Tanzen in den ro-
    manischen Sprachen," Beiheft zur Zeitschrift fur Romanische
    Philologie 75.

Agulera, D. C.
    1967   "Relationships between physical contact and verbal inter-
    action between nurses and patients," Journal of Psychiatric
    Nursing 5, pp. 5-21.

Aiello, John R.
    1974   "The development of personal space: proxemic behavior
    of children 6 through 16," Human Ecology 2, pp. 177-189.

Aiello, John R., and Stanley E. Jones
    1971   "Field study of the proxemic behavior of young school
    children in three subcultural groups," Journal of Personality
    and Social Psychology 19:3, pp. 351-356.

Akin, J., A. Goldberg, G. Myers, and J. Stewart
    1970   Language Behavior: A Book of Readings in Communica-
    tion. The Hague: Mouton, 359 pages.

Akiyama, Kazuyoshi, and Yumoto Kohzo
    1966   "A study of voice identification using Japanese speech,"
    Study of Sounds 12 (Tokyo), pp. 209-223.

Albert, Stuart, and James M. Dabbs, Jr.
    1970   "Physical distance and persuasion," Journal of Person-
    ality and Social Psychology 15:3, pp. 265-70.

Albright, Robert William
    1958   "The International Phonetic Alphabet: its backgrounds
    and development," International Journal of American Linguistics
    24:1, Part III (January), 78 pages.

Aldis, Owen
 1975 Play Fighting. New York: Academic Press, 320 pages.

Aldrich, Virgil C.
 1963 Philosophy of Art. Englewood Cliffs, N. J. : Prentice-Hall, 116 pages.

Aldridge, C. H.
 1963 "Sign-posts in diagnosis--application of the logoscope, " in Stella E. Mason, ed. , Signs, Signals and Symbols: A Presentation of a British Approach to Speech Pathology and Therapy. London: Methuen, pp. 93-100.

Alexandre, Pierre
 1967 "Note sur la réduction du système des classes dans les langues véhiculaires à fonds bantu, " La Classification nominale dans les langages Negro-Africaines. Paris: C. N. R. S. , pp. 277-290.

 1969 "Langages tambourines: une écriture sonore?" Semiotica 1, pp. 273-281.

Alfau, Felips
 1936 Locos: Comedy of Gestures [Spain]. New York: Farrar and Rinehart, 1966, 306 pages.

Allen, George D.
 1972 "The location of rhythmic stress beats in English: an experimental study: I, " Part I, Language and Speech 15 (January-March), pp. 72-100. Part II, Language and Speech 15 (April-June), pp. 179-195.

Allen, John Romily
 1887 Early Christian Symbolism in Great Britain and Ireland before the 13th Century. London, 408 pages.

Alloway, Thomas, Lester Krames, and Patricia Phiner
 1972 Communication and Affect: A Comparative Approach. New York: Academic.

Allport, Floyd H.
 1924 Social Psychology. Boston: Houghton Mifflin, 453 pages. Reprinted, New York: Johnson Reprint Corporation, 1967.

Allport, G. W. , and H. Cantril
 1934 "Judging personality from voice, " Journal of Social Psychology 5, pp. 37-55.

Allport, Gordon W. , and Philip E. Vernon
 1933 Studies in Expressive Movement. New York: Macmillan, 269 pages. Reprinted, New York: Hafner Publishing Company, 1967.

148 Bibliography

Alpert, Murray, Williams A. Frosch, and Saul H. Fisher
1967 "Teaching the perception of expressive aspects of vocal communication," American Journal of Psychiatry 124:2 (August), pp. 202-211.

Alrutz, S.
1908 "Die Kitzel und Juckempfindungen," Skandinaviska Archiv für Physiologie 20, pp. 371-410.

Altman, Irwin
1968 "Territorial behavior in humans: an analysis of the concept." Paper read at the Conference on Explorations of Spatial-behavioral-relationships as Related to Older People, Ann Arbor, Michigan.

1973 "An ecological approach to the functioning of socially isolated groups," in John E. Rasmussen, ed., Man in Isolation and Confinement. Chicago: Aldine Press, pp. 241-269.

1973 "Some perspectives on the study of man-environment phenomena," Representative Research in Social Psychology 4, pp. 109-126.

Altman, Irwin and William W. Haythorn
1967 "The ecology of isolated groups," Behavioral Science 12:3 (May), pp. 169-182.

Altman, Irwin, Dalmas A. Taylor, and Ladd Wheeler
1971 "Ecological aspects of group behavior in social isolation," Journal of Applied Social Psychology 1:1, pp. 76-100.

Altman, Stuart A., ed.
1967 Social Communication among Primates. Chicago: University of Chicago Press, 392 pages.

Altschule, Mark D.
1953 "Cutaneous functions," chapter 2, pp. 50-51, "Respiration," chapter 3, pp. 61-74, in Bodily Physiology in Mental and Emotional Disorders. New York: Grune and Stratton.

Amades, Joan
"El gesto a Cartalunia," Boletin del Instituto de Filosofia, Universidad de Cuyo, Argentina.

Ambrose, J. A.
1960 "The smiling response in early human infancy," Ph.D. thesis, London University, pp. 1-660.

1961 "The development of the smiling response in early infancy," in Brian M. Foss, ed., Determinants of Infant Behavior. London: Methuen.

1963 "The age of onset of ambivalence in early infancy:

indications from the study of laughing, " in Journal of Child Psychology and Psychiatry 4:3-4, pp. 167-184.

Ames, D. W. , E. A. Gregersen, and T. Neugebauer
1971   "Taaken Sàmàarii: a drum language of Hausa youth, " Africa 41, London, pp. 12-31.

Ames, Louise Bates
1949   "Development of interpersonal smiling responses in the pre-school years, " Journal of Genetic Psychology 74, pp. 273-291.

Amira, Karl von
1905   "Die Handgebärden in den Bilderhandschriften des Sachsenspiegels, " Abhandl. d. philos. -philol. Kl. d. Koniglich, bayerischen Akad. d. Wissenschaften 23:2, München, pp. 161-263.

Amman, John Conrade [1669-1724]
1694   The Talking Deaf Man: or A Method Proposed, Whereby He Who Is Born Deaf May Learn to Speak. London. Reprinted, Ann Arbor, Mich. : University Microfilms, 1969.

Anderson, J. D.
1920   "Collectanea: The language of gesture" in Folklore 31, pp. 70-71. [Bengali gestures]

Anderson, J. W.
1972   "Attachment behaviour out of doors, " in Nicholas G. Blurton Jones, ed. Ethological Studies of Child Behaviour. Cambridge University Press, pp. 199-215.

André, E.
1965   "Notes on 'Systems of prosodic and paralinguistic features in English'," in Revue du Phonétique Appliquée 1, pp. 7-13.

André, Edgar
1972   "Notes sur le statut linguistique des traits prosodiques et paralinguistiques, " Revue du Phonétique Appliquée 22, pp. 3-10.

Andrew, Richard J.
1963   "Evolution of facial expressions" in Science 142, (November 22), pp. 1034-1041. Reprinted in Bobbs-Merrill Reprint Series in Anthropology, A-256.

1963   "The origin and evolution of the calls and facial expressions of the primates, " Behaviour 20, Leiden, Netherlands, pp. 1-109. Reprinted as Evolution of Facial Expression: Two Accounts, New York: Arno Press, 1972. [Includes Ernst Huber.]

1965   "The origins of facial expressions," Scientific American
213 (October), pp. 88-94.

Andrews, Edward D.
1940   The Gift to Be Simple: Songs, Dances, and Rituals of
the American Shakers. J. J. Augustin Publisher. Reprinted,
New York: Dover Publications, 1962, 170 pages.

Andrews, T. G.
1948   "Some psychological apparatus: a classified bibliography," Psychological Monographs, Whole No. 289:62, pp. 1-38.

Angenot, Marc
1973   "Les traités de l'éloquence du corps," Semiotica 8,
pp. 60-82.

Anthony, David A.
1971   Seeing Essential English. Anaheim, California. Review by William C. Stokoe, Jr., Sign Language Studies 2
(1973), pp. 84-93.

Anthriotis, N. P.
1947   [Ancient and modern Greek hand and facial gestures],
Morphais (Thessaloniki), (February), pp. 90-92. [In Greek.]

Antrim, D. K.
1954   "The general who set victory to music," The Etude
(June), p. 14.

Appel, Victor H., Lawrence T. McCarron, and Bradley A. Manning
1968   "Eyeblink rate: Behavioral index of threat?" Journal of
Counseling Psychology 15:2, pp. 153-157.

Apple, Marianne M.
1972   "Kinesic training for blind persons: a vital means of
communication," The New Outlook for the Blind 66, pp. 201-
208.

Apuleius
1951   The Golden Ass, translated by Robert Graves. New
York: Farrar, Straus. [Chapter 11, page 150, kissing;
Hayes.]

Arbeau, Thoinet [Jean Taboureau/Jehan Tabourot, French Canon
of Langres]
1588   Orchesography: A Treatise in the Form of a Dialogue:
Whereby All Manner of Persons May Easily Acquire and Practise the Honourable Exercise of Dancing. Translation by Cyril
W. Beaumont. London: Beaumont, 1925, 174 pages. Translation by Mary Stewart Evans. Brooklyn, New York: Dance
Horizons, 1965; New York: Dover Publications, 1967, 266
pages.

Archer, Dane, Robert Rosenthal, J. Koivumaki, and P. Rogers
    Sensitivity to Nonverbal Communication: A Profile Approach to the Measurement of Differential Abilities.

Argyle, Michael
    1957   The Scientific Study of Social Behaviour. London: Methuen, 239 pages.

    1967   The Psychology of Interpersonal Behaviour. Harmondsworth: Penguin Books.

    1969   Social Interaction. London: Methuen; Chicago: Aldine Publ. Co., 504 pages. Review by Mark L. Knapp, Journal of Communication 21:1 (1971), pp. 101-102.

    1970   "Eye-contact and distance: a reply to Stephenson and Rutter," British Journal of Psychology 61, pp. 395-396.

    1973   "The syntaxes of bodily communication," Linguistics 112, pp. 71-91.

    1975   "Programme on social interaction." Final report to the Social Science Research Council, September 1970-August 1975, Oxford University, 34 pages.

    (in press)   Bodily Communication. London: Methuen; New York: International Universities Press.

Argyle, Michael, Florisse Alkema, and Robin Gilmore
    1971   "The communication of friendly and hostile attitudes by verbal and non-verbal signals" Eur. Journal Exp. Soc. Psychol. 1:3, pp. 385-402.

Argyle, Michael, and Mark Cook
    (in press)   Gaze and Mutual Gaze. Cambridge University Press.

Argyle, Michael, and Janet Dean
    1965   "Eye contact, distance, and affiliation," Sociometry 28:3, pp. 289-304.

Argyle, Michael, Ralph Exline, eds.
    1969   NATO Symposium on Non-verbal Communication. Wadham College, Oxford, 45 pages.

Argyle, Michael, and Roger Ingham
    1972   "Gaze, mutual gaze, and proximity," Semiotica 6, pp. 32-49.

Argyle, Michael, R. Ingham, F. Alkema, and M. McCallin
    1973   "The different functions of gaze," Semiotica 7, pp. 19-32.

Argyle, Michael, and Adam Kendon
    1967   "The experimental analysis of social performance," in
    L. Berkowitz (ed.), Advances in Experimental Social Psychol-
    ogy 3. New York: Academic Press, pp. 55-91.

Argyle, Michael, Mansur Lalljee, and Mark Cook
    1968   "The effects of visibility on interaction in a dyad,"
    Human Relations 21:1, pp. 3-17.

Argyle, Michael, Luc Lefebvre, and Mark Cook
    1975   "The meaning of five patterns of gaze," Language and
    Language Behavior Abstracts 9:2, 7501873.

Argyle, Michael, Veronica Salter, Hilary Nicholson, Marylin Wil-
    liams, and Philip Burgess
    1970   "The Communication of inferior and superior attitudes
    by verbal and non-verbal signals," British Journal of Social
    and Clinical Psychology 9, pp. 222-231.

Argyle, Michael, and Marylin Williams
    1969   "Observer or observed? A reversible perspective in
    person perception," Sociometry 32, pp. 396-412.

Arlow, J. A.
    1961   "Silence and the theory of technique," Journal of Ameri-
    can Psychoanalytic Association 9, pp. 44-55.

Armfield, Anne Constance (Smedley)
    1925   Greenleaf Theater Elements....   London: Duckworth &
    Co.

Armstrong, Edward A.
    1942   Bird Display and Behaviour: An Introduction to the
    Study of Bird Psychology. Lindsay Drummond. Reprinted,
    New York: Dover Publications, 1965, 431 pages. [The syn-
    chronization of male and female rhythms.]

Armstrong, Robert G.
    1955   "Talking instruments in West Africa," Explorations 4,
    pp. 140-153.

Arnals, Alexander d'.
    1932   Der Operndarsteller: Lehrgang zur musikalischen
    Darstellung in der Oper. Berlin: E. Bote & G. Bock, 114
    pages.

Árnason, Jón [1665-1743]
    1838   Dactylismus Ecclesiasticus: Edur, Fingra-rim,
    Vidvikjandi Kyrkju-Arsins Tímum....   Kaupmanna-Høfn:
    Utgefid af P. Jónnssyni, 256 pp. Reprinted in lithoprint,
    1946. [Sign-language in Iceland.]

Arrivé, Michel
1972   "Problèmes de sémiotique littéraire: les langages de
Jarry," Documents de Travail, numero 15, serie D, Università
di Urbino, Italia, Centro Internazionale di Semiotica e di
Linguistica.

Asano, Hachiro
1964   Faces Never Lie: The New Art of Japanese Physiognomy. Tokyo: Rikugei Publishing House, 153 pages.

Asher, James J., Jo Anne Kusudo, and Rita de la Torre
1974   "Learning a second language through commands: the
second field test," Modern Language Journal 58:1-2 (January),
pp. 24-32.

Ashihara, Eiryo
1964   The Japanese Dance. Tokyo: Japan Travel Bureau,
Inc., 1 Marunouchi 1-Chome, Chiyodaku.

Aubert, Charles
1901   The Art of Pantomime (translated from French Edition
of 1901). New York, 1927, 210 pages.

Auerbach, Alfred, ed.
1959   Schizophrenia: An Integrated Approach. New York:
Ronald Press, 224 pages.

Aungier, G. J. A.
1840   A History of Antiquities of Lyon Monastery in the Par-
ish of Isleworth. London: Nichols. [See pp. 405-419, A
table of signs used during silence by the sisters and brothers.]

Austerlitz, Robert
1956   "Gilyak nursery words" Word 12, pp. 260-279.

Austin, Gilbert see also Jonathan Barber

Austin, Gilbert
1806   Chironomia: Or a Treatise on Rhetorical Delivery:
Comprehending Many Precepts, Both Ancient and Modern, for
the Proper Regulation of the Voice, The Countenance, and
Gesture: Together with an Investigation of the Elements of
Gesture, and a New Method for the Notation Thereof: Illus-
trated by Many Figures. London, 583 pages. Reprinted,
Southern Illinois University Press, 1966.

1818   Die Kunst der rednerischen und theatralischen Declama-
tion, nach ältern und neuern Grundsätzen über die Stimme, den
Gesichtsausdruck und die Gesticulation aufgestellt und durch
152 Figuren erläutert für öffentliche Redner, Schauspieler und
Künstler. Leipzig: Baumgärtner, 184 pages.

Austin, J. L.
  1962   How to Do Things With Words: The William James
  Lectures Delivered at Harvard University in 1955. Cambridge,
  Mass.: Harvard University Press, 167 pages.

Austin, Mary
  1927   "Gesture in primitive drama," Theatre Arts Monthly 11
  (August), pp. 594-605.

Austin, William M.
  1965   "Some social aspects of paralanguage," Canadian Journal of Linguistics 11:1, pp. 31-9. Reprinted in Communication Barriers for the Culturally Deprived. USOE, 1966.

  1972   "The behavioral components of a two-way conversation,"
  in Lawrence M. Davis, ed., Studies in Linguistics in Honor of
  Raven McDavid, Jr. University of Alabama Press, pp. 231-
  237.

  1972   "Non-verbal communication," chapter 8 in A. L. Davis,
  ed., Culture, Class, and Language Variety. Urbana, Ill.:
  National Council of Teachers of English, pp. 140-169.

Aynesworth, Donald D.
  1974   "Silence, solitude, and language: Chateaubriand to
  Casmus," Dissertation Abstracts 35:5386A.

                              - B -

B., J. F.
  1946   "Say it with hands: pasimology, or the language of gestures," New York Times Magazine (December 22), p. 49.

Bacon, Albert M.
  1875   A Manual of Gesture: Embracing a Complete System
  of Notation, Together with the Principles of Interpretation and
  Selections for Practice. Chicago: S. C. Griggs and Company.

Bacon, Francis see Karl R. Wallace

Baden, T.
  1831   "Bemerkungen über das komische Gebärdenspiel der
  Alten nach den Originalen," Neue Jahrbücher fur Phil., Suppl.
  I, pp. 447-456.

Bailey, Flora L.
  1942   "Navaho motor habits," American Anthropologist 44:2
  (April-June), pp. 210-234.

Bakan, Paul
  1971   "The eyes have it," Psychology Today 4:11 (April),
  pp. 64-67, 96.

Baker, Charlotte [University of California at Berkeley]
  1975   "Regulators and turn-taking in American Sign Language
  discourse. "

Baker, Frank
  1888   "Anthropological notes on the human hand, " American
  Anthropologist, o. s. 1:1 (January), pp. 51-75.

Baker, Sidney J.
  1951   "Autonomic resistances in word association tests, "
  Psychoanalytic Quarterly 20, pp. 275-283.

Balázs, Béla
  1945   Theory of the Film: Character and Growth of a New
  Art. New York: Dover Publications, 291 pages.

Bales, Richard
  n. d.   The Confederacy. Columbia Records Legacy Series
  LS 1004. [The Rebel Yell is illustrated on Side 2--mentioned
  in Allen Walker Read, "The Rebel Yell.... "]

Balfour, Henry
  1948   "Ritual and secular uses of vibrating membranes as
  voice-disguisers, " Journal of the Royal Anthropological Institute of Great Britain & Ireland 78, pp. 45-69.

Balint, Michael
  1945   "Friendly expanses--horrid empty spaces, " International
  Journal of Psychoanalysis.

Ball, Donald W.
  1973   Microecology: Social Situations and Intimate Space.
  (Studies in Sociology) New York: Bobbs-Merrill, 38 pages.

Bally, Charles
  1952   Le Langage et la vie; Chapter 4, "Mecanisme de l'
  expressivité linguistique. " (Société de Publication Romanes et
  Francaises, No. 34) Geneva: Droz.

Banks, Ann
  1974   "French without language, " Harvard Today 181, pp. 4-
  6.

Barahal, Hyman S.
  1940   "The psychopathology of hair-plucking (Trichotillomania),"
  Psychoanalytic Review 27, pp. 291-310.

Barakat, Robert A.
  1969   "Gesture systems, " Keystone Folklore Quarterly 14
  (Fall), pp. 105-121.

  1973   "Arabic gestures, " Journal of Popular Culture 6:4
  (Spring), pp. 749-787.

1975   "On ambiguity in the Cistercian Sign Language," Sign Language Studies 8, pp. 275-289.

1976   The Cistercian Sign Language: A Study in Non-Verbal Communication. (Cistercian Studies Series 11) Dublin.

Barbara, Dominick A. , ed.
1960   Psychological and Psychiatric Aspects of Speech and Hearing. Springfield, Ill. : Charles C. Thomas, 756 pages.

1963   "Nonverbal communication," Journal of Communication 13:3 (September), pp. 166-173.

Barber, Jonathan
1831   A Practical Treatise on Gesture: Chiefly Abstracted from Austin's Chironomia.... Cambridge, Mass. : Hilliard and Brown, 116 pages.

Barber, T. X. , and M. J. Silver
1968   "Fact, fiction, and the experimenter bias effect," Psychological Bulletin Monograph Supplement 70, pp. 1-29.

Barbour, Alton, and Mele Koneya
(in press) Louder than Words.

Barker, Larry L. , and Nancy B. Collins
1970   "Nonverbal and kinesic research," in Philip Emmert and William D. Brooks, eds. , Methods of Research in Communication. Boston: Houghton Mifflin Co. , pp. 343-372.

Barker, Roger G. , ed.
1963   The Stream of Behavior as an Empirical Problem. New York: Appleton-Century-Croft, pp. 1-22.

Barlow, Jerry Dean
1969   "Pupillary size as an index of preference in political candidates," Perceptual and Motor Skills 28, pp. 587-590.

Barndt, Deborah
1974   "Toward a visual study of society," Technical Report, Social Science, Michigan State University, 67 pages.

Barnes, R. Bowling
1963   "Thermography of the human body: Infrared-radiant energy provides new concepts and instrumentation for medical diagnosis," Science 140:3569 (May 24), pp. 870-877.

Barnes, Susan van den Hoek
1973   "The use of sign language as a technique for language acquisition in autistic children: an applied model bridging verbal and nonverbal theoretical systems," Dissertation Abstracts 34:4651B, California School of Professional Psych. , 95 pages.

Barnlund, Dean C. , ed.
1968   "Nonverbal Interaction, " in Interpersonal Communication: Survey and Studies. Boston: Houghton-Mifflin, pp. 511-
610. [133-item list appears on pp. 536-542.]

Barrois, Jean Baptiste Joseph (1780-1855)
1850   Dactylologie et langage primitif restitués d'après les
monuments. Paris: Firmin Didot.

Bartenieff, Irmgard
1956   "Feuillet's l'art de decrire la danse: a modern notator
takes a look at the past, " Dance Notation Record 12. 5-6.

Bartenieff, Irmgard, and Martha Davis
1965   Effort-Shape Analysis of Movement: The Unity of Ex-
pression and Function. Bronx, New York: Albert Einstein
College of Medicine, 71 pages. Reprinted by Arno Press as
Research Approaches to Movement and Personality (includes
Philip Eisenberg and Martii Takala). New York, 1972.

1968   "An analysis of the movement behavior within a group
psychotherapy session, " presented at the Conference of the
American Group Psychotherapy Association, Chicago, 28 pages.
Dance Notation Bureau, 8 East 12th Street, New York 10003.

(in press) Four Adaptations of Effort Theory in Research and
Teaching. New York: Dance Notation Bureau.

Bartlett, John
1953   A Complete Concordance of Shakespeare. New York:
St. Martin's Press. [See under embrace, kiss, hand, etc. :
Hayes.]

Bartoli, D.
1679   Del Suono de'Tremori Armonici. Rome. [In the Frank
De Bellis Collection, Ostwald, Soundmaking, p. 159.]

Basler, A.
1912   "Experimentelle Untersuchungen über den Hautkitzel, "
Pflugers Arch 147, pp. 375-392. [Experimental investigation
of skin ticklishness.]

1912   "Über den Fussohlenkitzel, " Pflugers Arch 148, pp. 311-
318. [Ticklishness of the sole.]

Basmajian, J. V.
1965   "Man's posture, " Archives of Physical Medicine 46,
pp. 26-36.

Basso, Keith H.
1970   " 'To give up on words': silence in Western Apache
Culture, " Southwestern Journal of Anthropology 26:3 (Autumn),
pp. 213-230.

Basto, C.
1938   "A linguaguem dos gestos em Portugal," Revista Lusi-
tana 36, pp. 5-72.

Batchelor, James P., and George R. Goethals
1972   "Spatial arrangements in freely formed groups," Sociometry 35, pp. 270-279.

Bateson, Gregory
1958   "Language and psychotherapy: Frieda Fromm-Reich-
mann's last project," Psychiatry 21, pp. 96-100.

1959   "Cultural problems posed by a study of schizophrenic
process," in Alfred Auerbach, ed., Schizophrenia: An Integrated Approach. New York: Ronald Press, pp. 125-146.

1972   Steps to an Ecology of Mind. New York: Ballantine.

Bateson, Gregory, Don D. Jackson, Jay Haley, and John Weakland
1956   "Toward a theory of schizophrenia," Behavioral Science
1, pp. 251-264.

Bateson, Gregory and Margaret Mead
1942   Balinese Character: A Photographic Analysis. New
York: The New York Academy of Sciences, 277 pages. [Hand
postures in daily life, p. 96; hand postures in dance, p. 99;
prayer g., p. 81, 229, passim; bibliography pp. 255-256:
Hayes.]

Bateson, Mary Catherine
1963   "Kinesics and paralanguage," Science 139, p. 200.

1968   "Linguistics in the semiotic frame," Linguistics 39
(May), pp. 5-17.

1971   "The interpersonal context of infant vocalization,"
Quarterly Progress Report No. 100 (January), Cambridge,
Mass.: MIT Research Laboratory of Electronics, pp. 169-176.

Battison, Robbin
1974   "Phonological deletion in American sign language,"
Sign Language Studies 5, pp. 1-19.

Battison, Robbin and Harry Markowicz
"Sign aphasia and neurolinguistic theory."

Baudin, Maurice
1930   "Le visage humain dans la tragedie de La Calprenède,"
Modern Language Notes 45 (February), pp. 114-119.

Bauer, Ernest A.
1973   "Personal space: a study of blacks and whites,"
Sociometry 36, pp. 402-408.

Bauer, Leonhard
1898   "Einiges über Gesten der syrischen Araber," Zertschr.
d. deutschen Palaestina-Vereins (Leipzig) 8:21, pp. 59-64.

1903   Volkslegen im Lande der Bibel. Leipzig: Kommissions-
verlag von H. G. Wallmann. [Pp. 249-256: 48 Levantine gestures.]

Bauer, Paul
1950   Die Sprache der Hände: eine Einführung in die vernunft-
gemässe Deutung. Stuttgart, 116 pages.

Bauman, Richard
1972   "Speaking in the light: the role of the Quaker minister." Paper read at Conference on the Ethnography of Speaking, University of Texas.

Bäuml, Betty J. and Franz H. Bäuml
1975   A Dictionary of Gestures. Metuchen, N.J.: Scarecrow
Press, 249 pages.

Baxandall, Michael
1972   Painting and Experience in Fifteenth Century Italy.
Oxford: Clarendon Press.

Baxter, James C.
1970   "Interpersonal spacing in natural settings," Sociometry
33:4, pp. 444-456.

Baxter, James C., and Richard M. Rozelle
1975   "Nonverbal expression as a function of crowding during
a simulated police-citizen encounter," Journal of Personality
and Social Psychology 32:1, pp. 40-54.

Baxter, James C., Elaine P. Winters, and Robert E. Hammer
1968   "Gestural behavior during a brief interview as a function of cognitive variables," Journal of Personality and Social
Psychology 8:3 (March), pp. 303-307.

Bayley, Harold
1912   The Lost Language of Symbolism. 2 vols. London.
[II, 128 comments on tongue-protruding from mouth as a symbol of wisdom in Mexico and India. In Tibet a respectful salu-
tation is made by removing hat and lolling out the tongue:
Hayes.]

Bayley, Nancy
1965   "Comparisons of mental and motor test scores for ages
1-15 months by sex, birth order, race, geographical location
and education of parents," Child Development 36, pp. 379-411.

Beard, Daniel Carter
1918   The American Boys' Book of Signs, Signals and Symbols.

Philadelphia, 250 pages.

Beauchamp, Pierre
        [1666--Period of Louis XIV, French Act of Parliament
    recognizes Beauchamp for a system of dance notation: Pen-
    rod.]

Beaumont, Cyril W.
    1929 A Bibliography of Dancing. London: Dancing Times;
    New York: Benjamin Blom, 228 pages.

Beaumont, Cyril, ed. , and Serge Leslie, annotator
    1966-74 A Bibliography of the Dance Collection of Doris Niles
    and Serge Leslie. 3 vols. London: C. W. Beaumont.

Beck, Henry
    1971 "Minimal requirements for a biobehavioral paradigm,"
    Behavioral Science 16:5 (Sept. -Oct.), pp. 442-455.

Becker, Franklin D. , Robert Sommer, Joan Bee, and Bart Oxley
    1973 "College classroom ecology," Sociometry 36, pp. 514-
    525.

Bede, le Vénérable [672-735]
        see Putnam Fennell Jones, A Concordance to the His-
    toria Ecclesiastica of Bede. Cambridge, Mass. : 1929.

            De Computo vel Loquela Digitorum. (Migne: Patro-
    logiae latinae Cursus completus, t. 90, col. 295-298) Paris,
    1850.

            De Loquelá per Gestum Digitorum, sive de Indigitatione.

Bedichek, Roy
    1960 The Sense of Smell. New York: Doubleday and Co. ,
    271 pages.

Bedini, S.
    1964 "Holy smoke: the oriental fire clocks," New Scientist
    21:380 (Feb. 27), pp. 537-539. [Relation of time and senses
    --olfactory.]

Beebe, Steven A.
    1974 "Eye contact: a nonverbal determinant of speaker credi-
    bility," The Speech Teacher 23, pp. 21-25.

Beekman, Susan J. [California State University, Humboldt]
    1973 "Nonverbal behaviors in dyadic conversations in relation
    to subject sex and partner sex," University of Chicago, diss.

            "Sex differences in nonverbal behavior."

Beier, Ernest G.
1966 The Silent Language of Psychotherapy: Social Reinforcement of Unconscious Processes. Chicago: Aldine, 338 pages.

1974 "Nonverbal communication: how we send emotional messages," Psychology Today 8:5 (October), pp. 52-56.

Beier, E. G., E. E. Izard, D. C. Smock, and R. R. Tougas
1953 "Responses to the human face as a standard stimulus," Journal of Consulting Psychology 17, pp. 126-131.

1957 "Response to the human face as a standard stimulus: a reexamination," Journal of Consulting Psychology 21, pp. 165-170.

Beier, Ernst G., and Alexander J. Zautra
1972 "Identification of vocal communication of emotions across cultures," Journal of Consulting and Clinical Psychology 39, p. 166.

Beigel, Hugo G.
1952 "The influence of body position on mental processes," Journal of Clinical Psychology 8, pp. 193-199.

Beinhauer, Werner
1930 Spanische Umgangssprache. Berlin, Bonn: Ferd. Dümmlers Verlag, 1958 [Gestures, p. 113, 131, 170, 191, 202 ff.: Hayes]. El Español Coloquial. Madrid: Biblioteca Románica Hispanica, 1963, 445 pages.

1934 "Über 'Piropos': (Eine Studie über spanische Liebessprache)," Volkstum und Kultur der Romanen 7:2-3, pp. 111-163. [On women's glances, pp. 133-136; quotations from literature: Hayes.]

1942 El caracter español. Trans. of Der spanische Nationalcharakter, Madrid. ['Algo sobre el lenguaje' contains a few general remarks on Spanish gesticulation: Hayes.]

Beistle, James E., II
1974 "Proxemic patterns of school children," M.A. thesis, Colorado State University.

Bell, Alexander Graham [1847-1922]
1884 "Fallacies concerning the deaf, and the influence of such fallacies in preventing the amelioration of their condition," Bulletin of the Philosophical Society of Washington 6, pp. 48-77. Washington, D.C.: Smithsonian Inst. Misc. Coll. 33 (no. 543).

1898 "The question of sign-language." Reprinted as "The utility of signs in the instruction of the deaf," The Educator 5,

pp. 38-44.

Bell, Alexander Melville [1819-1905]
1852   Elocutionary Manual: The Principles of Articulation
and Orthoepy, the Art of Readings and Gesture.

1852   Exercises in Expressive Reading. "General Notation of
Gesture."

1867   Visible Speech: The Science of Universal Alphabetics.
Inaugural Edition, London. ["P. 50: the 'interjectional or
inarticulate utterances' of sighing, panting, fluttering, shudder-
ing, sobbing; the sneer, yawn, gasp, hiccough, pang, moan;
the murmur of ridicule, vexation, disgust; etc." Pike, p. 33.]

1887   The Principles of Elocution: with Exercises and Notations, 7th ed. Washington, D.C.: Volta, 240 pages.

Bell, Sir Charles
1806   Essays on the Anatomy and Philosophy of Expression:
as Connected with the Fine Arts, 6th ed., 1872; 7th ed., 1877.
London.

1806   Essays on the Anatomy of Expression in Painting. London.

1823   On the Motions of the Eye. London: Nicol.

1833   The Hand, Its Mechanism and Vital Endowments as
Evincing Design. Philadelphia, 213 pages.

Bell, David Charles
1878   The Modern Reader and Speaker: a Selection of Poetry
and Prose from the Writings of Eminent Authors, with copious
extracts for recitation; preceded by the principles of elocution,
comprising a variety of exercises from the simplest articulation to the utmost extent of vocal expression: with a system
of gesture, illustrated by diagrams and a plan of notation.
Dublin: M. H. Gill & Son, 464 pages.

Bell, R. Q. and N. S. Costello
1964   "Three tests for sex differences in tactile sensitivity in
the newborn," Biologia Neonatorum 1, pp. 335-347.

Bellugi, Ursula
1972   "Studies in Sign Language," in Psycholinguistics and
Total Communication, T. O'Rourke, ed. American Annals of
the Deaf.

Bellugi, Ursula, and Susan D. Fischer
1972   "A comparison of sign language and spoken language:
rate and grammatical mechanisms," Cognition: International
Journal of Cognitive Psychology 1:1, pp. 173-200.

Bellugi, Ursula and Edward S. Klima
1972 "The roots of language in the sign talk of the deaf,"
Psychology Today, 6:1, pp. 61-64, 76.

(in press) "Language in a different mode," Psychology Today.

Bellugi, Ursula and Patricia Siple
1971 "Remembering with and without words," in Current
Problems in Psycholinguistics. Paris: Centre National de la
Recherche Scientifique.

Bender, Arthur S., and George F. Mahl
1960 "Stress, feelings of identification, and dialect usage,"
mimeo, Yale University, 30 pages.

Bendor-Samuel, John T.
1966 "Grammatical prosodies?" in Kenneth L. Pike, ed.,
Tagmemic and Matrix Linguistics Applied to Selected African
Languages. Ann Arbor, Mich.: University of Michigan,
pp. 192-196.

Benesh, Rudolf and Joan
1956 An Introduction to Benesh Dance Notation. London:
Adam and Charles Black, 48 pages. Reprinted with additions,
Brooklyn, N.Y.: Dance Horizons, 1969, 56 pages.

Benesh see also Anon "Choreology...."; Anon "Notation, Choreology...."; Causley; Curl; Hall, Fernau; Morrice; Mossford;
Nadel and Nadel.

Bennet, David C.
1972 "Some observations concerning the locative-directional
distinction," Semiotica 5, pp. 31-57.

Benthall, Jonathan, and Ted Polhemus, eds.
1975 The Body as a Medium of Expression. New York:
Dutton; London: Allen Lane, 339 pages.

Benton, A. L., C. H. Hartman, and I. G. Sarason
1955 "Some relations between speech behavior and anxiety
level," Journal of Abnormal and Social Psychology 51, pp. 295-
297.

Benveniste, Emile
1953 "Animal communication and human language," Diogenes
1, pp. 1-7.

Berelson, Bernard, and Gary A. Steiner
1964 Human Behavior: An Inventory of Scientific Findings.
New York: Harcourt, Brace and World, 712 pages.

Berg, Charles
1936 "The unconscious significance of hair," International
Journal of Psycho-Analysis 17, pp. 73-88.

Berger, Milton M.
    1958   "Nonverbal communication in group psychotherapy,"
    International Journal of Group Psychotherapy 8, pp. 161-178.

Bergler, Edmund
    1956   Laughter and the Sense of Humor. New York: Inter-
    continental Medical Book Corporation. Reprinted, New York:
    Grune & Stratton, 1967, 297 pages.

Bergman, Eugene
    1972   "Autonomous and unique features of American Sign
    Language," American Annals of the Deaf 117:20-24.

Bergson, Henri Louis
    1900   Le Rire: essai sur la signification du comique.   Paris:
    Alcan.

    1911   Laughter. London: Macmillan.

    1956   "Laughter," in Comedy, ed. by Wylie Sypher. New
    York: Doubleday Anchor Books, pp. 61-190.

Berkson, Gershon
    1964   "Stereotyped movements of mental defectives. V:
    Ward behavior and its relation to an experimental task,"
    American Journal of Mental Deficiency 69, pp. 253-264.

    1967   "Abnormal stereotyped motor acts," Comparative Psy-
    chopathology, pp. 76-94.

Berkson, Gershon, and James D. Becker
    1975   "Facial expressions and social responsiveness of blind
    monkeys," Journal of Abnormal Psychology 84:5, pp. 519-523.

Berkson, Gershon, and Richard K. Davenport
    1962   "Stereotyped movements of mental defectives: I. initial
    survey," American Journal of Mental Deficiency 66, pp. 849-
    852.

Berkson, Gershon, and W. A. Mason
    1963   "Stereotyped movements of mental defectives: III, situ-
    ational effects," American Journal of Mental Deficiency 68,
    pp. 409-412.

    1964   "Stereotyped movements of mental defectives: IV. The
    effects of toys and the character of the acts," American Jour-
    nal of Mental Deficiency 68, pp. 511-524.

Berndt, R. M.
    1940   "Notes on the sign-language of the Jaralde tribe of the
    lower River Murray, South Australia," Royal Society of South
    Australia, Transactions and Proceedings and Report, Adelaide
    64:20, pp. 267-272.

Bernstein, Basil B.
1962   "Linguistic codes, hesitation phenomena and intelligence,"
Language and Speech 5 (Jan. -March), pp. 31-46.   Abstract:
International Journal of American Linguistics 34:1 (Jan. , 1968),
pp. 48-49.

Berque, Jacques
1961   "Expression et signification dans la vie arabe," L'Homme
1, pp. 50-67.

Bertalanffy, L. von
1955   "An essay on the relativity of categories," Philosophy
of Science 22:4 (October), pp. 243-263.

Best, Harry
1914   The Deaf. New York: T. Y. Crowell, 340 pages.
[On signs: Part II, chap. 19: Hayes.]

Betz, R.
1898   'Die Trommelsprache der Duala," Mitteilungen von
Forschungsreisenden und Gelehrten aus den deutschen
Schutzgebieten 11, pp. 1-86.

Bever, Thomas G.
1961   "Pre-linguistic behaviour: A systematic analysis and
comparison of early vocal and general development," Honors
Thesis, Harvard University.

1970   "The nature of cerebral dominance in speech behavior
of the child and adult," in Mechanisms of Language Development. New York: Academic Press.

Beym, Richard
1972   "El concepto de persona enfrentado con indicaciones de
espacio en español," Yelmo: La revista del profesor de
Español 4 (February/March), pp. 28-29.

Bhadbury, Manjulika
1945   The Art of the Hindu Dance. Calcutta: S. K. Chatter-
jee, 275 pages.

Bharata Muni
1951   The Natyashastra Ascribed to Bharata-Muni.   Tran-
scribed and trans. by Manomohan Ghosh.   (Bibliotheca Indica:
A Collection of Oriental Works, No. 272, Calcutta: Asiatic
Soc. of Bengal. [Basic g. of Hindu dance drama: West, p. 71.]

Bharata Muni, supposed author.
1936   Tāndava Laksanam: or, The fundamentals of ancient
Hindu dancing, being a translation into English of the fourth
chapter of the Natya sāstra of Bharata, with a glossary of the
technical dance terms compiled from the eighth, ninth, tenth
and eleventh chapters of the same work, illustrated with origi-

166 Bibliography

nal photographs of the sculptured dance poses in the great
temple of Siva Nataraja at Cidambaram, by Bijayeti Venkata
Narayanaswami Naidu and Pasupuleti Srinivasulu Naidu.
Madras, India.

Bharata Muni see also Naidu

Bharati, A.
1964 "Symbolik der Berührung in der hinduistisch-Buddhisti-
schen Vorstellungswelt," Studium Generale 17:10, pp. 609-620.

Bierwisch, Manfred
1967 "Some semantic universals of German adjectivals,"
Foundations of Language 3:1 (February), pp. 1-36.

Birdwhistell, Ray L.
1952 "Field methods and techniques: body motion research
and interviewing," Human Organization 2:1, pp. 37-38.

1952 Introduction to Kinesics: An Annotation System for
Analysis of Body Motion and Gesture. Foreign Service Inst.,
Dept. of State, Washington, D.C. Ann Arbor, Mich.: Uni-
versity Microfilms, 75 pages.

1955 "Background to Kinesics," ETC. 13:1 (Autumn), pp. 10-18.

1958 "Implications of recent developments in communication
research for evolutionary theory," Report on the Ninth Annual
Round Table Meeting on Linguistics and Language Studies, No.
11, Georgetown University.

1959 "Contribution of linguistic-kinesic studies to the understanding of schizophrenia," in Schizophrenia, ed. by Alfred
Auerbach. New York: Ronald Press, pp. 99-118, followed
by "Discussion" by Henry W. Brosin, pp. 118-123.

1960 "Kinesics and Communication," in Edmund Carpenter
and Marshall McLuhan, Explorations In Communication: An
Anthology. Boston: Beacon Press, pp. 54-64. Review by
Herbert Landar, American Anthropologist 63:4 (Aug. 1961),
pp. 874-875.

1961 "Paralanguage: 25 years after Sapir," Lectures on Experimental Psychiatry, ed. by Henry W. Brosin. Pittsburgh:
University of Pittsburgh Press, pp. 43-65.

1962 "An approach to communication," Family Process 1:2
(September), pp. 194-201.

1962 "Critical moments in the psychiatric interview," Research Approaches to Psychiatric Problems: A Symposium,
ed. by Thomas T. Tourlentes, et al. New York: Grune and
Stratton, pp. 179-188.

Birdwhistell   167

1963   "The kinesic level in the investigation of the emotions,"
in Expression of the Emotions in Man, Peter H. Knapp, ed.
New York: International Universities Press, chpt. 7, pp. 123-39.

1964   "Body behavior and communication," in International Encyclopedia of the Social Sciences. New York.

1964   "Communication without words," in L'Aventure Humaine,
ed. P. Alexandre.   Paris: Société d'Etudes Littéraires et
Artistiques.

1965   "Communication: group structure and process," Pennsylvania Psychiatric Quarterly (Spring), pp. 37-45.

1966   "Some relations between American kinesics and spoken
American English," in Alfred G. Smith, ed.   Communication
and Culture: Readings in the Codes of Human Interaction.
New York: Holt, Rinehart and Winston, pp. 182-189.

1967   "Some body motion elements accompanying spoken
American English," Communication: Concepts and Perspectives,
ed. Lee Thayer. New York: Spartan Books, Macmillan and
Co., chapter III, pp. 53-76.

1967-68   "Kinesics: inter- and intra-channel communication
research," in Julia Kristeva, Josette Rey-Debove, and Donna
Jean Umiker, eds., Essays in Semiotics (Essais de semiotique).
The Hague: Mouton, pp. 527-546.

1968   "L'analyse kinésique," Langage 10, pp. 101-106.

1968   "Kinesics," in David L. Sills, ed., International Encyclopedia of the Social Sciences. New York: Macmillan, vol.
8, pp. 379-385.

1968   "Kinesics: inter- and intra-channel communication research," Social Science Information 7, pp. 9-26.

1969   "Nonverbal communication in the courtroom: what message is the jury getting?" in Persuasion: The Key to Damages.
Ann Arbor, Mich.: The Institute of Continuing Legal Education,
pp. 189-204.

1970   Kinesics and Context: Essays on Body Motion Communication. Philadelphia: University of Pennsylvania Press, 338
pages. Reviews by Mary Catherine Bateson, Journal of Communication 24:1 (Winter 1974), pp. 127-130; Allen T. Dittmann,
Psychiatry 34 (1971), pp. 334-342; Adam Kendon, American
Journal of Psychology 85:3 (1972), pp. 441-455; Mark Hickson,
III, Journal of Communication 21:3 (September 1971), pp. 294-97.

1970   "Some meta-communicational thoughts about communica-
tional studies," in Johnnye Akin, et al., eds., Language

Behavior: a Book of Readings in Communication. The Hague:
Mouton, pp. 265-270.

1972 "A kinesic-linguistic exercise: the cigarette scene," in
John J. Gumperz, and Dell Hymes, eds., Directions in Sociolinguistics: the Ethnography of Communication. New York:
Holt, Rinehart and Winston, pp. 381-404. [Excerpt from Kinesics and Context.]

Birdwhistell see also Rosekrans

Birren, Faber
1969 Light, Color and Environment: a Thorough Presentation of Facts on the Biological and Psychological Effects of
Color. New York: Van Nostrand Reinhold, 131 pages.

Bjorn, D.
1973 "Notationer fra forskellige stadier i skabolsesprocessen
af et stykke balletkoreografi," Psykologisk Skriftserie 4.

Black, Harvey
1969 "Race and sex factors influencing the correct and er-
roneous perception of emotion," American Psychological Association Proceedings 4, pp. 363-364.

Black, John W.
1950 "The effect of room characteristics upon vocal intensity
and rate," Journal of Acoustical Society of America 22 (March),
pp. 174-176.

1961 "Relationships among fundamental frequency, vocal
sound pressure, and rate of speaking," Language and Speech
4:4 (Oct.-Dec.), pp. 196-199.

Black, Max
1949 Language and Philosophy: Studies in Method. Ithaca:
Cornell University Press.

Blackmur, R. P.
1935 Language as Gesture: Essays in Poetry. New York:
Harcourt, Brace and Co., 440 pages. Chap. 1, "Language as
Gesture," reprinted in: Kerker Quinn and Charles Shattuck,
eds., Accent Anthology: Selections from Accent: A Quarterly
of New Literature, 1940-45. New York: Harcourt, Brace,
1946, pp. 467-488.

1957 "The language of silence," in Ruth N. Anshen, ed.,
Language: an Enquiry into Its Meaning and Function. New
York: Harper, Vol. 8, pp. 134-152.

Blahna, Loretta J. [University of Minnesota, Morris]
1975 "A survey of the research on sex differences in nonverbal communication." Paper read at the Speech Communication Association, SISCOM Conference.

Blake

Blake, Robert W.
1973 "I see what you mean--but not by words: extraverbal communication," ETC. 30, pp. 233-243.

Blake, William Harold
1933 A Preliminary Study of the Interpretation of Bodily Expressions. (Contributions to Education, No. 574.) New York: Teachers College, Columbia University, 54 pages.

Blakely, Thomas D.
1972 " 'Proxemic' comparison of two visual anthropological records: the Dugum Dani and the Highland Balinese. "

Blankenship, Jane, and Christian Kay
1964 "Hesitation phenomena in English speech: a study in distribution," Word 20:3 (Dec.), pp. 360-372.

Blasis, C.
1830 The Code of Terpsichore: The Art of Dancing. Translated by R. Barton. London: Edward Bull, 548 pages.

Blass, Thomas [University of Maryland]
"A psycholinguistic comparison of speech, dictation and writing. "

Blatz, W. E., K. Allin, and D. Millichamp
1936 "A study of laughter in the nursery school child," University of Toronto Studies, Child Development Series 7.

Blau, Sidney
1964 "An ear for an eye: sensory compensation and judgments of affect by the blind," in Joel Robert Davitz, ed., The Communication of Emotional Meaning. New York: McGraw-Hill, pp. 113-127.

Blazer, John A.
1966 "Leg position and psychological characteristics in women," Psychology 3, pp. 5-12.

Bloom, Lois
1973 One Word at a Time: The Use of Single Word Utterances Before Syntax. The Hague: Mouton, 262 pages.

Bloomfield, Morton W., and Leonard Newmark
1963 A Linguistic Introduction to the History of English. New York: Alfred A. Knopf, pp. 82-83.

Blount, W. P.
1927 "Studies of the movements of the eyelids of animals: blinking," Quarterly Journal of Experimental Physiology 18, pp. 111-125. [See for definition of blink, wink, half-blink.]

Blum, Lucille H.
1972   Reading Between the Lines: Doctor-Patient Communication. New York: International Universities Press, 183
pages. [Esp. Part 2: The Flow of Reciprocal Response,
pp. 77-179.]

Blurton Jones see Jones, Nicholas G. Blurton

Boas, Franz, David Efron, and John P. Foley, Jr.
1936   "A comparative investigation of gestural behavior patterns in 'racial' groups living under different as well as similar environmental conditions," Psychological Bulletin 33,
p. 760.

Boas, Franziska, ed.
1944   The Function of Dance in Human Society. 52 pages.
To be reprinted by Dance Horizons Press, Brooklyn, New
York.

Bobele, Harvey Kenneth
1970   "An exploratory study of the use of body-movement as
a personal growth adjunct in sensitivity training." University
of California at Los Angeles, Dissertation.

Bödtker, A. T.
1913   "Questions of stress and pause in modern English,"
Anglia 37, pp. 27-40.

Boehn, Max Von
1929   Modes and Manners: Ornaments, Lace, Fans, Gloves,
Walking-Sticks, Parasols, Jewelry, and Trinkets. Philadelphia:
J. B. Lippincott, 293 pages. [Middle Ages to 18th century,
artifacts in gestures.]

Boese, Robert J.
1971   "Native Sign Language and the Problem of Meaning,"
University of California, Santa Barbara. Dissertation Abstracts
32, part 6, 6546 A, Order 72-7449, 395 pages.

Bogardus, E. S.
1933   "A social distance scale," Sociology and Social Research
17, pp. 265-271.

Bogardus, Emory Stephen
1959   Social Distance. Yellow Springs, Ohio: Antioch Press.

Bogen, Hellmuth, and Otto Lippmann, eds.
1931   "Gang und Charakter: Ergebnisse eines Preisausschrei-
bens," Beihefte zür Zeitschrift für Angewandte Psychologie 58.
Liepzig: Barth, pp. 1-122.

Bogen, Joseph E.
1969-72 "The other side of the brain," Bulletin of the Los

Angeles Neurological Society I: Vol. 34 (1969), pp. 73-105;
II: Vol. 34 (1969), pp. 135-162; III: Vol. 34 (1969), pp. 175-
195; IV: Vol. 37 (1972), pp. 49-61.

Boggs, R. S.
1934 "Gebärde, " in Lutz Mackensen, ed. , Handwörterbuch
des deutschen Marchens 2. Berlin, pp. 318-322.

Bogusɫawski, Wojciech [1757-1829]
1965 Mimika, Jacek Lipinski and Tadeusz Sivert, eds. Warsaw: Państwowy Instytut Wydawniczy, 224 pages.

Bokander, I.
1965 "Precognitive perception of facial photographs, " Scandinavian Journal of Psychology 6, pp. 103-108.

Bolinger, Dwight L.
1946 "Thoughts on 'Yep' and 'Nope', " American Speech 21:2
(April), pp. 90-95.

1960 "Linguistic science and linguistic engineering, " Word
16:3 (December), pp. 374-391.

1961 Generality, Gradience, and the All-Or-None. The
Hague: Mouton, 46 pages. Review by Robert Stockwell,
Language 39:1 (January-March), pp. 87-91.

1965 Forms of English: Accent, Morpheme, Order. Cambridge, Mass.: Harvard University Press. [Part I: "Accent
and related matters, " pp. 1-180.]

1968 Aspects of Language. New York: Harcourt, Brace and
World. ["Sound is embedded in gesture, " pp. 13-15. 2nd ed.
1975, pp. 18-22.]

1969 "The sound of the bell, " Kivung 2:3 (November), pp. 2-
7.

1972 Intonation: Selected Readings. Middlesex, England:
Penguin Books, 464 pages.

Böll, Heinrich
1966 18 Stories. New York: McGraw-Hill. "Murke's Collected Silences, " pp. 118-149.

Bolt, Richard H. , Franklin S. Cooper, Edward E. David, Jr. ,
Peter B. Denes, James M. Pickett, and Kenneth N. Stevens
1969 "Identification of a speaker by speech spectrograms:
how do scientists view its reliability for use as legal evidence?"
Science 166 (October 17), pp. 338-343.

1970 "Speaker identification by speech spectrograms: a scientists' view of its reliability for legal purposes, " Journal of
the Acoustical Society of America 47:2, pp. 597-612.

Bolton, H. Carrington
    1897   "The language used in talking to domestic animals,"
    American Anthropologist 10:3 (March), pp. 65-90; 10:4 (April
    1897), pp. 97-113.

Bolwig, Niels
    1963-64 "Facial expression in primates, with remarks on a
    parallel development in certain carnivores (a preliminary re-
    port on work in progress)," Behaviour 22, pp. 167-192.

Bond, Michael H., and Yasuo Iwata [Chinese University of Hong
    Kong]
             "Proxemics and observation anxiety in Japan: nonverbal
    and perceptual effects."

Bond, Michael H., and Hiroshi Komai
    1975   "Targets of gazing and eye-contact during interviews:
    effects on Japanese nonverbal behavior."

Bond, Michael H., and Daisuke Shiraishi
    1974   "The effect of body lean and status of an interviewer on
    the non-verbal behavior of Japanese interviewees," Internation-
    al Journal of Psychology 9:2, pp. 117-128.

Bonet, Juan Pablo
    1620   Reduction de las Letras, y Arte para enseñar á ablar
    los Mudos.   Madrid, 314 pages.

Bonifacio, Giovanni [1547-1635]
    1616   L'arte de cenni con la quale formandosi fauella visible,
    si tratta della muta eloquenza, che non e' aitro che un facondo
    silentio.   Vicenza, ca. 623 pages.   [Errors in paging] [Author
    explains meaning of several hundred gestures; gives copious
    notes from Dante, classic literature, and the Bible; divides
    gestures according to parts of body (v. g. Della barba, De gli
    occhi, Delle braccia, etc.):   Hayes.]

Boomer, Donald S.
    1963   "Speech disturbance and body movement in interviews,"
    Journal of Nervous and Mental Disease 136, pp. 263-266.

    1965   "Hesitation and grammatical encoding," Language and
    Speech 8, pp. 148-158.

Boomer, Donald S., and Allen T. Dittmann
    1962   "Hesitation pauses and juncture pauses in speech,"
    Language and Speech 5, pp. 215-220.

    1964   "Speech rate, filled pause, and body movement in inter-
    views," Journal of Nervous and Mental Disease 139, pp. 324-
    327.

Bordone-Sacerdote, C. , and G. G. Sacerdote
1969   "Some spectral properties of individual voices," Acus-
tica 21:4, pp. 199-210.

Boring, E. G. and E. B. Titchener
1923   "A model for the demonstration of facial expression,"
American Journal of Psychology 34:4 (October), pp. 471-485.
[Based on Piderit's model.]

Bornstein, Harry
1974   "Signed English: a manual approach to English language
development," Journal of Speech and Hearing Disorders 39:3
(August), pp. 330-343.

Bornstein, Harry, and Lillian B. Hamilton
1972   "Recent national dictionaries of signs," Sign Language
Studies 1, pp. 42-63.

Bosma, James F.
1964   "Respiratory motion patterns of the newborn infant in
cry," in Physical Diagnosis of the Newborn Infant Cry, Report
of the Forty-Sixth Ross Conference on Pediatric Research; J.
L. Kay, ed.   Columbus, Ohio: Ross Laboratories, pp. 103-
116.

Bosma, James F. , H. M. Truby, and John Lind
1965   "Cry motions of the newborn infant," in John Lind, ed. ,
Newborn Infant Cry, Acta Paediatrica Scandinavica, Supplement
163, Uppsala, pp. 62-92.

Bosmajian, Haig A. , ed.
1971   The Rhetoric of Nonverbal Communication: Readings.
Glenview, Ill.: Scott, Foresman and Co. , 180 pages.

Botkin, B. A.
n. d.   "Negro work songs and calls," [recording].   Library of
Congress, Recording Laboratory, AAFS L 8.

Boucher, Jerry D.
1969   "Facial displays of fear, sadness and pain," Perceptual
and Motor Skills 28, pp. 239-242.

Boucher, Jerry and Paul Ekman
1965   "A replication of Schlosberg's Evaluation of Woodworth's
Scale of Emotion."   Read at the Western Psychological Association.

Bouillard, G.
1930   Notes diverses sur les cultes en Chine: Les attitudes
des Bouddhas.   Peking.

Bouissac, Paul A. R.
1972   "What does the little finger do?   An appraisal of kinesics," Semiotica 6:3, pp. 279-288.

1973   La mesure des gestes: prolégomènes a la sémiotique
gestuelle. The Hague: Mouton, 295 pages.

Boulware, Marcus H. [Florida A and M University]
1969   "Bibliography on snoring," Tallahassee, Florida.

1972   Snoring: Causes, Medical Treatment, and Therapy.
American Faculty Press.

        The Riddle of Snoring. Mokelumme Hill, Calif.:
Health Research.

Bowen, J. Donald
1956   "A comparison of the intonation patterns of English and
Spanish," Hispania 39:1 (March), pp. 30-35.

Bowers, Faubion
1953   The Dance in India. New York: Columbia University
Press; reprinted, New York: AMS Press, 1967, 175 pages.

Bowers, Robert H.
1948   "Gesticulation in Elizabethan acting," Southern Folklore
Quarterly 12, pp. 267-277. [See for bibliog. on gesture in
Elizabethan times: Hayes.]

Bowler, Ned W.
1964   "A fundamental frequency analysis of harsh vocal quality," Speech Monographs 31:2, pp. 128-134.

Boynton, M. Adelia, and Florence L. Goodenough
1930   "The posture of nursery school children during sleep,"
American Journal of Psychology 42, pp. 270-278.

Boyvin de Vavrouy
1636   La Physionomie ou des indices que la nature a mis au
corps humain, par ou l'on peut découvrir les moeurs & les
inclinations d'un chacun: avec un traitté de la divination par
les palpitations, & un autre par les marques naturelles. Le
tout traduict du Grec d'Adamantius & de Melampe. Paris:
Louis de Vandosme, 8 vols. [A curious book, supposed to
have been translated by a boy of twelve; on the various signs
of human expression, and other subjects: Hayes.]

Brackbill, Yvonne
1958   "Extinction of the smiling response in infants as a
function of reinforcement schedule," Child Development 29,
pp. 115-124.

1970   "Acoustic variation and arousal level in infants,"
Psychophysiology 6:5 (March), pp. 517-526.

Brain, R.
1961   "The neurology of language," Brain 84:2 (June), pp. 145-
166.

Bram, Joseph
1955   Language and Society. (Studies in Sociology 8.) New
York: Random House. Reprinted 1966, 66 pages.

Brandt, E.
1965   Gruss und Gebet. Eine Studie zu Gebärden in der mino-
ischmykenischen und frühgriechischen Kunst. Waldassen, Ba-
varia: Stiftland Verlag.

Brandt, John F., and Kenneth F. Ruder
1969   "Vocal loudness and effort in continuous speech," Journal of the Acoustical Society of America 46:6 (Part 2) (December), pp. 1543-1548.

Brannigan, Christopher R. and David A. Humphries
1969   "I see what you mean...," New Scientist 42:650 (May),
pp. 406-408.

1972   "Human non-verbal behaviour; a means of communication," in Ethological Studies of Child Behaviour, ed. N. Blurton Jones. Cambridge University Press, pp. 37-64.

Brault, Gerard J. [Pennsylvania State University]
1963   "Kinesics and the classroom: some typical French gestures," The French Review 36:4 (February), pp. 374-382.

(in prep.) The Song of Roland [with gestures included].

Braun, Ilse, and Marjorie Crofts
1965   "Mundurukú phonology," Anthropological Linguistics 7:7
(October), pp. 23-39.

Braun, John T.
1971   The Apostrophic Gesture. The Hague: Mouton, 217
pages.

Brazelton, T. Berry, with Mary Main
1971   "Are there too many sights and sounds in your baby's
world?" Redbook (September), pp. 91, 149-151.

Brazelton, T. Berry, Mary Louise Scholl, and John S. Robey
1966   "Visual responses in the newborn," Pediatrics 37,
pp. 284-290.

Brazelton, T. Berry, Edward Tronick, Lauren Adamson, Heidelise
Als, and Susan Wise
1975   "Early mother-infant reciprocity," Parent-Infant Interaction. (Ciba Foundation Symposium 33.) Amsterdam: Elsevier, pp. 137-154.

Brazelton, T. Berry, and Grace C. Young
1964   "An example of imitative behavior in a nine week old
infant," American Academy of Child Psychiatry, Journal 3:1
(January), pp. 53-67.

Breed, George, and Victoria Colaiuta
    1974   "Looking, blinking, and sitting: nonverbal dynamics in
    the classroom," Journal of Communication 24, pp. 75-81.

Breger, Ilana
    1970   "Perception of sign language of the deaf," Perceptual
    and Motor Skills 31, p. 426.

Brend, Ruth M.
    1972   "Male-female differences in American English intona-
    tion," Proceedings of the 7th International Congress of Phonetic
    Sciences. The Hague: Mouton, pp. 866-870.

Brewer, W. D.
    1951   "Patterns of gesture among the Levantine Arabs,"
    American Anthropologist 53:2 (April-June), pp. 232-237.

Bridges-Adams, W.
    1957   The Irresistible Theatre. New York: World Publishing
    Company. [Plate between pp. 176-177, "The hand in rhetoric,"
    from Bulwer's Chirologia, 1644.]

Brilliant, Richard
    1963   Gesture and Rank in Roman Art: the Use of Gestures
    to Denote Status in Roman Sculpture and Coinage. New Haven:
    Memoirs of the Connecticut Academy of Arts & Sciences 14,
    238 pages.

Brislin, Richard W.
    1974   "Seating as a measure of behavior: you are where you
    sit," Topics in Culture Learning. Honolulu: East West Center,
    pp. 103-118.

Broadbent, Donald Eric
    1957   "Effects of noise on behavior," in Handbook of Noise
    Control; C. M. Harris, ed. New York: McGraw-Hill, 1031
    pages. [Chapter 10.]

    1958   Perception and Communication. New York: Pergamon
    Press, 338 pages.

    1962   "Attention and the perception of speech," Scientific
    American (April).

Broadbent, D. E., and Peter Ladefoged
    1960   "Vowel judgments and adaptation level," Proceedings
    Royal Society B 151, pp. 384-399.

Brock, Nancy
    1941   "Notation for dance," Musical Teachers National Asso-
    ciation, 35th Series, New York, pp. 336-340.

Brodey, Warren
1964   "Sound and space," American Institute of Architects
Journal 42:1 (July), pp. 58-60.

Brodsky, Gerry
1967   "The relation between verbal and nonverbal behavior
change," Behavior Research and Therapy 5, pp. 183-191.

Brody, Eugene B., Richard Newman and Fredrick C. Redlich
1951   "Sound recording and the problem of evidence in psychiatry," Science 113 (April 6), pp. 379-380.

Broeg, Bob
1957   "Signals, the secret language of baseball: in finger-tip
movies," Boston: The Gillette Company.

Bronowski, J.
1967   "Human and animal languages," in To Honor Roman
Jakobson. The Hague: Mouton, vol. I, pp. 374-394.

Brooks, Nelson
1964   Language and Language Learning. New York: Harcourt, Brace and World, pp. 16-18.

Brooks, Robert, Linda Brandt, and Morton Wiener
1969   "Differential response to two communication channels:
socioeconomic class differences in response to verbal rein-
forcers communicated with or without tonal inflection," Child
Development 40:2, pp. 453-470.

Brophy, John
1945   The Human Face. London: G. G. Harrap, 240 pages.

1962   The Human Face Reconsidered. London: Harrap.

1963   The Face in Western Art. London: George G. Harrap
and Company, 184 pages.

Brosin, Henry W.
        "Description of behavior by psychologists and others in-
terested in linguistics, body motion and related studies."

1956   "Abstract of linguistic-kinesic analyses and psychiatry,"
San Francisco Psychoanalytic Society.

1959   "Discussion" of R. L. Birdwhistell's paper: "Contribution of linguistic-kinesic studies to the understanding of schizophrenia," in Alfred Auerbach, ed., Schizophrenia: An Integrated Approach. New York: Ronald Press, pp. 118-123.

1966   "Linguistic-kinesic analysis using film and tape in a
clinical setting," American Journal of Psychiatry, suppl. 122:12
pp. 33-37.

Brosin, Henry W. and William S. Condon
  1970   "Micro linguistic-kinesic events in schizophrenic behavior," in Schizophrenia: Current Concepts and Research; D. V.
  Siva Sankar, ed. Hicksville, N.Y.: P J D Publications, Ltd.

Brosin, Henry W., William S. Condon and William D. Ogston
  1970   "Film recording of normal and pathological behavior,"
  in Hope: Psychiatry's Commitment, edited by A. W. R. Sipe.
  New York: Brunner-Mazel, pp. 137-150.

Brown, Dolores
  1970   "A two-syllable affective affirmation in spoken Spanish,"
  Studies in Language and Linguistics 1969-1970; Ralph W. Ewton
  and Jacob Ornstein, eds. University of Texas at El Paso,
  pp. 33-43.

Brown, Ellen
  1964   "What makes you blush?" Reader's Digest (October),
  pp. 53-54.

Brown, Moses True
  1886   The Synthetic Philosophy of Expression as Applied to the
  Arts of Reading, Oratory, and Personation. Boston: Houghton
  Mifflin, 297 pages.

Brown, Roger
  1958   Words and Things. New York: Free Press. [Chapter
  5 on animal communication.]

Browne, Ray B.
  1954   "Some notes on the southern 'holler'," Journal of American Folklore 67 (January-March), pp. 73-77.

Browning, Ann
  1973   "Some semantic and syntactic relationships between
  language and body motion." Paper read at Linguistic Society
  of America, Michigan.

Bruford, Rose
  1958   Teaching Mime. London: Methuen, 235 pages.

Brun, Jean
  1963   La Main et l'esprit. (Bibl. de Philosophie Contempo-
  raine) Paris: Presses Universitaires de France, 174 pages.

Brun, Theodore
  1969   The International Dictionary of Sign Language: A Study
  of Human Behaviour. London: Wolfe Publishing Co., 127
  pages.

Bruneau, Thomas J. [Eastern Michigan University]
  1973   "Communicative silences: forms and functions," Journal
  of Communication 23:1 (March), pp. 17-46.

1974   "Time and nonverbal communication," The Journal of
Popular Culture 8:3 (Winter), pp. 658-666.

"A representative bibliography on communicative silence."

Personal-Time: Man's Temporal Environment.

Bruner, Jerome S.
1973   Beyond the Information Given: Studies in the Psychology
of Knowing, intro. and ed. by Jeremey M. Anglin. London:
George Allen and Unwin, 502 pages. [On perception.]

Bruner, Jerome S., Rose R. Olver, and Patricia M. Greenfield
1966   Studies in Cognitive Growth. New York: John Wiley.

Bruner, Jerome S., and Leo Postman
1949   "On the perception of incongruity: a paradigm," Journal of Personality 18, pp. 206-223.

Bruner, Jerome S. and Renato Tagiuri
1954   "The perception of people," in Gardner Lindzey, ed.,
Handbook of Social Psychology 2, "Special Fields and Applications." Reading, Mass.: Addison-Wesley, pp. 634-654.

Brunvand, Jan Harold
1960   "More non-oral riddles" (Notes and Queries), Western
Folklore 19, pp. 132-133.

1968   The Study of American Folklore. New York: Norton.
IV "Nonverbal Folklore"; Chap. 16, "Folk Gestures," pp. 242-51.

Brusis, T.
1972   "Silbo Gomero--Eine gepfiffene Sprache," Zeitschrift
für Laryngologie, Rhinologie, Otologie und ihre Grenzgebiete
51, pp. 454-457.

Buch, Max
1909   "Die Bezeihungen des Kitzels zur Erotik," Archiv für
Physiologie 33 (Leipzig), pp. 27-33. [The erotic meaning of
ticklishness.]

Buch, Max
1909   "Über den Kitzel," Archiv für Physiologie 33 (Leipzig),
pp. 1-26. [On ticklishness.]

Buck, Ross W., V. J. Savin, R. E. Miller, and W. R. Caul
1972   "Communication of affect through facial expressions in
humans," Journal of Personality and Social Psychology 23:3,
pp. 362-371.

Budd, Richard W., and Brent D. Ruben, eds.
1972   Approaches to Human Communication. New York:
Spartan Books, 464 pages.

Bugental, Daphne E.
1974 "Interpretations of naturally occurring discrepancies between words and intonation," Journal of Personality and Social
Psychology 30:1, pp. 125-133.

Bugental, Daphne E., Leonore R. Love, and Robert M. Gianetto
1971 "Perfidious feminine faces," Journal of Personality and
Social Psychology 17, pp. 314-318.

Bugental, Daphne E., Leonore R. Love and Jaques W. Kaswan
1972 "Videotaped family interaction: differences reflecting
presence and type of child disturbance," Journal of Abnormal
Psychology 79:3, pp. 285-290.

Bugental, Daphne E., Leonore R. Love, Jaques W. Kaswan, and
Carol April
1971 "Verbal-nonverbal conflict in parental messages to normal and disturbed children," Journal of Abnormal Psychology
77, pp. 6-10.

Bühler, Charlotte
1933 "The social behavior of children," in A Handbook of
Child Psychology, ed. C. Murchison. Worcester, Mass.:
Clark University Press, pp. 374-416. Reprinted, New York:
Russell & Russell Publishers, 1967.

Bühler, Charlotte, and H. Hetzer
1928 "The first understanding of expression in the first year
of life," Zeitschrift für Psychologie 107, pp. 50-61.

Bühler, Karl
1929 Die geistige Entwicklung des Kindes. Jena: Gustav
Fischer, pp. 214-236.

1933 Ausdruckstheorie. Jena. Partially reprinted as "The
psychophysics of expression of Wilhelm Wundt," in Wilhelm
Wundt, The Language of Gestures, pp. 30-54.

1934 Sprachtheorie: die Darstellung der Sprache. Jena:
Fischer. Reprinted, Stuttgart: G. Fischer, 1965, 434 pages.

Bullowa, Margaret
1967 "The onset of speech." Paper read at Society for Research in Child Development.

1970 "The start of the language process," Actes du xe
Congres International des Linguistes, Bucarest, 1967. Editions
de l'Academie de la Republique Socialiste de Roumanie, pp. 191-
200.

1974 "Non-verbal communication in infancy." Paper read at
the First Congress of the International Association for Semiotic Studies, Milan.

Bullowa   181

Bullowa, Margaret, J. L. Fiedelholtz, and A. R. Kessler
1973 "Infant vocalization: communication before speech."
Read at the 9th International Congress of Anthropological and
Ethnological Sciences, Chicago.

Bullowa, Margaret, Lawrence G. Jones, and Thomas G. Bever
1964 "The development from vocal to verbal behavior in
children," in The Acquisition of Language; Ursula Bellugi and
Roger Brown, eds. Monographs of the Society for Research in
Child Development 29:1, pp. 101-114. Reprinted in Cognitive
Development in Children, Five Monographs of the Society for
Research in Child Development, University of Chicago Press,
1970, pp. 385-392.

Bullowa, Margaret, Lawrence G. Jones, and Audrey R. Duckert
1964 "The acquisition of a word," Language and Speech 7
(Part 2), (April-June), pp. 107-111.

Bullowa, Margaret, and E. Putney
1973 "A method for analyzing communicative behavior between
infant and adult from film." Read at the International Society
for the Study of Behavioral Development, Ann Arbor, Michigan.

Bulwer, John see Bridges-Adams; James William Cleary; H. J.
Norman

Bulwer, John
1644 Chirologia: Or The Natvrall Langvage of the Hand,
Composed of the speaking motions, and discoursing gestures
thereof. Whereunto is added Chironomia: or, The art of
manvall rhetoricke. Consisting of the naturall expressions,
digested by art in the hand, as the chiefest instrument of eloquence, by historicall manifesto's, exemplified out of the au-
thentique registers of common life, and civill conversation.
London. Reprinted, New York: AMS Press.

1648 Philocophus: or, the deafe and dumbe mans friend,
exhibiting ... the art which may inable one ... to heare what
any man speaks by the moving of his lips.... London.

Buning, E. J., and Cornelius H. van Schooneveld
1960 The Sentence Intonation of Contemporary Standard Russian. s'Gravenhage.

Bünning, Erwin
1964 The Physiological Clock: Endogenous Diurnal Rhythms
and Biological Chronometry. Berlin: Springer, 145 pages.
New York: Springer-Verlag, 1967, 167 pages.

Burgess, J.
1897 "Buddhist Mudras," Indian Antiquary 26 (Bombay).

Burgess, Thomas Henry
    1839   The Physiology or Mechanism of Blushing: Illustrative
    of the Influence of Mental Emotion on the Capillary Circulation:
    with a General View of the Sympathies. London: J. Churchill,
    202 pages.

Burhans, David T.
    1975   [Review article of five books on communication], Quar-
    terly Journal of Speech 61:2 (April), pp. 108-110.

Burke, Kenneth
    1966   "The thinking of the body," in Language as Symbolic
    Action: Essays on Life, Literature and Method. Berkeley:
    University of California Press, 514 pages.

    1969   A Grammar of Motives. Berkeley: University of Cali-
    fornia Press, 544 pages.

Burns, Kenton L., and Ernst G. Beier
    1973   "Significance of vocal and visual channels in the decod-
    ing of emotional meaning," Journal of Communication 23,
    pp. 118-130.

Burns, T.
    1969   "Nonverbal communication," Discovery 25:10.

Burns, Tom
    1964   "Nonverbal Communication," Discovery (October),
    pp. 31-35.

Bursack, Lois I.
    1971   "North American nonverbal behaviour as perceived in
    three overseas urban cultures," Dissertation Abstracts 32,
    572 A.

Burssens, Amaat
    1939   "Le Luba, langue à intonation, et le tambour-signal,"
    Proceedings of the Third Intern. Cong. of Phonetic Sciences,
    pp. 503-507.

Burton, Arthur, and Robert E. Kantor
    1964   "The touching of the body," Psychoanalytic Review 51,
    pp. 122-134.

Burton, Sir Richard Francis
    1862   The City of the Saints. New York: Harper, 574 pages.
    [List of Indian signs, with explanations, pp. 150-160--not
    illust.: Hayes.]

Busnel, René-Guy
    1966   "Human whistle language and sea mammal whistling,"
    in Whales, Dolphins and Porpoises, ed. Kenneth Norris.
    Berkeley: University of California Press, pp. 544-568.

1970   "Recherches expérimentales sur la langue sifflée de
Kuskoy," Revue du Phonétique Appliquée 14-15, pp. 41-75.

Busnel, René-Guy, Abraham A. Moles, and M. Gilbert
1962   "Un cas de langue sifflée dans les Pyrénées françaises,"
Logos 5, pp. 76-91.

Busnel, R. G., A. Moles, and B. Vallancien
1962   "Sur l'aspect phonétique d'une langue sifflée des
Pyrénées françaises," Proceedings of the 4th International Congress of Phonetic Sciences, Helsinki, 1961. The Hague:
Mouton.

Butterworth, Brian
1975   "Hesitation and semantic planning in speech," Journal
of Psycholinguistic Research 4, pp. 75-87.

Buytendijk, F. J. J.
1947   "De cerste glimlach van het kind." Nijmegen: Dekker
and v. d. Vegt.

1948   Algemene Theorie der Menselijke Houding en Beweging.
Utrecht: Het Sprectrum.

Buzby, Dallas E.
1924   "The interpretation of facial expression," American
Journal of Psychology 35 (October), pp. 602-604.

Buzby, Dallas E.   see also   Boring

Byers, Paul
1964   "Still photography in the systematic recording and analysis of behavioral data," Human Organization 23:1 (Spring),
pp. 78-84.

1971   "Sentics, rhythms, and a new view of man." Paper
read at 138th Annual Meeting of the American Association for
the Advancement of Science, Philadelphia.

Byers, Paul, and Happie Byers
1972   "Nonverbal communication and the education of children,"
in Functions of Language in the Classroom, ed. Courtney B.
Cazden, Vera P. John and Dell Hymes. New York: Columbia
University Teachers College Press, pp. 3-31.

- C -

Caballero, Ramón
n.d.   Diccionario de modismos. Madrid. [Contains nearly
300 Spanish phrases in which the hand figures, pp. 1181-1198:
Hayes.]

Cabibi, John V.
  1974   "Body talk: a group therapy approach to facilitate dyadic interaction," Dissertation Abstracts 35:5101B.

Cabrol, Fernand
  1907-53   "Imposition des mains, " in Dictionnaire d'archeologie
  chretienne et de liturgie, VII. Paris: Letouzey et Ané,
  15 vols.

Cajori, F.
  1926   "A notable case of finger-reckoning in America, " Isis
  8, pp. 325-327.

Call, Justin D.
  1965   "Contribution of longitudinal studies to psychoanalytic
  theory, " Journal of the American Psychoanalytic Association
  13, pp. 615-618.

  1968   "Lap and finger play in infancy, implications for ego
  development, " International Journal of Psycho-Analysis 49:2-3,
  pp. 375-378.

  1970   "Games babies play, " Psychology Today 3:8 (January),
  pp. 34-37, 54.

  (in press)   "Developmental and executive aspects of the point-
  ing gesture and the sound 'ush' in a 14-month-old infant, " in
  Samir Ghosh, ed. , The Biology of Language. New York:
  Academic Press.

Callan, Hilary
  1970   "On greeting, " chapter VII in Ethology and Society:
  Towards an Anthropological View. Oxford: Clarendon Press,
  pp. 104-124.

Callotto Resuscitato, II
  ca. 1720   Oder neu eingerichtetes Zwerchencabinet, cum priv.
  S. C. May, Augsburg. (Originally Le Monde plein de fols, ou
  Le Theatre des nains, en Francois et en Hollandois, Amsterdam, 1715.) [See gesticulation portrayed in engravings of gro-
  tesque figures: Hayes.]

Callow, Nicholas
  1971   "The Wolff System--An Appraisal, " The Teacher of the
  Deaf 69, pp. 331-333.

Cameron, James, Norman Livson, and Nancy Bayley
  1967   "Infant vocalizations and their relationship to mature intelligence, " Science 157, pp. 331-333.

Camina, V. B.
  1957-58   "Gestos (mímica), " Boletin da Comissão catarinense
  de folclore (Florianópolis Brasil) VIV:23-24, pp. 26-31.

Cammack 185

Cammack, Floyd M. and Hildebert van Buren
1967 "Paralanguage across cultures: some comparisons between Japanese and English, " The English Language Education
Council Bulletin (Kanda) 22 (November), pp. 7-10, 47.

Campbell, D. G.
1954 "Your actions speak so loudly, " Impulse, pp. 27-28.

Campbell, Donald T. , William H. Kruskal, and William P. Wallace
1966 "Seating aggregation as an index of attitude, " Sociometry
29, pp. 1-15.

Candido, Joseph
1972 "Language and gesture in the Chester Sacrifice of Issac,"
Comitatus 3 (University of California at Los Angeles), pp. 11-
18.

Canfield, D. Lincoln
1946 "The 'rúbrica' of the Hispanic culture pattern, " Hispania
29 (November), pp. 527-531.

Canna, D. J. , and Eugene Loring
1955 Kineseography: The Loring System of Dance Notation.
Academy Press, 57 pages.

Cardona, Miguel
1953-54 "Gestos o ademanes habituales en Venezuela, " Archi-
vos Venezolanos De Folklore, ano II-III, tomo II:3 (Caracas:
Univ. Central de Venezuela), pp. 159-166.

Carlile, John S. , compiler
1937-38 "Glossaries: Studio sign language, " Variety: Radio
Directory. Variety, Inc. (First Annual Edition), pp. 328-337.

Carlyle, Thomas
1833-34 Sartor Resartus.

Carmichael, L. , S. O. Roberts, N. Y. Wessell
1937 "A study of the judgment of manual expression as presented in still and motion pictures, " Journal of Social Psychology 8 (February), pp. 115-142.

Carpenter, C. R.
1958 "Territoriality: a review of concepts and problems, " in
Behavior and Evolution; A. Roe, and G. G. Simpson, eds.
New Haven, Conn. : Yale Univ. Press, pp. 224-250.

Carpenter, Charles
1932 "The sign language of railroad men, " American Mercury
25 (February), pp. 211-213.

Carpenter, Edmund, and Marshall McLuhan
1960 Explorations in Communication: An Anthology. Boston:

Beacon Press, 208 pages. Review by Herbert Landar, American Anthropologist 63:4 (August 1961).

Carr, Suzanne J. , and James M. Dabbs, Jr.
1974   "The effects of lighting, distance and intimacy on verbal and visual behavior, " Sociometry 37, pp. 592-600.

Carrington, John F.
1944   The Drum Language of the Lokele Tribe (African Studies) Witwatersrand: Witwatersrand Univ. Press.

1949   A Comparative Study of Some Central African Gong Languages. Brussels: Institut Royal Colonial Belge.

1949   Talking Drums of Africa. London: Carey Kingsgate Press. Reprinted, New York: Negro Universities Press, 1969, 96 pages. ["Shouting-at-a-distance" and whistle, pp. 74-77.]

1953   "Communication by means of gongs and other instruments in Central Africa, " Explorations 1, pp. 24-33.

1971   "The talking drums of Africa, " Scientific American 255:6, pp. 90-94.

Carruth, W. H.
1892   "The language used to domestic animals," Dialect Notes I, Part VI, pp. 263-268.

Carterette, Edward C. , ed.
1966   Brain Function, Vol. III, Speech, Language, and Communication. Berkeley: University of California Press.

Carus, Carl Gustav
1846   Über Grund und Bedeutung der verschiedenen Formen der Hand. Stuttgart. [First serious attempt to classify the hands and assoc. their types with personality, p. 241: Misiak and Franghiadi.]

1852   Symbolik der menschlichen Gestalt. Leipzig: Radebeul-Dresden, 1939.

Casa, Giovanni della [1503-1556]
1550-55   Galateo of Manners and Behaviours. Boston: Merrymount Press, 1914, 123 pages. [Contains numerous references on how Renaissance Italian gentlemen or ladies should walk, express themselves, and behave.]

Casagrande, Joseph B.
1948   "Comanche baby language, " International Journal of American Linguistics 14, pp. 11-14. Reprinted in Dell Hymes, Language in Culture and Society. New York: Harper and Row, 1964, pp. 245-248.

Cason, Hulsey
    1930   "Common annoyances: a psychological study of every-
    day aversions and irritations, " Psychological Monographs,
    Whole No. 182:40, pp. 1-218.

Cassota, L. , S. Feldstein, and J. Jaffe
    1968   "The stability and modifiability of individual vocal
    characteristics in stress and non-stress interviews, " Res.
    Bulletin 2 (New York: Wm. Alanson White Institute).

Castiglione, Baldesar
    1516   The Book of the Courtier, trans. by C. S. Singleton.
    Garden City, N.Y. : Anchor, 1959.

Catford, J. C.
    1939   "On the classification of stop consonants, " Le Maitre
    Phonetique 3rd series, No. 65 (January), pp. 2-5.

    1947   "Consonants pronounced with closed glottis, " Le Maitre
    Phonetique 3rd series, No. 87 (Jan. -June), pp. 4-6.

    1964   "Phonation types: the classification of some laryngeal
    components of speech production" in David Abercrombie, et al. ,
    eds. , In Honour of Daniel Jones: Papers Contributed on the
    Occasion of his Eightieth Birthday.   London: Longmans,
    pp. 26-37.

    1968   "The articulatory possibilities of man, " Manual of Pho-
    netics, ed. by Bertil Malmberg.   North-Holland Pub. Co. ,
    chap. 10, pp. 309-333.

Caudill, William
    ca. 1972   "Tiny dramas: vocal communication between mother
    and infant in Japanese and American families, " Proceedings,
    Second Conference on Culture and Mental Health; William
    Lebra, ed. Univ. of Hawaii: Social Science Research Institute.

Causley, Marguerite
    1967   An Introduction to Benesh Movement Notation: Its Gene-
    ral Principles and Its Use in Physical Education.   London:
    Max Parrish, 91 pages.

Cavendish, William
    1743   A General System of Horsemanship in All Its Branches.
    London. [A system of recording the steps of horses in the
    art of dressage: Lister, in Stepanov.]

Cazden, Courtney B. , Vera P. John, Dell Hymes, eds.
    1972   Functions of Language in the Classroom.   New York:
    Teachers College Press, 394 pages.

Chaitanya
    1968   "The school of silence, " Quest: A Quarterly of Inquiry,
    Criticism and Ideas 59 (Bombay, India), pp. 48-51.

Chalke, H. D. and J. R. Dewhurst
    1957 "Accidental coal-gas poisoning: loss of sense of smell
    as a possible contributory factor with old people," British
    Medical Journal II, pp. 915-917.

Chamberlain, Alexander F.
    1890 "Notes on Indian child-language," American Anthropolo-
    gist (o. s.) 3, pp. 237-241.

    1893 "Further notes on Indian child-language," American
    Anthropologist (o. s.) 6 (July), pp. 321-322.

Chance, Michael R. A.
    1962 "An interpretation of some agnostic postures: The role
    of 'out-off' acts and postures," Evolutionary Aspects of Animal
    Communication: Symposium of the Zoological Society of Lon-
    don 8, pp. 71-89.

Chance, Michael R. A. , and Clifford J. Jolly
    1970   Social Groups of Monkeys, Apes and Men.   New York:
    E. P. Dutton, 224 pages.

Chandola, Anoop Chandra
    1963 "Animal commands of Garhwali and their linguistic im-
    plications," Word 19:2 (August), pp. 203-207.

    1969 "Metalinguistic structure of Indian drumming: a study
    in musico-linguistics," Language and Style 2, pp. 288-295.

Chang, Chêng-ming [Tchang Tcheng-ming], B. S. J.
    1937   L'écriture chinoise et le geste humain: Essai sur la
    formation de l'écriture chinoise. (Variétés Sinologiques No.
    64) Paris, 205 pages. [Reproduction of 700 ancient characters.
    One of the fundamental works of gesture study: Hayes.]

Chang, Nien-Chuang T.
    1958 "Tones and intonation in the Chengtu dialect (Szechuan,
    China)," Phonetica 2:1/2, pp. 59-85.

Chao, Yuen Ren
    1953 "Speech and personality," in Levi-Strauss, et al. , eds. ,
    "Results of the Conference of Anthropologists and Linguists,"
    International Journal of American Linguistics 19:2, Memoir 8,
    (April), 67 pages.

    1956 "Tone, intonation, singsong, chanting, recitative, tonal
    composition, and atonal composition in Chinese," in For Roman
    Jakobson; Morris Halle, ed. The Hague: Mouton, pp. 52-59.

    1968   Language and Symbolic Systems.   London: Cambridge
    University Press, 240 pages.

Chapman, Antony J.
1973   "Funniness of jokes, canned laughter, and recall performance, " Sociometry 36, pp. 569-578.

Chapman, Ashton
1943   "Watch your gestures, " She: The Magazine for the
Modern Woman 1 (October), pp. 24-26.

1948   "Card-cataloguing man's gestures, " Profitable Hobbies
5 (November), pp. 30, 31, 54. [On Francis Hayes.]

Chapple, Eliot D. , with the collaboration of Conrad M. Arensberg
1940   "Measuring human relations: an introduction to the
study of interaction of individuals, " Genetic Psychology Monographs 22, pp. 3-147. [Special-usage terms ("action, " "event,"
"component, " and "set"); equipment for recording interaction
sequences; analysis of interaction patterns in various settings;
and interaction hierarchies, systems, and subsystems are defined and/or assessed.]

1942   Principles of Anthropology. New York: H. Holt and
Company.

1970   Culture and Biological Man: Explorations in Behavioral
Anthropology. New York: Holt, Rinehart and Winston.

Charlip, Remy, Mary Beth, and George Ancona
1974   Handtalk, An ABC of Finger Spelling and Sign Language.
New York: Parents' Magazine Press.

Charny, E. Joseph
1966   "Psychosomatic manifestations of rapport in psychotherapy, " Psychosomatic Medicine 28:4 (Part I), (July-Aug.),
pp. 305-315.

Chase, Stuart
1957   "The language of nods, " Saturday Review 40 (March 2),
pp. 17-18.

Chatman, Seymour
1966   "Linguistic analysis: A study of James Mason's interpretation of 'The Bishop Orders His Tomb', " in Thomas O.
Sloan, ed. , The Oral Study of Literature. New York: Random
House, pp. 94-133.

Chatterji, Usha (Srimati Usha)
1951   La danse Hindoue. Paris: Chez l'Auteur, Exclusive
Hachette.

Checkov, Michael
1953   To the Actor: On the Technique of Acting. New York:
Harper & Brothers, 201 pages.

Chen, Li-Ching Yen
1971   "Manual communication by combined alphabet and ges-
        tures," Archives of Physical Medicine and Rehabilitation 52,
        pp. 381-384.

Cherry, Colin
1957   On Human Communication: A Review, A Survey and A
        Criticism. New York: MIT and John Wiley, Science Editions,
        1961, 333 pages.

Chesneau, Albert
1975   "La notion de 'Sème Dormant'," Language and Language
        Behavior Abstracts 9:2, 7501908.

Chester, Sondra L., and Donald B. Egolf
1975   "Nonverbal communication and aphasia therapy," Langu-
        age and Language Behavior Abstracts 9:1, 7500804.

Cheyne, James A., and Michael G. Efran
1972   "The effect of spatial and interpersonal variables on the
        invasion of group controlled territories," Sociometry 35,
        pp. 477-489.

Chiba, Tsutomu and Masato Kajiyama
1941   The Vowel: Its Nature and Structure. Tokyo: Kaisei-
        kan Pub. Co., 1958, 236 pages. [Historical survey of theories:
        Willis, Wheatstone, Helmholtz, Hermann ... etc. --"sharp
        voice," "soft voice," pp. 13-23.]

Chisman, Isabel, and Hester Emilie Raven-Hart
n.d.   Manners and Movements in Costume Plays. London:
        H. F. W. Deane, 122 pages.

Chomentovskaja, O.
1938   "Le Comput digital: histoire d'un geste dans l'art de la
        renaissance italienne," Gazette des Beaux-Arts 20, pp. 151-
        172.

Chomsky, Noam
1967   "The general properties of language," in Brain Mecha-
        nisms Underlying Speech and Language, eds. Clark H. Millikan
        and Frederic L. Darley. New York: Grune and Stratton,
        pp. 73-88.

1968   Language and Mind. New York: Harcourt, Brace, and
        World. [Pp. 59-60, origin of language.]

Christian, Jane M. [University of Alabama]
        "Style and dialect selection in Hindi-Bhojpuri learning
        children."

Christiansen, Bjørn
1963   Thus Speaks the Body: Attempts Toward a Personology

from the Point of View of Respiration and Postures. Oslo,
Norway. Reprinted New York: Arno Press, 1972, 235 pages.

Chujoy, Anatole, and P. W. Manchester
1967   The Dance Encyclopedia. New York: Simon and Schuster (revised).

Churchill, J. C.
1951   "Do your gestures give you away?" Woman's Home
Companion (July), p. 14.

Cicourel, Aaron V.
1974   "Gestural sign language and the study of non-verbal
communication," Sign Language Studies 4, pp. 35-76.

(in press) "Sociolinguistic aspects of gestural sign language,"
in I. Schlesinger and L. Namir, eds. , Current Trends in
Studies of the Sign Language of the Deaf. The Hague: Mouton, in press.

Cicourel, Aaron V. , and Robert J. Boese
1972   "The acquisition of manual sign language and generative
semantics," Semiotica 5, pp. 225-256.

1972   "Sign language acquisition and the teaching of deaf
children," in Courtney B. Cazden, Vera P. John and Dell
Hymes, eds. , Functions of Language in the Classroom.
Teachers College Press, Columbia Univ. , pp. 32-62. Review
by Harry Markowicz, Sign Language Studies 3, (1973), pp. 72-
78.

Ciolek, T. M.
1975   "Human communication behavior: a bibliography," Sign
Language Studies 6:1, pp. 1-64.

Claiborn, William L.
1969   "Expectancy effects in the classroom: A failure to
replicate," Journal of Educational Psychology 60, pp. 377-383.

Clark, Leslie L.
1967   "The expression of emotion by the blind," The New Outlook, (May), Part I, pp. 155-163; (June), Part II, pp. 194-201.

Clark, Virginia P. , Paul A. Eschholz, and Alfred F. Rosa
1972   "Space and the language of the body," Language: Introductory Readings. New York: St. Martin's Press, pp. 457-
558.

Clark, Captain William Philo
1885   The Indian Sign Language: with Brief Explanatory Notes
of the Gestures Taught Deaf-Mutes in our Institutions for Their
Instruction: and a Description of Some of the Peculiar Laws,
Customs, Myths, Superstitions, Ways of Living, Code of Peace

and War Signals of Our Aborigines.   Philadelphia, 443 pages.
Reprinted, San Jose, Calif.:   The Rosicrucian Press, 1959.

Clarke, Roger T.
1934   "The drum language of the Tumba people," American
Journal of Sociology 40, pp. 34-48.

Classe, André
1957   "Phonetics of the Silbo Gomero," Archivium Linguisti-
cum 9:1 (Glasgow), pp. 44-61.

1957   "The unusual whistle language of the Canary Islanders,"
The UNESCO Courier No. 11, (November), pp. 30-32.

1957   "The whistled language of La Gomera," Scientific American 196:4 (April), pp. 111-120.

Clay, Vidal S.
1966   "The effect of culture on mother-child tactile communication," Teachers College, Columbia University.   Dissertation
Abstracts 28.1770B.

Cleary, James William
1956   [Dissertation on Bulwer, q.v.]   Dissertation Abstracts
16, No. 12, pp. 2552-2553.

Clevenger, T., and T. R. King
1961   "A factor analysis of visible symptoms of stage fright,"
Speech Monograph 28, pp. 290-298.

Cline, M. G.
1967   "The perception of where a person is looking," American Journal of Psychology 80, pp. 41-50.

Cline, Marvin G.
1956   "The influence of social context on the perception of
faces," Journal of Personality 25:1, pp. 142-158.

Clynes, Manfred
1970   "On being in order," Zygon: Journal of Religion and
Science 5:1 (March), pp. 63-84.

1972   "Sentic cycles: passions at your fingertips," Psychology
Today (May), pp. 59-72.

1974   "The pure pulse of musical genius," Psychology Today
(July), pp. 51-55.

Cobb, Jane
1940   "Clappers and hissers," New York Times Magazine
(April 21), p. 7.   [For audience response.]

Cocchiara, Giuseppe
1932   Il linguaggio del gesto. Turin: Fratelli Bocca, 131
pages. [See Hayes bibliography for chapter titles and review
notice.] Review by F. B., Zeitschrift für Volkskunde 44,
p. 299.

Cody, Iron Eyes, assisted by Ye-was
1952   How: Sign Talk in Pictures, illust. by Clarence Ellsworth. Hollywood, Calif.: Homer H. Boelter Lithography.

Coger, Leslie Irene
1972   "Physical actions and the oral interpreter," in Esther
M. Doyle, and Virginia H. Floyd, eds., Studies in Interpretation. Amsterdam: Rodopi N. V., pp. 275-286.

Coger, Leslie Irene, and Sharron Pelham
1975   "Kinesics applied to interpreter's theatre," The Speech
Teacher 24:2 (March), pp. 91-99.

Cohen, E., L. Namir, and I. M. Schlesinger
(in press) A New Dictionary of Sign Language. The Hague:
Mouton.

Cohen, Jerry L., Bernard Sladen, and Barbara Bennett
1975   "The effects of situational variables on judgments of
crowding," Sociometry 38, pp. 273-281.

Cohen, Lynn Renee [Queens College--CUNY]
        "An inquiry into the use of effort/shape analysis in the
exploration of leadership in small groups." Columbia University Dissertation.

Cohen, Marcel
1956   Pour une sociologie du langage. Paris. [Gestures,
p. 74.]

Cole, John T.
1963   "The sequential distribution of thanking in Aymara culture," in Viola E. Garfield, and Wallace L. Chafe, eds.,
Symposium on Language and Culture. American Ethnological
Society, pp. 64-68.

Coleman, Charles
1832   The Mythology of the Hindus. London, 401 pages.
[Numerous gestures, facial, manual, etc. Many gods and
goddesses have multiple arms and hands gesticulating. In
addition are Japanese, Egyptians, Dayak of Borneo: Hayes.]

Coleman, James C.
1949   "Facial expressions of emotion," Psychological Monographs 63:1 (whole No. 296), pp. 1-36. [Includes extensive
bibliography of early studies.]

Coleman, Roy, Milton Greenblatt, and Harry C. Solomon
1956   "Physiological evidence of rapport during psychotherapeutic interviews," Diseases of the Nervous System 17, pp. 71-
77.

Collier, John, Jr.
1967   Visual Anthropology: Photography as a Research Method. New York: Holt, Rinehart and Winston, 138 pages.

Comfort, Alex
1971   "Communication may be odorous," New Scientist and
Science Journal 49:740 (February 25), pp. 412-414.

Comstock, Andrew
1841   A System of Elocution, with Special Reference to Gesture, to the Treatment of Stammering, and Defective Articulation. Philadelphia, 364 pages.

Condon, John C., and Fathi S. Yousef
1975   An Introduction to Intercultural Communication. Indianapolis: Bobbs-Merrill, 306 pages.

Condon, William S.
1964   "Process in communication," 17 pages.

1968   "Linguistic-kinesic research and dance therapy," Ameri-
can Dance Therapy Association Proceedings, Third Annual
Conference, pp. 21-44. (Copies from ADTA, 5173 Phantom
Court, Columbia, Md. 21043.)

1970   "Method of Micro-analysis of Sound Films of Behavior,"
Behavioral Research Methods and Instrumentation 2:2, pp. 51-
54.

Condon, William S., and Henry W. Brosin
1969   "Micro linguistic-kinesic events in schizophrenic behavior," in Schizophrenia: Current Concepts and Research,
edited by D. V. Siva Sankar. Hicksville, N.Y.: PJD Publications, pp. 812-837.

Condon, William S., and William D. Ogston
1966   "Sound film analysis of normal and pathological behavior
patterns," Journal of Nervous and Mental Disease 143:4
pp. 338-347.

1967   "A method of studying animal behavior," Journal of
Auditory Research 7, pp. 359-365.

1967   "A segmentation of behavior," Journal of Psychiatric
Research 5, pp. 221-235.

1971   "Speech and body motion synchrony of the speaker-
hearer," in D. L. Horton and J. J. Jenkins, eds., Perception

of Language. Columbus, Ohio: Charles E. Merrill, pp. 150-173.

Condon, William S. , William D. Ogston, and Larry V. Pacoe
1969 "Three faces of Eve revisited: a study of transient microstrabismus, " Journal of Abnormal Psychology 74, pp. 618-620.

Condon, William S. , and Louis W. Sander
1974 "Synchrony demonstrated between movements of the neonate and adult speech, " Child Development 45, pp. 456-462.

1974 'Neonate movement is synchronized with adult speech: interactional participation and language acquisition, " Science 183 (January 11), pp. 99-101.

Conklin, Harold C.
1956 "Tagalog speech disguise, " Language 32:1 (January-March), pp. 136-139.

1959 "Linguistic play in its cultural context, " Language 35:4 (Oct. -Dec.), pp. 631-636. Reprinted in Dell Hymes, Language in Culture and Society. New York: Harper and Row, 1964, pp. 295-298.

Conn, L. K. , C. N. Edwards, R. Rosenthal, and D. Crowne
1968 "Perception of emotion and response to teachers' expectancy by elementary school children, " Psychological Reports 22, pp. 27-34.

Cook, Mark
1969 "Anxiety, speech disturbances and speech rate, " British Journal of Social and Clinical Psychology 8:1, pp. 13-21.

1969 "Transition probabilities and the incidence of filled pauses, " Psychonomic Science 16, pp. 191-192.

1970 "Experiments on orientation and proxemics, " Human Relations 23, pp. 61-76.

1971 "The Anatomy of um and er, " New Society No. 445 (April 8), pp. 577-579.

1971 "The incidence of filled pauses in relation to part of speech, " Language and Speech 14, pp. 135-139.

1971 Interpersonal Perception. London: Penguin Books, 168 pages.

Cook, Mark, and Mansur G. Lallgee
1972 "Verbal substitutes for visual signals in interaction, " Semiotica 6:3, pp. 212-221.

Cooke, Jean
    1959   "A few gestures encountered in a virtually gestureless
    society," Western Folklore 18, pp. 233-237.

Coomaraswamy   see   Nandikesvara

Coon, Carleton S.
    1966   "On Montagu's review of Conrad's 'The many worlds of
    man'," American Anthropologist 68:2 (Part 1), (April), p. 518.
    [On racial body odor.]

Corbin, Edwin I.
    1962   "Muscle action as nonverbal and preverbal communica-
    tion," Psychoanalytic Quarterly 31, pp. 351-363.

Coser, Lewis A. , ed.
    1965   Georg Simmel.   Englewood Cliffs, N. J. :   Prentice-Hall.

Coser, Rose Laub
    1959   "Some social functions of laughter: a study of humor in
    a hospital setting," Human Relations 12, pp. 171-182.

    1960   "Laughter among colleagues," Psychiatry 23 (Feb.),
    pp. 81-95.

Cosper, Wilma Baker
    1971   "An analysis of sex differences in teacher-student inter-
    action as manifest in verbal and nonverbal behavior cues,"
    Dissertation Abstracts 32:1-A (July), University of Tennessee.

Coss, R. G.
    1965   Mood Provoking Visual Stimuli.   University of California
    Press, Industrial Design Graduate Program, 55 pages.

    1968   "The ethological command in art," Leonardo I.   Elms-
    ford, N. Y. :   Pergamon Press, pp. 273-287.

Cossetta, Al
    1946   Natural Gestures and Postures in Speech.   Kansas City,
    Mo. :   Natural Gestures and Postures Association, 151 pages.

Costanzo, Frances S. , Norman N. Markel, and Philip R. Costanzo
    1969   "Voice quality profile and perceived emotion," Journal
    of Counseling Psychology 16:3, pp. 267-270.

Count, Earl W.
    1974   "On the phylogenesis of the speech function," with com-
    ments by Gordon Hewes, Frank B. Livingstone and A. E.
    Mourant, Current Anthropology 15:1, pp. 81-90.

Courogyer, B.
    1960   "Mettre sa main sur sa bouche, en Egypte et dans la
    Bible," Revue Biblique 67.

Courten, H. C.
1902   "Involuntary movements of the tongue," Yale Psychological Studies 10, pp. 93-96.

Covington, Virginia C.
1973   "Features of stress in American sign language," Sign Language Studies 2, pp. 39-50.

1973   "Juncture in American sign language," Sign Language Studies 2, pp. 29-38.

Cowan, George M.
1948   "Mazateco whistle speech," Language 24, pp. 280-286. Reprinted in Dell Hymes, Language in Culture and Society. New York: Harper and Row, 1964, pp. 305-311.

1952   "El idioma silbado entre los mazatecos de Oaxaca y los tepehuas de Hidalgo, México," Tlatoani, Revista de la Sociedad de Alumnos de la Escuela Nacional de Antropología 1:3-4, pp. 31-33.

1972   "Segmental features of Tepehua whistle speech," Proceedings of the 7th International Congress of Phonetic Sciences (Montreal, 1971). The Hague: Mouton, pp. 695-698.

Cowan, J. Milton
1936   "Pitch and intensity characteristics of stage speech," Archives of Speech, Supplement I, pp. 1-92.

Cowan, J. Milton and Bernard Bloch
1948   "An experimental study of pause in English grammar," American Speech 23:2 (April), pp. 89-99.

Craighead, Jean C.
1942   A System of Notation for the Modern Dance. Philadelphia. [Typewritten; Birdwhistell cited.]

Cranach, Mario von
1971   "The role of orienting behavior in human interaction," in Behavior and Environment: The Use of Space by Animals and Men, edited by A. H. Esser. New York: Plenum Publishing Corporation, pp. 217-237.

1974   Nonverbal Social Communication. New York: Academic Press.

Cranach, Mario, and Johann H. Ellgring
1973   "Problems in the recognition of gaze direction," in Mario von Cranach and Ian Vine, eds., Social Communication and Movement. London and New York: Academic Press, pp. 419-443.

Cranach, Mario von and Ian Vine, eds.
1973 Social Communication and Movement: Studies of Interaction and Expression in Man and Chimpanzees. London and
New York: Academic Press, 489 pages.

Cratty, Bryant J.
1967 Movement Behavior and Motor Learning. Philadelphia:
Lea & Febiger, 367 pages. [Valuable for its review of the
literature and a 1,000-title bibliography on motor skills and
learning.]

1971 Movement and Spatial Awareness in Blind Children and
Youth. Springfield, Ill.: Thomas, 240 pages.

Crawford, James M.
1970 "Cocopa baby talk," International Journal of American
Linguistics 36:1 (January), pp. 9-13.

Crawley, Alfred Ernest
1929 "The nature and history of the kiss," Studies of Savages
and Sex. London: Methuen. Reprinted New York: Johnson
Reprint Corporation, 1969.

Cresswell, Robert
1968 "Le geste manuel associé au langage," Langages 10,
pp. 119-127.

Crisari, Maurizio
1971 "Sul ruolo dei gesti in glottodidattica," Pensiero e
Linguaggio in Operazioni 2, pp. 128-132. [English trans.,
pp. 133-137.]

Critchley, Edmund
1967 Speech Origins and Development. Springfield, Ill.:
Charles C. Thomas.

Critchley, Macdonald
1938 "On the neurology of the gestures of a partial deaf-
mute," Brain 61, p. 163.

1939 The Language of Gesture. London: Edward Arnold,
128 pages. Review by Robert West, Quarterly Journal of
Speech 26 (1940), pp. 455-456.

1960 "The evolution of man's capacity for language," in Sol
Tax, ed., Evolution After Darwin. Chicago: University of
Chicago Press, pp. 289-308.

1961 "The nature of animal communication and its relation
to language in man," (Journal) Mount Sinai Hospital 28:3 (New
York), pp. 252-267.

1963   "Kinesics: gestural and mimic language: an aspect of
non-verbal communication," in Lipman Halpern, ed. , Problems
of Dynamic Neurology: An International Volume: Studies on
the Higher Functions of the Human Nervous System. Jerusalem: Dept. of Nervous Diseases of the Rothschild Hadassah
University Hospital and the Hebrew University Hadassah Medical School, pp. 181-200.

1975   The Silent Language. London: Butterworths, 231
pages.

Crittenden, Jerry B.
1974   "Categorization of cheremic errors in sign language reception," Sign Language Studies 5, pp. 64-71.

Croft, Kenneth
1961   English Stress and Intonation: for Students of English
as a Second Language. Washington, D.C. : English Language
Services, 81 pages.

Cronin, Morton
1958   "The tyranny of democratic manners," The New Repub-
lic 138 (Jan. 20), pp. 12-14.

Cross, Gertrude
1934   "A system of notation for recording dances," M.A.
thesis, Claremont Colleges, 78 pages. Printed in Research
Quarterly (American Physical Education Association) 6:3 (October 1935), pp. 45-62.

Crutchfield, Paul
1972   "Prospects for teaching English Det + N structures to
deaf students," Sign Language Studies 1, pp. 8-14.

Crystal, David [University of Reading]
        "Relative and absolute in intonation analysis," pp. 17-
28.

1963   "A perspective for paralanguage," Le Maitre Phonetique
73, pp. 25-29.

1964   "An approach to a reply," Le Maitre Phonetique 122,
pp. 23-24.

1966   "The linguistic status of prosodic and paralinguistic
features," Proceedings of the University of Newcastle Upon
Tyne Philosophical Society 1:8, pp. 93-108.

1969   Prosodic Systems and Intonation in English. Cambridge
University Press, 381 pages. Review by Norman N. Markel,
Contemporary Psychology 15:9 (Sept. 1970), pp. 547-548.

1970   "Intonation and semantic structure," Actes du Xe Congres

International des Linguistes (Bucarest 1967), Vol. II, pp. 415-422.

1970   "New perspectives for language study 2: semiotics,"
English Language Teaching 24, pp. 209-215.

1970   "Prosodic systems and language acquisition," Prosodic
Feature Analysis. Ottawa: Marcel Didier, pp. 77-90.

1971   "Prosodic and paralinguistic correlates of social categories," Social Anthropology and Language 10 (The Association
of Social Anthropologists of the Commonwealth; Edwin Ardener,
ed.) London: Tavistock, pp. 185-206.

1974   "Paralinguistics," Current Trends in Linguistics 12:1.
The Hague: Mouton, pp. 265-295.

        "Intonation and linguistic theory."

        "Intonation and metrical theory."

        "Non-segmental phonology and sociolinguistic distinctive-
ness: the importance of religious language."

Crystal, David, and Elma Craig
        "Contrived sign language," Current Trends in the Study
of Sign Languages of the Deaf. Schlesinger and Namir, eds.

Crystal, David, and Derek Davy
1969   Investigating English Style. Bloomington, Ind.: Indiana
University Press, 264 pages.

Crystal, David, and Randolph Quirk
1964   Systems of Prosodic and Paralinguistic Features in
English. The Hague: Mouton, 94 pages. Reviews by Kerstin
Hadding-Koch, International Journal of American Linguistics
33:2 (April 1967), pp. 176-178; Roger Fowler, Linguistics 32
(June 1967), pp. 106-109.

Cuceloglu, Dogan M.
1967   "A cross-cultural study of communication via facial expressions," dissertation, University of Illinois. Ann Arbor:
University Microfilms, No. 68-8046, 228 pages.

Cuisinier, Jeanne
1927   "The gestures in the Cambodian ballet: their traditional and symbolic significance," Indian Art and Letters, n.s., 1
(London), pp. 92-103.

Cullen, Lola Frances
1966   "Nonverbal communication in counseling an exploratory
study," Dissertation Abstracts 27, p. 2047. University of
Southern California.

Cundiff, Merlyn
1972   Kinesics: the Power of Silent Command.   West Nyack,
N.Y.: Parker Publishing Company, 233 pages.

Cuny, Xavier
1972   "L'approche psycho-sémiologique: Etude d'un code
gestuel de travail," Cahiers de Linguistique Théorique et
Appliquée 9, pp. 261-275.

Curl, Gordon F.
[1967]   "An enquiry into movement notation," Part I, Laban
and Benesh Movement Notations.

Currie, K. H., and C. R. Brannigan
1970   "Behavioural analysis and modification with an autistic
child," in Behaviour Studies in Psychiatry; C. Hutt and S. J.
Hutt, eds. Oxford: Pergamon.

Curry, Frederic K. W.
1967   "A comparison of left-handed and right-handed subjects
on verbal and nonverbal dichotic listening tasks," Cortex 3:3
(September), pp. 343-352.

Curtiss, Susan, Victoria Fromkin, Richard Harshman, and Stephen
Krashen
1975   "Language development in the mature (minor) right
hemisphere." Read at the Linguistic Society of America, San
Francisco.

Curtiss, Susan, Stephen Krashen, Victoria Fromkin, David Rigler,
and Marilyn Rigler
1973   "Language acquisition after the critical period: Genie
as of April 1973," Papers from the Ninth Regional Meeting,
Chicago Linguistic Society, pp. 98-103.

Cushing, Frank Hamilton
1892   "Manual concepts: a study of the influence of hand-
usage on culture-growth," American Anthropologist 5:4 (October), pp. 289-317.

- D -

Dabbs, James M., Jr.
1969   "Similarity of gestures and interpersonal influence,"
Proceedings of the 77th Annual Convention of the American
Psychological Association 4, pp. 337-338.

Da Costa, Maria I. L.
1946   "The Ozeretzky Tests: method, value, and results
(Portuguese adaptation)," Training School Bulletin 43-44,
pp. 1-13, 27-38, 50-59, 62-74.

Dale, Philip S.
    1975   'Hesitations in maternal speech," Language and Language
    Behavior Abstracts 9:3, 7502665.

Dalgarno, George [Aberdeen]
    1661   Ars Signorum, Vulgo Character Universalis et Lingua
    Philosophica. London. Reprinted in English Linguistics 1500-
    1800, No. 116. Yorks: Menston, 1968.

    1680   Didascalocophus: Deaf and Dumb Man's Tutor. Oxford.
    Reprinted Yorks: Menston, 1971, 136 pages.

    1834   The Works of George Dalgarno of Aberdeen. Edinburgh.

Dali, Salvador, and Philippe Halsman
    1954   Dali's Mustache: a Photographic Interview. New York:
    Simon and Schuster, 126 pages.

Danchin, Antoine [Centre Royaumont pour une science de l'homme]
            "Animal communication and human communication: the
    biological features of the problem. "

D'Angelo, Lou
    1969   How to Be an Italian. Los Angeles: Price, Stern,
    Sloan Publishers, 93 pages.

Daniell, Robert J. , and Philip Lewis
    1972   "Stability of eye contact and physical distance across a
    series of structured interviews, " Journal of Consulting and
    Clinical Psychology 39:1 (August), p. 172.

Daniel-Rops
    1951   "Les gestes de la priere et de l'imploration, " France
    Illustration 7 (December 1), pp. 599-606.

Daniels, Arthur
    1941   'Hand-made repartee, " New York Times (October 5).
    [Argentine, "ademanes"--with the hands.]

Dantzig, Tobias
    1930   Number: the Language of Science: a Critical Survey
    Written for the Cultured Non-mathematician. New York, 340
    pages. Revised and augmented, 1959. [Chapter 1 on the hand
    and counting. Illustrations of finger symbols of 16th century,
    p. 2: Hayes.]

D'Arcais, B. Flores
    1961   'Forming impressions of personality in situations of
    contrast between verbal and mimic expressions, " Acta Psycho-
    logia 19, pp. 494-495.

Darwin, Charles R.
    1872   The Expression of the Emotions in Man and Animals.

New York: Appleton, [1898]. Introduced by Margaret Mead in
1955. Preface by Konrad Lorenz. University of Chicago
Press, 1965, 372 pages.

Dashiell, J. F.
1927 "A new method of measuring reactions to facial expression of emotion," Psychological Bulletin 24, pp. 174-175.

Das Jain, Banarsi, and Stephen Jones
1926-28 "Musical accent and whisper," Bulletin of the School
of Oriental Studies, pp. 213-215.

Davenport, R. K., Jr., and G. Berkson
1963 "Stereotyped movements of mental defectives: II. Effects of novel objects," American Journal of Mental Deficiency
67, pp. 879-882.

Davey, R. C., and L. J. Taylor
1968 "The role of eye-contact in inducing conformity,"
British Journal of Social and Clinical Psychology 7:4, pp. 307-
308.

David-Neel, Alexandra
1926 "Behind the veil of Tibet: penetrating the inner life of
superstition-ruled families along the road to Lhasa," Asia and
the Americas 26:4. [P. 320, one photograph, Tibet greeting
to fellow traveller: thrust up thumb of right hand and thrust
out tongue.]

Davidson, Bill
1966 "Your eye can't lie," Saturday Evening Post (January
15), pp. 76-79.

Davidson, Levette Jay
1950 "Some current folk gestures and sign languages,"
American Speech 25:1 (February), pp. 3-9.

1951 A Guide to American Folklore. Denver: University of
Denver Press, 132 pages. Review by Daniel Hoffman, Journal
of American Folklore 65 (1952), pp. 198-199.

Davis, Anne
1966 The Language of Signs: A Handbook for Manual Communication With the Deaf. New York: Executive Council of the
Episcopal Church, 91 pages.

Davis, Flora
1969 "How to read body language," Reader's Digest (December), pp. 127-130. Condensed from Glamour (September 1969),
pp. 208-209, 267-274.

1973 Inside Intuition: What We Know About Nonverbal Communication. New York: McGraw-Hill, 245 pages. Review by

Donis A. Dondis, Journal of Communication 24 (1974), pp. 161-162.

Davis, Martha
   1972   Understanding Body Movement: An Annotated Bibliography. New York: Arno Press, 190 pages.

Davis, Martha, ed.
   1972   Body Movement: Perspectives in Research. New York: Arno Press. Series of reprinted works: Evolution of Facial Expression; Facial Expression in Children; Research Approaches to Movement and Personality.

Davis, R. C.
   1934   "The specificity of facial expressions," Journal of General Psychology 10 (January), pp. 42-58.

Davis, R. C., and Alexander M. Buchwald
   1957   "An exploration of somatic response patterns: stimulus and sex differences," Journal of Comparative and Physiological Psychology 50, pp. 44-52.

Davitz, Joel Robert, ed.
   1964   The Communication of Emotional Meaning. New York: McGraw-Hill, 214 pages.

   1966   "The communication of emotional meaning" [from the above, pp. 177-191], in Alfred G. Smith, ed., Communication and Culture: Readings in the Codes of Human Interaction, pp. 467-480.

   1969   The Language of Emotion. New York: Academic Press, 197 pages. Chapter 2, "A dictionary of emotional meaning," pp. 32-84. [Uganda--Luganda.]

Davitz, Joel Robert, and Lois Jean Davitz
   1959   "The communication of feelings by content-free speech," Journal of Communication 9, pp. 6-13. Reprinted in Dean C. Barnlund, ed., Interpersonal Communication: Survey and Studies. Boston: Houghton Mifflin, 1968, pp. 569-575.

   1961   "Nonverbal vocal communication of feeling," Journal of Communication 11, pp. 81-86.

Day, Merle E.
   1964   "An eye-movement phenomenon relating to attention, thought, and anxiety," Perceptual and Motor Skills 19, pp. 443-446.

   1967   "An eye-movement indicator of individual differences in the physiological organization of attentional processes and anxiety," The Journal of Psychology 66, pp. 51-62.

Dearborn, George V. N.
1900   "The nature of the smile and laugh," Science 11, pp. 851-856.

De Camp, L. Sprague
1957   "Language for time travelers," in Coming Attractions (Adventures in Science Fiction Series), ed. by Martin Greenberg. New York: Gnome Press, pp. 52-69.

Decroux, Étienne
1963   Paroles sur le mime. Paris: Gallimard, 200 pages.

De Haerne, D. D.
1875   "The natural language of signs," American Annals of the Deaf and Dumb 20-21. I: Vol. 20:2, pp. 73-87; II: Vol. 20:3, pp. 137-153; III: Vol. 20:3, pp. 216-228; IV: Vol. 21, pp. 11-16.

Delattre, Pierre
1964   "Comparing the vocalic features of English, German, Spanish, and French," International Review of Applied Linguistics 2:2, pp. 71-97.

1966   "A comparison of syllable-length conditioning among languages," International Review of Applied Linguistics 4:3, pp. 183-198.

1966   "Les dix intonations de base du français," The French Review 40:1 (October), pp. 1-14.

1970   "Syntax and intonation: a study in disagreement," Modern Language Journal 54, pp. 3-9.

Delattre, Pierre, Carroll Olsen, and Elmer Poenack
1962   "A comparative study of declarative intonation in American English and Spanish," Hispania 45, pp. 233-241.

Delaumosne, L'abbé
1892   The Delsarte System, trans. by Francis A. Shaw. New York: Werner.

de l'Epée   see   L'Epée, Charles Michel de

Dell, Cecily
1970   A Primer for Movement Description: Using Effort/ Shape and Supplementary Concepts. New York: Dance Notation Bureau 123 pages.

Delling, Hildegaard
1925   "Studien über die Gebärdensprache in der Dichtkunst und Bildkunst des frühen und hohen Mittelalters." Dissertation, Leipzig.

DeLong, Alton J.
1972   "The communication process: a generic model for man-
environment relations," Man-Environment Systems 2, pp. 263-
313.

1972   "Kinesic signals and utterance boundaries in preschool
children." Dissertation, Pennsylvania State University.

1974   "Kinesic signals at utterance boundaries in preschool
children," Semiotica 11, pp. 43-74.

Delsarte, Francois [1811-1871] see Delaumosne; Douailler;
LeMee; Parrish; Shawn; Stebbins; Warman; Zorn, John

De Mille, Agnes
1963   The Book of the Dance. New York: Golden Press,
252 pages.

DeMyer, Marian K., Nancy A. Mann, James R. Tilton, and Lois
H. Loew
1967   "Toy-play behavior and use of body by autistic and normal children as reported by mothers," Psychological Reports
21, pp. 973-981.

Dennis, Wayne
1935   "An experimental test of two theories of social smiling
in infants," Journal of Social Psychology 6, pp. 214-223.

Denzin, Norman K.
"Childhood as a conversation of gestures."

Deonna, W.
1914   L'Expression des sentiments dans l'arte grec. Paris:
H. Laurens.

Derlega, Valerian J.
1971   "Social penetration processes: the effects of acquaint-
ance, topic intimacy, and support of openness on nonverbal
behavior," Dissertation Abstracts 32, 6025B-26B. University
of Maryland, 161 pages.

Descartes, René [1596-1650]
Traité des passions, par Descartes, suivi de la corre-
spondance avec la princesse Elizabeth. Presentation et annotation par Francois Mizrachi. Paris: Union Generale d'editions,
1965. 375 pages. [First published under title: Les Passions
de l'ame, par Descartes.]

De Silva, Anil, and Otto von Simson, eds.
1968   The Human Face, Vol. 6 of Man Through His Art.
World Confederation of Organizations of the Teaching Profession. Greenwich, Connecticut: New York Graphic Society, 64
pages. [Anthology of reproductions of portraits.]

Dettering, Richard
1953   "Psychology as metalanguage," ETC. 10:3, pp. 176-182.

Deutsch, Felix
1947   "Analysis of postural behavior," Psychoanalytic Quarterly 16, pp. 195-213.

1949   "Thus speaks the body: I: an analysis of postural behavior," Transactions of the New York Academy of Science, New York Academy of Science Series 2, Vol. 12:2, pp. 58-62.

1952   "Analytic posturology," Psychoanalytic Quarterly 21, pp. 196-214. [4th in a series.]

1963   "Analytic posturology and synesthesiology: some important theoretical and clinical aspects," Psychoanalytical Review 50, pp. 40-67.

1966   "Some principles of correlating verbal and non-verbal communication," in Louis A. Gottschalk, and Arthur H. Auerbach, eds., Methods of Research in Psychotherapy. New York: Appleton-Century-Crofts, pp. 166-184. ["A fragment of a sound-filmed psychiatric interview demonstrating Dr. Felix Deutsch's concepts," pp. 170-188.]

Devereux, George
1948   "Mohave etiquette," Southwest Museum Leaflets 22, 9 pages. Highland Park, Los Angeles, Calif.: Southwest Museum.

1949   "Mohave voice and speech mannerisms," Word 5:3 (December), pp. 268-272. Reprinted in Dell Hymes, ed., Language in Culture and Society, pp. 267-271.

1949   "Some Mohave gestures" (brief communication), American Anthropologist 51:2, pp. 325-326.

1951   "Mohave Indian verbal and motor profanity," in Géza Róheim, Psychoanalysis and the Social Sciences, Vol. 3, pp. 99-127. New York: International Universities Press.

1956   "A note on the feminine significance of the eyes," Bulletin of the Philadelphia Association for Psychoanalysis 6:1, pp. 21-24.

Devi, Ragini
1928   Dances of India: with an Appendix on Indian Music. 3rd ed., 1962. Calcutta: S. Gupta, 87 pages. [Bibliography; hand gestures in sketch.]

DeVita, Phil
1971   "A partial investigation of the spatial forms of some Tuamotuan dialects," Anthropological Linguistics 13:8 (November), pp. 401-420.

DeVito, Joseph A.
   1968   "Kinesics: other codes, other channels," Today's
   Speech 16:2 (April), pp. 29-32.

   1971   Communication Concepts and Processes.   Englewood
   Cliffs, N.J.:   Prentice-Hall, 232 pages.

Dewey, Evelyn
   1935   Behavior Development in Infants: A Survey of the
   Literature on Prenatal and Postnatal Activity, 1920-1934.
   New York: Columbia University Press, 321 pages.

De Zoete, Beryl
   1960   The Other Mind: A Study of Dance in South India.
   Chapter II, "Abhinaya."   New York: Theatre Arts Books.
   [The gesture language of the body, pp. 32-37.]

Dickens, Milton, and Granville M. Sawyer
   1952   "An experimental comparison of vocal quality among
   mixed groups of whites and Negroes," Southern Speech Journal
   17, pp. 178-185.

Dickey, Elizabeth C., and Franklin H. Knower
   1941   "A note on some ethnological differences in recognition
   of simulated expressions of the emotions," American Journal
   of Sociology 47:2 (September), pp. 190-193.   [Mexico City.]

Dickson, David Ross
   1962   "An acoustic study of nasality," Journal of Speech and
   Hearing Research 5:2 (June), pp. 103-111.

Diebold, Richard A.
   1968   "Anthropological perspectives: anthropology and the
   comparative psychology of communicative behavior," in Thomas
   A. Sebeok, ed., Animal Communication.   Indiana University
   Press, chapter 19, pp. 525-571.

Diehl, Charles F.
   1949   "The effect of voice quality on communicativeness."
   State College of Pennsylvania, thesis.   University Microfilms
   No. 1441.   73 pages.

   1960   "Voice and personality: an evaluation," in Dominick A.
   Barbara, ed., Psychological and Psychiatric Aspects of Speech
   and Hearing.   Springfield, Ill.:   Charles C. Thomas, chapter
   IX, pp. 171-203.

Diehl, Charles F., and E. R. McDonald
   1956   "Effect of voice quality on communication," Journal of
   Speech and Hearing Disorders 21, pp. 233-237.

Diehl, Charles F., Richard White, and Kenneth W. Burk
   1959   "Voice quality and anxiety," Journal of Speech and Hearing Research 2, pp. 282-285.

Dierssen, Guillermo, Mary Lorenc, and Rose Marie Spitaleri
1961   "A new method for graphic study of human movements,"
Neurology 11, pp. 610-618.

Dieth, Eugen
1950   Vademekum der Phonetik. Bern, 96 pages. [Dieth
stated briefly that it is possible to indicate intonation in whisper to a certain extent ('einigermassen'), and tried to account
for this by postulating changes in air pressure, p. 187: Jensen.]

Dimitrovsky, Lilly
1964   "The ability to identify the emotional meaning of vocal
expressions at successive age levels," in Joel R. Davitz, ed.,
The Communication of Emotional Meaning. New York: McGraw-
Hill, pp. 69-86.

Ding, Gladys F., and Arthur T. Jersild
1932   "A study of the laughing and smiling of preschool
children," Journal of Genetic Psychology 40, pp. 452-72.

Dinges, Norman G., and Eugene R. Oetting
1972   "Interaction distance anxiety in the counseling dyad,"
Journal of Counseling Psychology 19:2 (March), pp. 146-149.

Disher, M. Willson
1925   Clowns and Pantomimes. Reprinted New York: Benjamin Blom, 1968.

Dittmann, Allen T.
1962   "The relationship between body movements and moods
in interviews," Journal of Consulting Psychology 26:5, p. 480.

1963   "Kinesic research and therapeutic processes," in Peter
Knapp, ed., Expression of the Emotions in Man. New York:
International Universities Press, pp. 140-147.

1966   "Speech and body movement: independent sources of
information." Paper read at American Psychological Association, New York.

1970   "The body movement-speech rhythm relationship as a
cue to speech encoding," in Studies in Dyadic Communication;
A. W. Siegman and B. Pope, eds., New York: Pergamon,
pp. 135-151.

1972   "Developmental factors in conversational behavior,"
Journal of Communication 22:4 (December), pp. 404-423.

1972   Interpersonal Messages of Emotion. New York:
Springer Publishing Company, 232 pages.

Dittmann, Allen T. , and Lynn G. Llewellyn
    1967   "The phonemic clause as a unit of speech decoding,"
    Journal of Personality and Social Psychology 6:3, pp. 341-349.

    1968   "Relationship between vocalizations and head nods as
    listener responses," Journal of Personality and Social Psychol-
    ogy 9:1, pp. 79-84.

    1969   "Body movement and speech rhythm in social conversa-
    tion," Journal of Personality and Social Psychology 11:2,
    pp. 98-106.

Dittmann, Allen T. , Morris B. Parloff, and Donald S. Boomer
    1965   "Facial and bodily expression: a study of receptivity
    of emotional cues," Psychiatry 28, pp. 239-244.

Dittmann, Allen, Seymour N. Stein, and David Shakow
    1966   "Sound motion picture facilities for research in commu-
    nication," Methods of Research in Psychotherapy; eds. Louis
    A. Gottschalk and Arthur H. Auerbach. New York: Appleton-
    Century-Crofts, pp. 25-33.

Dittmann, Allen T. and Lyman C. Wynne
    1961   "Linguistic techniques and the analysis of emotionality
    in interviews," Journal of Abnormal and Social Psychology 63,
    pp. 201-204. Reprinted in Louis A. Gottschalk, and Arthur H.
    Auerbach, eds. , Methods of Research in Psychotherapy. New
    York: Appleton-Century-Crofts, 1966, pp. 146-152.

Doat, Jan
    1944   L'expression corporelle du comédien. Grenoble: Les
    Éditions françaises nouvelles, Bordas frères, 72 pages.

Doehring, D. G.
    1957   "The relation between manifest anxiety and rate of eye-
    blink in a stress situation," USN School of Aviation Medical
    Research Report No. 6, Project NM 130199.

Dondis, Donis A.
    1973   A Primer of Visual Literacy. Cambridge, Mass. :
    MIT Press, 185 pages. Review by John M. Penrose, Journal
    of Communication 24:1 (Winter 1974), pp. 126-127.

Doob, Leonard W.
    1961   "Communication in Africa," in Communication in Africa.
    New Haven: Yale University Press, pp. 68-71. Reprinted in
    Haig A. Bosmajian, The Rhetoric of Nonverbal Communication.
    1971.

    1971   Patterning of Time. New Haven: Yale University Pres
    472 pages.

Dorcy   211

Dorcy, Jean
    1961   The Mime.   New York: Robert Speller and Sons, 116
    pages.

Dorson, Richard M.
    1956   "The art of Negro storytelling," in Negro Folktales in
    Michigan. Cambridge, Mass: Harvard University Press,
    chapter 2, pp. 19-30.

Douailler, Charles
    1911   Manuel technique et pratique du tragédien et comédien
    lyrique. Paris: Berger & Chausse, 67 pages.

Douty, H. I.
    "The influence of clothing on perceptions of persons in
    single contact situations. " Dissertation.

Downing, Bruce
    1970   "Syntactic structure and phonological phrasing in Eng-
    lish. " Dissertation, University of Texas.

Drag, Richard M. , and Marvin E. Shaw
    1967   "Factors influencing the communication of emotional
    intent by facial expressions," Psychonomic Science 8, pp. 137-
    138.

Draper, M. H. , Peter Ladefoged, and D. Whitteridge
    1959   "Respiratory muscles in speech," Journal of Speech and
    Hearing Research 2, pp. 16-27.

Drechsler, Paul
    1906   Sitte, Brauch, und Volksglaube in Schlesien. 2 vols.
    Leipzig: B. G. Teubner. [A number of Silesian gestures:
    Hayes.]

Dries, W. van den
    "The appeasing denials: a teleological approach to
    laughing and shrugging. " [In preparation: Hinde, p. 410.]

Dubin, Fraida
    1973   "The problem 'Who speaks next?' considered cross-
    culturally. " TESOL Convention, San Juan, Puerto Rico.

Dubner, Frances S.
    1972   "Nonverbal aspects of Black English," Southern Speech
    Communication Journal 37, pp. 361-374.

Dubois, Louis F.
    1824   Histoire civile, religieuse et littéraire de l'Abbaye de
    la Trappe. Paris, 386 pages. [pp. 248-258: Hayes.]

Duchenne, Guillaume Benjamin Amand
    1862   Mechanisme de la physionomie humaine: ou, Analyse

électrophysiologique de l'expression des passions applicable à
la pratique de arts plastiques.   Paris: Renouard, 70 pages.

1949   Physiology of Motion.   (Translation.)   Philadelphia:
J. P. Lippincott.

Dudeck, James E.
1974   "A developmental study of haptic-tactual perceptual skill
utilization among sighted, partially sighted, and blind children,"
Dissertation Abstracts International 35:5151B.

Duffy, Elizabeth
1932   "The measurement of muscular tension as a technique
for the study of emotional tendencies," American Journal of
Psychology 44, pp. 146-162.

Duffy, Robert J. , and Marcia C. Moore
1971   "The relationship between intelligence and gestural behavior in a mentally retarded population," Journal of Genetic
Psychology 119, pp. 195-202.

Duke, Charles R.
1974   "Nonverbal behavior and the communication process,"
College Composition and Communication 25, pp. 397-404.

Dumas, Georges
1948   La vie affective: physiologie, psychologie, sociolisation.
Paris: Alcan, 408 pages. ["Les mimiques," pp. 339-405.]

Dumont, Robert V. , Jr.
1972   "Learning English and how to be silent: studies in
Sioux and Cherokee classrooms," in Courtney B. Cazden, Vera
P. John, and Dell Hymes, eds. , Functions of Language in the
Classroom.   Columbia University: Teachers College Press,
pp. 344-369.

Dunbar, William
1801   "On the language of signs among certain North American
Indians," Transactions of the American Philosophical Society
No. 1, pp. 1-8. [About 60 signs, communicated by Thomas
Jefferson, President of the Society.]

Duncan, Melba H.
1945   "An experimental study of some of the relationships between voice and personality among students of speech," Speech
Monographs 12, pp. 47-60.

1947   "Personality adjustment techniques in voice therapy,"
Journal of Speech Disorders 12, pp. 161-167.

Duncan, Starkey D. , Jr.
1965   "Paralinguistic behaviors in client-therapist communication in psychotherapy. " Dissertation, University of Chicago.

1969   "Nonverbal communication," Psychological Bulletin 72:2,
pp. 118-137.

1970   "Towards a grammar for floor apportionment: a system approach to face-to-face interaction," in Proceedings of
the 2nd Annual Environmental Design Research Association
Conference, pp. 225-235. Philadelphia: Environmental Design
Research Association.

1972   "Some signals and rules for taking speaking turns in
conversations," Journal of Personality and Social Psychology
23:2, pp. 283-292.

1973   "Toward a grammar for dyadic conversations," Semiotica
9:1, pp. 29-46.

1974   "On the structure of speaker-auditor interaction during
speaking turns," Language in Society 3:2 (October), pp. 161-
180.

Duncan, Starkey, Jr., and George Niederehe
        "On signalling that it's your turn to speak."

Duncan, Starkey, Jr., Laura N. Rice, and John M. Butler
1968   "Therapists' paralanguage in peak and poor psychotherapy hours," Journal of Abnormal Psychology 73:6, pp. 566-570.

Duncan, Starkey, Jr., Milton J. Rosenberg, and Jonathan Finkel-
stein
1969   "The paralanguage of experimenter bias," Sociometry
32:2 (June), pp. 207-219.

Duncan, Starkey, Jr., and Robert Rosenthal
1968   "Vocal emphasis in experimenters' instruction reading
as unintended determinant of subjects' responses," Language
and Speech 11:1 (January-March), pp. 20-26.

Dundes, Alan
1968   Every Man His Way: Readings in Cultural Anthropology.
Englewood Cliffs, N.J.: Prentice-Hall, 551 pages.

Dunlap, Knight
1927   "The role of eye-muscles and mouth-muscles in the
expression of emotion," Genetic Psychology Monographs 2:3,
pp. 199-233.

Dunning, G. B.
1975   "Research in nonverbal communication," Language and
Language Behavior Abstracts 9:2, 7501879.

Dupouy, Walter
1953   "Algunos casos de postura nilótica (Nilotenstellung) entre
indios de Venezuela," Boletín Indigenista Venezolano 1, pp. 287-
297. Venezuela: Comisión Indigenista.

1957   "Die Nilotenstellung bei Venezuelanischen Indianern, "
Zeitschrift für Ethnologie 82, pp. 191-201.

Durbin, Marshall, and Michael Micklin
1968   "Sociolinguistics: some methodological contributions
from linguistics, " Foundations of Language 4:3 (August),
pp. 319-331.

Dusenbury, Delwin, and Franklin H. Knower
1938   "Experimental studies of the symbolism of action and
voice--I: A study of the specificity of meaning in facial expression, " Quarterly Journal of Speech 24, pp. 424-436.

Dyke, Jennie
1939   "Dance notation: a comparative analysis and evaluation
of various systems. "   M. S. thesis (in Hygiene and P. E.),
Wellesley.

                                - E -

Earley, Kathleen
1975   "The voice of Neanderthal, " The Sciences 15:2 (March),
pp. 11-15.

Eberlein, P. J.
1910   "Die Trommelsprache auf der Gazellehalbinsel, " (Neu-
pommern), Anthropos 5, pp. 635-642.

Eboué, F.
1935   "La clef musicale des langages tambourinés et sifflés, "
Bulletin du Comité de L'Afrique Occidentale Française 18,
pp. 353-360.

Echtermeyer, Th
1835   Über Namen und symbolische Bedeutung der Finger bei
den Griechen und Römern.   Programm des Pädagogiums in
in Halle.

Eco, Umberto
1968   La Struttura Assente: Introduzione Alla Ricerca Semio-
logica.   Milan: Bompiani.   La estructura ausente.   Barcelona.

1972   La structure absente.   Paris: Mercure de France.
[Section C on proxemics.]

1974   "Bibliographia semiotica, " Special Issue, VS: Quaderni
Di Studi Semiotici 8/9 (May-December), 280 pages.

Eco, Umberto, L. Jonathan Cohen, Tullio de Mauro, Thomas Sebeok, and Todorov Tzvetan
1973   "A Survey of Semiotics" [a series of articles by the authors listed], The Times Literary Supplement (October 5),
pp. 1149-50, 1161-62, 1169-70, 1179-81, 1187-89.

Eder, P. Ferencz Xaver [Francisco Javier]
1791   Descriptio provinciae Mojitarum.   Budapest.   Translated by P. Fray Nicolas Armentia as: Description de la
provincia de los Mojos.   La Paz, 1888, 109 pages.   [Men-
tions sign language of South American Indians.]

Edwards, E. D.
1957   "Principles of whistling, " Bulletin of the School of
Oriental and African Studies 20, pp. 217-229.

Edwards, Harold T.
1972   "Synthesized voice cues to sex identification, " Dissertation Abstracts 32, 4746A.   University of Washington.

Efran, Jay S.
1968   "Looking for approval: effects on visual behavior of
approbation from persons differing in importance, " Journal of
Personality and Social Psychology 10, pp. 21-25.

Efran, Jay S. , and Andrew Broughton
1966   "Effect of expectancies for social approval on visual behavior, " Journal of Personality and Social Psychology 4:1,
pp. 103-107.

Efron, David
1941   Gesture and Environment: A Tentative Study of Some
of the Spatio-Temporal and "Linguistic" Aspects of the Gestural
Behavior of Eastern Jews and Southern Italians in New York
City, Living under Similar as well as Different Environmental
Conditions.   New York: Kings' Crown Press, 184 pages.
Sketches by Stuyvesant Van Veen; preface by Franz Boas.   Reprinted as Gesture, Race and Culture.   The Hague: Mouton,
1972, 226 pages.   [Added 35 pages of illustrations of gestures.]
Gesto, raza y cultura.   Buenos Aires: Ediciones Nueva Vision,
1970.   Gesto, razza e cultura.   Milan: Casa Editrice, Valen-
tino Bompiani, 1974.   Reviews by Allen T. Dittmann, "Style
in conversation, " Semiotica 9:3 (1973), pp. 241-251; Mary
Ritchie Key, Linguistics 163 (1975), pp. 70-77. Gardner Murphy,
Annals of the American Academy 220 (March 1942), pp. 268-269;
Everett V. Stonequist, American Sociological Review 7 (April
1942), pp. 279-280; Alfred M. Tozzer, American Anthropologist
44 (October 1942), pp. 715-716.

Efron, David, and John P. Foley, Jr.
1937   "Gestural behavior and social setting, " Zeitschrift für
Sozialforschung 6:1 (New name: Studies in Philosophy and Social Science), pp. 152-161.

Eggen, Paul Duane
        "A comparison of student affect and kinesic behavior. "
University Microfilms No. 72-27,626, 215 pages.

Eibl-Eibesfeldt, Irenäus [Max Planck Institute]
    1964   "Experimental criteria for distinguishing innate from
    culturally conditioned behavior," in F. S. C. Northrop, and
    Helen H. Livingston, eds., Cross-Cultural Understanding:
    Epistemology in Anthropology. New York: Harper and Row,
    pp. 297-307.

    1967   "Concepts of ethology and their significance in the study
    of human behavior," in Early Behavior; Harold W. Stevenson,
    Eckhard H. Hess and H. L. Rheingold, eds. New York: John
    Wiley and Sons.

    1967   Grundriss der vergleichenden Verhaltensforschung.
    Munich: Piper. English translation, New York: Holt, Rine-
    hart and Winston, 1969.

    1968   "Universality of Emotional Expression."

    1968   "Zur Ethologie des menschlichen Grussverhaltens, I:
    Beobachtunger an Balinesen, Papuas und Samoanern, nebst
    Vergleichenden Bemerkungen," Zeitschrift für Tierpsychologie
    25, pp. 727-744.

    1969   "Culture-Independent Invariables in Human Greeting Be-
    havior," in Michael Argyle, and Ralph Exline, eds., NATO
    Symposium on Non-verbal Communication. Oxford. [Tongue
    play in flirt situations, p. 13.]

    1970   Ethology: The Biology of Behavior. New York: Holt,
    Rinehart and Winston, 530 pages.

    1971   Love and Hate: The Natural History of Behavior Pat-
    terns. New York: Holt, Rinehart and Winston, 276 pages.

    1973   "The expressive behaviour of the deaf-and-blind-born,"
    in Von Cranach and Vine, eds., Social Communication and
    Movement, pp. 163-194.

Eibl-Eibesfeldt, I. and H. Hass
    1967   "Neue Wege der Humanethologie," Homo 18, pp. 13-23.

Eimas, Peter D., Einar R. Siqueland, Peter Jusczyk, and James
    Vigorito
    1971   "Speech perception in infants," Science 171, pp. 303-
    306.

Eisenberg, Abne M., and Ralph R. Smith
    1971   Nonverbal Communication. Indianapolis: Bobbs-Merrill,
    133 pages.

Eisenberg, Philip
    1937   "Expressive movements related to feeling of dominance,"
    Archives of Psychology 30:211 (May), pp. 1-73. Reprinted,

New York: Arno Press, 1972, as Research Approaches to Movement and Personality (includes Irmgard Bartenieff, and M. Davis, and Martti Takala).

Eisenberg, Philip and Philip B. Reichline
1939   "Judgments of dominance-feeling from motion pictures of gait," Journal of Social Psychology 10, pp. 345-357.

Eisenson, Jon, and Paul H. Boase
1950   "Nonverbal communication," in Basic Speech. New York: Macmillan, chapter 4, pp. 47-49.

1967   "Speech: gesture and communication," in Arthur F. Beringhause, and Daniel K. Lowenthal, The Range of College Reading. Boston: Houghton Mifflin, chapter 16, pp. 78-82.

Eisler see Goldman-Eisler

Ekman, Paul
1957   "A methodological discussion of nonverbal behavior," Journal of Psychology 43, pp. 141-149.

1964   "Body position, facial expression, and verbal behavior during interviews," Journal of Abnormal and Social Psychology 68:3, pp. 295-301. Also in D. C. Barnlund, Interpersonal Communication. Boston: Houghton Mifflin, 1968, pp. 576-586.

1965   "Communication through nonverbal behavior: a source of information about an interpersonal relationship," in Silvan S. Tomkins, and Carroll E. Izard, eds., Affect, Cognition, and Personality. New York: Springer Press, pp. 390-442.

1965   "Differential communication of affect by head and body cues," Journal of Personality and Social Psychology 2:5 (November), pp. 726-735.

1971   "Universals and cultural differences in facial expressions of emotion," in James K. Cole, ed., Nebraska Symposium on Motivation. University of Nebraska Press, Vol. 19, pp. 207-284.

1973   Darwin and Facial Expression: A Century of Research in Review. New York: Academic Press, 273 pages.

1975   "The universal smile: face muscles talk every language," Psychology Today 9:4 (September), pp. 35-39.

Ekman, Paul, and Wallace V. Friesen
1967   "Head and body cues in the judgment of emotion: a reformulation," Perceptual and Motor Skills 24, pp. 711-724.

1968   "Nonverbal behavior in psychotherapy research," in J.
Shlien, ed., Research in Psychotherapy. Washington, D. C. :
American Psychological Association, Vol. 3, pp. 179-216.
["The hands," pp. 201-212.]

1969   "Nonverbal leakage and clues to deception," Psychiatry
32:1 (February), pp. 88-106.

1969   "The repertoire of nonverbal behavior: categories,
origins, usage and coding," Semiotica 1:1, pp. 49-98.

1969   "A tool for the analysis of motion picture film or video
tape," American Psychologist 24:3 (March), pp. 240-243.

1971   "Constants across cultures in the face and emotion,"
Journal of Personality and Social Psychology 17:2, pp. 124-129.

1972   "Hand movements," Journal of Communication 22 (December), pp. 353-374.

1974   "Detecting deception from the body or face," Journal of
Personality and Social Psychology 29:3, pp. 288-298.

1974   "Nonverbal behavior and psychopathology," in R. J.
Friedman and M. M. Katz, eds. , The Psychology of Depres-
sion: Contemporary Theory and Research.   Washington, D. C. :
Winston and Sons, pp. 203-232.

1975   Unmasking the Face.   Englewood Cliffs, N. J. : Prentice-
Hall, 212 pages.

Ekman, Paul, Wallace V. Friesen, and Phoebe Ellsworth
    1972   Emotion in the Human Face: Guidelines for Research
and an Integration of Findings.   New York: Pergamon Press,
191 pages.   Review by C. E. Izard, Psychiatry 36:2 (May),
pp. 219ff.

Ekman, Paul, Wallace V. Friesen, and Thomas G. Taussig
    1969   "VID-R and SCAN: tools and methods for the automated
analysis of visual records," in The Analysis of Communication
Content: Developments in Scientific Theories and Computer
Techniques; eds. George Gerbner, Ole R. Holsti, Klaus Krip-
pendorff, William J. Paisley, and Philip J. Stone.   New York:
John Wiley and Sons, pp. 297-312.

Ekman, Paul, Wallace V. Friesen, and Silvan S. Tomkins
    1971   "Facial affect scoring technique: a first validity study,"
Semiotica 3, pp. 37-58.

Ekman, Paul, Robert M. Liebert, Wallace V. Friesen, Randall
Harrison, Carl Zlatchin, Edward J. Malstrom, and Robert A.
Baron
    1972   "Facial expressions of emotion while watching televised

violence as predictors of subsequent aggression," Television
and Social Behavior: A Report to the Surgeon General's Scientific Advisory Committee. Washington, D.C. , Vol. 5, pp.
22-58.

Ekman, Paul, E. Richard Sorenson and Wallace V. Friesen
1969   "Pan-cultural elements in facial displays of emotion,"
Science 164:3875 (April), pp. 86-88. [Happiness, anger, fear,
disgust, surprise, sadness.]

Eldernbosch, P. A.
1953   De Opleging der Handen. Den Haag.

Eldred, S. H. and D. B. Price
1958   "A linguistic evaluation of feeling states in psychotherapy," Psychiatry 21, pp. 115-121.

Elerick, Charles
1970   "The contrastive semology of Spanish and English verbs
of visual perception," in Ralph W. Ewton, and Jacob Ornstein,
eds. , Studies in Language and Linguistics: 1969-1970. University of Texas at El Paso, pp. 93-125.

Elkin, A. P. [further note by William Fagg]
1953   "The one-leg resting position in Australia," Man 53:No.
95 (April), p. 64. [Australian occurrences of one-leg resting
position.]

Ellis, Havelock
1929   "The art of dancing," in The Dance of Life. New York:
Modern Library, pp. 34-63.

Ellsworth, Phoebe, and J. Merrill Carlsmith
1968   "The effects of eye contact and verbal content on affective response to a dyadic interaction," Journal of Personality
and Social Psychology 10:1, pp. 15-20.

Ellsworth, Phoebe C. , J. Merrill Carlsmith, and Alexander Hen-
son
1972   "The stare as a stimulus to flight in human subjects,"
Journal of Personality and Social Psychology 21:3, pp. 302-311.

Ellsworth, Phoebe and Linda M. Ludwig
1972   "Visual behavior in social interaction," Journal of Communication 22:4 (December), pp. 375-403.

Elworthy, Frederick Thomas
1895   The Evil Eye. London: John Murray.

1900   Horns of Honour: And Other Studies in the By-Ways of
Archaeology. London: John Murray, 315 pages.

Emerson, Charles Wesley
    1900   Expressive Physical Culture; or, Philosophy of Gesture.
    Boston: Emerson College of Oratory Publishing Department,
    189 pages.

Enders, A. C.
    1927   "A study of the laughter of the pre-school child in the
    Merrill-Palmer Nursery School," Michigan Academy of Science,
    Art and Letters 8, pp. 341-356.

Engebretson, Darold, and Daniel Fullmer
    1970   "Cross-cultural differences in territoriality: interaction
    distances of native Japanese, Hawaii Japanese, and American
    Caucasians," Journal of Cross-Cultural Psychology 1 (Septem-
    ber), pp. 261-269.   Reprinted in Larry A. Samovar and
    Richard E. Porter, eds., Intercultural Communication. Bel-
    mont, Calif.: Wadsworth, 1972, pp. 220-226.

Engel, Johann Jakob [1741-1802]
    1785-86 Ideen zu einer mimik. 2 vols. Berlin: Auf Kosten
    des verfassers.

    1788-89 Idées sur le geste et l'action théatrale; suivies d'une
    lettre du même auteur, sur la peinture musicale le tout traduit
    de l'allemand. 2 vols. Paris: Barrois.

    1822   Practical Illustrations of Rhetorical Gesture and Action.
    Reprinted, New York, B. Blom, 1968. ["Embellished with
    sixty-nine engravings, expressive of the various passions."
    Translation of Ideen zu einer Mimik.]

    1845   J. J. Engel's Mimik. Neu herausgegeben und eingeleitet
    von Theodor Mundt.... Berlin: Mylius.

Engel, Walburga von Raffler
    1964   Il prelinguaggio infantile. Brescia: Paideia Editrice,
    115 pages.

    1970   "The LAD, our underlying unconscious, and more on
    'Felt sets'," Language Sciences 13, pp. 15-18. [LAD = Lan-
    guage Acquisition Device.]

    1971   "Verbal and kinesic correlations in dialect switching."
    Chicago, American Dialect Society.

    1972   "Some phono-stylistic features of Black English,"
    Phonetica 25:1, pp. 53-64.

    1974   "The acquisition of kinesics." Paper read at the 25th
    Annual Kentucky Foreign Language Conference, University of
    Kentucky.

Engen

221

1974 "Children's acquisition of kinesics" [film]. New York: Campus Film Distributors.

1975 "Kinesics and topic," Language Sciences 37, p. 39.

Engen, Trygg, and Nissim Levy
1956 "Constant-sum judgments of facial expressions," Journal of Experimental Psychology 51, pp. 396-398.

Engen, Trygg, Nissim Levy, and Harold Schlosberg
1957 "A new series of facial expressions," American Psychologist 12, pp. 264-266.

1958 "The dimensional analysis of a new series of facial expressions," Journal of Experimental Psychology 55, pp. 454-458.

Engen, Trygg, Nissim Levy, Harold Schlosberg, and H. Woodworth
1960 "Scale values of the Lightfoot pictures of facial expression," Journal of Experimental Psychology 60, pp. 121-125.

Enjoy, Paul d'
1900 "Le rôle de la main dans les gestes de responsabilité," Revue Scientifique 4:14, pp. 81-83. Paris.

Epée see L'Epée, Charles Michel de

Epstein, Aubrey and John H. Ulrich
1966 "The effect of high- and low-pass filtering on the judged vocal quality of male and female speakers," Quarterly Journal of Speech 52, pp. 267-272.

Erb, Russell C.
1968 The Common Scents of Smell: How the Nose Knows and What It All Shows. Cleveland: World Publishing Co.

von Erhardt-Siebold, Ericka
1932 "Harmony of the senses in English, German and French romanticism," Publications of the Modern Language Association 47, pp. 577-592.

Erickson, Frederick [Harvard]
1971 "Cognitive anthropology, ethnomethodology, and the school counseling interview: a search for a generative grammar of talk about social structure." Paper read at American Anthropological Association, New York.

1972 "F'get you Honkie," in Arthur L. Smith, Language, Communication, and Rhetoric in Black America. New York: Harper and Row, pp. 18-27.

Ervin, Charles R., Jr.
1971 "When being close counts: the role of physical proxim-

ity, attitude similarity to a communicator, and audience self-
esteem in mediating compliance." Dissertation Abstracts 31,
6873 B. University of Texas.

Eschbach, A.
    1974   Zeichen - Text - Bedeutung: Bibliographie zur Theorie
und Praxis der Semiotik. München: Fink-Verlag. [Has 15
pages of bibliography on NVC.]

Escholz, Paul A.
    1973-74 "Mark Twain and the language of gesture," Mark
Twain Journal 17:1, pp. 5-8.

Eshkol, Noa see also Golani Zeidel
    1971   The Hand Book: The Detailed Notation of Hand and
Finger Movements and Forms. Tel Aviv: Movement Notation
Society, 135 pages.

Eshkol, Noa, and Racheli Nul
    1968   Eshkol Wachmann Movement Notation. Tel Aviv: Israel
Music Institute, 100 pages.

Eshkol, Noa, and Abraham Wachmann
    1958   Movement Notation. London: Weidenfeld and Nicolson,
203 pages.

Essen, O. von
    1956   Grundzüge der hochdeutschen Satzintonation. Ratingen.

    1961   "Die phonetische Dokumentation der Nasalität und des
offenen Näselns," Folia Phoniatrica 13, pp. 269-275.

Esser, Aristide H., ed.
    1971   Behavior and Environment: The Use of Space by Ani-
mals and Men. International symposium on the use of space
by animals and men, AAAS, Dallas, 1968. New York: Plenum Press, 411 pages.

Esser, Aristide H., S. Amparo, R. N. Chamberlain, E. D. Chapple, and N. S. Kline
    1964   "Territoriality of patients on a research ward," Recent
Advances in Biological Psychiatry 7, pp. 37-44.

Estes, Stanley G.
    1938   "Judging personality from expressive behavior," Jour-
nal of Abnormal and Social Psychology 33, pp. 217-236.

Etzel, Barbara C., and J. L. Gewirtz
    1967   "Extinction of crying with reinforcement of eye contact
and smiling," Journal of Experimental Child Psychology 5,
pp. 303-317.

Evans, Bessie, and May G. Evans
1931   American Indian Dance Steps.   New York: A. S.
Barnes, 104 pages.

Evans, Gary W. , and Roger B. Howard
1973   "Personal space," Psychological Bulletin 80:4, pp. 334-
344.

Ex, J. and Adam Kendon
"A notation for facial postures and bodily positions in
the social performance." Appendix to Appendix II of Progress
Report to Dept. of Scientific and Industrial Research for the
Social Skills Project, Institute of Experimental Psychology, Ox-
ford University.

Exline, Ralph V.
1960   "Effects of sex, norms, and affiliation motivation upon
accuracy of interpersonal preferences," Journal of Personality
28, pp. 397-412.

1962   "Need affiliation and initial communication behavior in
problem-solving groups characterized by low interpersonal visibility," Psychological Reports 10, pp. 79-89.

1963   "Explorations in the process of person perception: visual interaction in relation to competition, sex, and need for
affiliation," Journal of Personality 31:1 (March), pp. 1-20.

1972   "Visual interaction: the glances of power and preference," in James K. Cole, ed. , Nebraska Symposium on Motivation.   University of Nebraska Press, Vol. 19, pp. 163-206.

Exline, Ralph V. , and Yellin M. Absalom [University of Delaware]
"Eye contact as a sign between man and monkey."

Exline, Ralph V. , and E. Clark
1967   "Effects of two patterns of a speaker's visual behavior
upon the perception of the authenticity of his verbal message."
Paper read at the Eastern Psychological Association, Boston,
Mass. , 10 pages.

Exline, Ralph V. , David Gray, and Dorothy Schuette
1965   "Visual behavior in a dyad as affected by interview
content and sex of respondent," Journal of Personality and Social Psychology 1, pp. 201-209.   Reprinted in D. C. Barnlund,
ed. , Interpersonal Communication.   Boston: Houghton-Mifflin,
1968.

Exline, Ralph V. , and David Messick
1967   "The effects of dependency and social reinforcement
upon visual behavior during an interview," British Journal of
Social and Clinical Psychology 6:3, pp. 256-266.

Exline, Ralph V. , John Thibaut, Carole Brannon, and Peter Gumpert
1961   "Visual interaction in relation to machiavellianism and
an unethical act, " Technical Report No. 16, University of Dela-
ware, Contract Nonr-2285(02), Office of Naval Research.
American Psychologist 16:7, p. 396 [abstract].   Reprinted in
R. Christie, and F. Geis, eds. , Studies in Machiavellianism.
New York: Academic Press, 1970.

Exline, Ralph V. , and L. C. Winters
1965   "Affective relations and mutual glances in dyads, " in
Silvan S. Tomkins and Carroll E. Izard, eds. , Affect, Cognition and Personality. New York: Springer, pp. 319-350.

                            - F -

Fabbri, Paolo
1968   "Considérations sur la proxémique, " Langages 10,
pp. 65-75.

Faber, Albrecht
1953   Laut- und Gebärdensprache bei Insekten.   Stuttgart,
198 pages.

Fabricant, Noah D.
1960   "Sexual functions and the nose, " American Journal of
the Medical Sciences 239 (April), pp. 498-502.

Fabun, Don
1965   Communications: The Transfer of Meaning.   Beverly
Hills: The Glencoe Press, 48 pages.

1971   "The silent languages, " in Joseph A. De Vito, ed. ,
Communication: Concepts and Processes.   Englewood Cliffs,
N. J. : Prentice-Hall, pp. 127-133.

Fagg see Lindblom

Fairbanks, Grant
1942   "An acoustical study of the pitch of infant hunger wails, "
Child Development 13, pp. 227-232.

Fairbanks, Grant, E. C. Herbert, and J. M. Hammond
1949   "An acoustical study of vocal pitch in seven- and eight-
year-old girls, " Child Development 20, pp. 71-78.

Fairbanks, Grant, and LeMar W. Hoaglin
1941   "An experimental study of the durational characteristics
of the voice during the expression of emotion, " Speech Monographs 8, pp. 85-90.

Fairbanks, Grant, and Wilbert Pronovost
1939   "An experimental study of the pitch characteristics of
the voice during the expression of emotion," Speech Monographs
6, pp. 87-104.

Fairbanks, Grant, J. H. Wiley, and F. M. Lassman
1949   "An acoustical study of vocal pitch in seven- and eight-
year-old boys," Child Development 20, pp. 63-69.

Faltico, Gary James
1969   "The vocabulary of nonverbal communication in the
psychological interview." UCLA Dissertation.

Fant, Louie J.
"Ameslan, an introduction to American sign language."

1964   Say It With Hands. Washington, D. C. : Department of
Education, Gallaudet College.

Farquhar, M.
1950   "The African hand," WADA 27 (Rhodesia), pp. 25-30.

Fast, Julius
1970   Body Language. New York: M. Evans, 192 pages.
Review by Edward A. Schmerler, ETC. 29:2 (June 1972),
pp. 215-217.

Fay, P. J. , and W. C. Middleton
1940   "Judgment of intelligence from the voice as transmitted
over a public address system," Sociometry 3, pp. 186-191.

Feldenkrais, Moshé
1949   Body and Mature Behavior: A Study of Anxiety, Sex,
Gravitation and Learning. London: Routledge and Kegan Paul,
167 pages. New York: International Universities Press, 1966.

Feldman, Sandor S.
1922   "Über Erröten," Int. Zeitschrift PSA 8, pp. 14-34. [On
blushing.]

1926   "A ticroel," Magyar Orvosi Archivum 17, Budapest.
[On the tic.]

1941   "The Blessing of the Kohenites," American Imago 2,
pp. 296-322. [Pp. 315-318 for gestures.]

1941   "On blushing," Psychiatric Quarterly 15, pp. 249-261.

1956   "Crying at the happy ending," Journal American Psychoanalytic Association 4, pp. 477-485.

1959   Mannerisms of Speech and Gestures in Everyday Life.
New York: International Universities Press, 301 pages.

226   Bibliography

Feldman, Shel, and Robert E. Kleck [Dartmouth College]
    "Nonverbal behavior as a function of impression sets. "

Feldstein, Stanley
    1972 "Temporal patterns of dialogue: basic research and
    reconsiderations, " in Aron Wolfe Siegman, and Benjamin Pope,
    eds. , Studies in Dyadic Communication. New York: Pergamon
    Press, pp. 91-113.

Feleky, Antoinette
    1914 "The Expression of the emotions, " Psychological Review
    21:1 (January), pp. 33-41.

    1922 Feelings and Emotions. New York: Pioneer Publishing
    Co. , 245 pages.

Felipe, Nancy Jo, and Somers, Robert
    1966 "Invasions of personal space, " Social Problems 14:2
    (Fall), pp. 206-214.

Ferdon, Constance Etz
    1946 "Mind your manners, " The Inter-American V (July),
    pp. 19-20, 40.

Ferenczi, Sandor
    1913 "Flatus as an adult prerogative, " Zeitschrift 1, p. 380.
    Reprinted in Further Contributions to the Theory and Technique
    of Psycho-Analysis. London: Hogarth Press, 1926, p. 325.

    1914 "Embarrassed hands, " Zeitschrift 2, p. 378. Re-
    printed in Further Contributions to the Theory and Technique
    of Psycho-Analysis. London: Hogarth Press, 1926, pp. 315-
    316.

    1915 "Psychogenic anomalies of voice production, " Zeitschrift
    3:24. Reprinted in Further Contributions to the Theory and
    Technique of Psycho-Analysis. London: Hogarth Press, 1926,
    pp. 105-109.

    1919 "Thinking and muscle innervation, " in Further Contribu-
    tions to the Technique and Theory of Psycho-Analysis. Lon-
    don: Hogarth Press, 1926.

Ferenczi, Victor, M. -J. Gyselings, J. -P. Jaumot, and M. -N. Thill
    1973 "Le langage sans parole comme procédure expérimen-
    tale, " Revue du Phonétique Appliquée 26, pp. 19-41.

Ferguson, Charles A.
    1956 "Arabic baby talk, " Morris Halle, et al. , eds. , For
    Roman Jakobson. The Hague: Mouton, pp. 121-128.

    1964 "Baby talk in six languages, " American Anthropologist
    66:6 (December), (Part 2) Special Publication, The Ethnography
    of Communication, pp. 103-114.

Fernandez Mines, Rose [New Mexico State University, Las Cruces]
  1976   "Non-verbal communication and the Chicano." Paper
  read at the conference of the English Language Institute, Ann
  Arbor, Michigan.

Fernberger, Samuel W.
  1927   "Six more Piderit faces," American Journal of Psychology 39, pp. 162-166.

  1928   "False suggestion and the Piderit model," American
  Journal of Psychology 40 (October), pp. 562-568.

  1930   "Can an emotion be accurately judged by its facial expression alone?" Journal of Criminal Law, Criminology and
  Police Science 20 (February), pp. 554-564.

Fernberger, Samuel W., and E. Jarden
  1926   "The effect of suggestion on the judgment of facial expression of emotion," American Journal of Psychology 37,
  pp. 565-570.

Feüillet, Raoul Auger [fl. 1700]
  For the Further Improvement of Dancing.

  1706   Orchesography, or the Art of Dancing: by characters
  and demonstrative figures wherein the whole art is explain'd;
  with compleat tables of all steps us'd in dancing, and rules
  for the motions of the arms, &. whereby any person (who
  understands dancing) may of himself learn all manner of
  dances. Being an exact and just translation from the French
  of Monsieur Feuillet, by John Weaver, dancing-Master, London. Republished by Farnborough, Hants: Gregg International
  Publishers, 1971, 59 pages.

Feüillet, Raoul Auger see also Bartenieff

Feves, Angene
  1974   "Reconstruction of renaissance dances," New Merrye
  News & Tidings: The Newsbill of the Renaissance Centre,
  San Francisco, Calif., (Midsummer), pp. 4-5.

Fickett, Joan G., and George L. Trager [Fairleigh-Dickinson Uni-
  versity]
  ca. 1972   "Neighbors and kin."

Field, C.
  1918   "Salutes and saluting, naval and military," Journal of
  the Royal United Service Institution 63, pp. 42-49.

Fielding, William J.
  1960   "Kissing customs," in Strange Customs of Courtship and
  Marriage. New York: Garden City Books, pp. 53-66.

Fields, Sidney J.
    1953   "Discrimination of facial expression and its relation to
    personal adjustment," Journal of Social Psychology 38, pp. 63-
    71.

Fillmore, Charles J.
    1971   "Types of lexical information," in Danny D. Steinberg,
    and Leon A. Jakobovits, eds., Semantics: An Interdisciplinary
    Reader in Philosophy, Linguistics and Psychology. Cambridge
    University Press, pp. 370-392.

Fine, Leon J.
    1959   "Nonverbal aspects of psychodrama," in Progress in
    Psychotherapy; J. H. Masserman and J. L. Moreno, eds.
    New York: Grune & Stratton, Vol. 4, pp. 212-218.

Firestone, Marsha Larrie
    1972   "Farewell behavior: a descriptive analysis of nonverbal
    farewell encounters." Columbia University dissertation. Dis-
    sertation Abstracts International 36:2939A (1975).

Firestone, Shulamith
    1970   The Dialectic of Sex. New York: William Morrow and
    Co.

Firth, J. R.
    1950   "Personality and language in society," Sociological Re-
    view 42, pp. 37-52.

Firth, Raymond William
    1970   "Postures and gestures of respect," Échanges et com-
    munications: Mélanges offerts à Claude Lévi-Strauss à l'occa-
    sion de son 60eme anniversaire; Jean Pouillon, and Pierre Ma-
    randa, eds. The Hague: Mouton, Vol. I, pp. 188-209.

    1972   "Verbal and bodily rituals of greeting and parting," in
    J. S. La Fontaine, ed., Interpretation of Ritual: Essays in
    Honour of I. A. Richards. London: Tavistock Publications,
    pp. 1-38.

    1973   Symbols: Public and Private. Cornell University Press.
    [Chapter 8, "Hair as private asset and public symbol," pp. 262-
    298; Chapter 9, "Bodily symbols of greeting and parting,"
    pp. 299-327.]

Fischer, Capt. Harold E., Jr.
    1955   "My case as a prisoner was 'different'," Life 38:26
    (June 27), pp. 146-160.

Fischer, Herbert
    1958   "Die offene Kreuzhaltung im Rechtsritual: Beiträge zur
    Geschichte einer archetypischen Armgebärde," Festschrift Artur

Steinwenter. Graz-Köln: Grazer Rechts- und Staatswissen-
schaftliche Studien, Band 3, pp. 9-57.

1959   "Die eheliche Verantwortung und das Schultersymbol,"
Antaios: Zeitschrift Für Eine Freie Welt (Stuttgart) 1:2 (July),
pp. 186-208.

1960   "Heilgebärden," Antaios 2:4 (November), pp. 318-347.

1960   "Leben und Tod in alter Mittelfingersymbolik," Sonn-
tagsblatt 43, 54 Nr. 462 (Sonntag 30, Oktober).

1961   "Das Wort im Nacken," Zeitschrift für Ganzheitsfor-
schung (Vienna), Neue Folge 5 (March), pp. 125-133.

1962   "Die kosmurgische Symbolik der Sonnen-Erde-Stellung
(vornehmlich im mittleren und südöstlichen Europa)," Symbolon:
Jahrbuch für Symbolforschung 3, pp. 89-107. Stuttgart: Benno
Schwabe.

1962   "Rot und Weiss als Fahnenfarben," Antaios (Stuttgart)
4:2 (July), pp. 136-153.

1963   "Indogermanischer Kriegeryoga," Festschrift Walter
Heinrich. Graz, Austria: Akademische Druck-U. Verlagsan-
stalt, pp. 65-97.

Fischer, Liselotte K.
1958   "The significance of atypical postural and grasping behavior during the first year of life," American Journal of Or-
thopsychiatry 28, pp. 368-375. [Central African countries.]

Fischer, Susan
        "Sign language and linguistic universals," in Proceedings
of the 5th Conference on Phenomenology. Duquesne University
Press.

1973   "Two processes of reduplication in the American sign
language," Foundations of Language 9:3, pp. 469-480.

        "Verb inflections in American sign language and their
acquisition by the deaf child."

(in press) "Influences on word order change in American sign
language," in Charles N. Li, ed., Word Order and Word Order
Change. University of Texas Press.

Fisher, Gerald H.
1967   "The development of visual and tactile-kinesthetic perception," in W. Wathen-Dunn, ed., Models for the Perception
of Speech and Visual Form. Proceedings of a Symposium,
1964. Cambridge, MIT, pp. 259-262.

Fisichelli, Vincent R. , Samuel Karelitz, John Eichbauer, and
Laura S. Rosenfeld
1961 "Volume-unit graphs: their production and applicability
in studies of infants' cries, " Journal of Psychology 52, pp. 423-
427.

Flachskampf, Ludwig
1938 "Spanische Gebärdensprache, " Romanische Forschungen
52, pp. 205-258. Reprinted in Erlangen, 1938. Reviewed by
Joseph E. Gillet, in Hispanic Review 8:1 (January 1940),
pp. 86-87.

Flack, Michael J.
1966 "Communicable and uncommunicable aspects in personal
international relationships, " Journal of Communication 16:3
(September), pp. 283-290.

1967 The Role of Culture in International Operations. Pittsburg: University of Pittsburg, 60 leaves. [Also in French,
Centre D'Echanges Technologiques Internationaux.]

Fleming, Gerald
1971 "Gesti e movimenti come mediatori di significato nei
nuovi sistemi visuali per l'insegnamento delle lingue, " Pensiero
e Linguaggio in Operazioni 2, pp. 31-43.

1971 "Gesture and body movement as mediators of meaning in
our new language teaching systems, " Contact 16, pp. 15-22.

Fletcher, Harvey
1953 Speech and Hearing in Communication. New York: Van
Nostrand, 461 pages.

Fliess, Robert
1949 "Silence and verbalization: a supplement to the theory
of the 'Analytic Rule', " International Journal of Psycho-Analysis
30, pp. 21-30.

Flint, E. H.
1970 "The influence of prosodic patterns upon the mutual intelligibility of aboriginal and general Australian English, "
Pacific Linguistic Studies in Honour of Arthur Capell (Canberra),
Series C, 13, pp. 717-740.

Flögel, Karl Friedrich
1788 Geschichte des Grotesk-komischen, ein Beitrag zur
Geschichte der Menschheit. Leipzig, 322 pages.

Florenz, K.
1899 "Ancient Japanese rituals, " Asiatic Society of Japan,
Transactions 27. [Continuation of the work of Sir Ernest Satow, q. v.]

Flügel, J. C.
1929   "On the mental attitude to present-day clothes: report
on a questionnaire," British Journal of Medical Psychology 9,
Part II, pp. 97-149.

1930   The Psychology of Clothes. New York: International
Universities Press, Inc., [1969 ed.], 257 pages.

Foa, Uriel G.
1967   "Differentiation in cross-cultural communication," in
Lee Thayer, ed., Communication: Concepts and Perspectives.
Washington, D.C.: Spartan Books, chapter VI, pp. 135-151.

Foley, John P.
1935   "Judgment of facial expression of emotion in the chimpanzee," Journal of Social Psychology 6, pp. 31-67.

Fónagy, Ivan
1956   "Ueber den Verlauf des Lautwandels," Acta Linguistica
Academiae Scientiarum Hungaricae 6 (Budapest), pp. 173-278.

1962   "Mimik auf glottaler Ebene," Phonetica 8, pp. 209-219.

1963   Die Metaphern in der Phonetik. The Hague: Mouton,
132 pages.

1967   "Hörbare mimik," Phonetica 16, pp. 25-35.

1970   "Les bases pulsionnelles de la phonation," Revue Française de Psychanalyse 34:1 (January), pp. 101-136.

1971   "Bases pulsionnelles de la phonation," Revue Française
de Psychanalyse 35:4 (July), pp. 543-591.

1971   "Synthèse de l'ironie," Phonetica 23, pp. 42-51.

1975   "Analyses semiotique de la voix humaine," Semiotica
13:1, pp. 97-108.

Fónagy, Ivan, and Judith Fónagy
1966   "Sound pressure level and duration," Phonetica 15:1,
pp. 14-21.

1970   "Distribution of phonemes in word-sets contrasting in
meaning," in David Cohen, ed., Mélanges Marcel Cohen. The
Hague: Mouton, pp. 66-72.

Fónagy, Ivan, and Klara Magdics
1960   "Speed of utterance in phrases of different lengths,"
Language and Speech 3, pp. 179-192.

1963   "Emotional patterns in intonation and music," Zeitschrift
für Phonetik 16:1-3, pp. 293-326.

Ford, Barbara
    1970   "Body language: what it reveals about you," Science
    Digest 68:2 (August), pp. 16-21.

Forer, B.
    1969   "The taboo against touching in psychotherapy," Psycho-
    therapy: Theory, Research and Practice 6:5.

Forrest, William Craig
    1968   "The kinesthetic feel of literature," Bucknell Review
    13:3 (December), pp. 91-106.

    1969   "Literature as aesthetic object: the kinesthetic stra-
    tum," Journal of Aesthetics and Art Criticism 27:4, pp. 455-
    459.

    1969   "The poem as a summons to performance," British
    Journal of Aesthetics 9:3 (July), pp. 298-305.

Forston, Robert F., and Charles U. Larson
    1968   "The dynamics of space: an experimental study in
    proxemic behavior among Latin Americans and North Ameri-
    cans," Journal of Communication 18:2 (June), pp. 109-116.

Foss, Brian M., ed.
    1963   Determinants of Infant Behaviour. Vol. 2. London:
    Methuen & Co.; New York: John Wiley & Sons, 248 pages.

Fouché, P.
    1930   "Rapport du congrès international de linguistique de
    Rome de 1930," MS. [Enlarges the concept of the word
    'language' to include gesture communication: Hayes.]

Fouts, R. S.
    1974   "Language, origins, definitions and chimpanzees,"
    Journal of Human Evolution 1.

Frachtenberg, Leo J.
    1917   "Abnormal types of speech in Quileute," International
    Journal of American Linguistics 1:4, pp. 295-299.

Frahm, J. H.
    1970   "Verbal-nonverbal interaction analysis: exploring a new
    methodology for quantifying dyadic communication systems."
    Ph.D. Dissertation, Michigan State University. Ann Arbor:
    University Microfilms, No. 71-2069.

Fraisse, Paul
    1973   "Temporal isolation, activity rhythms, and time esti-
    mation," in John E. Rasmussen, ed., Man in Isolation and
    Confinement. Chicago: Aldine, pp. 85-97.

Frank, Lawrence K.
1957 "Tactile communication," Genetic Psychology Monographs 56:2, pp. 209-255. Reprinted in Alfred G. Smith, ed.,
Communication and Culture: Readings in the Codes of Human
Interaction. New York: Holt, Rinehart & Winston, 1966,
pp. 199-209. ETC: A Review of General Semantics 16:1
(Autumn), 158, pp. 31-79; Haig A. Bosmajian, ed., The Rhetoric of Nonverbal Communication. 1971; partially reprinted
in Larry A. Samovar and Richard E. Porter, eds., Intercultural Communication: A Reader. Belmont, Calif.: Wadsworth,
1972, pp. 200-205.

1960 "Tactile communication," in Edmund Carpenter and
Marshall McLuhan, eds., Explorations in Communication: An
Anthology. Boston: Beacon Press, pp. 4-11.

Frankel, Steven A., and Ellen B. Frankel
1970 "Nonverbal behavior in a selected group of Negro and
White males," Psychosomantics 11, pp. 127-132.

Franklin, William G.
1971 "An experimental study of the acoustic characteristics
of simulated emotion," Dissertation Abstracts 32, 575 A.
Pennsylvania State University.

Fraser, J. T., ed.
1966 The Voices of Time: a Cooperative Survey of Man's
Views of Time as Expressed by the Sciences and by the Humanities. New York: George Braziller. [Especially Part II,
"Communications, rhythm, and behavior."]

1972 The Study of Time. Vol. 1. New York: Springer Verlag.

1975 Of Time, Passion and Knowledge. New York: George
Braziller, 506 pages.

Fraser, J. T., and N. Lawrence, eds.
1975 The Study of Time II: Proceedings of the Second Conference of the International Society for the Study of Time.
New York: Springer-Verlag, 486 pages.

Frazer, Sir James George
1919 "The silent widow," Folk-Lore in the Old Testament:
Studies in Comparative Religion, Legend and Law. New York:
Macmillan, Vol. I, pp. 71-81. Vol. II, "Weeping as a Salu-
tation," pp. 82-93.

1961 The New Golden Bough: A New Abridgment of the Classic Work. New York: Anchor Books. [Original 1922.]

Freedman, Daniel G.
1964 "Smiling in blind infants and the issue of innate vs.

acquired," Journal of Child Psychology and Psychiatry 5,
pp. 171-184. Reprinted in The New Outlook (May 1967),
pp. 156-163; (June 1967), pp. 194-201.

1965   "Hereditary control of early social behavior," in Foss,
B. M. , ed. , Determinants of Infant Behaviour. London:
Methuen.

1969   "The survival value of the beard: there's status in it--
and sexual magnetism," Psychology Today 3:5 (October), pp. 36-
39.

Freedman, Lawrence Z. , and August B. Hollingshead
1957   "Neurosis and social class," American Journal of Psychiatry 113:9 (March), pp. 769-775.

Freedman, Norbert
1972   "The analysis of movement behavior during the clinical
interview," in A. Siegman and B. Pope, eds. , Studies in Dyadic Communication. New York: Pergamon Press, pp. 153-
175.

Freedman, Norbert, Thomas Blass, Arthur Rifkin, and Frederic
Quitkin
1973   "Body movements and the verbal encoding of aggressive
affect," Journal of Personality and Social Psychology 26:1,
pp. 72-85.

Freedman, Norbert, and Stanley P. Hoffman
1967   "Kinetic behavior in altered clinical states: approach
to objective analysis of motor behavior during clinical interviews," Perceptual and Motor Skills 24, pp. 525-539.

Freedman, Norbert, James O'Hanlon, Philip Oltman, and Herman
A. Witkin
1972   "The imprint of psychological differentiation on kinetic
behavior in varying communicative contexts," Journal of Abnormal Psychology 79:3, pp. 239-258.

French, Norman R. , Charles W. Carter, Jr. , and Walter Koenig,
Jr.
1930   "The words and sounds of telephone conversations,"
Bell System Technical Journal 9, pp. 290-324.

French, Patrice
1973   "Kinesics in communication: black and white," Language
Sciences 28 (December), pp. 13-16.

French, Patrice, and Walburga van Raffler Engel
1973   "Kinesic dialect? Language and paralanguage in Black
English speakers." Paper read at American Dialect Society,
Midwest Regional.

Fretz, Bruce R.
1966   "Personality correlates of postural movements," Journal
of Counseling Psychology 13:3, pp. 344-347.

1966   "Postural movements in a counseling dyad" Journal of
Counseling Psychology 13:3, pp. 335-343.

Frey, Siegfried, and Mario von Cranach
1973   "A method for the assessment of body movement variability," in von Cranach and Vine, eds., Social Communication
and Movement, pp. 398-418.

Fridman, Ruth
?   Los comienzos de la conducta musical.   Argentina.

Friederici, Georg
1907   Der Tränengruss der Indianer.   Leipzig: Simmel, 22
pages.

Friedlander, Bernard Z.
1968   "The effect of speaker identity, voice inflection, and
message redundancy on infants' selection of focal reinforcement," Journal of Experimental Child Psychology 6:3, pp. 443-
459.

Friedman, Lynn A.
        "On the semantics of space, time and person reference
in the American Sign Language. " M. A. thesis, University of
California at Berkeley.

1975   "Space, time, and person reference in American Sign
Language," Language 51:4 (December), pp. 940-961.

1975   "The manifestation of subject and object in American
Sign Language. " Paper read at the Linguistic Society of America, San Francisco.

Friedrich, Paul
1969   "On the meaning of the Tarascan suffixes of space,"
International Journal of American Linguistics 35:4, Memoir 23
(October), pp. 1-48.

Fries, Charles Carpenter
1952   The Structure of English.   New York: Harcourt, Brace
and World.

Frijda, Nico H.
1953   "The understanding of facial expression of emotion,"
Acta Psychologica 9, pp. 294-362.

1958   "Facial expression and situational cues," Journal of Abnormal and Social Psychology 57, pp. 149-154.

236   Bibliography

1961   "Facial expression and situational cues: a control,"
Acta Psychologica 18:3, pp. 239-244.

1965   "Mimik und pantominik," in R. Kirchhoff, ed., Handbuch der Psychologie 5.   Gottingen: Hogrefe, pp. 351-421.

1968   "Emotion and recognition of emotion." Contribution to
the third Feelings and Emotions Symposium, Loyola University,
Chicago.   Mimeo, 15 pages.

1969   "Recognition of emotion," in L. Berkowitz, ed., Advances in Experimental Social Psychology 4.   New York:
Academic Press, Inc., pp. 167-223.

1973   "The relation between emotion and expression," in von
Cranach and Vine, eds., Social Communication and Movement,
pp. 325-339.

Frijda, Nico H., and E. Philipszoon
1963   "Dimensions of recognition of expression," Journal of
Abnormal and Social Psychology 66, pp. 45-51.

Frijda, Nico H., and John P. Van De Geer
1961   "Codability and recognition: an experiment with facial
expressions," Acta Psychologica 18, pp. 360-367.

Frink, Orrin
1962   "Substandard 'yes' and 'no' in spoken American English,"
American Speech 37, pp. 230-232.

Frishberg, Nancy
1975   "Arbitrariness and iconicity: historical change in
American Sign Language," Language 51:3 (September), pp. 696-
719.

Frois-Wittmann, J.
1930   "The judgment of facial expression," Journal of Experimental Psychology 13:2 (April), pp. 113-151. [Cf. Hulin and
Katz.]

From, F.
1973   "Tillaerte gestus: karakteristiske for dansk befolkning,"
Psykologisk skriftserie 4.

Fry, D. B.
1956   "Perception and recognition in speech," in For Roman
Jakobson; Morris Halle, ed.   The Hague: Mouton, pp. 169-
173.

Fugita, Stephen S.
1974   "Effects of anxiety and approval on visual interaction,"
Journal of Personality and Social Psychology 29, pp. 586-592.

Fugita 237

Fugita, Stephen S. , Kenneth N. Wexley, and Joseph M. Hillery
1974 "Black-white differences in nonverbal behavior in an interview setting, " Journal of Applied Social Psychology 4:4, pp. 343-350.

Fujimoto, Edward K.
1971 "The comparative communicative power of verbal and nonverbal symbols, " Dissertation Abstracts 32, 4152A. Ohio State University.

Fulcher, J. S.
1942 " 'Voluntary' facial expression in blind and seeing children, " Archives of Psychology 38, no. 272, pp. 1-49.

Fussell, Paul, Jr.
1955 "The Gestic symbolism of T. S. Eliot, " A Journal of English Literary History 22, pp. 194-211.

- G -

Gaines, Jack
1950 "El lenguaje silencioso de la radio, " La Voz de los Estados Unidos (September-October), pp. 2-4, U. S. Department of State.

Galas, Evangeline M.
1961 "The language teacher as choral director: suggestions on the use of gestures, " Hispania 44 (December), pp. 787-789.

Gallini, Giovanni Andrea
1762 A Treatise on the Art of Dancing. Reprinted, New York: Broude Brothers, 1967, 292 pages.

Gallois, Cynthia, and Norman N. Markel
1975 "Turn taking: social personality and conversational style, " Journal of Personality and Social Psychology 6, pp. 1134-1140.

Galloway, Charles M.
1962 "An exploratory study of observational procedures for determining teacher nonverbal communication. " Thesis, University of Florida, 23, 3811.

1966 "Teacher non-verbal communication, " Educational Leadership 24:1, pp. 55-63.

1968 "Nonverbal communication, " Theory into Practice 7:4 pp. 172-175.

Galper, Ruth E.
1970 "Recognition of faces in photographic negatives, " Psychonomic Science 19:4, pp. 207-211.

Ganguly, S. N.
    1968   "Culture, communication and silence," Philosophy and
    Phenomenological Research 29, pp. 182-200.

Gardiner, William
    1832   The Music of Nature: Or an Attempt to Prove that
    What Is ... Pleasing in the Art of Singing ... Is Derived from
    the Animated World. Boston, Wilkins and Carter, 505 pages.

Gardner, Martin
    1968   "Counting systems and the relationship between numbers
    and the real world," Scientific American (September), pp. 218-
    229.

Gardner, R. Allen, and Gardner, Beatrice T.
    1969   "Teaching sign language to a chimpanzee," Science 165,
    pp. 664-672.

    1971   "Two-way communication with an infant chimpanzee,"
    in Allan Schrier, Harry F. Harlow, and Fred Stollnitz, eds.,
    Behavior of Nonhuman Primates. New York: Academic Press,
    vol. IV, chapter 3.

    1975   "Early signs of language in child and chimpanzee,"
    Science 187, pp. 752-753.

Gartner, Jane E.
    1972   "A study of verbal, vocal, and visual communication,"
    Dissertation Abstracts 33, 2343B-44B.   127 pages.

Garvin, Paul L., and Sidney Bertram
    1965   "Linguistic and engineering aspects of automatic speech
    recognition," Phonetica 13, pp. 37-39.

Garvin, Paul L. and Peter Ladefoged
    1963   "Speaker identification and message identification in
    speech recognition," Phonetica 9:4, pp. 193-199.

Garwood, R., A. Z. Guirora, and N. Kalter
    1970   "Manifest anxiety and perception of micro-momentary
    expression," Studies in Language and Language Behavior 6,
    pp. 1-7.

Gary, Patricia E.
    1969   "Kinesics," Quest: Perspectives for Sport, Monograph
    12 (May), pp. 71-72.

Gason, Samuel
    1874   The Dieyerie Tribe of Australian Aborigines.   Adelaide.
    [Sign language on p. 35.]

Gates, Alice
    1968   A New Look at Movement: A Dancer's View.   Minne-
    apolis: Burgess Publishing Co., 187 pages.

Gates, Georgina S.
1925   "A test for the ability to interpret facial expression, "
Psychological Bulletin 22, p. 120.

Gazzaniga, Michael S.
1970   The Bisected Brain.   New York: Appleton-Century-
Crofts, 172 pages.

Gazzaniga, Michael S. , and Steven A. Hillyard
1971   "Language and speech capacity of the right hemisphere, "
Neuropsychologia 9, pp. 273-280.

Geertsma, Robert H. , and Ronald S. Reivich
1969   "Auditory and visual dimensions of externally mediated
self-observation, " Journal of Nervous and Mental Disease
148:3, pp. 210-223.

Geertz, Clifford
1960   "The background and general dimension of Prijaji belief
and etiquette"; "Linguistic etiquette, " in The Religion of Java.
Glencoe, Ill. :   The Free Press, pp. 248-260.

Geiger, Paul, and Richard Weiss
1951   Atlas de folklore suisse.   Basel, 76 pages.   [See distribution of greeting formulas.]

Geizer, Ronald S.
1971   "Interaction context and the perception of nonverbal dyadic communication systems, " Dissertation Abstracts 32, 6584A.
Ohio State University, 146 pages.

Geldard, Frank A.
1953   The Human Senses.   New York: John Wiley and Sons,
365 pages.   [Reprinted 1972.]

1957   "Adventures in tactile literacy, " The American Psychologist 12, pp. 115-124.

1960   "Some neglected possibilities of communication, " Science
131:3413 (May 27), pp. 1583-1588.

1961   "Cutaneous channels of communication, " in Walter A.
Rosenblith, ed. , Sensory Communication: Contributions to the
Symposium on Principles of Sensory Communication.   MIT
Press, pp. 73-87.   [Revision of "Some neglected possibili-
ties.... "]

1968   "Body English, " Psychology Today 2:7, pp. 42-47.

Gellen, Nicolaus Adamuslet Wikblad
1801   De Actione ad Sacras Orationes Applicata.   Upsaliae:
J. F. Edmon, 12 pages.

Genders, Roy
    1972   Perfume Through the Ages. New York: G. P. Put-
    nam's Sons, 238 pages.

Genot, Gérard
    1973   "Tactique du sens," Semiotica 8:3, pp. 193-219.

George, S. S.
    1916   "The gesture of affirmation among the Arabs," Ameri-
    can Journal of Psychology 27 (July), pp. 320-232. [Corrects
    the error of H. Petermann, in Reisen im Orient, 1860:
    Hayes.]

Gerland, Georg Karl Cornelius
    1883   Die Zeichensprache der Indianer. Berlin: Gebrüder
    Paetel, pp. 258-272.

Germanovič, A. I.
    1969   "Zvukovye žesty: etjud o razgovornoj reči" [Sound ges-
    tures: study of conversational language], in N. A. Meščerskij,
    P. A. Dmitriev, et al., eds., Voprosy teorii i istorii jazyka:
    Sbornik statej, posvjaščennyj pamjati B. A. Larina. Lenin-
    grad U. P., pp. 291-297.

Gerstner-Hirzel, Arthur
    1957   The Economy of Action and Word in Shakespeare's Plays.
    (The Cooper Monographs on English and American Language
    and Literature, 2) Bern: Francke, 134 pages.

Geschwind, Norman
    1964   "The development of the brain and the evolution of
    language," Monograph Series on Languages and Linguistics 17
    (Georgetown University Press), pp. 155-169.

    1970   "The organization of language and the brain," Science
    170 (November), pp. 940-944.

    1972   "Language and the brain," Scientific American 226
    (April), pp. 76-83.

Gewirtz, J. L.
    1965   "The course of infant smiling in four child-rearing en-
    vironments in Israel," in Paul Henry Mussen, John Janeway
    Conger, and Jerome Kagan, eds., Readings in Child Develop-
    ment and Personality. New York: Harper and Row, pp. 146-
    170.   Also in B. M. Foss, ed., Determinants of Infant Be-
    haviour 3. London: Methuen, pp. 205-259.

Ghosh, Manomohan see Nandikesvara [translation of the Natya
    Shastra]

Ghosh, Samir K., ed.
    1972   Man, Language and Society: Contributions to the

Sociology of Language. The Hague: Mouton, 264 pages.

Gianotti, G. , and R. Ibba
1972 "La comprensione del significato dei gesti simbolici negli afasici, " _Minerva Psichiatrica e Psicologica_ 13, pp. 1-9.

Gibson, James J.
1950 _The Perception of the Visual World._ Boston: Houghton Mifflin, 242 pages.

1962 "Observations on active touch, " _Psychological Review_ 69:6 (November), pp. 477-491.

Gibson, James J. , and Anne Danielson Pick
1963 "Perception of another person's looking behavior, " _American Journal of Psychology_ 76:3 (September), pp. 386-394.

Giedt, F. Harold
1955 "Comparison of visual, content, and auditory cues in interviewing, " _Journal of Consulting Psychology_ 19:6, pp. 407-416.

Giese, Fritz
1928 _Psychologie der Arbeitshand._ Berlin-Wien: Urban Schwartzenburg, 325 pages.

Giet, Franz
1956 "Kann Man in einer Tonsprache flüstern?" _Lingua_ 5, pp. 372-381.

1950 _Zur Tonität nordchinesischer Mundarten._ Studia Instituti Anthropos, Wien/Freiberg. Wien: Mödling: Verlag der Missionsdruckerei St. Gabriel, pp. 95-97.

Gilbert, Harvey R. , and Gary G. Weismer
1974 "The effects of smoking on the speaking fundamental frequency of adult women, " _Journal of Psycholinguistic Research_ 3:3, pp. 225-231.

Gilmore, Art, and G. Y. Middleton
1949 _Television and Radio Announcing._ Hollywood, Calif. : Hollywood Radio Publishers, 283 pages.

Giner de los Ríos, Gloria
1955 _Cumbres._ New York: Holt, Rinehart and Winston. [Illustrations of gestures from the Hispanic peninsula from Roman times on, see pp. 58, 61, 62, 93, 100, 114, 157, 188, 191: Hayes.]

Gitin, Sharon R.
1970 "A dimensional analysis of manual expression, " _Journal of Personality and Social Psychology_ 15, pp. 271-277.

242   Bibliography

Gladstones, W. H.
    1962 "A multidimensional study of facial expression of emo-
    tion," Australian Journal of Psychology 14:2, pp. 95-100.
    [Western Australia.]

Glasersfeld, E. von
    1974 "Signs, communications and language," Journal of Hu-
    man Evolution 1.

Glasgow, George M.
    1944 "The effects of nasality on oral communication," Quar-
    terly Journal of Speech 30:3 (October), pp. 337-340.

Glassow, Ruth B.
    1966 "Kinesiology: modern dance and kinesiology," Journal
    of Health, Physical Education, and Recreation 37:1 (January),
    pp. 65-68.

Glaze, John Arthur
    1928 "Sensitivity to odors and other phenomena during a
    fast," American Journal of Psychology 40 (October), pp. 569-
    575.

Gleason, Jean Berko
    1971 "Code switching in children's language." Paper pre-
    sented at the Linguistic Society of America.

Glixon, Patricia
    1974 "Eye contact and intimacy," Dissertation Abstracts Inter-
    national 35:4203B.

Goffman, Erving
    1956 "The nature of deference and demeanor," American An-
    thropologist 58:3 (June), pp. 473-502.

    1959 The Presentation of Self in Everyday Life. New York:
    Doubleday Anchor, 255 pages.

    1961 Encounters. Indianapolis: Bobbs-Merrill, 152 pages.

    1963 Behavior in Public Places: Notes on the Social Organi-
    zation of Gatherings. New York: Free Press, 248 pages.
    Chapter 6, "Face engagements," pp. 83-111 [eye].

    1964 "The neglected situation," in Gumperz and Hymes, eds.,
    The Ethnography of Communication, pp. 133-136; American
    Anthropologist 66:6 (Part 2), (December).

    1964 "On face-work: an analysis of ritual elements in social
    interaction," in Warren G. Bennis, E. H. Schein, D. E. Ber-
    lew, F. I. Steele, eds., Interpersonal Dynamics. Homewood,
    Ill.: Dorsey Press, 736 pages.

1967   Interaction Ritual: Essays on Face-to-Face Behavior.
Garden City, N.Y.: Doubleday Anchor. 270 pages.

1971   Relations in Public: Microstudies of the Public Order.
New York: Harper Colophon Books, 396 pages. Review by
John Fought, Language in Society 1:2 (October 1972), pp. 266-
271.

Golani, Ilan, and Shmuel Zeidel
1969   The Golden Jackal. Tel Aviv: Movement Notation Society, 124 pages.

Goldberg, Gordon N., Charles A. Kiesler, and Barry E. Collins
1969   "Visual behavior and face-to-face distance during interaction," Sociometry 32 (March), pp. 43-53.

Goldberg, Susan, and Michael Lewis
1969   "Play behavior in the year-old infant: early sex differences," Child Development 40:1 (March), pp. 21-31. Reprinted in Judith M. Bardwick, ed., Readings on the Psychology of Women. New York: Harper and Row, 1972, pp. 30-
33.

Goldfinger, Ernö
1941   "The sensation of space: urbanism and spatial order,"
Architectural Review (November), pp. 129-131.

1942   "The elements of enclosed space," Architectural Review
91 (January), pp. 5-9.

1942   "Urbanism and spatial order," Architectural Review
(January), pp. 163-166.

Goldman-Eisler, Frieda
1952   "Individual differences between interviewers and their
effect on interviewees' conversational behavior," Journal of
Mental Science 98 (October), pp. 660-671.

1954   "On the variability of the speed of talking and on its
relation to the length of utterances in conversations," British
Journal of Psychology 45, pp. 94-107.

1954   "A study of individual differences and of interaction in
the behaviour of some aspects of language in interviews,"
Journal of Mental Science 100, pp. 177-197.

1955   "Speech-breathing activity--a measure of tension and
affect during interviews," British Journal of Psychology 46,
pp. 53-63.

1956   "The determinants of the rate of speech output and their
mutual relations," Journal of Psychosomatic Research 1, pp.
137-143.

1957   "Speech production and language statistics," Nature
180:4600 (December), p. 1497.

1958   "The predictability of words in context and the length
of pauses in speech," Language and Speech 1, pp. 226-231.

1958   "Speech analysis and mental processes," Language and
Speech 1, pp. 59-75.

1958   "Speech production and the predictability of words in
context," Quarterly Journal of Experimental Psychology 10,
pp. 96-106.

1961   "A comparative study of two hesitation phenomena,"
Language and Speech 4:1 (January-March), pp. 18-26.

1961   "Continuity of speech utterance, its determinants and
its significance," Language and Speech 4:4 (October-December),
pp. 220-231.

1961   "The distribution of pause durations in speech," Language and Speech 4:4 (October-December), pp. 232-237.

1961   "Hesitation and information in speech," in Information
Theory: 4th London Symposium, pp. 162-174, ed. by Colin
Cherry.   Papers Read at a Symposium on 'Information Theory'
Held at the Royal Institution, London.   [With 8 pages of car-
toons used in exp.]

1961   "The significance of changes in the rate of articulation,"
Language and Speech 4, pp. 171-174.

1967   "Sequential temporal patterns and cognitive processes in
speech," Language and Speech 10, pp. 122-132.

1968   Psycholinguistics: Experiments in Spontaneous Speech.
New York: Academic Press, 170 pages.

Goldring, Paul
1967   "Role of distance and posture in the evaluation of interactions," Proceedings of the 75th Annual Convention, APA 2,
pp. 243-244.

Goldschmidt, Walter
1972   "An ethnography of encounters: a methodology for the
enquiry into the relation between the individual and society,"
Current Anthropology 13:1 (February), pp. 59-78.

Goldstein, Alvin G. , and June E. Chance
1964   "Recognition of children's faces," Child Development 35,
pp. 129-136.

1965 "Recognition of children's faces: II," Perceptual and Motor Skills 20, pp. 547-548.

Goldstein, Alvin G., and Edmund J. Mackenberg
1966 "Recognition of human faces from isolated facial features: a developmental study," Psychonomic Science 6:4, pp. 149-150.

Goldstein, Kurt
1939 The Organism: A Holistic Approach to Biology Derived from Pathological Data in Man. New York: American Book Company, 533 pages. Reprinted by Boston: Beacon Press, 1963.

1957 "The smiling of the infant and the problem of understanding the 'other'," The Journal of Psychology 44, pp. 175-191.

Goldziher, I.
1866 "Ueber Gebärden- und Zeichensprache bei den Arabern," Zeitschrift für Völkerpsychologie 16:4, pp. 369-386.

Golomb, Solomon W.
1961 "Extraterrestrial linguistics," Astronautics (American Rocket Society). Reprinted in Word Ways: The Journal of Recreational Linguistics 1:4 (November 1968), pp. 202-205.

Gombrich, Sir Ernst H.
1964 "Moment and movement in art," Journal of the Warburg and Courtauld Institutes 27, pp. 293-306.

1966 "Ritualized gesture and expression in art," Royal Society of London, Philosophical Transactions B, No. 772, pp. 393-401.

1969 "The evidence of images," in Interpretation: Theory and Practices, ed. Charles S. Singleton. Baltimore: Johns Hopkins Press, pp. 35-104.

1972 "The visual image," Scientific American (September), pp. 82-96.

Gombrich, Ernst Hans Josef, Julian Hochberg, and Max Black
1972 Art, Perception and Reality. Baltimore: Johns Hopkins Press, 132 pages.

Gomme, Alice B.
1894 Children's Singing Games: With the Tunes to Which They Are Sung. New York: Dover Publications, 1967, 70 pages. [With directions for actions.]

Gondal, I. L.
1912 Parlons ainsi de la voix et du geste. Paris. [Pp. 407-419: Hayes.]

Goodall, Jane see Lawick-Goodall, Jane van

Goodenough, Florence L.
1931   "The expression of the emotions in infancy," Child Development 2, pp. 96-101.

1932   "Expression of the emotions in a blind-deaf child,"
Journal of Abnormal and Social Psychology 27, pp. 328-333.
Reprinted, New York: Arno Press, 1972, as Facial Expression in Children: Three Studies. (Includes R. W. Washburn,
and René A. Spitz.)

Goodenough, Florence L. , and Miles A. Tinker
1931   "The relative potency of facial expression and verbal
description of stimulus in the judgment of emotion," Journal
of Comparative and Physiological Psychology 12 (December),
pp. 365-370.

Goodland, Roger
1931   A Bibliography of Sex Rites and Customs: An Annotated Record of Books, Articles, and Illustrations in all Languages. London: George Routledge and Sons, 752 pages.

Goodman, Felicitas D.
1969   "The acquisition of glossolalia behavior. " New Orleans:
American Anthropological Association.

1969   "Glossolalia: speaking in tongues in four cultural settings," Confinia Psychiatrica 12, pp. 113-129.

1969   "Phonetic analysis of glossolalia in four cultural settings," Journal for the Scientific Study of Religion 8:2, pp. 227-
239.

1969   "Tactile behavior: application of semantic theory to a
problem of anthropological analysis. " Mimeo, 21 pages.

1972   Speaking in Tongues: A Cross-Cultural Study of Glosso-
lalia. University of Chicago Press, 175 pages. Reviews by:
William J. Samarin, Language 50, pp. 207-214; Walt Wolfram,
Language in Society 3:1 (April 1974), pp. 123-126.

1975   "Touching behavior: the application of semantic theory
to a problem of anthropological analysis. " Paper read at the
Conference on Culture and Communication, Temple University.

Goodman, Nelson
1968   Languages of Art: An Approach to a Theory of Symbols.
Indianapolis: Bobbs-Merrill, 277 pages.

Goody, Esther
1973   "Verbal and nonverbal aspects of greeting in a stratified
society in West Africa. " London School of Economics.

Gordon, H. W.
1970   "Hemispheric asymmetries in the perception of musical
chords," Cortex 6:4 (December), pp. 387-398.

Gostynski, E.
1951   "A clinical contribution to the analysis of gestures,"
International Journal of Psychoanalysis 32, pp. 310-318.

Gottschalk, Louis A.
1974   "The psychoanalytic study of hand-mouth approxima-
tions," in Psychoanalysis and Contemporary Science. New
York: Macmillan Company, vol. 3, pp. 269-291.

Gottschalk, Louis A., and Arthur H. Auerbach, eds.
1966   Methods of Research in Psychotherapy. New York:
Appleton-Century-Crofts. 654 pages.

Goude, Jean-Paul
1973   "Les beaux gestes," Esquire (April), pp. 124-127.

Graf, Heinz Joachim
1939   "Untersuchungen zur Gebärde in der Islendingasaga."
Dissertation, Universität Bonn.

Graham, Jean Ann, and Michael Argyle
1975   "A cross-cultural study of the communication of extra-
verbal meaning by gestures," International Journal of Psychology 10:1, pp. 57-67.

Graham, Jean Ann, Pio Ricci Bitti, and Michael Argyle
1975   "A cross-cultural study of the communication of emotion by facial and gestural cues," Journal of Human Movement
Studies 1, pp. 68-77.

Grajew, Felix
1934   "Untersuchungen über die Bedeutung der Gebärden in
der griechischen Epik." Dissertation, Freiburg.

Grambye, Chr., and Harly Sonne
1973   "Greimas til hverdag," Meddelelser fra Dansklaererfo-
reningen, pp. 34-39.

Grant, Ewan C.
1968   "An ethological description of non-verbal behaviour during interviews," British Journal of Medical Psychology 41,
pp. 177-184.

1969   "Human facial expression," Man 4:4 (n.s.), (December),
pp. 525-536.

Grassi, Letizia
1973   "Kinesic and paralinguistic communication," Semiotica
7, pp. 91-96.

Gratiolet, Louis Pierre
    1865   De la physionomie et des mouvements d'expression.
    Paris, 436 pages.

Gray, Giles Wilkeson
    1934   "Problems in the teaching of gesture," Quarterly Jour-
    nal of Speech Education 10, pp. 238-252.

Gray, Philip H.
    1958   "Theory and evidence of imprinting in human infants,"
    Journal of Psychology 46 (July), pp. 155-166.

Green, B. P.
    1916   A Handbook in the Manual Alphabet and the Sign-Langu-
    age of the American Deaf.   Ohio.

Green, Jerald R.
    1968   A Gesture Inventory: for the Teaching of Spanish.
    Philadelphia: Chilton Books, 114 pages.

    1971   "A focus report: kinesics in the foreign-language class-
    room," Foreign Language Annals 5:1 (October), pp. 62-68.

Green, Lili
    1929   Einführung in das Wesen unserer Gesten und Bewegungen.
    Berlin: Oesterheld & Company, 152 pages.

Green, Ruth M.
    1966   The Wearing of Costume: The Changing Techniques of
    Wearing Clothes and How to Move in Them, from Roman
    Britain to the Second World War.   London: Pitman, 171 pages.

Greenbaum, Marvin
    1956   "Manifest anxiety and tachistoscopic recognition of facial
    photographs," Perceptual and Motor Skills 6, pp. 245-248.

Greenberg, Joanne
    1972   In This Sign.   New York: Holt, Rinehart and Winston.
    Review by: Ursula Bellugi, Psychology Today 4:11 (April
    1971), pp. 10-12.

Greene, Donovan R.
    1959   "The effects of aging on the component movements of
    human gait."   Ph. D. Dissertation, University of Wisconsin.
    (Datrix order no. 59-3192).   129 pages.

Greene, Gordon K.
    1972   "From mistress to master: the origins of polyphonic
    music as a visible language," Visible Language 6:3 (Summer),
    pp. 229-252.

Greenfield, Sarah C.
    1975   "Notation systems for transcribing verbal and nonverbal

behavior in adult education research: linguistics (phonetics and phonemics), paralinguistics, proxemics, the micro analysis of the organized flow of behavior, haptics, dance notations, and kinesics. " Dissertation, Arizona State University.

Greenwald, Harold
1958   The Call Girl: A Social and Psychoanalytic Study.
New York: Ballantine Books.

Gregory, Joshua Craven
1924   The Nature of Laughter.   Chapter III, "Laughter of Relief, " pp. 20-40; Chapter IV, "Laughter and Tickling, " pp. 41-51. New York: Harcourt, Brace, 241 pages.

Greimas, A. J.
1968   "Conditions d'une sémiotique du monde naturel, " Langages 10 (June), pp. 3-35.

1968   "Pratiques et langages gestuels, " (ed. Special issue) Langages 10 (June).

1968   Sign, Language, Culture.   The Hague: Mouton, 723 pages.

Greimas, A. J.   see also   Grambye and Sonne

Grice, H. P.
1968   "Utterer's meaning, sentence-meaning, and word-meaning, " Foundations of Language 4:3 (August), pp. 225-242.

Griffin, Donald R.
1958   Listening in the Dark: The Acoustic Orientation of Bats and Men. Yale University Press.   Chapter 12, "Echolocation by the Blind, " pp. 297-322.

1959   Echoes of Bats and Men.   Garden City, N.Y.: Doubleday Anchor Book, 156 pages.

Griffitt, William, and Russell Veitch
1971   "Hot and crowded: influences of population density and temperature on interpersonal affective behavior, " Journal of Personality and Social Psychology 17, pp. 92-98.

Grigsby, Donald L.
1974   "The prisoner's dilemma: interpersonal trust in a nonverbal situation, " Dissertation Abstracts International 35:4726A. [Male-female differences.]

Grimes, Joseph E.
1955   "Style in Huichol structure, " Language 31:1-2, pp. 31-35.

1959   "Huichol tone and intonation," International Journal of American Linguistics 25:4 (October), pp. 221-232.

Grimes, Joseph E.   see also   Hamp

Grinde, Nick
    1948   "Handmade language," Saturday Evening Post 221 (July 10), pp. 34-35, 117-120.

Grohne, Ernst
    [1936]   "Gruss und Gebärde," in Wilhelm Pessler, ed., Handbuch der deutschen Volkskunde. Potsdam: Akademische, vol. 1, pp. 315-324.

Grolleau, Charles, and Guy Chastel
    1932   L'ordre de citeau: la Trappe.   Paris.

Groschuf, G.
    1756   Abhandlung von den Fingern, deren Verrichtungen und Symbolische Bedeutung.   Leipzig und Eisenach.

Groslier, George
    1913   Danseuses cambodgiennes, anciennes et modernes. Paris, 178 pages.

Gross, Leonard R.
    1959   "Effects of verbal and nonverbal reinforcement in the Rorschach," Journal of Consulting Psychology 23, pp. 66-68.

Grotowski, Jerzy
    1968   Towards a Poor Theatre. Holstebro, Denmark: Odin Teatrets Forlag, 262 pages. New York: Simon & Schuster, 1969.

Grover, David H.
    1965   "Elocution at Harvard: the saga of Jonathan Barber," Quarterly Journal of Speech 51:1 (February), pp. 62-67.

Gruber, Jeffrey S.
    1966   "Playing with distinctive features in the babbling of infants," Quarterly Progress Report of the Research Laboratory of Electronics, MIT, No. 81 (April), pp. 181-186. Reprinted in Charles A. Ferguson and Dan Isaac Slobin, eds., Studies of Child Language Development. New York: Holt, Rinehart and Winston, 1973, pp. 4-12.

    1967   "Functions of the lexicon in formal descriptive grammars." Technical Memorandum TM-3770/000/00, System Development Corporation, Santa Monica, 62 pages.

    1967   "Look and see," Language 43:4 (December), pp. 937-947.

Gruhle   251

1965   "Studies in lexical relations. " Dissertation, MIT. Reproduced by the Indiana University Linguistics Circle, mimeo, January 1970.

Gruhle, H. W.
1939   "Antlitz, Gestalt, Haltung, Gebärden des Verbrechers, " Monatsschrift für Kriminologie und Strafrechtsreform, 30.

Gubar, G.
1966   "Recognition of human facial expressions judged live in laboratory setting, " Journal of Personality and Social Psychology 4, pp. 108-111.

Guilford, J. P.
1929-30   "An experiment in learning to read facial expression, " Journal of Abnormal and Social Psychology 24, pp. 191-202.

1958   "A system of the psychomotor abilities, " American Journal of Psychology 71, pp. 164-174.

Guilford, J. P. , and Margaret Wilke
1930   "A new model for the demonstration of facial expressions, " American Journal of Psychology 42, pp. 436-439.

Guilhot, J.
1962   La dynamique de l'expression et de la communication: la voix, la parole, les mimiques et gestes auxiliaires. The Hague: Mouton, 230 pages.

Gulick, Charlotte Emily (Vetter)
1915   Air Pictures (Sign Language). New York: The Campfire Outfitting Co. , 37 pages.

Guillaume, Paul
1926   Imitation in Children, trans. from L'imitation chez l'enfant. Paris: Universitaires de France, 235 pages. Chicago: University of Chicago Press, 1971, 214 pages.

Guillén, Claudio
1971   "Stylistics of silence, " in Literature as System. Princeton University Press, pp. 221-279.

Guilliver, P. H.
1958   "Counting with the fingers by two East African tribes, " Tanganyika Notes and Records 51, pp. 259-262.

Gumperz, John J. , and Dell Hymes, eds.
1964   "The ethnography of communication, " American Anthropologist 66:6 (December), Special Issue.

Gunkle, G.
1968   "An experimental study of some vocal characteristics of spontaneity in acting, " Speech Monographs 35, pp. 159-165.

Gunnell, Pamela, and Howard M. Rosenfeld
1971 "Distribution of nonverbal responses in a conversational regulation task. " Paper read at Western Psychological Association, San Francisco.

Gunter, Richard
1966 "On the placement of accent in dialogue: a feature of context grammar," Journal of Linguistics 2:2 (October), pp. 159-179.

Gunther, Bernard
1968 Sense Relaxation: Below Your Mind. New York: Collier Books, 191 pages.

Gurnee, Herbert
1934 "An analysis of the perception of intelligence in the face," Journal of Social Psychology 5 (February), pp. 82-90.

Gustason, Gerilee, Donna Pfetzing, and Esther Zawolkow
1972 Signing Exact English. California: Modern Signs Press.

Guttentag, Marcia
1972 "Negro-White differences in children's movement," Perceptual and Motor Skills 35, pp. 435-436.

Guyssens, Eric
1967 La communication et l'articulation linguistique. Brussells, Belgium: Univ. Libre de Bruxelles, Trav. de la Fac. de Philos. et Litt. Tom. 31.

- H -

Haas, Mary R.
1946 "Techniques of intensifying in Thai," Word 2:2 (August), pp. 127-130.

1972 "The expression of the diminutive," in M. Estellie Smith, ed. , Studies in Linguistics: in Honor of George L. Trager. The Hague: Mouton, pp. 148-152.

Haase, Richard F. , and Donald T. Tepper, Jr.
1972 "Nonverbal components of empathic communication," Journal of Counseling Psychology 19:5, pp. 417-424.

Habicht, Werner
1959 Die Gebärde in englischen Dichtungen des Mittelalters. München: Verlag der Bayerischen Akademie der Wissenschaften, 168 pages.

Hackett, Francis
1935 Francis I. New York. [Describes coronation gestures, pp. 139-140: Hayes.]

Hacks, Charles
1892   Le geste. Paris: E. Flammarion, 492 pages. ["A
comprehensive survey of g. types from infant to pathological
from a psychological point of view," p. 102: West.]

Haddon, A. C. , ed.
1907   "The gesture language of the Eastern Islanders," Cambridge Anthropological Expedition to Torres Straits, Reports,
vol. 3, pp. 261-262.

Hadley, Lewis F.
1887   A List of the Primary Gestures in Indian Sign-Talk.
Anadarko, Indian Territory.

1890   A Lesson in Sign Talk. Fort Smith, Arkansas.

1890   Wolf Lame and the White Man, by In-go-nom-pa-shi,
[pseud.]. Fort Smith, Arkansas, 9 pages.

1893   Indian Sign Talk. Chicago: Baker. [Only 75 copies
issued.]

Hagen, Chris, Wyne Porter, and Joyce Brink
1973   "Nonverbal communication: an alternate mode of communication for the child with severe cerebral palsy," Journal
of Speech and Hearing Disorders 38, pp. 448-455.

Haggard, Ernest A. , and Kenneth S. Isaacs
1966   "Micromomentary facial expressions as indicators of
ego mechanisms in psychotherapy," in Louis A. Gottschalk and
Arthur H. Auerbach, eds. , Methods of Research in Psychotherapy. New York: Appleton-Century-Crofts, pp. 154-165.

Haiding, Karl
1955   "Von der Gebärdensprache der Märchenerzähler," Folklore Fellowship Communications. Helsingfors, Finland, Suo-
malainen Tiedeakatemia Academia Scientiarum Fennica, no.
155, 16 pages.

n.d.   Kinderspiel und Volksüberlieferung. München.

Haith, Marshall M.
1966   "A semiautomatic procedure for measuring changes in
position," Journal of Experimental Child Psychology 3, pp. 289-
295.

Hald, P. Tetens
1906   "The nose in literature," The Lancet 1 (January 27),
p. 246.

Haldane, J. B. S.
1955   "Animal communication and the origin of human language," Science Progress 43, pp. 385-401.

254   Bibliography

Haliburton, R. G.
    1863   "New materials for the history of man." Halifax, Nova
    Scotia. [Quoted by Tylor, 1878, p. 238, superstitions con-
    nected with the sneeze.]

Hall, Edward T.
    1949   "The Freudian error as an aid in determining atti-
    tudes," International Journal of Opinion and Attitude Research
    3:1, pp. 113-122.

    1955   "The anthropology of manners," Scientific American
    192:4 (April), pp. 84-90. Reprinted in Alan Dundes, Every
    Man His Way: Readings in Cultural Anthropology. Englewood
    Cliffs, N.J.: Prentice-Hall, 1968, pp. 511-518.

    1959   The Silent Language. New York: Doubleday, 192 pages.

    1960   "The language of space," Landscape (Fall). Reprinted
    in Journal of the American Institute of Architects, (February
    1961).

    1962   "The madding crowd," Landscape (Fall).

    1962   "Our silent language: 'ocultos' speak louder than
    words," Americas 14:2, pp. 5-8.

    1963   "Proxemics--the study of man's spatial relationship,"
    in Iago Galdston, ed., Man's Image in Medicine and Anthro-
    pology. New York: International Universities Press. Re-
    printed in Larry A. Samovar and Richard E. Porter, eds.,
    Intercultural Communication, pp. 205-220.

    1963   "Quality in architecture--an anthropological view," Jour-
    nal of the American Institute of Architects (July).

    1963   "A system for the notation of proxemic behavior,"
    American Anthropologist 65:5 (October), pp. 1003-
    1026.

    1964   "Adumbration as a feature of intercultural communica-
    tion," The Ethnography of Communication (Special Publ.) pp.
    154-163; American Anthropologist 66:6 (part 2), (December),
    ed. John J. Gumperz, and Dell Hymes. Reprinted in Haig A.
    Bosmajian, ed., The Rhetoric of Nonverbal Communication,
    1971.

    1964   "An anthropological view of space: proxemics," Office
    Design (July), pp. 16-20.

    1964   "Silent assumptions in social communication," Disorders
    of Communication, vol. 42, ed. by David McK. Rioch and
    Edwin A. Weinstein. Baltimore: Williams and Wilkins Co.,
    pp. 41-55. Reprinted in Floyd W. Matson, and Ashley Montagu,

eds., The Human Dialogue. New York: The Free Press, 1967, pp. 491-505.

1966 "The anthropology of space," The Architectural Review, No. 835, vol. 142, pp. 163-166.

1966 The Hidden Dimension. New York: Doubleday, 201 pages.

1967 "To each his own: the manpower potential in our ethnic groups," Employment Service Review 4:10 (October), pp. 24-29.

1968 "Human needs and inhuman cities," The Fitness of Man's Environment: Smithsonian Annual II. Washington, D. C., pp. 161-172. Reprinted in Ekistics 27:160 (March 1969).

1968 "Proxemics," Current Anthropology 9:2-3 (April-June), pp. 83-108.

1969 "Listening behavior: some cultural differences," Phi Delta Kappan (March). Reprinted in The Bridge: A Center for the Advancement of Intercultural Studies (Occasional Paper No. 2) (March 1970), pp. 1-8.

1972 "Architectural implications of the thermal qualities of the human skin," Ekistics 33:198 (May), pp. 352-354.

1972 "Art, space, and the human experience," in Gyorgy Kepes, ed., Arts of the Environment. New York: George Braziller, pp. 52-59.

1974 Handbook for Proxemic Research. Washington, D. C.: Studies in the Anthropology of Visual Communication, 124 pages. Review by O. Michael Watson, Reviews in Anthropology 2:4 (November 1975), pp. 515-519.

? "Supuestos implicitos en la comunicación social," in Ricardo Zuñiga B., ed., La influencia social primaria. (Psicología Social 8, Serie Reimpresiones) Valparaiso: Ediciones Universitarias, pp. 9-29.

Hall, Edward, and Mildred
(in press) "The sounds of silence," in Ed Rintye, ed., Centering a Lopsided Egg: Reflections on Communication Balance. Allyn and Bacon.

Hall, Edward T., Jr. and George L. Trager
1953 The Analysis of Culture. Washington, D. C.: American Council of Learned Societies, 62 pages.

Hall, Edward T., and William Foote Whyte
1960 "Intercultural communication: a guide to men of action," Human Organization 19:1 (Spring), pp. 5-12. Reprinted in

Alfred G. Smith, ed. , Communication and Culture: Readings
(Reprint Series in the Social Sciences A-303) Bobbs-Merrill;
and Social Processes in International Relations. New York:
John Wiley, 1968.

Hall, Fernau
1964 "Dance notation and choreology, " British Journal of
Aesthetics (January).

1965 "An alphabet of movement notation, " New Scientist
(October 28).

1966 "Benesh movement notation and choreology, " Dance
Scope (Fall).

1967 "Benesh notation and ethnochoreology, " Journal of Ethnomusicology 11:2 (May), pp. 188-198.

1967 "Institute of choreology, " Ballet Today 1:17 (January-
February), p. 13.

Hall, G. Stanley, and Arthur Allin
1897 "The psychology of tickling, laughing and the comic, "
American Journal of Psychology 9:1 (October), pp. 1-41.

Hallar, M.
1973 "Gestikulationen i comedia del 'arte, " Psykologisk
skriftserie 4.

Halliday, M. A. K.
1967 Intonation and Grammar in British English. The Hague:
Mouton, 61 pages.

Hallowell, A. I.
1942 "Some psychological aspects of measurement among the
Saulteaux, " American Anthropologist 44, pp. 62-78.

Hallpike, C. R.
1969 "Social hair, " Man 4:2 (June), pp. 256-264.

Halpern, Lipman, ed.
1963 Problems of Dynamic Neurology: An International
Volume: Studies on the Higher Functions of the Human Nervous System. Jerusalem: Department of Nervous Diseases
of the Rothschild Hadassah University Hospital and the Hebrew
University Hadassah Medical School, 509 pages.

Halprin, Lawrence
1972 "Notes on a system, " Notebooks: 1959-1971. MIT
Press, pp. 95-104.

Halsman, Philippe
1948 The Frenchman: a Photographic Interview with Fernan-
del. New York: Simon and Schuster.

1959   Jump Book. New York: Simon and Schuster, 94 pages.

Halsman, Philippe see also Salvador Dali

Hamalian, Leo
  1965   "Communication by gesture in the Middle East," ETC.
  22:1 (March), pp. 43-49.

Hamayon, Roberte
  1970   "Façons de s'asseoir," Etudes Mongoles 1, pp. 135-
  141. [Manual gestures.]

  1971   "Protocol manuel," Etudes Mongoles 2, pp. 145-207.

Hamid, Paul N.
  1968   "Style of dress as a perceptual cue in impression formation," Perceptual and Motor Skills 26, pp. 904-906.

Hammes, John A.
  1965   "Judgment of emotional facial expressions as a function
  of manifest anxiety and sex," Perceptual and Motor Skills 17,
  pp. 601-602.

Hamp, Eric P.
  1957   "Stylistically modified allophones in Huichol," Language
  33:2 (April-June), pp. 139-142. [Comments on Grimes' 1955
  article.]

Hanawalt, Nelson G.
  1942   "The role of the upper and lower parts of the face as a
  basis for judging facial expressions: I. In painting and sculpture," Journal of General Psychology 27, pp. 331-346.

  1944   "The role of the upper and the lower parts of the face
  as the basis for judging facial expressions: II. In posed expressions and 'candid camera' pictures," Journal of General
  Psychology 31, pp. 23-36.

Hanley, Theodore D.
  1954   "Time measurements in speech analysis," Report of the
  5th Annual Round Table Meeting on Linguistics and Language
  Teaching, ed. by Hugo J. Mueller. Washington, D.C.:
  Georgetown University Press, pp. 83-97.

Hanna, Jay
  1935   "Sign talk speeds radio drama," Popular Mechanics 63
  (May), pp. 702-704.

Hansen, Marian
  1948   "Children's rhymes accompanied by gestures," Western
  Folklore 7, pp. 50-53.

258   Bibliography

Hargreaves, W. A. and J. A. Starkweather
1964   "Voice quality changes in depression," Language and
        Speech 7, 84-88.

Hargreaves, W. A. , J. A. Starkweather, and K. H. Blacker
1965   "Voice quality in depression," Journal of Abnormal Psy-
        chology 70, pp. 218-220.

Harmon, Leon D.
1973   "The recognition of faces," Scientific American 229:5
        (November), pp. 70-82.

Harms, L. S.
1961   "Listener judgments of status cues in speech," Quarter-
        ly Journal of Speech 47:2, pp. 164-168.

Harrington, John P.
1938   "The American Indian Sign Language" Indians at Work
        (March) Section I, 5:7, pp. 8-15; (July) Section 2, Part 1,
        5:11, pp. 28-32; (August) Section 2, Part 2, pp. 25-30; (Sep-
        tember) 6:1, pp. 24-32; (November) 6:3, pp. 24-29.

1941   "The Indian's greatest invention," in Robert (Gray-Wolf)
        Hofsinde, "Talk-Without-Talk," Natural History 47, pp. 32-
        39.

Harris, Herbert I.
1957   "Telephone anxiety," Journal of the American Psycho-
        analytic Association 5, pp. 342-347.

Harris, Richard M.
1972   "Paralinguistics," Language Sciences 19 (February),
        pp. 8-11.

Harrison, Randall P.
1964   "Pictic analysis: toward a vocabulary and syntax for
        the pictorial code: with research on facial communication."
        Ph.D. Dissertation, Michigan State University. Ann Arbor:
        University Microfilms, no. 65-6079.

1965   "Nonverbal communication: explorations into time,
        space, action, and object," in Dimensions in Communication:
        Readings, ed. by James H. Campbell, and Hal W. Hepler.
        Belmont, Calif. : Wadsworth, pp. 158-174.

1972   "Nonverbal behavior: an approach to human communi-
        cation," in Richard W. Budd, and Brent D. Ruben, eds. ,
        Approaches to Human Communication. New York: Spartan
        Books, pp. 253-268.

1973   "Nonverbal communication," in Handbook of Communica-
        tion, ed. by Ithiel de Sola Pool, et al. Chicago: Rand-
        McNally, pp. 93-115.

1974   Beyond Words: An Introduction to Nonverbal Communication. Englewood Cliffs, N.J.: Prentice-Hall, 210 pages.

Harrison, Randall P. , Akiba A. Cohen, Wayne W. Crouch, B. K.
L. Genova, and Mark Steinberg
1972   "The nonverbal communication literature," Journal of
Communication 22:4 (December), pp. 460-476.

Harrison, Randall P. , and Mark L. Knapp, eds.
1972   The Journal of Communication, "A special issue on nonverbal communication," 22:4 (December).

Harshbarger, H. C.
1925   "The significance of gestures in public speaking. "
Master's thesis, Columbia University.

Hart, Ronald J. , and Bruce L. Brown
1974   "Interpersonal information conveyed by the content and
vocal aspects of speech," Speech Monographs 41:4, pp. 371-
380.

Hartmann, Johann Ludwig
1678   Pastorale Evangelicum. Nuernberg. [Chapter 14 on
prayer gestures: Hayes.]

Harwood, Eliza Josephine
1933   How We Train the Body; The Mechanics of Pantomimic
Technique. Boston: Walter H. Baker, 142 pages.

Haskell, Arnold L.
1960   The Wonderful World of Dance. New York: Garden
City Books, 93 pages.

Hasler, Juan A.
1960   "El lenguaje silbado," La Palabra y el Hombre: Reviste
de la Universidad Veracruzana, no. 15 (Xalapa, Mexico), pp.
23-36.

Hastings, James
1961   "Silence, " Encyclopaedia of Religion and Ethics. New
York: Charles Scribner's Sons, vol. XI, pp. 512-513.

Hastorf, Albert H. , Charles E. Osgood, and Hiroshi Ono
1966   "The semantics of facial expressions and the prediction
of the meanings of stereoscopically fused facial expressions,"
Scandinavian Journal of Psychology 7, pp. 179-188. [Second
of series; I, Osgood; III, Ono, Hastorf, and Osgood.]

Hattwick, M. S.
1932   "A preliminary study of pitch inflection in the speech
of pre-school children, " Proceedings Iowa Academy Science
39, pp. 237-242.

260   Bibliography

Haugen, Einar
    1942   "Baby talk," Norwegian Word Studies, vol. I, part III.
    Mimeo, on deposit, Library of Congress.

Hawkins, P. R.
    1971   "The syntactic location of hesitation pauses," Language
    and Speech 14:3, pp. 277-288.

Hayakawa, S. I.
    1950   Symbol, Status and Personality. New York: Harcourt,
    Brace and World, 188 pages.

Hayes, Alfred S.
    1962   "A tentative schematization for research in the teaching
    of cross-cultural communication," International Journal of
    American Linguistics 28:1, Part II (January), pp. 155-167.

    1964   "Paralinguistics and kinesics: pedagogical perspectives,"
    in Sebeok, et al., eds., Approaches to Semiotics, pp. 145-172.

    1965   "New directions in foreign language teaching," Modern
    Language Journal 49:5 (May), pp. 281-293.

Hayes, Francis C.
    1940   "Should we have a dictionary of gestures?" Southern
    Folklore Quarterly 4, pp. 239-245.

    1941   "Beckoning" American Notes and Queries 1 (December),
    p. 142.

    1942   "Just a gesture," Collier's 109 (January 31), pp. 14-15.
    [Poses by Harpo Marx.]

    1951   "Gestos o ademanes folklóricos," Folklore Americas 11,
    pp. 15-21.

    1957   "Gestures: a working bibliography," Southern Folklore
    Quarterly 21:4 (December), pp. 218-317.

    1959   "Guia para el que recoge ademanes o gestos," Folklore
    Americas 19:1 (June), pp. 1-6.

    1964   "Gesture," Encyclopedia Americana. [Originally in
    1941.]

    1975   "Gesticulation: a plan of classification." Paper read
    at AATSP, Chicago.

Hayes, K. J.
    1968   "Spoken and gestural language learning in chimpanzees."
    Paper read at Psychonomic Society Meetings.

Hayman, David
  1974   "Language of/as gesture in Joyce," in Louis Bonnerot,
  ed., <u>Ulysses: cinquante ans après.</u> Paris: Didier, pp. 209-
  221.

Hayworth, Donald
  1928   "The social origin and function of laughter," <u>Psychologi-</u>
  <u>cal Review</u> 35:5, pp. 367-384.

Hazen, Barry Martin
  1972   "The effects of changing phonetic context on the voiceprint identification technique," <u>Dissertation Abstracts Interna-</u>
  <u>tional</u> 33:1868A-69A. State University of New York, 91 pages.

Hearn, G.
  1957   "Leadership and the spatial factor in small groups,"
  <u>Journal of Abnormal and Social Psychology</u> 104, pp. 269-272.

Hearn, Lafcadio
  1894   "The Japanese smile," in <u>Glimpses of Unfamiliar Japan.</u>
  2 vols. New York. [Quoted in <u>Klineberg, Race Differences,</u>
  page 285.]

Hecaen, Henri
  1967   "Approche sémiotique des troubles du geste," <u>Langages</u>
  5, pp. 67-83.

  1971   "La Sémiotique non-linguistique." [Rev. of Sebeok, et
  al., eds. <u>Approaches to Semiotics</u>], in Julia Kristeva, Josette
  Rey-Debove, and Donna Jean Umiker, eds., <u>Essays in Semi-</u>
  <u>otics.</u> The Hague: Mouton, pp. 519-526.

Hedgepeth, William
  1970   "Growl to me softly and I'll understand," <u>Look</u> 34 (January 13), pp. 46-50.

Heepe, M.
  1920   "Die Trommelsprache der Jaunde in Kamerun," <u>Zeit-</u>
  <u>schrift Für Kolonialsprachen</u> 10, pp. 43-60.

Hegedüs, L.
  1953   "On the problem of the pauses of speech," <u>Acta Lin-</u>
  <u>guistica</u> 3, pp. 1-34.

Heim, Edgar, Peter H. Knapp, Louis Vachon, Gordon G. Globus,
  and S. Joseph Nemetz
  1968   "Emotion, breathing and speech," <u>Journal of Psychoso-</u>
  <u>matic Research</u> 12, pp. 261-274.

Heine-Geldern, Robert T.
  1933   "Trommelsprachen ohne Trommeln," <u>Anthropos</u> 28,
  pp. 485-487.

Heinitz, Wilhelm
    1943   "Probleme der afrikanischen Trommelsprache,"
    Beiträge Zur Kolonialforschung 4, pp. 69-100.

Heller, Morton A.
    1974   "Some observations on passive touch," Dissertation Ab-
    stracts International 35:5156B.

Helmholtz, Hermann L. F.
    1862   On the Sensations of Tone: As a Physiological Basis
    for the Theory of Music. Reprinted by Dover Publications,
    New York, 1954, 576 pages.

Hemsterhuis, Franz
    1793   Vorlesungen über den Ausdruck der verschiedenen
    Leidenschaften durch die Gesichtszüge. Berlin.

Henderson, A. , Frieda Goldman-Eisler, and A. Skarbek
    1965   "The common value of pausing time in spontaneous
    speech," Quarterly Journal of Experimental Psychology 17,
    pp. 343-345.

    1966   "Sequential temporal patterns in spontaneous speech,"
    Language and Speech 9, pp. 207-216.

Henley, Nancy M.
    1972   "The politics of touch," Women: A Journal of Libera-
    tion 3:1, pp. 7-8.

    1973   "Power, sex, and nonverbal communication," Berkeley
    Journal of Sociology 18, pp. 1-26.

    1973   "Status and sex: some touching observations," Bulle-
    tin of the Psychonomic Society 2:2 (August), pp. 91-
    93.

Hennings, Dorothy Grant
    1974   Smiles, Nods, and Pauses; Activities to Enrich Chil-
    dren's Communication Skills. New York: Citation Press, 232
    pages.

Henry, Jules
    1936   "The linguistic expression of emotion," American Anthro-
    pologist 38:2 (April-June), pp. 250-256.

    1965   "White people's time, colored people's time," Trans-
    Action 2:3 (March-April), pp. 31-34.

Henser, Mary I.   [Harvard University]
        "A study of gestures and their meaning in medieval
    art. " Dissertation.

Heraeus, Wilhelm
1904 "Die Sprache der römischen Kinderstube," Archiv für Lateinische Lexikographie 13, pp. 149-172. Reprinted in Kleine Schriften von Wilhelm Heraeus, ed. by J. B. Hoffmann. Heidelberg: Carl Winters, 1937, pp. 158-180.

Herrgot
1726   Vetus Disciplina Monastica.   Paris.

Hertweck, E. R.
1966 "Semantic differential ratings of counselor nonverbal and verbal communication." Thesis, Arizona State University.

Hertz, Robert
1909   La Prééminence de la main droite: étude sur la polarité religieuse. In R. Needham and C. Needham, Robert Hertz: Death and the Right Hand. London, 1960. Translation of essays in Mélange de la sociologie religieuse et folklore. Paris, 1928.

Herzog, George
1934 "Speech-melody and primitive music," Musical Quarterly 20:4 (October), pp. 452-466. Abstract in Africa 8 (1935), pp. 375-377.

1945 "Drum signaling in a West African tribe," Word 1:3 (December), pp. 217-238. Reprinted in Dell Hymes, ed., Language in Culture and Society, 1964, pp. 312-323.

1949 "Linguistic approaches to personality," in Stephen Stansfeld Sargent and Marian W. Smith, eds., Culture and Personality. New York: Wenner-Gren Foundation for Anthropological Research, pp. 93-102.

Heshka, Stanley, and Yona Nelson
1972 "Interpersonal speaking distance as a function of age, sex, and relationship," Sociometry 35, pp. 491-98.

Heslin, Richard, and Diane Boss [Purdue University]
ca. 1975 "Nonverbal boundary behavior at the airport."

Hess, Eckhard H.
1958 " 'Imprinting' in animals," Scientific American 198:3 (March), pp. 81-90.

1959 "Imprinting," Science 130, pp. 133-141.

1965 "Attitude and pupil size," Scientific American 212 (April), pp. 46-54.

1966 "Changes in pupil size as a measure of taste difference," Perceptual and Motor Skills 23:2, pp. 451-455.

1968   "Pupillometric assessment," in Research in Psychotherapy. Vol. III, edited by J. M. Schlien. Washington, D.C.:
American Psychological Association, pp. 573-583.

1973   Imprinting: Early Experience and the Developmental
Psychobiology of Attachment. New York: Van Nostrand Reinhold.

1975   "The role of pupil size in communication," Scientific
American 233:5 (November), pp. 110-119.

Hess, Eckhard H., and James M. Polt
1960   "Pupil size as related to interest value of visual stimuli," Science 132 (August), pp. 349-350.

Hess, Eckhard H., A. L. Seltzer, and J. M. Shlien
1965   "Pupil response of hetero and homosexual males to pictures of men and women: a pilot study," Journal of Abnormal
Psychology 70:3, pp. 165-168.

Hewes, Gordon W.
1953   "The one-leg resting position," Man 53 (November),
Article No. 280, p. 180.

1955   "World distribution of certain postural habits," American Anthropology 57:2 (Part 1), (April), pp. 231-244.

1957   "The anthropology of posture," Scientific American
196:2 (February), pp. 123-132.

1966   "The domain posture," Anthropological Linguistics 8
(November), pp. 106-112.

1970   "New light on the gestural origin of language." Paper
read at the American Anthropological Association, San Diego,
10 pages.

1973   "An explicit formulation of the relationship between
tool-using, tool-making, and the emergence of language,"
Visible Language 7:2 (Spring), pp. 101-127.

1973   "Primate communication and the gestural origin of
language," Current Anthropology 14:1-2 (February-April), pp. 5-
24.

1974   "Gesture language in cultural contact," Sign Language
Studies 4, pp. 1-34.

1975   Language Origins: A Bibliography. (Approaches to
Semiotics 44) The Hague: Mouton, 890 pages.

1975   "The current status of the gestural theory of language
origin." MS.

Hiat, Alice B.
  1971   "Explorations in personal space," Dissertation Abstracts
  International 31:7572B.

Hicks, Clifford B.
  1965   "Your mysterious nose," Today's Health 43 (October),
  pp. 35-37, 89.

Higgins, Dan D.
  1942   How to Talk to the Deaf; the Language of Gestures, Expression, Impersonation, Pantomime or Acting, Used by All
  Peoples in All Ages and Everywhere.   Chicago: J. S. Paluch,
  91 pages.

Hildebrand
  1869   "Die Sitte des Hutabnehmens," Germania 14, pp. 125-
  128.   [Miscellen, by Ludwig Bossler.]

Hill, Archibald A.
  1955   "Linguistics since Bloomfield," Quarterly Journal of
  Speech 41 (October), pp. 253-260.   Reprinted in Harold B.
  Allen, ed., Readings in Applied English Linguistics.   New
  York: Appleton-Century-Crofts, 1958, pp. 14-23.

  1958   Introduction to Linguistic Structures: From Sound to
  Sentence in English.   New York: Harcourt, Brace and Co.,
  pp. 408-409.

Hill, Jane H.
  1972   "On the evolutionary foundations of language," American
  Anthropology 74:3 (June), pp. 308-317.

Hinchliffe, Mary K., M. Lancashire, and F. J. Roberts
  1971   "Depression: defence mechanisms in speech," British
  Journal of Psychiatry 118:545, pp. 471-472.

  1971   "A study of eye contact changes in depressed and re-
  covered psychiatric patients," British Journal of Psychiatry
  119:549, pp. 213-215.

Hinde, Robert A., ed.
  1972   Non-Verbal Communication.   Cambridge University
  Press, 443 pages.   Reviews by Edward O. Wilson, Science
  176 (May), pp. 625-627; Georges Mounin, Journal of Linguistics
  10:1 (February 1974), pp. 201-206.

Hindmarch, Ian
  1973   "Eyes, eye-spots and pupil dilation in nonverbal communication," in Social Communication and Movement, ed. by
  von Cranach and Ian Vine.   London/New York: Academic
  Press, pp. 299-321.

Hinds, John [Seishin Joshi Daigaku, Tokyo]
    "Non-verbal modalities of communication."

Hirsch, P.
    1923   Die Gebärdensprachen des Hörenden und ihre Stellung
    zur Lautsprache. Charlottenburg.

Hirsh, Ira J.
    1967   "Information processing in input channels for speech
    and language: the significance of serial order of stimuli," in
    Brain Mechanisms Underlying Speech and Language, eds.
    Clark H. Millikan, and F. L. Darley. New York: Grune and
    Stratton, pp. 21-38.

Hjortsjö, Carl Herman
    1970   Man's Face and Mimic Language. Lund: Student
    Literatuer.

Hobbs, William
    1967   Stage Fight: Swords, Firearms, Fisticuffs and Slap-
    stick. New York: Theatre Arts Books, 96 pages.

Hobson, G. N., K. T. Strongman, D. Bull, G. Craig
    1973   "Anxiety and gaze aversion in dyadic encounters,"
    British Journal of Social and Clinical Psychology 12:2, pp. 122-
    129.

Hochberg, Julian, and Ruth Ellen Galper
    1967   "Recognition of faces: I, An exploratory study," Psy-
    chonomic Science 9, pp. 619-620.

Hockett, Charles F.
    1950   "Peiping morphophonemics," Language 26, pp. 63-85.
    [Fast and slow speech in Chinese, page 75.]

    1957   "How to learn Martian," Coming Attractions. (Adven-
    tures in Science Fiction Series, ed. by Martin Greenberg)
    New York: Gnome Press, pp. 38-51.

    1958   "Ethnolinguistic implications of studies in linguistics
    and psychiatry," Report of the Ninth Annual Round Table Meet
    ing on Linguistics and Language Study 11-12 (Georgetown Uni-
    versity) (April), pp. 175-193.

    1960   "The origin of speech," Scientific American 203:3
    (September), pp. 89-96.

Hodder, Margaret George [Claremont Graduate School]
    1971   "Strategems in establishing Right-to-Speak in interac-
    tion situations: an observational study of one facet of social
    structure as rule-governed behavior." MS.

Hodgson, Kenneth W.
1953   The Deaf and Their Problems: A Study in Special Education. London: Watts, 364 pages.

Hoffer, A. , and H. Osmond
1962   "Olfactory changes in schizophrenia, " American Journal of Psychiatry 119, pp. 72-75.

Hoffman, M.
1965   "The effects of training on the judgment of non-verbal behavior. " Dissertation, Harvard University.

Hoffman, S. P.
1968   "An empirical study of representational hand movements. " Dissertation, New York University.

Hoffman, Walter James
1895   The Beginnings of Writing. New York.   [Chap. VI, "Gesture signs and attitudes": Hayes.]

Hoffman-Krayer, Eduard, and H. Bächtold-Stäubli
1927   Handwörterbuch des deutschen Aberglaubens. Berlin and Leipzig. [Vol. 3, pp. 327-338, under Gebärde, see Gebet, Kreuzzeichen, Feige, Eid, etc. Vol. 10 contains Index: Hayes.]

Hofsinde, Robert (Gray-Wolf)
1941   "Talk-without-talk, " Natural History 47, pp. 32-39. [Pictures posed by the author.] Includes "The Indian's greatest invention, " by John P. Harrington, BAE, Smithsonian.

1956   Indian Sign Language. New York: Morrow Junior Books, 96 pages. [Indian sign language for boys.]

Hogan, Peter, and Ian Alger
1969   "The impact of videotape recordings on insight in group psychotherapy, " International Journal of Group Psychotherapy 19:2 (April), pp. 158-164.

Hogben, Lancelot
1952   "Astraglossa: or first steps in celestial syntax, " Journal British Interplanetary Society 11:6 (November), pp. 258-274.

Holder, William [1616-1698]
1669   Elements of Speech: an Essay of Inquiry into the Natural Production of Letters, with an Appendix Concerning Persons Deaf and Dumb. Reprinted, Menston, England: The Scolar Press, 1967, pp. 151-153.

Höllerer, Walter
1975   "World of language as example, " VS: Quaderni di Studi Semiotici 10, pp. 78-85. [Commentary on the exposition, "Welt aus Sprache, " Academy of Arts, Berlin.]

Holm, A.
1972   "The Danish mouth-hand system," Teacher of the Deaf
70, pp. 486-490.

Holmes, Thomas H., Helen Goodell, S. Wolf, and H. Wolff
1950   The Nose: an Experimental Study of Reactions within
the Nose in Human Subjects during Varying Life Experiences.
Springfield, Ill.: Thomas, 154 pages.

Holzkapp, K.
1956   "Ausducksverstehen an Phanomen, Funktion und Leis-
tung," Journal of Psychological Psychotherapy 4, pp. 297-323.

Holzman, Phillip S.
1969   "On hearing and seeing oneself," Journal of Nervous and
Mental Disease 148, pp. 198-209.

Hong, Woong Sun
1967   "Interrelationships among selected verbal and nonverbal
communication activities of third- and fourth-grade teachers in
socially, economically or ethnically different schools." Thesis,
University of Washington.

Honikman, Beatrice
1964   "Articulatory settings," in David Abercrombie, et al.,
eds., In Honour of Daniel Jones. London: Longmans, pp. 73-
84.

Honkavaara, Sylvia
1961   "The psychology of expression: dimensions in human
perception," British Journal of Psychology, Monograph Supplement, No. 32, 96 pages.

Hooton, E. A.
1925   "Whistling language," The Ancient Inhabitants of the
Canary Islands. (Harvard African Studies 7), pp. 61-63.

Hopkins, E. Washburn
1907   "The sniff-kiss in ancient India," Journal of the American Oriental Society 28, pp. 120-134 [Kiss/lick/taste/touch/
stroke/sniff/smell/breathe in.]

Hoppál, Mihály
1972   "Gesztus-kommunikáció," Altalános Nyelvészeti Tanu-
lmányok 8, pp. 71-84.

Hoppe, Ruth
1937   "Die romanische Geste im Rolandslied," Schriften der
Albertus Magnus Universität 10 (Königsberg), 184 pages.

Hore, Terry
1970   "Social class differences in some aspects of the nonverbal communication between mother and preschool child,"
Australian Journal of Psychology 22:1, pp. 21-27.

Horetsky, O.
1966   "Pantomime in group psychotherapy," International Journal of Sociometry and Sociatry, vol. 1.

Horner, A. Musgrave
1970   Movement, Voice and Speech. London: Methuen, 142 pages.

Horowitz, Mardi J.
1965   "Human spatial behavior," American Journal of Psychotherapy 19:1 (January), pp. 20-28. [Nonverbal communication in group psychotherapy.]

Horowitz, Mardi J., D. F. Duff, and L. O. Stratton
1964   "Body--buffer zone: exploration of personal space," Archives of General Psychiatry 11, pp. 651-656.

Horton, David L., and James J. Jenkins, eds.
1971   Perception of Language. Columbus, Ohio: Charles E. Merrill, 267 pages.

Horton, John
1967   "Time and cool people," Trans-Action (April), pp. 5-12. Reprinted in Lee Rainwater, ed., Black Experience: Soul. Aldine Publishing Co., 1970, pp. 31-50.

Houde
        A Study of Tongue Body Motion During Selected Speech Sounds. Speech Communications Research Lab, No. 2. Santa Barbara.

Howard, Jane
1970   Please Touch: A Guided Tour of the Human Potential Movement. New York: Dell, 271 pages.

Howell, Richard
1968   "Linguistic choice and levels of social change," American Anthropologist 70, pp. 553-559.

Howell, Richard W., and Harold J. Vetter
1969   "Hesitation in the production of speech," Journal of General Psychology 81, pp. 261-276.

Howell, Richard W., and Harold J. Vetter
1975   Language in Behavior. New York: Human Sciences Press, Behavioral Publications.

Howitt, Alfred W.
1890-91 "Note on the use of gesture language in Australian tribes," (Proceedings) Australian and New Zealand Association for the Advancement of Science 2, pp. 637-646.

1904   "Messengers and message sticks--Barter and trade
centers--Gesture language. " The Native Tribes of South-East
Australia. London; New York: Macmillan, chap. XI, pp.
678-735.

Huber, Ernst
1931   Evolution of Facial Musculature and Facial Expression.
Baltimore: Johns Hopkins Press, 184 pages. Reprinted, New
York: Arno Press, 1972, as Evolution of Facial Expression:
Two Accounts. [Includes R. J. Andrew.]

Hughes, Henry
1900   Die Mimik des Menschen auf grund voluntarischer Psychologie. Frankfurt: J. Alt, 423 pages.

Hughes, Russell Meriweather [La Meri]
1941   The Gesture Language of the Hindu Dance. New York:
B. Blom, 1964.

1948   Spanish Dancing. New York: A. S. Barnes, 188 pages.
Reprinted Pittsfield, Mass. : Eagle Printing and Binding Co. ,
1967, 157 pages. [Bracero, arm postures, and gestures:
Hayes.]

Hughey, Jim D. , and Arlee W. Johnson
1975   Speech Communication. New York: Macmillan. Chapter 11 "Nonverbal outputting. "

Hulin, Wilbur S. , and Daniel Katz
1935   "The Frois-Wittmann pictures of facial expression, "
Journal of Experimental Psychology 18 (August), pp. 482-498.
[See also Frois-Wittmann.]

Hulstaert, Gustaaf
1935   "Notes sur les instruments de musique à l'Equateur, "
Congo.

1935   "De telefoon der Nkundo (Belgische Kongo), " Anthropos
30, pp. 655-668.

Humphrey, Doris
1959   The Art of Making Dances. New York: Rinehart and
Company, 189 pages; New York: Grove Press, 1962.

Humphries, David A.
1970   "Ethology and linguistic communication, " Technology and
Society 6:1, pp. 27-33.

Hunt, Valerie
1964   "Movement behavior: a model for action, " Quest 2:1
(April), pp. 69-91.

1968   "The biological organization of man to move, " Impulse

1968: Dance, A Projection for the Future.   San Francisco:
Impulse Publications, pp. 51-63.

Huntley, C. W.
1940   "Judgments of self based upon records of expressive
behavior," Journal of Abnormal and Social Psychology 35:3,
pp. 398-427.

Hurley, William M.
1968   "The Kickapoo whistle system: a speech surrogate,"
Plains Anthropologist 13, pp. 242-247.

Hutcheson, Smith
1935   The Elements of the Universal Sign Language and U.S.L.
Phonetic Alphabet, and St. John's Gospel in Interlinear of English and Universal Sign Language.   Toronto: University of
Toronto Press, 122 pages.

Hutchinson, Ann
1954   Labanotation: The System for Recording Movement.
New York: Theatre Arts Books, 274 pages.   Revised, 1970,
528 pages.

1965   "Dance notation," Encyclopaedia Britannica 7, pp. 41-42.

Hutt, Clelia
1968   "Étude d'un corpus: dictionnaire du langage gestuel
chez les trappistes," Langages 10, special issue, pp. 107-118.

Hutt, Corrinne, and Ounsted, C.
1966   "A behavioural and electroencephalographic study of
autistic children," Journal of Psychiatric Research 3, pp. 181-
197.

1966   "The biological significance of gaze aversion, with particular reference to the syndrome of infantile autism," Behavioral Science 11, pp. 346-356.

Hutt, Sidney John, and Corrinne Hutt
1970   Direct Observation and Measurement of Behavior.
Springfield, Ill.:   Charles C. Thomas.

Huttar, George L.
1967   "An experimental study of some relations between the
emotions and the prosodic parameters of speech," Dissertation
Abstracts 28, 2665A-66A.   University of Michigan, 202 pages.

1967   Some Relations Between Emotions and the Prosodic
Parameters of Speech.   Santa Barbara, California: Speech
Communications Research Laboratory.

1968   "Relations between prosodic variables and emotions in
normal American English utterances," Journal of Speech and
Hearing Research 11, pp. 418-487.

Hutton, J. H.
    1950   "Pygmaeogeranomachia and Nilotenstellung," Man 50,
    No. 216 (September), p. 132. [In answer to Fagg's review of
    Lindblom.]

Huxley, Aldous
    1945   "Silence," The Perennial Philosophy. New York:
    Harper, pp. 216-219.

Hymes, Dell H.
    1961   "Functions of speech: an evolutionary approach," in
    Anthropology and Education, ed. by Frederick Gruber. Uni-
    versity of Pennsylvania Press, pp. 55-83. Bobbs-Merrill re-
    print, No. A-124.

    1961   "Linguistic aspects of cross-cultural personality study,"
    in Bert Kaplan, ed., Studying Personality Cross-Culturally.
    New York: Row, Peterson and Co., chap. 10, pp. 313-359.
    Partially reprinted as "The functions of speech," in John P.
    De Cecco, The Psychology of Language, Thought, and Instruc-
    tion. New York: Holt, Rinehart and Winston, 1967, pp. 78-
    84; condensed in Norman N. Markel, Psycholinguistics.
    Homewood, Ill.: Dorsey Press, 1969, pp. 285-317.

    1962   "The ethnography of speaking," in Thomas Gladwin,
    and William C. Sturtevant, eds., Anthropology and Human Be-
    havior. The Anthropological Society of Washington, D.C., pp.
    13-53. Reprinted in Joshua A. Fishman, ed., Readings in the
    Sociology of Language. The Hague: Mouton, 1968, pp. 99-
    138.

    1964   Language in Culture and Society: A Reader in Linguis-
    tics and Anthropology. New York: Harper and Row, 764 pages.

                                - I -

Ikegami, Yoshihiko
    1971   "A stratificational analysis of the hand gestures in In-
    dian classical dancing," Semiotica 4, pp. 365-391.

Illingworth, R. S.
    1955   "Crying in infants and children," British Medical Jour-
    nal 1, pp. 75ff.

Illyés, Sándor
    1972   "A jelnyelvvel történő képlerrás néhány gondolkodás-
    lélektani vonása," Magyar Pszichológiai Szemle 29:1, pp. 21-
    25.

Ingram, David
    1971   "Transitivity in child language," Language 47:4 (Decem-
    ber), pp. 888-910.

Ingram, Robert [Detroit Hearing and Speech Center]
1973   "A model of sociolinguistic variation in sign language forms." Paper read at Linguistic Society of America, Michigan.

1974   "A communication model of the interpreting process," Journal of Rehabilitation of the Deaf (January).

Inui, T.
1937   "On the temporal structure in the judgment of facial expression," Japanese Journal of Psychology 12, pp. 465-482.

Irizawa, Tatsukichi
1920-21   "Nihonjin no suwari-kata ni tsuite," Shigaku-zasshi 31:8. [Asiatic sitting postures: Hewes.]

Irwin, Francis W.
1932   "Thresholds for the perception of difference in facial expression and its elements," American Journal of Psychology 44:1, pp. 1-17.

Irwin, Orvis C.
1941   "Research on speech sounds for the first six months of life," Psychological Bulletin 38:5 (May), pp. 277-285.

1947   "Development of speech during infancy: curve of phonemic frequencies," Journal of Experimental Psychology 37:2, pp. 187-193.

1947   "Infant speech: consonantal sounds according to place of articulation," Journal of Speech Disorders 12, pp. 397-401.

1957   "Phonetical description of speech development in childhood," in L. Kaiser, ed., Manual of Phonetics. Amsterdam: North-Holland Publishing Company, chap. 26, pp. 403-425.

Irwin, Orvis C., and Han Piao Chen
1941   "A reliability study of speech sounds observed in the crying of newborn infants," Child Development 12, pp. 351-368.

1946   "Development of speech during infancy: curve of phonemic types," Journal of Experimental Psychology 36, pp. 431-436.

Isačenko, A. V., and H. J. Schädlich
1970   A Model of Standard German Intonation. The Hague: Mouton, 80 pages.

Ishii, Satoshi
1973   "Characteristics of Japanese nonverbal communicative behavior," Journal of the Communication Association of the Pacific 2:3, University of Hawaii.

Island, D. D.
    1966   "The development and analysis of categories of non-
    verbal behavior of counselors in filmed interviews." Thesis,
    University of Minnesota.

Izard, Carroll E.
    1968   "Cross-cultural research findings on development in
    recognition of facial behavior," Proceedings of the 76th Annual
    Convention of the American Psychological Association 3, p. 727.

    1968   "The emotions and emotion constructs in personality and
    culture research," in R. D. Cattell, ed., Handbook of Modern
    Personality Theory. Chicago: Aldine.

    1971   The Face of Emotion. New York: Appleton-Century-
    Crofts, 468 pages.

                                - J -

Jablonko, Allison P.
    1968   "Dance and daily activities among the Maring people of
    New Guinea: a cinematographic analysis of body movement
    style." Dissertation Abstracts 29, B 3594, B-95 B. Columbia
    University. Microfilm 69-3077.

Jackson, C. V.
    1954   "The influence of previous movement and posture on sub-
    sequent posture," Quarterly Journal of Experimental Psychology
    6:2, pp. 72-78.

Jacobson, Edith
    1946   "The child's laughter," The Psychoanalytic Study of the
    Child 2. New York: International Universities Press, pp. 39-
    60.

Jaeger, E.
    1942   "An Indian V," Nature Magazine (November), p. 469.

Jaffe, Joseph, and Stanley Feldstein
    1970   Rhythms of Dialogue. New York: Academic Press,
    156 pages.

Jaffe, Joseph, Stanley Feldstein and L. Cassota
    1967   "A stochastic model of speaker switching in natural dia-
    logue," in Kurt Salzinger and Suzanne Salzinger, eds., Re-
    search in Verbal Behavior and Some Neurophysiological Impli-
    cations. New York: Academic Press, pp. 281-294.

Jaffe, Joseph, Daniel N. Stern and J. Craig Peery
    1973   " 'Conversational' coupling of gaze behavior in prelin-
    guistic human development," Journal of Psycholinguistic Re-
    search 2, pp. 321-329.

Jakobson, Roman
1960   "Closing statement: linguistics and poetics," in Thomas
A. Sebeok, ed. , Style in Language. Massachusetts Institute of
Technology Press, 1966, pp. 350-377.

1962   "Why 'mama' and 'papa'?" in Selected Writings, vol. 1.
The Hague: Mouton, pp. 538-545.

1964   "On visual and auditory signs," Phonetica 11, pp. 216-
220.

1967   "About the relation between visual and auditory signs,"
in Weiant Wathen-Dunn, ed. , Models for the Perception of
Speech and Visual Form. Proceedings of a Symposium, 1964.
Cambridge: Massachusetts Institute of Technology, pp. 1-7.

1970   "Linguistics," in Main Trends of Research in the Social
and Human Sciences: Part One: Social Sciences. The Hague:
Mouton, chap. 6, pp. 419-463.

1971   'Da i net v mimike," in Selected Writings, II: Word
and Language. The Hague: Mouton, pp. 360-365. [Gestures
for yes and no.]

1971   'I am a linguist: nothing in language is alien to me,"
Brown: Alumni Monthly 71:4 (January), pp. 13-17. [A series
of photographs of Jakobson's gestures while lecturing.]

1972   "Motor signs for 'yes' and 'no'," Language in Society
1:1 (April), pp. 91-96.

James, William
1890   The Principles of Psychology. New York: H. Holt,
1950. [Chapter 23, the production of movement: Hayes.]

James, William T.
1932   "A study of the expression of bodily posture," Journal
of General Psychology 7, pp. 405-437.

Janet, Pierre
1936 L'intelligence avant le langage. Paris, pp. 102-104,
202-211, 228.

Jaquith, James R.
1967   "Toward a typology of formal communicative behavior:
glossolalia," Anthropological Linguistics 9:8, pp. 1-8.

Jarcho, Julius
1934   Postures and Practices during Labor among Primitive
Peoples. New York: Paul B. Hoeber.

Jarden, Ellen, and Samuel W. Fernberger
1926   "The effect of suggestion on the judgment of facial

expression of emotion," American Journal of Psychology 37
(October), pp. 565-570. [Continued experiment with Piderit
model.]

Jaspan, M. A.
1967 "Symbols at work: aspects of kinetic and mnemonic
representation in Redjang ritual," Bijdragen tot de Taal-,
Land- en Volkekunde 123, pp. 476-516.

Jassem, Wiktor, and L. Frackowiak
1968 "Czestotliwości formantów jako cechy osobnicze głosu
ludzkiego," Biuletyn Polskiego Towarzystwa Jezykoznawczego
26, pp. 67-99. [Formant frequencies as special characteristics of human voice.]

Jay, Leticia
1957 "A stick-man notation," Danse Observer 24:1 (January),
pp. 7-8.

Jay, Phyllis C., ed.
1968 Primates: Studies in Adaptation and Variability. New
York: Holt, Rinehart and Winston, 529 pages.

Jecker, J. D., N. Maccoby, and H. S. Breitrose
1965 "Improving accuracy in interpreting nonverbal cues of
comprehension," Psychology in the Schools 2, pp. 239-244.

Jefferson, Gail
1973 "A case of precision timing in ordinary conversation:
overlapped tag-positioned address terms in closing sequences,"
Semiotica 9, pp. 47-96.

Jelgerhuis, Johannes
1827 Theoretische lessen over de gesticulatie en mimiek,
gegeven aan de kweekelingen van het fonds ter opleiding en
onderrichting van tooneel-kunstenaars aan den stads schouwburg
te Amsterdam. Amsterdam: P. M. Warnars.

Jelliffe, Smith E.
1940 "The Parkinsonian body posture: some considerations
in unconscious hostility," Psychoanalytic Review 27, pp. 467-
479.

Jenness, Arthur
1932 "Differences in the recognition of facial expression of
emotion," Journal of General Psychology 7:1 (July), pp. 192-
196.

1932 "The effects of coaching subjects in the recognition of
facial expressions," Journal of General Psychology 7 (July),
pp. 163-178. [A repetition of Allport's experiment, criticism
of conclusions: Hayes.]

1932   "The recognition of facial expressions of emotion,"
Psychological Bulletin 29, pp. 324-350.

Jensen, J. Vernon
1973   "Communicative functions of silence," ETC. 30 (September), pp. 249-257.

Jensen, Martin Kloster
1958   "Recognition of word tones in whispered speech," Word
14:2-3, pp. 187-196. [Norwegian, Swedish, Slovenian, Chinese
(Mandarin); cf. Miller on Vietnamese.]

Jepson, Stanley
1970   'India says it with signs," The Rotarian 117:5 (November), p. 30.

Jespersen, Otto
1921   Language: Its Nature, Development and Origin. New
York: W. W. Norton, 1964 reprint.

Jóhannesson, Alexander
1952   Gestural Origin of Language. Reykjavik and Oxford,
234 pages.

1963   The Third State in the Creation of Human Language.
Oxford: B. H. Blackwell, 134 pages.

Johnson, David L.
1973   "A report of a study of teacher and student classroom
interaction and student-in-classroom verbal creativity," Classroom Interaction Newsletter, Philadelphia, Pennsylvania, (December).

Johnson, Donald Barton
1970   "Verbs of body position in Russian," The Slavic and
East European Journal 14:4 (Winter), pp. 423-435. [Sit/set,
lie/lay, stand, hang.]

Johnson, H. G.
       "A classification schema for the function of gestures in
an interaction. "

Johnson, Kenneth R.
1971   "Black kinesics: some non-verbal communication patterns in the Black culture," The Florida Foreign Language Reporter 9:1-2 (Spring/Fall), pp. 17-20, 57. Reprinted in Larry
A. Samovar, and Richard E. Porter, eds., Intercultural Communication: A Reader, pp. 181-189.

Johnson, Pam
1976   "The use of para-linguistic features in the teaching of
Spanish to English speakers," The Informant 8:2 (Winter), pp.
1-8. [Newsletter, Dept. of Linguistics, Western Michigan
University.]

Johnson, Robinson (Whirling Thunder), Winnebago
    1930   "Some 200 signs used effectively in Indian sign langu-
    age," The American Indian 4:4 (January), p. 14.

Jones, Frank P., and John A. Hanson
    1961   "Time-space pattern in gross body movement," Perpet-
    ual and Motor Skills 12, pp. 35-41.

Jones, Harold E.
    1950   "The study of patterns of emotional expression," in
    Feelings and Emotions ed. by M. L. Reymert. New York:
    McGraw-Hill, pp. 161-168.

Jones, Harry
    1968   Sign Language. (Teach Yourself Books) London: Eng-
    lish Universities Press, 180 pages.

Jones, Hugh Percy, ed.
    1925   Dictionary of Foreign Phrases and Classical Quotations.
    Edinburgh: J. Grant, 93 pages. Revised, 1908, 532 pages.
    [Pollice verso, thumbs down.]

Jones, Marshall R.
    1943   "Studies in 'nervous' movements: I, The effect of men-
    tal arithmetic on the frequency and patterning of movements,"
    Journal of General Psychology 29, pp. 47-62.

    1943   "Studies in 'nervous' movements: II, The effect of in-
    hibition of micturition on the frequency and patterning of move-
    ments," The Journal of General Psychology 29, pp. 303-312.

Jones, Nicholas G. Blurton
    1967   "An ethological study of some aspects of social be-
    haviour of children in nursery school," in Desmond Morris,
    ed., Primate Ethology. London: Weidenfeld and Nicolson;
    Chicago: Aldine Publishing Company, pp. 347-368.

    1971   "Criteria for use in describing facial expressions,"
    Human Biology 43:3 (September), pp. 365-413.

    1972   Ethological Studies of Child Behaviour. London: Cam-
    bridge University Press, 400 pages.

    1972   "Non-verbal communication in children," in R. A. Hinde,
    ed., Non-Verbal Communication. Cambridge University Press,
    chap. 10, pp. 271-296.

Jones, Nicholas G. Blurton, and Gill M. Leach
    1972   "Behaviour of children and their mothers at separation
    and greeting," in Nicholas G. Blurton Jones, ed., Ethological
    Studies of Child Behaviour. London: Cambridge University
    Press, pp. 217-247.

Jones

1971   "A comparative proxemics analysis of dyadic interaction in selected subcultures of New York City," Journal of
Social Psychology 84, pp. 35-44.

Jones, Stanley E., and John R. Aiello
1973   "Proxemic behavior of black and white first-, third-,
and fifth-grade children," Journal of Personality and Social
Psychology 25:1, pp. 21-27.

Jordan, Irving K.
1973   "The referential communication of facial characteristics by deaf and normal-hearing adolescents," Dissertation
Abstracts 34, 4083 B-84B. University of Tennessee, 67 pages.

Jorio, Andrea De
1832   La mimica degli antichi investigata nel gestire Napole-
tano. Naples, 384 pages. [21 plates--some colored aquatints.]

Joseph, Bertram Leon
1952   Elizabethan Acting. London: Oxford University Press,
156 pages.

Josephs, Herbert
1969   Diderot's Dialogue of Language and Gesture. Ohio
State University Press, 228 pages.

Jourard, Sidney M.
1966   "An exploratory study of body-accessibility," British
Journal of Social and Clinical Psychology 5, pp. 221-231.

1971   Self-Disclosure: an Experimental Analysis of the
'Transparent Self'. New York: Wiley-Interscience, 248 pages.

Jourard, Sidney M., and Jane E. Rubin
1968   "Self-disclosure and touching: a study of two modes of
interpersonal encounter and their inter-relation," Journal of
Humanistic Psychology 8:1 (Spring), pp. 39-48.

Jousse, Marcel
1925   "Études de psychologie linguistique: le style oral,
rythmique et mnémotechnique chez les verbo-moteurs,"
Archives de philosophie 2:4. Paris: G. Beauchesne, 240 pages.

1936   "Le mimisme humain et l'anthropologie du langage,"
Revue Anthropologique 7-9 (July-September), pp. 201-215.

Jucker, Ines
1956   Der Gestus des Aposkopein: ein Beitrag zur Gebärdensprache in der antiken Kunst. Zurich: Juris-Verlag, 136 pages.

Justine, Florence
1932   "A genetic study of laughter-provoking stimuli," Child
Development 3, pp. 114-136.

- K -

K. , W.
1971   'Ingressive speech reported in Newfoundland 'Mummer-
talk', " Regional Language Studies 3 (January), St. Johns:
Memorial University of Newfoundland, p. 24.

Kaeppler, Adrienne L.
1967   "The structure of Tongan dance, " Dissertation Abstracts
28, 1772B. University of Hawaii.

1972   "Method and theory in analyzing dance structure with
an analysis of Tongan dance, " Ethnomusicology 16:2 (May),
pp. 173-217.

Kagan, Jerome
1965   "The growth of the 'face' schema: theoretical significance and methodological issues. " Paper read at the American Psychological Association, Chicago.

1970   "A sexual dimorphism in vocal behavior in infants, "
in Norman Kretchmer, and Dwain N. Walcher, eds. , Environmental Influences on Genetic Expression: Biological and Behavioral Aspects of Sexual Differentiation (A Symposium).
Washington, D. C. : Superintendent of Documents, pp. 155-169.

1972   'Do infants think?" Scientific American (March), pp. 74-
82.

Kagan, Jerome, B. Henker, A. Hen-Tov, J. Levine, and M. Lewis
1966   'Infant's differential reactions to familiar and distorted
faces, " Child Development 37, pp. 519-532.

Kagan, Jerome, and M. Lewis
1965   "Studies of attention in the human infant, " Merrill-
Palmer Quarterly 11, pp. 95-127.

Kahn, Malcom
1970   'Non-verbal communication and marital satisfaction, "
Family Process 9:4, pp. 449-456.

Kaiser, L. , ed.
1957   Manual of Phonetics.   Amsterdam: North-Holland Pub.
Co. , 460 pages.

Kakumasu, Jim
1968   "Urubú sign language, " International Journal of American Linguistics 34:4 (October), pp. 275-281.

Kalisch, Beth
1970   "A study of non-verbal interaction in the classroom, "
Developmental Center for Autistic Children, 120 North 48th
St. , Philadelphia, Pa. 19139.

Kalmus, Hans
1958   "The chemical senses," Scientific American 198 (May),
pp. 97-106.

Kalmus, Hans, and S. J. Hubbard
1960   The Chemical Senses in Health and Disease.   Springfield, Ill.: Thomas, 95 pages.

Kalogerakis, M. G.
1963   "The role of olfaction in sexual development," Psychosomatic Medicine 25, pp. 420.

Kamin, Sally, comp.
1954   "Check list of books on dance notation from the 16th to
the 20th century." (Foreword by Ann Hutchinson) (Danceo-
mania 43) New York: Kamin Dance Bookshop.

Kanfer, Frederick H.
1959   "Verbal rate, content and adjustment ratings in experimentally structured interviews," Journal of Abnormal and Social Psychology 58:3, pp. 305-311.

1960   "Verbal rate, eyeblink, and content in structured psychiatric interviews," Journal of Abnormal and Social Psychology 61, pp. 341-347.

Kanner, Leo
1931   "Judging emotions from facial expressions," Psychological Monographs 41:3, Whole No. 186, 91 pages.

Kantner, Claude E., and Robert West
1933   Phonetics: An Introduction to the Principles of Phonetic
Science from the Point of View of English Speech. New York:
Harper and Bros., revised, 1960, 433 pages.

Kany, Charles E.
1960   American-Spanish Euphemisms. University of California
Press. [Appendix II: Illustrations of gestures, pp. 205-210;
many references within the text (see index).]

Kaplan, Eleanor
1969   "The role of intonation in the acquisition of language."
Dissertation, Cornell University.

Kaplan, Robert A.
1972   "The effects of manipulating nonverbal behavior of interviewers on the nonverbal behavior of interviewees." Dissertation Abstracts 32, 5425B-26B. Michigan State University.

Kapsalis, Peter T.
1946   "Gestures in Greek art and literature." Dissertation,
Johns Hopkins University, 103 pages.

Karelitz, Samuel
    n.d.   "Infant vocalizations," phonograph record C 12669 A.
    Long Island Jewish Hospital.

Karelitz, Samuel, and Vincent R. Fisichelli
    1969   "Infants' vocalizations and their significance," Clinical
    Proceedings of Children's Hospital 25:11 (December), pp. 345-
    361.

Karlgren, H.
    1962   "Speech rate and information theory," Proceedings of
    the 4th International Congress of Phonetic Science. The Hague:
    Mouton, pp. 671-677.

Kashinsky, Marc, and Morton Wiener
    1969   "Tone in communication and the performance of children
    from two socioeconomic groups," Child Development 40:4,
    pp. 1193-1202.

Kasl, Stanislav V., and George F. Mahl
    1965   "The relationship of disturbances and hesitations in
    spontaneous speech to anxiety," Journal of Personality and So-
    cial Psychology 1:5, pp. 425-433.

Katz, R.
    1964   "Body language: a study on unintentional communica-
    tion." Dissertation, Harvard University.

Kauffman, Lynn E.
    1969   "Tacesics, the study of touch: a model for proxemic
    analysis. Sacramento State University, M.A. thesis, 49 pages.

    1971   "Tacesics, the study of touch: a model for proxemic
    analysis," Semiotica 4, pp. 149-161.

Kaulfers, Walter Vincent
    1931   "Curiosities of colloquial gestures," Hispania 14:4 (Octo-
    ber), pp. 249-264.

    1932   "A handful of Spanish," Education 52 (March), pp. 423-
    428.

Kauranne, Urpo
    1964   "Quantitative factors of facial expression," Scandinavian
    Journal of Psychology 5, pp. 136-142.

Kavanagh, James F., and James E. Cutting
    1975   The Role of Speech in Language. Cambridge, Mass.:
    MIT Press, 335 pages.

Kealiinohomoku, Joann Wheeler
    1965   "A comparative study of dance as a constellation of

motor behaviors among African and United States Negroes. "
Master's thesis, Northwestern University.

Kealiinohomoku, Joann W. , and Frank J. Gillis
1970 "Special bibliography: Gertrude Prokosch Kurath, "
Ethnomusicology 14, pp. 114-128.

Keesing, Felix, and Marie M. Keesing
1956 Elite Communication in Samoa: A Study of Leadership.
Stanford: Stanford University Press. Review by Ward H.
Goodenough, Language 33:3 (1957), pp. 424-429.

Kelkar, Ashok R.
1964 "Marathi baby talk, " Word 20:1 (April), pp. 40-54.

Keller, Helen
1902 The Story of My Life. New York: Doubleday & Company, 382 pages.

1908 "Sense and sensibility, " Century 75 (February).

1930 Midstream: My Later Life. New York: Doubleday,
Doran & Company, pp. 164-166, 291. [Olfactory.]

Keller, Kathryn C.
1971 Instrumental Articulatory Phonetics. Santa Ana, Calif. :
Summer Institute of Linguistics, 145 pages.

Kelley, Samuel R.
1885 Tableaux d'Art Consisting of Instantaneous Changes of
the Emotions, for Public Entertainment. Boston.

Kelly, Joseph P.
1934 "Studies in nasality, " Archives of Speech (January),
pp. 26-42.

Kempf, Edward John
1921 The Automatic Functions and the Personality. New
York: Nervous and Mental Disease Publ. Co. , 156 pages.

Kenderdine, Margaret
1931 "Laughter in the pre-school child, " Child Development
2, pp. 228-30.

Kendon, Adam [Australian National University]
1967 "Some functions of gaze-direction in social interaction, "
Acta Psychologica 26, pp. 22-63.

1970 "Movement coordination in social interaction: some
examples described, " Acta Psychologica 32:2, pp. 101-125.

1972 "Some relationships between body motion and speech:
an analysis of an example, " in Aron Wolfe Siegman and

Benjamin Pope, eds. , Studies in Dyadic Communication.
Elmsford, N.Y.: Pergamon Press, pp. 177-210.

1973   "The role of visible behaviour in the organization of social interaction, " in M. Von Cranach and Ian Vine, eds. , Social Communication and Movement.   New York: Academic
Press, pp. 29-74.

"The face-formation system: spatial-orientational relations in face-to-face interaction. "

"Some functions of the face in a kissing round. "

"The study of the behaviour of social interaction. "

Kendon, Adam, and Mark Cook
1969   "The consistency of gaze patterns in social interaction, "
British Journal of Psychology 60, pp. 481-494.

Kendon, Adam and Andrew Ferber
1973   "A description of some human greetings, " in R. P.
Michael and J. H. Crook, eds. , Comparative Ecology and Behaviour of Primates.   London: Academic Press.

Kendon, Adam, Richard M. Harris, and Mary Ritchie Key
1975   Organization of Behavior in Face-to-Face Interaction.
(World Anthropology Series; Sol Tax, ed.)   The Hague: Mouton, 509 pages.

Kennard, David W. , and Gilbert H. Glaser
1964   "An analysis of eyelid movements, " Journal of Nervous
and Mental Disease 139, pp. 31-48.

Kepes, Gyorgy
1944   Language of Vision.   Chicago: Paul Theobald, 1961,
228 pages.

1965   The Nature and Art of Motion.   (Vision + Value Series.)
New York: George Braziller, 195 pages.

1965   Structure in Art and in Science.   (Vision + Value
Series.)   New York: George Braziller.

Kesson, John
1854   The Cross and the Dragon: or the Fortunes of Christi-
anity in China: with Notices of the Christian Missions and
Missionaries: and Some Account of the Chinese Secret Societies.   London, 282 pages.   [Chapter 18:   Hayes.]

Kestenberg, Judith S.
1965   "The role of movement patterns in development: I,
Rhythms of movement, " Psychoanalytic Quarterly 34, pp. 1-36.

Kester

1965   "The role of movement patterns in development: II, flow of tension and effort," Psychoanalytic Quarterly 34, pp. 517-563.

Kester, Judy [San Jose State University]
       "Why women talk that way: cultural influences on male-female verbal behavior."

Key, Mary Ritchie
1962   "Gestures and responses: a preliminary study among some Indian tribes of Bolivia," Studies in Linguistics 16:3-4, pp. 92-99.

1970   "Preliminary remarks on paralanguage and kinesics in human communication," La Linguistique 6:2, pp. 17-36.

1971   "Differences between written and spoken language." Paper read at the American Dialect Society, Chicago.

1974   "An abstract of differences between written and spoken languages," Claremont Reading Conference 38th Yearbook, Claremont Graduate School, pp. 94-96.

1974   "The relationship of verbal and nonverbal communication," Proceedings of the Eleventh International Congress of Linguists (August 1972), Bologna, vol. II, pp. 103-110.

1975   "Nonverbal, extra-linguistic messages," Male/Female Language. Metuchen, N.J.: Scarecrow Press, pp. 107-116.

1975   Paralanguage and Kinesics (Nonverbal Communication): with a Bibliography. Metuchen, N.J.: Scarecrow Press, 246 pages.

Khan, M. Masud R.
1963   "Silence as communication," Bulletin of the Menninger Clinic 27, pp. 300-313, 314-317.

Khatchadourian, Haig
1966   "Gestures as expression in the Middle East," ETC. 23:3 (September), pp. 358-361.

Kiener, F.
1952   Ausdruck und liturgische Sprache, Liturgie und Mönchtum. Laacher Hefte. Freiberg: Verein der Förderer und Freunde des Abt-Herwegen-Instituts.

1953   Die Verehrung des Göttlichen im Ausdruck. Christliche Welt als Verkundigung. Maria Leach.

Kiener, Franz
1962   Hand, Gebärde und Charakter; ein Beitrag zur Ausdruckskunde der Hand und ihrer Gebärden. München: E. Reinhardt, 366 pages.

Kiger, John A. , ed.
   1972   The Biology of Behavior.   Proceedings of a Colloquium.
   Corvallis: Oregon State University Press, 182 pages.

Kightlinger, Flora N.
   ca. 1892   The Star Speaker: a Complete and Choice Collection of
   the Best Productions by the Best Authors; with an Exhaustive
   Treatise on the Subject of Vocal and Physical Culture and Gesturing.   Jersey City, pp. 63-109.

Kimball, Linda Amy
   1966   "An application of generative grammar to nonverbal behavior: a preliminary study. "   M. A. thesis, Ohio State University.

Kimura, Doreen
   1961   "Cerebral dominance and the perception of verbal stimuli, " Canadian Journal of Psychology 15:3 (September), pp. 166-
   171.

   1967   "Functional asymmetry of the brain in dichotic listening. "
   Cortex 3:2 (June), pp. 163-178.

   1973   "The asymmetry of the human brain, " Scientific American 228:3 (March), pp. 70-78.

Kimura, Doreen, R. Battison, and B. Lubert
   n. d. [ca. 1975]   "Impairment of nonlinguistic hand movements
   in a deaf aphasic, " Research Bulletin 338, Psychology, University of West Ontario, London, Canada. (ISSN 0316-4675.)

King, William S.
   1949   (Notes and Queries):   "Hand gestures, " Western Folklore 8 (July), pp. 263-264.

Kingson, W. K. , and Rome Cowgill
   1950   Radio Drama Acting and Production: a Handbook.   New
   York, pp. 358-363. ["Studio sign language. "]

Kinross, Martha·
   1930   "The inarticulate sense, " English Review (July).

Kirby, Percival R.
   1937   "The musical practices of the native races of South
   Africa, " in I. Schapera, ed. , The Bantu-Speaking Tribes of
   South Africa: An Ethnographical Survey.   London: G. Routledge, chap. 12, pp. 271-289.

Kirchhoff, Robert
   1957   Allgemeine Ausdruckslehre, Prinzipien und Probleme
   der allgemeinen Ausdruckstheorie; ein Beitrag zur Grundle-
   gung der Wissenschaft vom Ausdruck.   Göttingen: C. J.
   Hogrefe, 277 pages.

Kirchhoff
Kirchhoff, R.
1965   Handbuch der Psychologie: V. Ausdruckspsychologie.
Gottingen, Germany: Verlag fur Psychologie, 596 pages.

Kirchner, Paul C.
1726   Jüdisches Ceremoniell.   Nurnberg, 226 pages.

Kirk, Lorraine
1973   "An analysis of speech imitations by Gã children, "
Anthropological Linguistics 15:6 (September), pp. 267-275.

Kirk, Lorraine, and Michael Burton
1975   "Ethnoclassification of minimally context-bound kine-
morphs: an application of judged similarities measures to
nonverbal performance. " Paper read at the Mathematical Social Science Board Conference, Coloma, California.

(in press)   "Maternal kinesic behavior and cognitive development in a child, " Annals of the New York Academy of Sciences.

Kirstein, Lincoln Edward
1935   The Dance.   New York: G. P. Putnam, 369 pages.
["The dance as a language with a structure similar to language. "]

Kishimoto, Suehiko
1964   "A brief note on the language of gesture, " Memoirs of
Osaka Gakugei University No. 13, pp. 62-67.

1965   "The seen height, " Memoirs of Osaka Gakugei University 14, pp. 33-37.

Kitchen, Curtis
1975   "Proxemic interaction in spare-changing, " Sociolinguistics Newsletter 6:1, pp. 11-12.

Kjellén, Nicolaus A. W.
1801   De Actione ad Sacras Orationes Applicata.   Upsaliae,
12 pp. [New York Public Library.]

Klaus, Marshall H. , John H. Kennell, Nancy Plumb, and Steven
Zuehlke
1970   "Human maternal behavior at the first contact with her
young, " Pediatrics 46, pp. 187-202.

Kleck, Robert E.
1968   "Physical stigma and nonverbal cues emitted in face-to-
face interaction, " Human Relations 21:1 (February), pp. 19-28.

1969   "Physical stigma and task oriented interactions, " Human Relations 22:1, pp. 53-60.

1970   'Interaction distance and non-verbal agreeing responses,"
British Journal of Social and Clinical Psychology 9, pp. 180-
182.

Kleck, Robert E., and William Nuessle
1968   "Congurence between the indicative and communicative
functions of eye contact in interpersonal relations," British
Journal of Social and Clinical Psychology 7, pp. 241-246.

Kleen, Tyra
1924   'Hand-poses of the priests of Bali," Asia and the Americas 24 (February), pp. 129-131.

1924   Mudrās: The Ritual Hand-Poses of the Buddha Priests
and the Shiva Priests of Bali. London: K. Paul, Trench,
Trubner, 42 pages. [60 full-page drawings.]

1947   Wayang (Javanese Theatre). Stockholm: Ethnographical
Museum of Sweden (Statens Etnografiska Museum), New Series,
Publication No. 4, 36 pages.

Klein, Sanvel Eben
1967   "The message in the Medium Activation-Level; meaning
and style in the nonverbal communication of affect." Thesis,
Columbia University.

Kleinpaul, Rudolf
1869   "Zur theorie der Gebärdensprache," Zeitschrift fur
Völkerpsycholo Sprachwissenschaft 6, pp. 353-375.

1888-93 Sprache ohne Worte: Das Leben der Sprache und
ihre Weltstellung. Leipzig. Reprinted as Sprache ohne Worte:
Idee einer allgemeinen Wissenschaft der Sprache. The Hague:
Mouton, 1972, 456 pages.

Klima, Edward S., and Ursula Bellugi
1972   "The signs of language in child and chimpanzee," in
Thomas Alloway, Lester Krames, and Patricia Pliner, eds.,
Communication and Affect: a Comparative Approach. New
York: Academic Press, pp. 67-96.

Kline, Linus W. and Dorothea E. Johannsen
1935   "Comparative role of the face and of the face-body-
hands as aids in identifying emotions," Journal of Abnormal
Psychology 29 (January), pp. 415-26.

Kline, Peter, and Nancy Meadors
1971   Theatre Student: Physical Movement for the Theatre.
New York: Richards Rosen Press, 156 pages.

Klineberg, Otto
1927   "Racial differences in speed and accuracy," Journal of
Abnormal and Social Psychology 22, pp. 273-277.

1935   "Emotional expression," Race Differences. New York:
Harper and Bros., chap. 15, pp. 278-289.

1938   "Emotional expression in Chinese literature," Journal
of Abnormal and Social Psychology 33, pp. 517-20.

Klitgaard, C.
1934   "Skaeldsord og foragtelig gestus" [Gestures of insult and
contempt], Danske Studier (Copenhagen), pp. 88-89.

Kloek, J.
1961   "The smell of some steroid sex hormones and their
metabolites: reflections and experiments concerning the significance of smell for the mutual relation of the sexes,"
Psychiatria Neurologia Neurochirurgia 64, pp. 309ff.

Klopfer, Peter H.
1969   Habitats and Territories: A Study of the Use of Space
by Animals. New York: Basic Books, 117 pages.

Kluckhohn, Clyde
1943   "Covert culture and administrative problems," American
Anthropologist 45, pp. 213-229.

Knapp, Mark L.
1972   Nonverbal Communication in Human Interaction. New
York: Holt, Rinehart and Winston, 213 pages.

Knapp, Mark L., Roderick P. Hart, Gustav W. Friedrich, and
Gary M. Shulman
1973   "The rhetoric of goodbye: verbal and nonverbal correlates of human leave-taking," Speech Monographs 40:3 (August),
pp. 182-198. Comment in Psychology Today (October 1974),
pp. 26-28.

Knapp, Peter H., ed.
1963   Expression of the Emotions in Man. New York: International Universities Press, 351 pages.

Knapp, Robert H.
1965   "The language of postural interpretation," Journal of
Social Psychology 67, pp. 371-377.

Kniep, Emily H., Winona L. Morgan, and Paul Thomas Young
1931   "Individual differences in affective reactions to odors,"
American Journal of Psychology 43:3, pp. 406-421.

Knight, David J., Daniel Langmeyer, and David C. Lundgren
1973   "Eye-contact, distance, and affiliation: the role of observer bias," Sociometry 36, pp. 390-401.

Knight, Richard Payne
1876   The Symbolical Language of Ancient Art and Mythology.
New York, 240 pages. [Manu cornuta, the fig.]

Knower, Franklin H.
1941 "Analysis of some experimental variations of simulated
vocal expressions of the emotions," Journal of Social Psychology 14, pp. 369-372.

Knowles, James Sheridan
1830? Appendix to Rudiments of Gesture: Consisting of a Debate on the Character of Julius Caesar. London?

1873 Lectures on Oratory, Gesture and Poetry; to Which Is
Added a Correspondence with Four Clergymen, in Defence of
the Stage. London, 249 pages.

Knowles, James Sheridan see Russell

Knowlson, James R.
1965 "The idea of gesture as a universal language in the
XVIIth and XVIIIth centuries," Journal of the History of Ideas
26:4 (October-December), pp. 495-508.

Knust, Albrecht
1957 Abriss der Kinetographie Laban. Leipzig: Friedrich
Hofmeister, 2 vols. 227, 116 pages.

Koch, Christian
Semiotics and the Cinema. The Hague: Mouton.

Koch, Helen L.
1935 "An analysis of certain forms of so-called 'nervous
habits' in young children," Journal of Genetic Psychology 46,
pp. 139-170.

Koch, Walter A.
1971 Varia Semiotica. New York: G. Olms, 632 pages.

Kochman, Thomas, ed.
1968 "The kinetic element in Black idiom." Paper read at
American Anthropological Association, Seattle, Washington.

1972 Rappin' and Stylin' Out: Communication in Urban Black
America. Urbana: University of Illinois Press, 424 pages.

1973 "Orality and literacy as factors of 'black' and 'white'
communicative behavior."

Koechlin, B.
1968 "Techniques corporelles et leur notation symbolique,"
Langages 10, pp. 36-47.

Koenig, F., and M. Capps
1969-70 "Response to kinesic patternings and semantic differentiation of significant others," Actes du Xe Congres International des Linguistes (Bucarest), vol. III, pp. 297-300.

Koht, Paul
    1962   (Letter to the editor), New Yorker (February 24),
    p. 125.

Kolshanskii, G. V. [Kolshansky]
    1973   "Funktsii paralingvisticheskikh sredstv v yazykovoi
    kommunikatsii" [The functions of paralinguistic means in verb-
    al communication], Voprosy Jazykoznanija 1, pp. 16-25.

    (in press) Paralinguistiki. Academy of Sciences, Moscow, 5
    leaves.

Koneya, Mele
    1973   "The relationship between verbal interaction and seat
    location of members of large groups." Dissertation, Univer-
    sity of Denver.

Kool, Jaap
    1927   Tanzschrift. Sevres: Editions Allard, 27 pages.

Kortholt, Chr.
    1693   De Sacris Publicis, Debita cum Reverentia Praestantisque
    Numinis Metu Colendis Diatribe Ascetica. Kiel. [Prayer ges-
    tures.]

Kowal, Sabine, Daniel C. O'Connell, and Edward J. Sabin
    1975   "Development of temporal patterning and vocal hesita-
    tions in spontaneous narratives," Journal of Psycholinguistic
    Research 4, pp. 195-207.

Kozel, Nicholas J.
    1969   "Perception of emotion: race of expressor, sex of re-
    ceiver, and mode of presentation," American Psychological
    Association Proceedings (77th) 4, pp. 39-40.

Kramer, E. E.
    1955   The Main Stream of Mathematics. New York: Oxford
    University Press, pp. 10-12.

Kramer, Ernest
    1963   "Judgment of personal characteristics and emotions from
    nonverbal properties of speech," Psychological Bulletin 60:4,
    pp. 408-420.   Partially reprinted in Norman N. Markel, Psy-
    cholinguistics. Homewood, Ill.: Dorsey Press, 1969, pp. 353-
    372.

    1964   "Elimination of verbal cues in judgments of emotion
    from voice," Journal of Abnormal and Social Psychology 68:4,
    pp. 390-396.

    1964   "Personality stereotypes in voice: a reconsideration of
    the data," Journal of Social Psychology 62, pp. 247-251.

Krames, Lester, Thomas Alloway, and Patricia Pliner
    Advances in the Study of Communication and Affect.
    Vol. 1, Nonverbal Communication. New York: Plenum Pub-
    lishing Corporation, 212 pages.

Krapp, George Phillip
    1919   The Pronunciation of Standard English in America.
    New York: Oxford University Press, 235 pages. ["Sounds not
    used in articulate speech": sigh, cough, cluck, click, sniff,
    hmph, huh, eh, hm, calling a cat, starting a horse, p. 143.]

Krashen, Stephen
    1972   "Language and the left hemisphere," Working Papers in
    Phonetics 24, University of California at Los Angeles, 72
    pages.

Krashen, Stephen, Victoria Fromkin, Susan Curtiss, David Rigler,
    and S. Spitz
    1972   "Language lateralization in a case of extreme psycho-
    social deprivation," Journal of the Acoustical Society of Ameri-
    ca 53 (Abstract), p. 367.

Krebs, Richard L.
    1970   "Mother and child: Interruptus," Psychology Today 3:8,
    p. 33.

Kretsinger, Elwood A.
    1952   "An experimental study of gross bodily movement as an
    index to audience interest," Speech Monograph 19:4, pp. 244-
    248.

Krim, Alaine
    1953   "A study in non-verbal communications: expressive
    movements during interviews," Smith College Studies in Social
    Work (Smith College, Northampton, Mass.), pp. 41-80.

Kris, Ernst
    1940   "Laughter as an expressive process," International
    Journal of Psychoanalysis 21, pp. 330-331. Reprinted in
    Psychoanalytic Explorations in Art. New York: International
    Universities Press, 1952, pp. 217-239.

Kris, Ernst, and Ernst Gombrich
    1938   "The principles of caricature," British Journal of Medi-
    cal Psychology 17, pp. 319-342. Revised and reprinted in
    Ernst Kris, Psychoanalytic Explorations in Art. New York:
    International Universities Press, 1952, pp. 189-203.

Kriss-Rettenbeck, Lenz
    1964-65 "Probleme der volkstümlichen Gebärdenforschung,"
    Bayerische Jahrbuch für Völkskunde, pp. 14-47.

Kristeva, Julia
1968   "Le geste, pratique ou communication?" Langages 10, pp. 48-64.

Kristeva, Julia, Josette Rey-Debove, and Donna Jean Umiker
1971   Essays in Semiotics. The Hague: Mouton, 639 pages.

Kroeber, A. L.
1958   "Sign language inquiry," International Journal of American Linguistics, 24:1, pp. 1-19. Reprinted in Garrick Mallery, Sign Language among North American Indians. The Hague: Mouton, 1972.

Krout, Maurice H.
1931   "Personality testing in the light of the situational approach," American Journal of Psychiatry 10, pp. 839-855.

1931   "Symbolic gestures in the clinical study of personality," Transactions of the Illinois State Academy of Science 24, pp. 519-523.

1935   "Autistic gestures: an experimental study in symbolic movement," Psychological Monographs 46:4, Whole No. 208, pp. 1-126.

1935   "The social and psychological significance of gestures (A differential analysis)," Journal of Genetic Psychology 47, pp. 385-412.

1937   "Further studies on the relation of personality and gesture: a nosological analysis of autistic gestures," Journal of Experimental Psychology 20:3 (March), pp. 279-287.

1939   "Understanding human gestures," The Scientific Monthly 49 (August), pp. 167-72.

1942   Introduction to Social Psychology. New York: Harper and Brothers. Partially reprinted as "Symbolism," in Haig A. Bosmajian, The Rhetoric of Nonverbal Communication, 1971, pp. 15-33.

1954   "An experimental attempt to determine the significance of unconscious manual symbolic movements," Journal of General Psychology 51, pp. 121-152.

1954   "An experimental attempt to produce unconscious manual symbolic movements," Journal of General Psychology 51, pp. 93-120.

Krumboltz, John D., Barbara B. Varenhorst, and Carl E. Thoren-sen
1967   "Nonverbal factors in the effectiveness of models in

counseling," Journal of Counseling Psychology 14:5, pp. 412-
418.

Kruse, Otto Friedrich
    1853   Ueber Taubstumme: Taubstummen-Bildung und Taubstu-
mmen-Anstalten: nebst Notizen aus meinem Reisetagebuch.
Schleswig, 51 pages.

Kuepper, Karl J.
    1970   "Gesture and posture as elemental symbolism in Kafka's
The Trial," Mosaic 3:4 (Summer), pp. 143-52.

Kulovesi, Y.
    1939   'Die Ausdrucksbewegungen der Bejahung und der Vernei-
nung," Internationale Zeitschrift für Psychoanalyse 24 (Vienna),
pp. 446-447. [The expressive movements of confirmation and
denial.]

Kumin, Libby, and Martin Razar
             "Acquisition of nonverbal behavior: the encoding and de-
coding of emblems in young children."

Kummer, Hans
    1970   "Spacing mechanisms in social behavior," Social Science
Information 9, pp. 109-22.

Kuno, Yas
    1934   The Physiology of Human Perspiration.   London:
Churchill, [p. 129].

    1956   Human Perspiration.   Springfield, Ill.: C. C. Thomas,
416 pages.

Kurath, Gertrude Prokosch
    1950   "A new method of choreographic notation," American
Anthropologist 52, pp. 120-123.

    1960   "Panorama of dance ethnology," Current Anthropology
1:3 (May), pp. 233-254.

Kurath, Gertrude Prokosch see also Kealiinohomoku

Kurtz, J. H.
             "The sounds of a day-old baby." Tape-recording from
Langley Porter Neuropsychiatric Institute, San Francisco,
California.

Kurylowicz, Jerzy
    1972   "The role of deictic elements in linguistic evolution,"
Semiotica 5:2, pp. 174-183.

Kuschel, Rolf
    1973   "The silent inventor: the creation of a sign language

Kuschel

by the only deaf-mute on a Polynesian island," Sign Language Studies 3, pp. 1-27.

1974 A Lexicon of Signs from a Polynesian Outliner Island. Copenhagen: Psykologisk Laboratorium, Københavns Universitet, 187 pages.

Kuschel, Rolf see also Valerie Sutton

Kuttikrishna, M.
1937 "Hand symbols in Kathakali," Modern Review (June).

Kwint, L.
1934 "Ontogeny of motility of the face," Child Development
5:1-12.

- L -

Laban see Bartenieff; Bartenieff and Davis; Curl; Dell; Hutchinson; Knust; Kurath (1960); Lamb; Nadel and Nadel; North; Preston; Preston-Dunlop; Redfern; Thornton; Topaz

Laban, Juana de
1946 "Dance notation," Dance Index 5:4, pp. 89-131.

Laban, Rudolf von
1928 Laban's Dance Notation Charts: Basic Symbols Taken from Dance Notation Scripts. New York: Associated Music Publishers.

1928 Schrifttanz.

1950 The Mastery of Movement, revised by Lisa Ullmann. London: Macdonald and Evans, 200 pages.

1956 Principles of Dance and Movement Notation. London: Macdonald and Evans, 56 pages. Reprinted Brooklyn, New York: Dance Horizons.

1966 Choreutics. London: Macdonald and Evans, 224 pages.

1968 Modern Educational Dance, revised by Lisa Ullmann. London: Macdonald and Evans, 128 pages.

Laban, Rudolf, and F. C. Lawrence
1947 Effort. London: Macdonald and Evans, 88 pages. Reprinted 1967, 104 pages.

La Barre, Weston
1947 "The cultural basis of emotions and gestures," Journal of Personality 16:1 (September), pp. 49-68. Bobbs-Merrill Reprint Series in the Social Sciences S-157. Reprinted in

D. G. Haring, ed., Personal Character and Cultural Milieu.
Syracuse, N.Y.: Syracuse University Press, 1956, pp. 554-
561.

1954   The Human Animal. University of Chicago Press.

1964   "Paralinguistics, kinesics, and cultural anthropology,"
in Thomas Seboek, et al., eds. Approaches to Semiotics,
pp. 191-237. Reprinted in Floyd W. Matson and Ashley Montagu, eds., The Human Dialogue. New York: The Free Press,
1967, pp. 456-490. Partially reprinted in Larry A. Samovar
and Richard E. Porter, eds., pp. 172-180.

1972   "Ethology and ethnology," Semiotica 6:1, pp. 83-96.

?   "Paralingüística, kinésica, y antropología cultural," in
Ricardo Zuñiga B., ed., La influencia social primaria. (Psi-
cología Social 8, Serie Reimpresiones) Valparaiso: Ediciones
Universitarias, 131 pages.

Labarta de Chaves, Teresa, and Jorge L. Soler
1974   "Pedro Ponce de León, first teacher of the deaf," Sign
Language Studies 5, pp. 48-63.

Labouret, H.
1923   "Langage tambouriné et sifflé," Comite d'études histori-
ques et scientifiques de l'Afrique occidentale française 6, pp.
120-158.

LaCuisse, M.
1763   Le Repertoire du ballets. Paris.

Ladefoged, Peter
1964   "Tone and intonation," A Phonetic Study of West African Languages: An Auditory-Instrumental Survey. Cambridge
University Press, pp. 41-42.

1967   Three Areas of Experimental Phonetics: Stress and
Respiratory Activity, the Nature of Vowel Quality, Units in the
Perception and Production of Speech. Oxford University Press,
180 pages.

Ladefoged, Peter, and D. E. Broadbent
1957   "Information conveyed by vowels," Journal of the Acoustical Society of America 29:1 (January), 98-104.

Ladner, Gerhart B.
1961   "The gestures of prayer in Papal iconography of the
13th and early 14th century," Didascaliae: Study in Honour of
Anselmo Maria Albareda. New York: Bernard M. Rosenthal,
pp. 245-275.

Lado, Robert
1957 Linguistics Across Cultures. Chapter 6, "How to compare two cultures." Ann Arbor: University of Michigan Press, pp. 110-123.

1964 "How to test cross-cultural understanding," in Studies in Languages and Linguistics: in Honor of Charles C. Fries, ed. by Albert H. Marckwardt. Ann Arbor, Mich.: English Language Institute, pp. 353-362.

Laffal, Julius
1965 Pathological and Normal Language. New York: Atherton Press, 249 pages.

La Fin
1692 Sermo Mirabilis, or the Silent Language. London.

LaFrance, Marianne, and Clara Mayo [Boston College, Massachusetts]
1973 "Gaze direction in interracial dyadic communication." Paper read at the Eastern Psychological Association, Washington, D. C.

LaFrancois, Guy R.
1973 Of Children. Belmont, Calif.: Wadsworth Publishing Company.

Laikin, Paul
1963 A Hand Guide to Language, with a Guide to Famous International Hand Gestures. New York: Sloves & Frey.

Lajard, M.
1891 "Communications: le langage sifflé des Canaries," Bulletin de la societe d'anthropologie de Paris 4:2, pp. 469-483.

Lakin, M., and C. Eisdorfer
1960 "Affective expression among the aged," Journal of Projective Techniques 24, pp. 403-408.

Lallgee, Mansur G., and Mark Cook
1969 "An experimental investigation of the function of filled pauses in speech," Language and Speech 12 (Part I), (January-March), pp. 24-28.

1973 "Uncertainty in first encounter," Journal of Personality and Social Psychology 26:1, pp. 137-141.

1975 "Filled pauses and floor-holding: the final test," Language and Language Behavior Abstracts 9:3, 7502781.

Lamb, Warren
1965 Posture and Gesture: An Introduction to the Study of Physical Behaviour. London: Gerald Duckworth.

Lamb, Warren, and David Turner
    1969   Management Behaviour. New York: International Uni-
    versities Press, 177 pp.

Lambert, Louis C.
    n. d.   Mimetic Expression: A Study of Gesture. The Expres-
    sion Company.

Lambert, William W., and Wallace E. Lambert
    1964   Social Psychology. New York: Prentice-Hall. ["The
    perception of the line of regard," pp. 32-33; "The perception
    of facial expression," pp. 33-34.]

La Meri   see   Russell Meriweather Hughes

Lance, Long [Chief Buffalo Child, Blackfoot]
    1930   How to Talk in the Indian Sign Language. Akron, Ohio:
    B. F. Goodrich Rubber Company. [In Krout, 1942, 2 pages of
    photos, pp. 320-321.]

Landar, Herbert J.
    1959   "The Navaho intonational system," Anthropological
    Linguistics 1:9, pp. 11-19.

    1967   "The language of pain in Navaho culture," in Dell H.
    Hymes, ed., Studies in Southwestern Ethnolinguistics. The
    Hague: Mouton, pp. 117-144.

Landis, Carney
    1924   "Studies in emotional reactions: I, A preliminary study
    of facial expression," Journal of Experimental Psychology 7,
    pp. 325-341.

    1924   "Studies of emotional reactions: II, General behavior
    and facial expression," Journal of Comparative Psychology 4:5,
    pp. 447-509.

    1929   "The interpretation of facial expression in emotion,"
    Journal of General Psychology 2:1 (January), pp. 59-72.

    1934   "Emotion: II, The expressions of emotion," in Hand-
    book of General Experimental Psychology, ed. by C. Murchi-
    son. Clark University Press, pp. 312-351. Reprinted, New
    York: Russell and Russell, 1969.

Landis, Carney, and William A. Hunt
    1939   The Startle Pattern. New York. Reprinted by Johnson
    Reprint Corporation, 1968, 168 pages.

Landreth, C.
    1941   "Factors associated with crying in young children in the
    nursery school and the home," Child Development 12, pp. 81-
    97.

Lane, Harlan, and William Sheppard
1966 "Development of the prosodic features of infants' vocalizing," Studies in Language and Language Behavior.

Lane, Harlan, and Bernard Tranel
1971 "The Lombard sign and the role of hearing in speech," Journal of Speech and Hearing Research 14:4, pp. 677-709.

Langdon, Margaret
1971 "Sound symbolism in Yuman languages," University of California Publications in Linguistics 65, pp. 149-173.

Langdon, S.
1919 "Gesture in Sumerian and Babylonian prayers," Royal Asiatic Society of Great Britain and Ireland, Journal, pp. 531-556.

Lange, Carl G., and William James
1922 The Emotions. Vol. I. Baltimore: The Williams and Wilkins Company, 135 pages.

Lange, Fritz
1937 Die Sprache des menschlichen Antlitzes: eine wissenschaftliche Physiognomik und ihre praktische Verwertung im Leben und in der Kunst. München/Berlin, 228 pages. Translated by Luis Miracle, El lenguaje de Rostro. Barcelona.

Langer, Jonas, and B. G. Rosenberg
1964 "Non-verbal representation of verbal referents," Perceptual and Motor Skills 19, pp. 363-370.

Langer, Susanne K.
1942 Philosophy in a New Key. New York: New American Library, a Mentor book.

1942 Feeling and Form--a Theory of Art. New York: Scribner's, 431 pages.

1957 Problems of Art: Ten Philosophical Lectures. New York: Charles Scribner's Sons.

1958 Reflections on Art: a Source Book of Writings by Artists, Critics, and Philosophers. Baltimore: The Johns Hopkins Press.

1960 "Origins of speech and its communicative function," Quarterly Journal of Speech 46:2 (April), pp. 121-134.

Lange-Seidl, Annemarie
1975 "Ansatzpunkte für Theorien nichtverbaler Zeichen," Sprachtheorie 2, pp. 241-275.

Langfeld, Herbert Sidney
    1918   "The judgment of emotions from facial expressions,"
    Journal of Abnormal Psychology 13, pp. 172-184.

    1918   "Judgments of facial expression and suggestion," Psy-
    chological Review 25, pp. 488-494.

Lanigan, Richard L.
    1972   Speaking and Semiology: Maurice Merleau-Ponty's
    Phenomenological Theory of Existential Communication. The
    Hague: Mouton, 257 pages. [See also Merleau-Ponty.]

Lanzetta, John T., and Robert E. Kleck
    1970   "Encoding and decoding of nonverbal affect in humans,"
    Journal of Personality and Social Psychology 16:1, pp. 12-19.

LaPiere, Richard T. and Paul R. Farnsworth
    1936   Social Psychology. Chapter 4, "Symbolic behavior: I,
    gesture." New York: McGraw-Hill, pp. 77-97.

Largey, Gale Peter, and David Rodney Watson
    1972   "The sociology of odors," American Journal of Sociology
    77:6, pp. 1021-1034.

La Riviere, Conrad L.
    1972   "Some acoustic and perceptual correlates of speaker
    identification," Dissertation Abstracts, 32, 7116A. University
    of Florida. Also in Proceedings of the 7th International Con-
    gress of Phonetic Sciences. The Hague: Mouton.

Larsen, Dave
    1961   "Do you like to be whistled at?" in the column "The
    Question Man," San Francisco Chronicle (Monday, July 3),
    p. 15.

Larsen, Eleanor W.
    1947   "The fatigue of standing," American Journal of Psychol-
    ogy 150, pp. 109-121.

Larsen, Kay
    1949   "Huasteco baby talk," El Mexico Antiguo 7, pp. 295-
    298.

Lasaulx, E. de
    1842   Die Gebete der Griechen und Römer. Würzburg.

Lashley, Karl S.
    1929   Brain Mechanisms and Intelligence. Chicago: Univer-
    sity of Chicago Press.

    1951   "The problem of serial order in behavior," in Lloyd A.
    Jeffress, ed., Cerebral Mechanisms in Behavior. New York:
    Wiley, pp. 112-136. Reprinted, New York: Hafner, 1967,

pp. 112-146. Reprinted in: Frank A. Beach, Donald O. Hebb, Clifford T. Morgan, The Neuropsychology of Lashley. New York: McGraw-Hill, 1960, pp. 506-528; and Sol Saporta, ed., Psycholinguistics. New York: Holt, Rinehart and Winston, 1961, pp. 180-198.

Lassen, Carol L.
1969 "Interaction distance and the initial psychiatric interview: a study in proxemics," Dissertation Abstracts 31.1542B. Yale University, 172 pages.

1973 "Effect of proximity on anxiety and communication in the initial psychiatric interview," Journal of Abnormal Psychology 81:3, pp. 226-232.

Lassner, Rudolf
1948 "Annotated bibliography on the Oseretsky tests of motor proficiency," Journal of Consulting Psychology 12, pp. 37-46.

Laufer, Asher
1969 "Chironomy and head movement in reciting the Hebrew Scriptures," Proceedings of the Fifth World Congress of Jewish Studies, vol. 4. Jerusalem: The Hebrew University.

Laurendeau, Monique, and Adrien Pinard
1970 The Development of the Concept of Space in the Child. Introduction by Jean Piaget. New York: International Universities Press, 465 pages.

Laurie, Alec
1965 "Visual communication," in Sir Gerald Barry, et. al., eds., Communication and Language: Networks of Thought and Action. London: Macdonald.

Lavater, John C.
1774 Physiognomoniques Fragmente. 3 vols., 1783-1787.

1815 Le Lavater des dames: ou, L'Art de connoitre les femmes sur leur physionomie, suivi d'un essai sur les moyens de procréer des enfans d'esprit. Paris.

1815 Le Lavater portatif: ou Précis de l'art de connaitre les hommes par les traits du visage. (Original German title, Physiognomische.)

1853 Essays on Physiognomy: Designed to Promote the Knowledge and the Love of Mankind. 8th rev. ed. London: William Tegg, 507 pages.

Laver, John D. M.
1968 "Voice quality and indexical information," British Journal of Disorders of Communication 3, pp. 43-54.

1970 "The synthesis of components in voice quality," Proceedings of the Symposium on Intonology Sponsored by International Association of Phonetic Sciences. Prague, pp. 523-525.

1972 "A semiotic approach to the analysis of spoken communication," Work in Progress (Linguistics Department, Edinburgh University) 5, pp. 34-47.

Laver, John and Sandy Hutcheson, eds.
1972 Communication in Face to Face Interaction. Middlesex: Penguin Books, 418 pages.

Lawick-Goodall, Jane Van
1968 "A preliminary report on expressive movements and communication in the Gombe stream chimpanzees," in Phyllis C. Jay, ed., Primates: Studies in Adaptation and Variability. New York: Holt, Rinehart and Winston, pp. 313-374.

1971 In the Shadow of Man. New York: Dell, 304 pages.

Lawrence, Robert Means
1898 The Magic of the Horse-Shoe: with Other Folk-Lore Notes. Boston, 344 pages. [Gestures described, e.g., the folklore of common salt: Hayes.]

Lawrence, Telete Z.
1970 "Regional speech of Texas: a description of certain paralinguistic features," Xth International Congress of Linguists, Bucharest, 1967, pp. 125-130.

Lawson, Joan
1953 European Folk Dances. Toronto and London: Pitman.

1957 Mime: the Theory and Practice of Expressive Gesture, with a Description of Its Historical Development. New York: Pitman, 167 pages.

Lay, C. H., and A. Paivio
1969 "The effects of task difficulty and anxiety on hesitation in speech," Canadian Journal of Behavioral Sciences 1, pp. 25-37.

Laziczius, Gyula
1966 Selected Writings of Gyula Laziczius, ed. by Thomas Sebeok. The Hague: Mouton, 226 pages.

Leach, E. R.
1958 "Magical hair," Man, n.s. 88, pp. 147-164.

Leach, Maria see Potter, Charles Francis

Le Bidois, M. G.
1900 De l'action dans la tragedie de Racine. Paris.

LeBrun, Charles [1619-1690]
1667   Conférences sur l'expression des différents caractères
des passions.   Paris: ed. Lavater, by Moreau, 1820. Vol. 9.

1689   Conference sur l'expression générale et particulière.
Paris: E. Picart.

1727   Expressions des passions de l'âme représentées en
plusieurs testes gravées d'aprés les desseins de feu Monsieur
de Brun.   Paris.

1916   La physionomie humaine comparée a la physionomie des
animaux.   Paris: Laurens.

LeBrun, Charles   see also   Montagu, J.

Lee, Ernest W.
1963   "Inches, feet and yards in Northern Roglai," Anthropological Linguistics 5:9 (December), pp. 14-16.

Lefcourt, Herbert M., Francine Rotenberg, Barbara Buckspan,
and Richard A. Steffy
1967   "Visual interaction and performance of process and re-
active schizophrenics as a function of the examiner's sex,"
Journal of Personality 35, pp. 535-46.

Lefevre, Carl A.
1964   Linguistics and the Teaching of Reading.   New York:
McGraw-Hill, 252 pages.

Lehrer, Adrienne
1974   "Extended meanings of a body-part terms," International
Journal of American Linguistics 40:2 (April), pp. 135-137.

Leibman, Miriam
1970   "The effects of sex and race norms on personal space,"
Environment and Behavior 2, pp. 208-246.

Leibniz, G. G. [1646-1716]
1768   Opera Omnia, vol. 6, part 2.   Geneva, p. 207.
[Description of signs by Cistercian monks.]

Lekis, Lisa
1956   "The origin and development of ethnic Caribbean dance
and music."   University of Florida, dissertation, 282 pages.

Le Mée, Katharine
1967   "Studies in communication," in Mario Pei, ed.,
Language Today.   New York: Funk and Wagnalls, chap. 4,
pp. 98-127.

1973   "Francois Delsarte, 19th century teacher of vocal and
body behavior."   Northeastern Modern Language Association.

Lemoine, Jean-Gabriel
   1932   "Les anciens procédés de calcul sur les doigts en
   Orient et en Occident, " Revue des études islamiques, pp. 1-
   60.

Lemoine, M.
   1865   La Physionomie et la parole.   Paris.

Lenneberg, Eric H.
   1962   "A laboratory for speech research at the Children's
   Hospital Medical Center, " New England Journal of Medicine
   266:8, pp. 385-392.

   1964   New Directions in the Study of Language.   Cambridge,
   Mass. :   MIT Press, 194 pages.

   1967   "Prelanguage development, " Biological Foundations of
   Language.   New York: John Wiley and Sons, pp. 276-280.

   1970   "An acoustic analysis of the Turkish whistling languages
   of Kusköy, " Revue du phonétique appliquée 14-15, pp. 25-39.

   1970   "Brain correlates of language, " in F. O. Schmitt, ed. ,
   The Neurosciences: Second Study Program.   New York:
   Rockefeller University Press.

   1971   "Of language, knowledge, apes, and brains, " Journal of
   Psycholinguistic Research 1:1, pp. 1-29.

   1971   "The importance of temporal factors in behavior, " in
   D. L. Horton, and J. J. Jenkins, eds. , Perception of Language.   Columbus, Ohio: Charles E. Merrill, pp. 174-184.

Leonard, Carolyn [Harvard University]
          "A method for film analysis of ethnic communication
   style. "   13 pages.

Leonhard, Karl
   1949   Ausdruckssprache der Seele, Darstellung der Mimik,
   Gestik und Phonik des Menschen.   Berlin: K. F. Haug, 507
   pages.

   1968   Der menschliche Ausdruck.   Leipzig: J. A. Barth,
   320 pages.

Leont'ev, Alessei Alessejevič
   1974   The Psychology of Communication [in Russian].   Tartu:
   Tartu State University Press, 219 pages.

L'Épée, Abbé Charles Michel de [1712-1789]
   1776   Institution des sourds et muets, par la voie des signes
   méthodiques.   Paris.

1860   "The true method of educating the deaf and dumb,"
American Annals of the Deaf 12:1 (January), pp. 1-60; 12:2
(April), pp. 61-132.

Lepper, John Heron
n.d.   Famous Secret Societies.   London, 344 pages.

Lerman, J. W. and P. H. Damsté
1969   "Voice pitch of homosexuals," Folia Phoniatrica 21,
pp. 340-346.

Leroi-Gourhan, André
1965   Le geste et la parole.   Dessins de l'auteur.   Paris:
A. Michel.

Leroy, Ch.
1970   "An ecological study," Revue du phonétique appliquée
14-15, pp. 13-24.

1970   "Etude de phonétique comparative de la langue turque
sifflée et parlée," Revue du phonétique appliquée 14-15,
pp. 119-161.

Lersch, Phillip
1928   "Die Bedeutung des mimischen Ausdruckserscheinungen
für die Beurteilung der Personalichkeit," Industrielle Psycho-
technik 5, pp. 178-183.

1932   Gesicht und Seele: Grundlinien einer mimischen Diag-
nostik.   München: Reinhardt, 167 pages.

Leuba, Clarence
1941   "Tickling and laughter: two genetic studies," Journal
of Genetic Psychology 58, pp. 201-209.

Leventhal, Howard, and Kurt Fischer
1970   "What reinforces in a social reinforcement situation--
words or expressions?" Journal of Personality and Social Psychology 14, pp. 83-94.

Leventhal, Howard, and Elizabeth Sharp
1965   "Facial expressions as indicators of distress," in S. S.
Tomkins and C. E. Izard, eds., Affect, Cognition, and Personality.   New York: Springer, pp. 296-318.

Levin, H. and I. Silverman
1965   "Hesitation phenomena in children's speech," Language
and Speech 8, pp. 67-85.

Levin, Harry, Irene Silverman, and Boyce L. Ford
1967   "Hesitations in children's speech during explanation and
description," Journal of verbal learning and verbal behavior
6:4, pp. 560-564.

Levin, R. H. and T. T. Stigall
    1965   "Effect of nonverbal social reinforcement on rate of
    speech in a free-operant design. " Paper presented at APA.

Levitt, Eugene A.
    1964   "The relationship between abilities to express emotion-
    al meanings vocally and facially, " in Joel R. Davitz, The
    Communication of Emotional Meaning. New York: McGraw-
    Hill, pp. 87-100.

Levy, Kata
    1958   "Silence in the analytic session, " International Journal
    of Psychoanalysis 39, pp. 50-58.

Levy, Leon H. , Thomas B. Orr, and Sanford Rosenzweig
    1960   "Judgments of emotion from facial expressions by col-
    lege students, mental retardates, and mental hospital patients, "
    Journal of Personality 28, pp. 342-349.

Levy, Nissim and Harold Schlosberg
    1960   "Woodworth scale values of the Lightfoot pictures of
    facial expression, " Journal of Experimental Psychology 60:2,
    pp. 121-125.

Lévy-Bruhl, Lucien
    1910   Les Fonctions mentales dans les Sociétés inférieures.
    Paris: F. Alcan, 461 pages. How Natives Think. London:
    G. Allen and Unwin, 1926, 392 pages.

Lewis, Jack W.
    1970   "The tonal system of remote speech, " Le Maitre
    phonétique 134, pp. 31-36.

Lewis, M. M.
    1936   Infant Speech: A Study of the Beginnings of Language.
    Harcourt, Brace and Co. , 335 pages. London, 1951, 383
    pages.

    1963   Language, Thought and Personality: In Infancy and
    Childhood. New York: Basic Books.

Lewis, M.
            "Infants' responses to facial stimuli during the first
    year of life, " Developmental Psychology.

Lewis, Phillip V.
    1973   "Body language: nonverbal behavior as a communicative
    stimulus, " ETC. 30, pp. 245-247.

Lichtenberg, Georg Christoph [1742-1799]
    1773   Über Physiognomik wider die Physiognomen.

1966   The World of Hogarth ... Commentaries on Hogarth's
Engravings.   Boston: Houghton Mifflin, 297 pages.   Review
by Matthew Hodgart, The New York Review 15:3 (Aug. 13,
1970), pp. 13-15.

      Hogarth on High Life: the Marriage à la Mode Series.
Commentaries, translated and ed. by Arthur S. Wensinger,
with W. B. Coley.   Wesleyan, 208 pages.

Licklider, J. C. R., and George A. Miller
1951   "The perception of speech," Handbook of Experimental
Psychology, ed. Stanley Smith Stevens.   New York: John
Wiley and Sons, chap. 26, pp. 1040-1074.

Lieberman, Philip
1967   "Intonation and the syntactic processing of speech," in
Weiant Wathen-Dunn, ed., Models for the Perception of Speech
and Visual Form.   Proceedings of a Symposium, (1964).   Cambridge: MIT Press, pp. 314-319.

1967   Intonation, Perception, and Language.   Cambridge,
Mass.:   MIT Press, chap. 3, "Intonation in infant speech,"
pp. 38-47.

1970   "A study of prosodic features," Haskins Lab. Status Report on Speech Research 23, pp. 179-208.

1972   The Speech of Primates.   The Hague: Mouton, 133
pages.

1975   On the Origins of Language: an Introduction to the Evolution of Human Speech.   New York: Macmillan, 196 pages.

Lieberman, Philip and Edmund S. Crelin
1971   "On the speech of Neanderthal man," Linguistic Inquiry
2:2 (Spring), pp. 203-222.

Lieberman, Philip, Edmund S. Crelin and Dennis H. Klatt
1972   "Phonetic ability and related anatomy of the newborn
and adult human, Neanderthal Man, and the chimpanzee,"
American Anthropologist 74:3 (June), pp. 287-307.

Lieberman, Philip and S. B. Michaels
1962   "Some aspects of fundamental frequency, envelope amplitude and the emotional content of speech," Journal of the
Acoustical Society of America 34, pp. 922-927.

Lieth, Lars von der
1967   Dansk Døve-Tegnsprog.   Copenhagen: Akademisk Forlag.

1972   "Experimental social deafness," Scandinavian Audiology
1, pp. 81-87.

1972-73   "Hearing tactics," Scandinavian Audiology 1-2, pp.
155-160, 209-213.

1973   "Le geste et la mimique dans la communication totale,"
Bulletin de Psychologie 26:5-9, pp. 494-500.

1973   "Om notationssytemer: I, " Psykologisk Skriftserie 4.

Lieth, Lars von der, ed.
Nonverbal Kommunikation. Copenhagen: Psykologisk
Laboratorium, Københavns Universitet, No. 4.

Tekster om gestikulation.

Lifar, Serge
1940   Annotation of Movement: Kinetography [in Russian].
Moscow: Art Publishing House.

1951   Lifar on Classical Ballet. London: Allan Wingate.
Chapter 9, "Jumps."

Liggett, John
The Human Face. Constable, 287 pages. Review by
David Piper, Times Literary Supplement (November 15, 1974),
p. 1275.

Liles, Bruce L.
1975   An Introduction to Linguistics. Englewood Cliffs, N. J. :
Prentice-Hall. [Chapter on NVC.]

Lilly, John C.
1972   The Center of the Cyclone: an Autobiography of Inner
Space. New York: Julian Press. [Perception.]

Lin, Nan
1973   The Study of Human Communication. Indianapolis:
Bobbs-Merrill, 247 pages, especially pp. 68-74.

Lind, John, ed.
1965   "Newborn infant cry," Acta Paediatrica Scandinavica,
Supplement 163, pp. 1ff.

Lindblom, K. Gerhard
1949   The One-Leg Resting Position (Nilotenstellung), in
Africa and Elsewhere. Stockholm: Statens Etnografiska Museum, 34 pages. Review by William Fagg, Man 50:64 (April,
1950), pp. 51-52.

Lindenfeld, Jacqueline
1971   "Verbal and non-verbal elements in discourse," Semiotica 3:3, pp. 223-233.

1973   "Affective states and the syntactic structure of speech,"
Semiotica 8, pp. 367-376.

1974   "Syntactic structure and kinesic phenomena in communicative events," Semiotica 12:1, pp. 61-73.

Lindner, Gerhart, and Eva-Maria Reusz
1975   "Artikulation und Daktylzeichen," Language and Language
Behavior Abstracts 9:1, 7500585.

Liphan, J. N., and D. C. Francke
1966   "Nonverbal behavior of administrators," Educational Ad-
ministration Quarterly, pp. 101-109.

Lipinski, Jacek
1970   "Mimika i gest," Dialog no. 10 (Warsaw), pp. 95-105.

Lister, J.
1853   Quarterly Journal of Microscopical Science 1, p. 266ff.
[From Darwin, p. 199.]

Little, Kenneth B.
1965   "Personal space," Journal of Experimental Social Psychology 1, pp. 237-247.

Little, L.
1963   "The syntax of vocalized pauses in spontaneous cultivated speech." Ph. D. dissertation, George Peabody College
for Teachers.

Livant, W. P.
1963   "Antagonistic functions of verbal pauses: filled and
unfilled pauses in the solution of additions," Language and
Speech 6, pp. 1-4.

Livingstone, Frank B.
1973   "Did the Australopithecines sing?" Current Anthropology
14:1-2, pp. 25-26.

Ljung, Magnus
1965   "Principles of a stratificational analysis of the Plains
Indian sign language," International Journal of American Linguistics 31:2, pp. 119-127.

Llewellyn, T. E., and E. Stasiak
1964   "Eye movements and body images," Canadian Psychiatry
Association Journal 9, pp. 336-344.

Lloyd, Donald J., and Harry R. Warfel
1956   American English in Its Cultural Setting.   New York:
Alfred A. Knopf, pp. 61-64.

310   Bibliography

Locke, John [1632-1704]
1690 Essay Concerning Human Understanding.

Lodge, Oliver
1935 'Džamutra, or the bridegroom: some marriage customs in the villages around Tetovo in Serbian Macedonia or
Southern Serbia," Folk-Lore 96, Part I, pp. 244-267; Part II,
pp. 306-330.

Loeb, Felix F.
1968 "The fist: The microscopic film analysis of the function of a recurrent behavioral pattern in the psychotherapeutic
session," Journal of Nervous and Mental Disease 147:6,
pp. 605-618.

Loeb, Loretta R., Felix F. Loeb, Jr., and David S. Ross
1972 "Grasping as an adult communication signal," Journal
of Nervous and Mental Disease 154:5, pp. 368-386.

Lomax, Alan, ed.
1968 Folk Song Style and Culture: A Staff Report on Canto-
metrics. (AAAS Publications 88) Washington, D.C.: American
Association for the Advancement of Science, 363 pages.

Lomax, Alan, Irmgard Bartenieff and Forrestine Paulay
1969 "Choreometrics: a method for the study of cross-
cultural pattern in film," Research Film 6:6, pp. 505-517.

Lommatzsch, Erhard
1890 "Gebärden," Verhandlungen der Berliner Gesellschaft
für Anthropologie, Ethnologie und Urgeschichte, pp. 329ff.

1910 System der Gebärden: dargestellt auf Grund der
mittelalterlichen Literatur frankreichs. Diss., Berlin. [Only
the preface and Chap. D were printed: Taylor.]

Long, Joseph Schuyler
1910 "The sign language: a manual of signs, being a descriptive vocabulary of signs used by the deaf of the U.S. and
Canada," American Annals of the Deaf, 1908-1910.

Long, Major Stephen H.
1823 "Indian language of signs," in Account of an Expedition
from Pittsburgh to the Rocky Mountains, compiled by Edwin
James, vol. I, pp. 378-394. [Gives 104 signs.]

Longfellow, Layne A.
1970 "Body talk: the game of feeling and expression,"
Psychology Today 4:5 (October), pp. 45-54. [A game.]

Longstreet, Wilma
1972 "Multiforms of communication in interpersonal understanding," Educational Leadership 30:2, pp. 175-177.

Loomis, C. Grant
1956   "Folklore in the news--sign language of truck drivers,"
Western Folklore 5, pp. 205-206.

Lorand, A. S.
1931   "Aggression and flatus," International Journal of Psychoanalysis 12, p. 368.

Lorenz, Konrad Z.
1937   "The companion in the bird's world," Auk 54, pp. 245-
273.

1943   "Die angeborenen Formen möglicher Erfahrung," Zeitschrift Für Tierpsychologie 5, pp. 235-409.

1963   On Aggression. New York: Bantam, 306 pages.

1970   Studies in Animal and Human Behaviour.   Cambridge,
Mass.: Harvard University Press.

Lorenz, Konrad Z. , and Paul Leyhausen
1973   Motivation of Human and Animal Behavior: an Ethological View. New York: Van Nostrand Reinhold, 423 pages.

Lotman, Juri
1973   "Different cultures, different codes," Times Literary
Supplement 3:736 (October 12), pp. 1213-1215.

Lott, Dale F. , and Robert Sommer
1967   "Seating arrangements and status," Journal of Personality and Social Psychology 7, pp. 90-95.

Lounsbury, Floyd G.
1954   "Pausal, juncture and hesitation phenomena," in Charles
E. Osgood, and Thomas A. Sebeok, eds. , Psycholinguistics.
Indiana University Press, pp. 98-101.

Lourié, Anton
1964   "The systematic interpretation of gesture," in For Max
Weinreich on His Seventieth Birthday: Studies in Jewish Languages, Literature, and Society. . The Hague: Mouton.

Lourie, Reginald S.
1949   "The role of rhythmic patterns in childhood," American
Journal of Psychiatry 105, pp. 653-660.

Love, Kenneth
1955   "Egyptian land reform," New York Times (October 23,
1955), Section I, p. 9.   [A fellah speaks about his gestures and
liberty: Hayes.]

Love, Robert E.
1972   "Failure of inadvertent nonverbal behaviors to reflect

attitudes toward communication," Dissertation Abstracts
33, 1822B.

Löw, Immanuel
1921   "Der Kuss," Monatsschrift für Geschichte und Wissenschaft des Judentums 65, pp. 253-276, 323-349.

Löw, J.
1900   "Die Finger in Literatur und Folklore der Juden,"
Gedenkbuch zur Erinnerung an D. Kaufmann.   Breslau.

Lozier, J. D.
1967   "Perception of politeness in non-verbal behavior." M. A.
thesis, University of Minnesota.

Lubbock, Sir J.
1870   The Origin of Civilization, p. 355.   [Weeping among
aboriginals: Darwin, p. 154.]

Lubienska de Lenval, Hélène
1956   La liturgie du geste.   Tournai: Casterman, 100 pages.

Luce, Gay Gaer
1970   Biological Rhythms in Psychiatry and Medicine.   (Public
Health Service Publication No. 2088) U. S. Government Printing
Office, pp. 4, 36-38.

1971   Body Time: (Physiological Rhythms and Social Stress).
New York: Pantheon Books, 394 pages.

1971   "Understanding body time in the twenty-four hour city,"
New York (November 15), pp. 38-43.

Luchsinger, R.
1957   "Phonetics and pathology," in L. Kaiser, Manual of
Phonetics.   Amsterdam: North-Holland, pp. 339-363.

Luck, J. E.
1969   "Automatic speaker verification using Cepstral measurements," Journal of Acoustical Society of America 46, pp. 1026-
32.

Lucretius, T.
1917   De Rerum Natura, Book I.   Berkeley.

Luft, Joseph
1966   "On nonverbal interaction," Journal of Psychology 63,
pp. 261-268.

Lummis, Robert C.
1972   "Speaker verification: a step toward the 'checkless'
society," Bell Laboratories Record 50 (September), pp. 254-259.

Lurçat   313

Lurçat, Liliane
1972/73 'Du geste au langage," Bulletin de Psychologie 26,
pp. 501-05.

Luria, Aleksándr R.
1966 Higher Cortical Functions in Man. New York: Basic
Books, 513 pages.

1970 "The functional organization of the brain," Scientific
American 222:3 (March), pp. 66-78.

Lutz, Frank E.
1908 "The inheritance of the manner of clasping the hands,"
American Naturalist 42, pp. 195-196.

Lutz, H. F.
1936 "Speech consciousness among Egyptians and Babylonians,"
Osiris 2:1, pp. 1-27.

Lyall, Archibald
1956 "The Italian sign language," 20th Century 159, (June),
pp. 600-604.

Lynge Nielsen, L.
1973 "Om notationssystemer: II," Psykologisk skriftserie 4.

1973 "Problemer vedrørende udvikling af en dansk tegnspro-
gsordbog," Psykologisk skriftserie 4.

Lynip, Arthur W.
1951 "The use of magnetic devices in the collection and analysis of the preverbal utterances of an infant," Genetic Psychology Monographs 44, pp. 221-262.

Lynn, John G.
1940 "An apparatus and method for stimulating, recording,
and measuring facial expression," Journal of Experimental
Psychology 27, pp. 81-88.

Lyons, John
1972 'Human language," in R. A. Hinde, ed., Nonverbal
Communication. Cambridge University Press, pp. 49-85.

Lyons, Joseph, and Stanley Goldman
1966 "An experimentally generated set of expressive photographs," Journal of Psychology 62, pp. 67-82.

- M -

McBride, Glenorchy
       "Crowding without stress," Australian Veterinary Jour-
nal 47, pp. 564-567.

1966   "Society evolution," Proceedings of the Ecological Society of Australia 1, pp. 1-13.

1968   "On the evolution of human language," Social Science Information 7:5, pp. 81-85.

1970   "Social adaptation to crowding in animals and man," in S. V. Boyden, ed., The Impact of Civilization on the Biology of Man. Australian National University Press, pp. 142-154.

1971   "The evolution of human language," in J. Kristeva, J. R. DeBove, and D. J. Umiker, eds., Essays in Semiotics. The Hague: Mouton.

McBride, Glenorchy, M. G. King and J. W. James
1965   "Social proximity effects on Galvanic skin responses in adult humans," Journal of Psychology 61 (Sept.), pp. 153-157.

McCall, Elizabeth A.
1965   "A generative grammar of sign." M. A. thesis, University of Iowa.

MacCannell, Dean
1973   "A note on hat tipping," Semiotica 7, pp. 300-312.

McCardle, Ellen S.
1974   Nonverbal Communication. (Communication Science and Technology Series, 2) Dekker.

McCarthy, Dorothea
1946   "Language development in children," in Leonard Carmichael, ed., Manual of Child Psychology. New York: John Wiley and Sons, [1954], chap. 9, pp. 492-630.

McCartney, William
1968   Olfaction and Odours: an Osphresiological Essay. New York, Berlin: Springer-Verlag, 249 pages.

Maccoby, N., J. Jecker, H. Breitrose, and E. Rose
1964   "Sound film recordings in improving classroom communications: experimental studies in nonverbal communication." Unpublished report, Stanford University, Institute for Communication Research.

McConnell, O. L.
1967   "Control of eye contact in an autistic child," Journal of Child Psychology and Psychiatry 8, pp. 249-255.

McCord, Charlotte
1948   "Gestures," Western Folklore 7, pp. 290-292.

McCraw, Charles B.
1964   Scoreography. Ann Arbor, Mich.: Edwards Brothers, 58 pages.

McCray, John M.
1964   Cutaneous Communications. Fort Monmouth, N. J. :
U. S. Army Electronics Command, National Technical Information Service, Ad-710 949, 166 pages.

McCroskey, James C. , Carl E. Larson, and Mark L. Knapp
1971   An Introduction to Interpersonal Communication. Englewood Cliffs, N. J. : Prentice-Hall, 246 pages.

McDavid, Raven I. , Jr.
1955   "The grunt of negation, " American Speech (February),
p. 56.

1965   "The cultural matrix of American English, " Elementary
English 42:1 (January), pp. 13-21, 41.

McDermott, Raymond P.
        "A biobehavioral ethnography of learning disabilities in
urban classrooms. " Ms.

1972   "Selective attention and the politics of everyday life: a
biosocial inquiry into school failure and the persistence of
pariah minorities across generations. " M. S. , Stanford University, 42 pages. Read at the American Political Science Association, Washington, D. C.

MacDougald, Duncan, Jr.
1961   "Language and sex, " in Albert Ellis and Albert Abar-
banel, eds. , The Encyclopedia of Sexual Behavior, vol. 2,
pp. 585-598.

McDowall, Joseph J.
1974   "The reliability of ratings by linguistically untrained subjects in response to stress in speech, " Journal of Psycholinguistic Research 3, pp. 247-259.

McGehee, Frances
1944   "An experimental study of voice recognition, " Journal
of General Psychology 31, pp. 53-65.

MacGowan, D. G.
1866   [List of gestures of American Indians], Historical Magazine 10 (March), pp. 86-87.

McGrady, H. J. , Jr.
1964   "Verbal and nonverbal functions in school children with
speech and language disorders. " Thesis, Northwestern University.

McGrew, W. C.
1969   "An ethological study of agonistic behaviour in preschool
children, " Proceedings of 2nd International Congress Primatol
Behaviour 1, pp. 149-159.

1972 "Aspects of social development in nursery school
children with emphasis on introduction to the group," in N. G.
B. Jones, Ethological Studies of Child Behaviour. Cambridge
University Press, pp. 129-156.

McGrew, William Clement
1972 An Ethological Study of Children's Behavior. New York:
Academic Press, 257 pages.

Machotka, Pavel
1965 "Body movement as communication," Dialogues, Behavioral Science Research, 2. Boulder, Col.: Western Interstate
Commission for Higher Education.

McKay, F.
1929 "Time variability in speaking," Vox 15 (Hamburg), pp.
50-60.

McKelvey, D. P.
1953 "Voice and personality," Western Speech 17, pp. 91-94.

Mackworth, Norman and Muriel Bagshaw
1970 "Eye catching in adults, children and monkeys," Perception and Its Disorders. (Association for Research in Nervous and Mental Disease, 48) Baltimore: Williams and Wilkins, pp. 201-213.

Maclay, Howard, and Charles E. Osgood
1959 "Hesitation phenomena in spontaneous English speech,"
Word 15:1 (April), pp. 19-44. Reprinted in Leon A. Jakobo-
vitz and Murray S. Miron, eds., Readings in the Psychology
of Language. Englewood Cliffs, N.J.: Prentice-Hall, 1967,
pp. 305-324.

MacLeod, C.
1972 "A deaf man's sign language--its nature and position
relative to spoken languages," York Papers in Linguistics 2,
University of York (May).

Macleod, Catriona
1973 "A deaf man's sign language--its nature and position
relative to spoken languages," Linguistics 101, pp. 72-88.

McLure, Erica F.
1975 "Ethno-anatomy: the structure of the domain," Anthropological Linguistics 17:2, pp. 78-88.

McNeil, E. B.
1956 "Social class and the expression of emotion," Papers of
the Michigan Academy of Science, Arts, and Letters 41, pp.
341-348.

McNeill, David
1970 "The biological background" [animal], Chapter 4; "Sound development," Chapter 9, in The Acquisition of Language: the Study of Developmental Psycholinguistics. New York: Harper and Row.

McQuown, Norman A.
'Natural history method--a frontier method. " Mimeo, 12 pages.

1954 "Analysis of the cultural content of language materials," in H. Hoijer, ed., Language in Culture. University of Chicago Press, pp. 20-31.

1957 "Linguistic transcription and specification of psychiatric interview materials," Psychiatry 20:1 (Feb.), pp. 79-86.

1964 "Micro-analysis of speech and body-motion from sound-filmed interview. " Mimeo, 8 pages.

1972 "The nature of culture," in Estellie M. Smith, ed. , Studies in Linguistics in Honor of George L. Trager. The Hague: Mouton, pp. 19-24.

McQuown, Norman A. , ed. , with Gregory Bateson, Ray L. Bird-whistell, Henry W. Brosin, and Charles F. Hockett
1971 The Natural History of an Interview. (Microfilm Collection of Manuscripts on Cultural Anthropology, 15 series) Chicago: The University of Chicago, Dept. of Photoduplication.

Magdics, Klára
1963 "Research on intonation during the past ten years," Acta Linguistica 13, pp. 133-165.

1964 "First findings in the comparative study of intonation of Hungarian dialects," Phonetica 11:2, pp. 101-115.

Maginnis, Maria
1958 "Gesture and Status," Group Psychotherapy 11, pp. 105-109. [Abstracted from diss. , UCLA, Education ... Gestures of 301 Children, K-6 grades.]

Magriel, Paul David
1936 A Bibliography of Dancing. New York: H. W. Wilson.

Mahgoub, Fatma M.
1970 "A kinemorphological study of Cairene gestures: with pedagogical applications. " Dissertation Abstracts 31, 6036A, University of Texas.

Mahl, George F.
1956 'Disturbances and silences in the patient's speech in psychotherapy," Journal of Abnormal and Social Psychology 53:1 (July), pp. 1-15.

1958   "On the use of 'ah' in spontaneous speech: quantitative developmental, characterological, situational, and linguistic aspects, abstracted," American Psychologist 13, p. 349.

1959   "Measuring the patient's anxiety during interviews from 'expressive' aspects of his speech," (Transactions), New York Academy of Science 21, pp. 249-257.

1961   "Measures of two expressive aspects of a patient's speech in two psychotherapeutic interviews," in Louis A. Gottschalk, ed. , Comparative Psycholinguistic Analysis of Two Psychotherapeutic Interviews. New York: International Universities Press, pp. 91-114, 174-188.

1961   "Sensory factors in the control of expressive behavior: an experimental study of the function of auditory self-stimulation and visual feedback in the dynamics of vocal and gestural behavior in the interview situation," Acta Psychologica 19, pp. 1-2.

1963   "The lexical and linguistic levels in the expression of the emotions," Expression of the Emotions in Man, ed. Peter Knapp. New York: International Universities Press, pp. 77-105.

1964   "Some observations about research on vocal behavior," in Disorders of Communication, Vol. 42, Research Publications, Assn. for Research in Nervous and Mental Disease, chap. 32, pp. 466-483.

1967   "Some clinical observations on nonverbal behavior in interviews," Journal of Nervous and Mental Disease 144:6, pp. 493-505.

1968   "Gestures and body movements in interviews," Research in Psychotherapy 3 (American Psychological Association), pp. 295-346.

1972   "People talking when they can't hear their voices," in A. Siegman, and B. Pope, eds. , Studies in Dyadic Communication. New York: Pergamon Press, chap. 10, pp. 211-264.

Mahl, George F. see also Alpert, Murray, et al.

Mahl, George F. , Burton Danet, and Nea Norton
1959   "Reflection of major personality characteristics in gestures and body movements" (Abstract), American Psychologist 14, p. 357.

Mahl, George F. and Gene Schulze
1964   "Psychological research in the extralinguistic area," in Sebeok, et al. , Approaches to Semiotics. The Hague: Mouton, pp. 51-143. Partially reprinted in Norman N. Markel,

Maisel

Psycholinguistics.   Homewood, Ill. :   Dorsey Press, 1969,
pp. 318-352.

Maisel, Edward
   1970   The Resurrection of the Body: The Writings of F.
   Matthias Alexander.   New Hyde Park, N. Y. :   University Books,
   204 pages.

Malecot, Gaston Louis
   1927   "A note on gesture and language, " Quarterly Journal of
   Speech Education 13, pp. 439-442.

Malinowski, Bronislaw
   1935   The Language of Magic and Gardening.   Vol. II of
   Coral Gardens and Their Magic.   Indiana University Press,
   (1965), 350 pages.

Mallery, Colonel Garrick
   1879-80   Sign Language among North American Indians: Compared with That among Other Peoples and Deafmutes.   Washington: Bureau of Ethnology I (1881), pp. 263-552.   Reprinted,
   The Hague: Mouton, 1972.   [Includes pictures from de Jorio.]
   Reviews by Mary Ritchie Key, Linguistics 132 (July 1974),
   pp. 116-123; and Georges Mounin, Semiotica 7 (1973), pp. 154-
   162.

   1880   "A collection of gesture-signs and signals of the North
   American Indians, with some comparisons, " Miscellaneous
   Publications (Bureau of Am Ethnology 1), 329 pages.   [Only
   250 copies printed; mentioned on p. 396 of Sign Language
   among. . . .]

   1880   Gesture Signs and Signals of the North American Indians.
   Bureau of American Ethnology, Smithsonian Institute, 330 pages.

   1880   Introduction to the Study of Sign Language among the
   North American Indians: as Illustrating the Gesture Speech of
   Mankind.   Washington, D. C. , Smithsonian Institution--Bureau
   of Ethnology, 72 pages.   [Mentioned on p. 395, Sign Language
   among. . . .]

   1881   "The gesture speech of man, " Proceedings of the American Association for the Advancement of Science 30, pp. 283-
   313.

   1884   "Sign language, " Internationale Zeitschrift für Allegmeine
   Sprachwissenschaft 1, pp. 193-210.

   1891   "Greeting by gesture, " Popular Science Monthly (Feb. -
   March), pp. 477-490.

Malmberg, Bertil, ed.
   1968   Manual of Phonetics.   Amsterdam: North-Holland

Publishing Co. , 568 pages. [Completely revised and extended
edition of Manual of Phonetics, ed. L. Kaiser, 1957.]

Malmo, Robert B.
    1950 "Experimental studies of mental patients under stress,"
    in Feelings and Emotions, ed. , M. L. Reymert. New York:
    McGraw-Hill, pp. 169-180.

Mandler, George, and William Kessen
    1959 The Language of Psychology. New York: John Wiley
    & Sons, 301 pages. Review by Roger Brown, Language 35:4
    (Oct. -Dec.), pp. 717-721.

Mantegazza, Paolo
    1885 La Physionomie et L'expression des sentiments. Paris.
    (Eng. translation, Physiognomy and the Expression of Emotions.
    London, 1904; New York, 1906, 327 pages.)

    1888 Physiologie de la douleur. Paris, 350 pages.

Marañón, Gregorio
    1937 Psicología del gesto. Habana: Cultural, 86 pages.
    Translated as "The Psychology of Gesture," Journal of Nervous
    and Mental Disease 112:6 (Dec. 1950), pp. 469-497. Abstracted
    in Psychological Abstracts 25 (1951), item no. 4535. Re-
    printed in MD (March 1972), pp. 71-72.

    1947 Ensayos liberales. Madrid: Espasa-Calpe, 158 pages.

Marden, Luis
    1946 "Land of the painted oxcarts," National Geographic Mag-
    azine 90:4 (October), pp. 413-417. [Costa Rica.]

Maresca, Carol J.
    1966 "Gestures as meaning in Sherwood Anderson's 'Wines-
    burg, Ohio'," College Language Association Journal 9:3
    (March), pp. 279-283.

Marey, Étienne Jules
    1894 Le Mouvement. Paris: Masson. Translated as Move-
    ment. London, 1895.

Marinus, Albert
    1952 "Langage et manuelage, II," Tesaur 4 (July-Dec.). [A
    study of the relationship of gesture to language: Hayes.]

Markel, Norman N.
    1965 "The reliability of coding paralanguage: pitch, loudness,
    and tempo," Journal of Verbal Learning and Verbal Behavior
    4:4 (August), pp. 306-308.

    1968 "The paralinguistic framework," in Alan Lomax, ed. ,
    Folk Song Style and Culture. Washington, D. C. : American

Association for the Advancement of Science No. 88, pp. 114-116.

1969   Psycholinguistics: An Introduction to the Study of Speech and Personality. Homewood, Ill.: The Dorsey Press, 400 pages.

1969   "Relationship between voice-quality profiles and MMPI profiles in psychiatric patients," Journal of Abnormal Psychology 74:1, pp. 61-66.

Markel, Norman N., Monte F. Bein, William W. Campbell, Marvin E. Shaw
       "The relationship between self-rating of expressed inclusion and speaking time," Language and Speech.

Markel, Norman N., Monte F. Bein, and Judith A. Phillis
1973   "The relationship between words and tone-of-voice," Language and Speech 16, Part I (Jan.-March), pp. 15-21.

Markel, Norman N., Richard M. Eisler, and Hayne W. Reese
1967   "Judging personality from dialect," Journal of Verbal Learning and Verbal Behavior 6:1 (Feb.), pp. 33-35.

Markel, Norman N., Murray Meisels, and John E. Houck
1964   "Judging personality from voice quality," Journal of Abnormal and Social Psychology 69:4 (Oct.), pp. 458-463.

Markel, Norman N., Judith A. Phillis, Robert Vargas, and Kenneth Howard
1972   "Personality traits associated with voice types," Journal of Psycholinguistic Research 1:3, pp. 249-255.

Markel, Norman N., Layne D. Prebor, and John F. Brandt
1972   "Biosocial factors in dyadic communication: sex and speaking intensity," Journal of Personality and Social Psychology 23:1, pp. 11-13.

Markel, Norman N., and Gloria L. Roblin
1965   "The effect of content and sex-of-judge on judgments of personality from voice," International Journal of Social Psychiatry 11:4 (Autumn), pp. 295-300.

Markel, Norman N., and Clair Ann Sharpless
1972   "Socio-economic and ethnic correlates of dialect differences," in M. Estellie Smith, ed. Studies in Linguistics: In Honor of George L. Trager. The Hague: Mouton, pp. 313-323.

Markowicz, Harry
1972   "Some sociolinguistic considerations of American sign language," Sign Language Studies 1, pp. 15-41.

1973   "Aphasia and deafness," Sign Language Studies 3, pp.
61-71.

Marks, Harold Eugene
1971   "The relationship of eye contact to congruence and em-
pathy." Dissertation, University of California at Los Angeles.

Marks, Sita P.
1974   "A silent morality: non-verbal expression in 'The Am-
bassadors'," South Atlantic Bulletin 39:2, pp. 102-106.

Marone, Silvio
1967   Psicologia dos gestos das mãos: contribuicão para o
seu estudo, sua importancia em medicina. Sao Paulo: Editora
Mestre Jou, Universidade de São Paulo, 124 pages.

Marouzeau, J.
1923   "Langage affectif et langage intellectuel," Journal de
Psychologie: Normale et Pathologique 20, pp. 560-578.

Marquis, Dorothy Postle
1933   "A study of activity and postures in infants' sleep,"
Journal of Genetic Psychology 42, pp. 51-69.

Marshack, Alexander
1972   The Roots of Civilization: The Cognitive Beginnings of
Man's First Art, Symbol and Notation. New York: McGraw-
Hill, 413 pages.

Marshall, Lorna
1968   "Sharing, talking, and giving: relief of social tensions
among Kung Bushmen," Joshua A. Fishman, ed. , Readings in
the Sociology of Language. The Hague: Mouton, pp. 179-184.

Martí, Samuel
1971   Mudrā manos simbólicas en Asia y América. Mexico,
D. F. : Litexa.

Martin, Howard R. , and Kenneth L. Pike
"Analysis of the vocal performance of a poem: a classification of intonational features," Language and Style.

Martin, James G.
1970   "On judging pauses in spontaneous speech," Journal of
Verbal Learning and Verbal Behavior 9, pp. 75-78.

1972   "Rhythmic (hierarchical) versus serial structure in
speech and other behavior," Psychological Review 79:6, pp. 487-
509.

Martin, James G. and Strange, W.
1968   "Determinants of hesitations in spontaneous speech,"
Journal of Experimental Psychology 76, pp. 474-479.

Martin, W. H.
1931   "Rating the transmission performance of telephone cir-
cuits, " Bell System Technical Journal 10, pp. 116-131.

Martín de Castañega, R. P. Fray
1529   Tratado de las supersticiones y Hechicerías.   Madrid:
Sociedad de Bibliófilos Españoles, 1946, vol. 17, chap. 14:
"Que el aojar es cosa natural y no hechicería. " Originally
published in Logroño.

Martinet, André
1957   "Phonetics and linguistic evolution, " in L. Kaiser,
Manual of Phonetics.   Amsterdam: North-Holland Publishing
Company, pp. 252-273.

Martinet, Jeanne
1973   Clefs pour la semiologie.   Paris: Editions Seghers,
243 pages.

Maser, Siegfried
1974   "Bedeutungsreinheit und Bedeutungshöhe: eine Analogie
aus der visuellen Kommunikation, " Poetics 10, pp. 85-96.

Mas-Latrie, Louis de
1854   Dictionnaire de paléographie, de cryptographie, de
dactylologie, d'hiéroglyphie, de sténographie et de télégraphie.
Paris: J. P. Migne. [Pp. 179-366: Seton.]

Maslow, A. H.
1949   "The expressive component in behavior, " Psychological
Review 56, pp. 261-272.

Maslyko, E. A.
1970   "K psikholingvisticheskoy prirode paralingvisticheskikh
yavleniyakh" [Toward the psycholinguistic nature of paralinguistic phenomena], Materialy Tretyego Vsesoyuznogo simpo-
siuma po psikholingvistike [Materials of the Third symposium
on psycholinguistics]. Moscow.

Mason, Bernard S.
1944   Dances and Stories of the American Indian.   New York:
A. S. Barnes.

Mason, Stella E. , ed.
1963   Signs, Signals and Symbols: A Presentation of a British
Approach to Speech Pathology and Therapy.   London: Methuen,
212 pages.   Review by Eric Lenneberg, Language 41:1 (Jan. -
March, 1965), pp. 91-94.

Masson-Oursel, P.
1930   "Le rôle des attitudes dans la conception indienne de la
vie, " Psychologie et Vie 4, pp. 23-24.

Masure, Em
    1954   Le signe, le passage du visible à l'invisible: Psycho-
    logie, histoire [et] mystère. Paris: Bloud & Gay, 336 pages.

Matarazzo, Joseph D.
    1968   Speech Characteristics as Indices of Attitude, Mood,
    and Motivational State. Portland, Ore.: University of Port-
    land Medical School. Available from the Clearinghouse for
    Federal Scientific and Technical Information, AD-669 830.

Matarazzo, Joseph D., G. Saslow, A. N. Wiens, M. Weitman,
    and B. V. Allen
    1964   "Interviewer head nodding and interviewee speech dura-
    tions," Psychotherapy: Theory Research and Practice 1, pp.
    54-63.

Matarazzo, Joseph D., and A. N. Wiens
    1967   "Interviewer influence on durations of interviewee si-
    lence," Journal of Experimental Research in Personality 2:1,
    (February), pp. 56-69.

    1972   The Interview: Research on its Anatomy and Structure.
    Chicago: Aldine-Atherton, 183 pages.

Matarazzo, Joseph D., Arthur N. Wiens, Russell H. Jackson, and
    Thomas S. Manaugh
    1970   "Interviewee speech behavior under different content
    conditions," Journal of Applied Psychology 54:1, pp. 15-26.

Matarazzo, Joseph D., Arthur N. Wiens, Ruth G. Matarazzo, and
    George Saslow
    1968   "Speech and silence behavior in clinical psychotherapy
    and its laboratory correlates," in John M. Schlein, et al., eds.,
    Research in Psychotherapy: Proceedings of the Third Con-
    ference (Chicago, 1966), vol. 3. Washington, D.C.: Ameri-
    can Psychological Association, pp. 347-394. [Interruptions.]

Mathieu, G.
    1964   "Pitfalls of pattern practice: an exegesis," Modern
    Language Journal 48:1 (Jan.), pp. 20-24.

Mathon, C.
    1969   "Pour une semiologie du geste en Afrique Occidentale,"
    Semiotica 1, pp. 245-255.

Matluck, Joseph H. [University of Texas]
    1975   "Sociolinguistic aspects of verbal and nonverbal commu-
    nication in Spanish." Paper read at AATSP, Chicago.

Matoré, Georges
    1961   L'espace humain: L'expression de l'espace dans la vie,
    la pensée et l'art contemporains. Paris: Editions La Colombe.

Matson, Floyd W. and Ashley Montagu, eds.
1967 The Human Dialogue: Perspectives on Communication.
New York: Free Press, 595 pages.

Mattingly, Ignatius G.
1966 "Speaker variation and vocal-tract size," Journal of the
Acoustical Society of America 39:6 (June), p. 1219.

1972 "Speech cues and sign stimuli: an ethological view of
speech perception and the origin of language," American Scientist 60:3, pp. 327-337.

Mauss
1921 L'expression obligatoire des sentiments. [Australians
cry for their dead only at certain hours, and only certain close
relatives are required to cry.]

Mauss, Marcel
1935 "Les techniques du corps," Journal de Psychologie:
Normale et Pathologique 32:3, pp. 271-293. Reprinted in Sociologie et anthropologie. Paris: Presses Universitaires, 1960,
pp. 363-386.

Mawer, Irene
1932 The Art of Mime: Its History and Technique in Education and the Theatre. London: Methuen, 244 pages. [Chap.
II, "Gesture and the gesture apparatus: hands, wrist, elbows
and shoulders": Hayes.]

May, Helen S.
1938 "A study of emotional expression among Chinese and
Americans." M.A. thesis, Columbia University.

May, L. Carlyle
1956 "A survey of glossolalia and related phenomena in non-
Christian religions," American Anthropologist 58:1 (February),
pp. 75-96.

Maynard, Olga
1959 The American Ballet. Philadelphia: Macrae Smith.
[Kineseography, pp. 296-304.]

Mazur, Allan and Leon S. Robertson
1972 Biology and Social Behavior. New York: Macmillan
(Free Press); London: Collier-Macmillan, 200 pages.

Mead, George H.
1922 "A behavioristic account of the significant symbol,"
Journal of Philosophy 19 (January-December), pp. 157-163.
Reprinted in the Bobbs-Merrill Series in the Social Sciences, S-188.

1934 Mind, Self and Society: from the Standpoint of a Social
Behaviorist. Chicago: University of Chicago Press, 401 pages.

[See index, "conversation of gestures" and "gestures," pp. xii-
viii. No. 3, "The behavioristic significance of gestures," pp.
13-18. Part II, Mind: "Wundt and the concept of the gesture,"
pp. 42-68.]

Mead, Margaret
    1935   Sex and Temperament: in Three Primitive Societies.
New York: Dell.

    1954   "The swaddling hypothesis: its reception," American
Anthropologist 56, pp. 395-409.

    1961   "Four families": a documentary film on family life in
India, France, Japan, and Canada. (Wirtten and produced for
the National Film Board of Canada by Ian MacNeill. Commentary by Dr. Margaret Mead. (Comment on) in Visual Communications: International: A Report on the Fifth Communications Conference of the Art Directors Club of New York; Frank
Baker and Edward S. Morse, eds. New York: Communication
Arts Books, pp. 29-36.

    1969   "From intuition to analysis in communication research,"
Semiotica 1, pp. 13-25.

Mead, Margaret, and Paul Byers
    1968   The Small Conference: An Innovation in Communication.
The Hague: Mouton, 126 pages.

Mead, Margaret and Frances MacGregor
    1951   Growth and Culture: A Photographic Study of Balinese
Childhood. New York: G. P. Putnam.

Mead, Margaret and Rhoda Metraux, ed.
    1953   The Study of Culture at a Distance. Chicago: Univer-
sity of Chicago Press.

Meerloo, Joost A. M.
    1955   "Archaic behavior and the communicative act (the mean-
ing of stretching, rocking, yawning and other fetal behavior in
therapy)," Psychiatric Quarterly 29, pp. 60-73.

    1959   "Psychoanalysis as an experiment in communication,"
Psychoanalytic Review 46, pp. 2-16.

    1960   "Some conversational patterns with the neurotic," in
Dominick A. Barbara, ed., Psychological and Psychiatric Aspects of Speech and Hearing. Springfield, Ill.: Charles C.
Thomas, chap. 21, pp. 456-470. ["Speaking in silence,"
pp. 462-465.]

    1961   Dance Craze and Sacred Dance. London: Peter Owen,
151 pages. New York: Humanities Press, 1962.

1961 "Rhythm in babies and adults: its implications for mental contagion," Archives of General Psychiatry 5, pp. 169-175.

1964 Unobtrusive Communication: Essays in Psycholinguistics. Assen, the Netherlands: Van Gorcum Ltd. [Part 1. "Psychoanalysis as an experiment in communication," pp. 11-28; "Patterns of silence," pp. 19-23. Part 13. "A world of smells," pp. 166-169.]

Meggitt, Mervyn
1954 "Sign language among the Walbiri of Central Australia," Oceania 25:1-2 (Sept. -Dec.), pp. 2-16.

Mehegan, Charles, and Fritz E. Dreifuss
1972 "Hyperlexia: exceptional reading ability in brain-damaged children," Neurology 22:11 (November), pp. 1105-1111.

Mehling, R.
1957 "Attitude changing effect of verbal and nonverbal elements in selected news and photo combinations." Thesis, Stanford University.

Mehrabian, Albert
1968 "Communication without words," Psychology Today 2:4 (September), pp. 52-55.

1968 "The inference of attitudes from the posture, orientation and distance of a communicator," Journal of Consulting and Clinical Psychology 32, pp. 296-308.

1969 "Methods and designs: some referents and measures of nonverbal behavior," Behavior Research Methods and Instrumentation 1, pp. 203-207.

1969 "Significance of posture and position in the communication of attitude and status relationships," Psychological Bulletin 71:5, pp. 359-372.

1971 Silent Messages. Belmont, Calif. : Wadsworth, 152 pages.

1972 Nonverbal Communication. Chicago: Aldine-Atherton, 226 pages. Review by Murray Melbin, Semiotica 10:3 (1974), pp. 293-304.

Mehrabian, Albert and Shirley G. Diamond
1971 "Seating arrangement and conversation," Sociometry 34, pp. 281-289.

Mehrabian, Albert, and Morton Wiener
1967 "Decoding of inconsistent communications," Journal of Personality and Social Psychology 6, pp. 109-114.

Mehrabian, Albert and Martin Williams
    1971   "Piagetian measures of cognitive development for
    children up to age two," Journal of Psycholinguistic Research
    1:1, pp. 113-126.

Mehrotra, R. R. [Banaras Hindu University]
            " 'Hattha': the finger language of diamond dealers. "
    MS.

            "Modes of greeting in Hindi: a sociolinguistic state-
    ment. " MS.

    1975   "Hindi speech community of North India," Sociolinguis-
    tics Newsletter 6:1, pp. 13-15.

Mehta, S. S.
    1914   "Modes of salutation," Journal of the Anthropological
    Society of Bombay 10:4, pp. 263-272.

Meijer, D. H.
    1935   "Das Alarmsystem der javanischen Dorfpolizei," Archiv
    für Anthropologie: Volkerforschung und Kolonialon Kulturwandel,
    n. s. 23, pp. 285-295.

Meissner, Martin, and Stuart B. Philpott
    1975   "The sign language of sawmill workers in British Co-
    lumbia, " pp. 291-308; "A dictionary of sawmill workers' signs,"
    pp. 309-347, Sign Language Studies 9.

Melbin, Murray
    1972   Alone and with Others: a Grammar of Interpersonal Be-
    havior. New York: Harper & Row, 333 pages.

Melly, George
    1965   "Gesture goes classless," New Society (June 17), pp.
    26-27.

Melo, Verissimo de
    1960   Gestos populares. Natal: Edicões "Cactus," 36 pages.

Meltzer, Leo and William N. Morris
    1971   "Interruption outcomes and vocal amplitude: explora-
    tions in social psychophysics, " Journal of Personality and So-
    cial Psychology 18, pp. 392-402.

Mencken, H. L.
    1946   Treatise on the Gods. New York: A. A. Knopf.
    [Prayer gestures, pp. 117ff.]

Mendelson, Jack H. , L. Siger, E. Kubzansky, and P. Soloman
    1964   "The language of signs and symbolic behavior of the
    deaf, " in Disorders of Communication 42, Research publica-
    tions, Association for Research in Nervous and Mental Disease.

Mendelson, Jack H. , Leonard Siger, and Philip Solomon
1960   "Psychiatric observations on congenital and acquired
deafness: symbolic and perceptual processes in dreams, "
American Journal of Psychiatry 116 (April), pp. 883-888.

Mendoza, George
1970   The Marcel Marceau Alphabet Book.   New York:
Doubleday.

Meo-Zilio, Giovanni
1960   El lenguaje de los gestos en el Rio de La Plata.
Montevideo, 154 pages.

1961   "El lenguaje de los gestos en el Uruguay, " Boletin de
Filologia 13 (University of Chile), pp. 75-163. [Especially,
pp. 90-97.]

Merleau-Ponty, Maurice
1964   "Indirect language and the voices of silence, " in Signs.
Transl. by R. C. McCleary.   Evanston, Ill. : Northwestern
University Press, chap. 1.

Merleau-Ponty, Maurice   see also   Lanigan

Merrill, Bruce R.
1952   "Childhood attitudes toward flatulence and their possible
relation to adult character, " Yearbook of Psychoanalysis 8,
pp. 213-224.

Merryman, Montgomery
1945   "The eloquence of Brazilian hands, " in Portuguese: A
Portrait of the Language of Brazil.   Rio de Janeiro, chap. 10,
pp. 154-162.

Meschke, Kurt
1927-42 "Gebärde, " in Handwörterbuch des Deutschen
Aberglaubens.   Berlin, 10 vols. [See III, 1930-31, cols. 328-
337.]

Messing, Simon D.
1960   "The nonverbal language of the Ethiopian toga, " Anthropos 55:3-4, pp. 558-560.

Methany, Eleanor
1968   Movement and Meaning.   New York: McGraw-Hill,
126 pages.

Metz, Christian
1968   Film Language: A Semiotics of the Cinema (Translation of Essais sur la significance au cinema).   Oxford University Press.

Meunier, Antoine
   1931   La danse classique. Paris: Firmin-Didot. [Details of
   Saint-Leon's notation and of several other methods: Lister, in
   Stepanov.]

Meyer, Donald R., Harry P. Bahrick, and Paul M. Fitts
   1953   "Incentive, anxiety, and the human blink rate," Journal
   of Experimental Psychology 45:3 (March), pp. 183-187.

Meyer-Eppler, W.
   1957   "Realization of prosodic features in whispered speech,"
   Journal of the Acoustical Society of America 29:1 (January),
   pp. 104-106.

Mezey, A. G., and P. H. Melville
   1960   "Adaptation to postural change in psychiatric patients,"
   Journal of Neurology, Neurosis, and Psychiatry 23, pp. 162-
   169.

Michael, Geraldine, and Frank N. Willis, Jr.
   1968   "The development of gestures as a function of social
   class, education and sex," Psychological Record 18:4, pp. 515-
   519.

   1969   "The development of gestures in three subcultural
   groups," Journal of Social Psychology 79:1, pp. 35-41.

Michael, William, and C. C. Crawford
   1927   "An experiment in judging intelligence by the voice,"
   Journal of Educational Psychology 18:1 (Jan.), pp. 107-114.

Michaels, J. W.
   1923   A Handbook of the Sign Language of the Deaf.   Atlanta.

Michel, Arthur
   1937   "The oldest dance notation," Dance Observer (November),
   pp. 111-112.

Michel, Karl
   1910   Die Sprache des Körpers. Leipzig: J. J. Weber, 167
   pages. [Several hundred photos: Hayes.]

Michels, Th.
   1967   Segensgestus od. Hoheitsgestus? Festschrift für Alois
   Thomas. (Archäolog., kirchen-u., kunsthistor. 39) Trier,
   484 pages.

Michelsson, Katarina
   1971   "Cry analyses of symptomless low birth weight neonates
   and of asphyxiated newborn infants," Acta Pediatrica Scandinavica, Supplementum 216, Helsinki.

Middlemore, Mary P.
1941   The Nursing Couple. London: Cassell.

Miles, W. R.
1925   "Eyeball reflex movement associated with voluntary and
reflex winking," American Journal of Physiology 72, p. 239.

1941   "Correlation of reaction and coordination speed with
age in adults," American Journal of Psychology 43, pp. 377-
391.

Miller, C. B.
1925   "Whispering in Chinese," Le Maitre Phonetique 40,
p. 4.

Miller, Charles Boardman
1934   An Experimental-phonetic Investigation of Whispered Conversation, Considered from the Linguistic Point of View. Bo-
chum-Langendreer: H. Pöppinghaus, 77 pages.

Miller, George A., Eugene Galanter, and Karl H. Pribam
1960   Plans and the Structure of Behavior. New York: Holt,
Rinehart and Winston.

Miller, John D.
1961   "Word tone recognition in Vietnamese whispered speech,"
Word 17:1 (April), pp. 11-15. [Based on Jensen, q.v.]

Miller, Neal Elgar, and John Dollard
1941   Social Learning and Imitation. Institute of Human Relations. New Haven: Yale University Press. [See esp. Appendix 2: Cherry.]

Miller, Robert E., John V. Murphy, and I. Arthur Mirsky
1959   "Nonverbal communication of affect," Journal of Clinical
Psychology 15, pp. 155-158.

Miller, Roy Andrew
1967   " 'Special and notable' utterances," The Japanese Language. University of Chicago Press, pp. 268-307.

Millikan, Clark H. (Chairman), and Frederic L. Darley, ed.
1967   Brain Mechanisms Underlying Speech and Language.
Proceedings of a Conference held at Princeton, New Jersey
(1965). New York: Grune and Stratton, 261 pages.

Millum, Trevor
1971   "A bibliography of non-verbal communication," Working
Papers in Cultural Studies 1 (University of Birmingham), pp.
132-137.

Milmoe, Susan
1965   "Characteristics of speakers and listeners as factors in

nonverbal communication." Senior honors thesis, Harvard University, Department of Social Relations.

Milmoe, Susan, M. S. Nowey, J. Kagan, and R. Rosenthal
1968   "The mother's voice: postdictor aspects of her baby's behavior," Proceedings of the 76th Annual Convention of the American Psychological Association, pp. 463-464.

Milmoe, Susan, Robert Rosenthal, Howard T. Blane, Morris E. Chafetz, and Irving Wolf
1967   "The doctor's voice: postdictor of successful referral of alcoholic patients," Journal of Abnormal Psychology 72:1, pp. 78-84.

Minkowski, M.
1921   "Sur les mouvements, les reflexes, les reactions musculaires du foetus humain de 2 a 5 mois et leur relations avec le systeme nerveux foetal," Revue Neurologique 37, pp. 1105-1135.

Mira, Emilio
1940   "Myokinetic psychodiagnosis: a new technique of exploring the conative trends of personality," Proceedings of the Royal Society of Medicine 33, pp. 173-194.

Mira y Lopez, Emilio
1958   M. K. P.: Myokinetic psychodiagnosis. New York: Logos Press, 186 pages. [One of the first "applied" works on kinesics, trans. from French. Foreword by Gordon W. Allport.]

Mira y Lopez, Emilio see also Takala, Martti

Misiak, Henryk, and George J. Franghiadi
1953   "The thumb and personality," Journal of General Psychology 48 (April), pp. 241-244.

Mitchell, J. C.
1968   "Dermatological aspects of displacement activity: attention to the body surface as a substitute for fright or flight," Canadian Medical Association Journal 98, pp. 962-964.

Mittlemann, Bela
1954   "Motility in infants, children and adults," Psychoanalytic Study of the Child 9, pp. 142-177.

1955   "Motor patterns and genital behavior: fetishism," Psychoanalytic Study of the Child 10, pp. 241-263.

Mobbs, N. A.
1968   "Eye contact in relation to social introversion/extraversion," British Journal of Social and Clinical Psychology 7, pp. 305-306.

Modi, Shams-Ul-Ulma, Dr. Jivanji Jamshedji
1914   "Tibetan salutations and a few thoughts suggested by them," Journal of the Anthropological Society of Bombay 10:3, pp. 165-178. [Tongue protruding.]

Modiliani, Andre
1971   "Embarrassment, facework, and eye contact: testing a theory of embarrassment," Journal of Personality and Social Psychology 17:1 (January), pp. 15-24.

Modley, Rudolf
1974   "World language without words," Journal of Communication 24, pp. 59-66.

Moe, James D.
1971   "Social status cues in the voice," Dissertation Abstracts 32, p. 580A. Wayne State University.

Moles, Abraham A.
1964   "Les voies cutanées, compléments informationnels de la sensibilité de l'organisme," Studium Generale 17:10, pp. 589-595.

1970   "Etude sociolinguistique de la langue sifflée de Kusköy," Revue du phonétique appliquée 14-15, pp. 77-118.

1972   Theorie de l'information et perception esthétique. Paris: Editions Denoël, 328 pages.

Moles, Abraham A., and R.-G. Busnel
1972   "A phonetic and linguistic study of the whistled speech of Kuskoy, Turkey," Proceedings of the Seventh International Congress of Phonetic Sciences (Montreal, 1971). The Hague: Mouton, pp. 737-742.

Moles, Abraham A., and Elisabeth Rohmer
1972   Psychologie de l'espace. Paris: Casterman, 164 pages.

Moncrieff, Robert Wighton
1944   The Chemical Senses. London: L. Hill, 424 pages.

1965   "Changes in olfactory preferences with age," Revue de Laryngologie--Otologie--Rhinologie, pp. 895-904.

Monrad-Krohn, G. H.
1963   "The third element of speech prosody and its disorders," in Lipman Halpern, ed., Problems of Dynamic Neurology: An International Volume: Studies on the Higher Functions of the Human Nervous System. Jerusalem, pp. 101-118.

Montagna, William
1956   The Structure and Function of Skin. London, New York: Academic Press, 454 pages.

Montagu, Ashley
1953   "The sensory influences of the skin," Texas Reports on
Biology and Medicine 2, pp. 291-301.

1959   "Natural selection and the origin and evolution of weeping in man," Science 130:3388, pp. 1572-1573.

1960   "Why man laughs," Think 26:4 (April), pp. 30-32.

1966   "A reply to Coon," American Anthropologist 68:2 (Part
1), (April), pp. 518-519. [On racial body odor.]

1971   Touching: The Human Significance of the Skin.   Columbia University Press, 338 pages.

Montagu, J.
"Charles LeBrun's conference sur l'expression." Ph.D.
thesis, University of London.

Montaigne, Michel de
1580   Selected Essays, translated, and with introduction and
notes by Donald M. Frame.   New York: D. Van Nostrand Co.,
1943, 364 pages.

Montenovesi, Ottorino
1933   Il Linguaggio dei Sordomuti in una Pergamena Veronese
del 1472.   Italy, vol. 2, pp. 217-222.

Moor, Edward
1810   The Hindu Pantheon.   London, 466 pages.

Moore, W. E.
1939   "Personality traits and voice quality deficiencies,"
Journal of Speech and Hearing Disorders 4, pp. 33-36.

Moores, Donald F.
1974   "Nonvocal systems of verbal behavior," in Richard L.
Schiefelbusch and Lyle L. Lloyd, eds., Language Perspectives:
Acquisition, Retardation, and Intervention.   Baltimore, Md.:
University Park Press.

Moores, Donald F., Cynthia K. McIntyre and Karen Weiss
1973   "Gestures, signs and speech in the evaluation of pro-
grams for hearing impaired children," Sign Language Studies
2, pp. 9-28.

Morawski, J.
1965   "Gestowe i mimiczne kody przestepcow," Problemy
Kryminalistyki 58.

Mordkoff, A. M.
1967   "A factor analytic study of the judgment of emotion

from facial expression," Journal of Experimental Research in Personality 2, pp. 80-85.

Moreno Villa, José
1952 Cornucopia de Mexico. Mexico, 149 pages. [Chap. 6, gestures for: time, money, space, height of human being, animal, inanimate object.]

Morey, Edward, and Frederick Koenig
1970 "Paralinguistic and kinesic cues in a word association game," Language and Speech 13:4 (October-December), pp. 279-284.

Morrice, Norman
1967 "Advantages of Benesh notation to a choreographer," Ballet Today 1:17 (January-February), p. 14.

Morris, Charles W.
1946 Signs, Language, and Behavior. New York: George Braziller, Inc., 365 pages.

1964 Signification and Significance: A Study of the Relations of Signs and Values. M.I.T. Press, 99 pages.

1971 Writings on the General Theory of Signs. (Approaches to Semiotics 16) The Hague: Mouton, 486 pages. [Rptd. writings, incl. Foundations of the Theory of Signs (1938) and Signs, Language, and Behavior (1946).]

Morris, Desmond
1967 The Naked Ape: A Zoologist's Study of the Human Animal. New York: Dell, 205 pages.

1971 Intimate Behavior. New York: Random House, 253 pages.

Morris, Kenneth T., and Kenneth M. Cinnamon
1975 A Handbook of Non-verbal Group Exercises. Springfield, Ill.: Charles C. Thomas, 299 pages.

Morris, Margaret
1928 The Notation of Movement: Text, Drawings, and Diagrams. London: Kegan Paul, Trench, Trubner & Co., 103 pages.

Morsbach, Helmut
1973 "Aspects of non-verbal communication in Japan," Journal of Nervous and Mental Disease 157:4 (October), pp. 262-277.

Mortensen, David G.
1972 Communication: The Study of Human Interaction. New York: McGraw-Hill.

Moscovici, Serge
    1967   "Communication processes and the properties of langu-
    age," in Leonard Berkowitz, ed., Advances in Experimental
    Social Psychology, 3. New York: Academic Press, pp. 225-
    270.

Moser, Oskar
    1954   "Zur Geschichte und Kenntnis der volkstümlichen Ge-
    bärden," Carinthiai: Geschichtliche und volkskundliche
    beiträge zur heimatkunde kärntens 144:1-3, pp. 735-774.
    [Searching through the protocols of the county courts of Carin-
    thia, the years 1570-1670, Moser partially reconstructs the
    daily life ... provides some illustrations and many descrip-
    tions of court gestures, ear-gestures (Ohrfeige), gestures of
    scorn, insult, greeting, with special emphasis on the sign of
    the fig which was used both for protection from the evil eye
    and as an insult: Hayes.]

Moses, Paul J.
    1954   The Voice of Neurosis. New York: Grune and Stratton,
    131 pages.

    1958   "Psychosomatic aspects of inspiratory voice," Archives
    Otolaryngology 67, pp. 390-393.

    1960   "Emotional causes of vocal pathology," in Dominick A.
    Barbara, ed., Psychological and Psychiatric Aspects of Speech
    and Hearing. Springfield, Ill.: Charles C. Thomas, chap. 10,
    pp. 204-231.

    1961   "Modern trends in singing." Paper presented at the 1st
    International Congress of Audiology and Phoniatrics (Mexico
    City).

Mosher, Harris D.
    1951   "The expression of the face and man's type of body as
    indicators of his character," Laryngoscope 61, pp. 1-38.

Mosher, Joseph A.
    1916   The Essentials of Effective Gesture: for Students of
    Public Speaking. New York: Macmillan, 188 pages. Re-
    printed in Mosher, Joseph A., Effective Public Speaking: The
    Essentials of Extempore Speaking and of Gesture, Part II.

    1917   Effective Public Speaking: The Essentials of Extempore
    Speaking and of Gesture, Part I. Macmillan, 207 pages; Part
    II, The Essentials of Effective Gesture: for Students of Public
    Speaking, 188 pages. (Part II is also published separately,
    q.v.)

    1931   Complete Course in Public Speaking. New York: Mac-
    millan, 631 pages. [Part II, Gesture, pp. 1-82.]

Moss, Howard A.
1967 "Sex, age, and state as determinants of mother-infant interaction," Merrill-Palmer Quarterly of Behavior and Development 13:1, pp. 19-36. Reprinted in Judith M. Bardwick, ed., Readings on the Psychology of Women. New York: Harper and Row, 1972, pp. 22-29.

Mossford, Lorna
1967 "Advantages of Benesh notation to a ballet company," Ballet Today 1:17 (January-February), pp. 13-14.

1967 "Choregraphie: Fussball nach Noten," Der Spiegel (May 1), Hamburg.

Moulton, Robert H.
1916 "Trading by signs," (Frank) Leslies Illustrated Weekly Newspaper 122 (June 29), New York, pp. 816-817. [Buying grain.]

Mounin, Georges
1959 "Les systèmes de communication non-linguistiques et leur place dans la vie du XXe siecle," Bulletin de la Société de Linguistique de Paris 54:1, pp. 176-200.

Mountford, C. P.
1938 "Gesture language of the Ngada Tribe of the Warburton Ranges, Western Australia," Oceania 9:2, pp. 152-155.

Mowat, Barbara
1970 "The beckoning ghost: stage gesture in Shakespeare," Renaissance Papers, Southeastern Renaissance Conference (Columbia: University of South Carolina), pp. 41-54.

Mowrer, Priscilla
1970 "Notes on Navajo silence behavior." M.A. thesis, University of Arizona.

Müller, E., H. Hollien, and T. Murray
1974 "Perceptual responses to infant crying: identification of cry types," Journal of Child Language 1:1, pp. 89-95.

Müller, (Friedrich) Max [1823-1900]
["Max Müller properly calls touch, scent, and taste the palaioteric [paleo-?], and sight and hearing the neoteric senses..."--Mallery, Sign Language among North American Indians, p. 281.]

Müller, Günter
1939 "Ueber die geographische Verbreitung einiger Gebärden im östlichen Mittelmeergebiet und dem näheren Osten," Zeitschrift für Ethnologie 71, pp. 99ff.

Müller, H.
    1937   "Darstellung von Gebärden auf Den Mälern der alten
    Reiche," Mitteilungen des Deutschen Institutus für Ägyptische
    Altertumskunde in Kairo 7.

Müller, Johannes
    1848   The Physiology of the Senses, Voice and Muscular Mo-
    tion with the Mental Faculties. (Trans. from Handbuch der
    Physiologie des Menschen für Vorlesungen) London: Taylor,
    Walton and Maberly.

Munn, Norman L.
    1940   "The effect of knowledge of the situation upon judgment
    of emotion from facial expressions," Journal of Abnormal and
    Social Psychology 35, pp. 324-328.

Murai, Jun-Ichi
    1960   "Speech development of infants: analysis of speech
    sounds by sona-graph," Psychologia 3, pp. 27-35.

Murdock, George P., Clellan S. Ford, Alfred E. Hudson, Raymond
    Kennedy, Leo W. Simmons, John W. M. Whiting
    1961   Outline of Cultural Materials. New Haven: Human Re-
    lations Area Files, 164 pages. [Sections: during sleep 513;
    during elimination 514; in the arts 535, 536; sexual inter-
    course 833.]

Murphy, Gardner
    1947   Personality: a Biosocial Approach to Origins and Struc-
    ture. New York: Harpers.

Murphy, Robert F.
    1964   "Social distance and the veil," American Anthropologist
    66, pp. 1257-1274.

Murray, Elsie
    1908   "A qualitative analysis of tickling," American Journal
    of Psychology 19:3 (July), pp. 289-344.

                                - N -

Nachson, Israel, and Seymour Wapner
    1967   "Effect of eye contact and physiognomy on perceived lo-
    cation of other person," Journal of Personality and Social
    Psychology 7, pp. 82-89.

Nadel, Myron Howard, and Constance Gwen Nadel
    1970   The Dance Experience: Readings in Dance Appreciation.
    New York: Praeger, 388 pages.

Naidu, Pasupuleti Srinivasulu
    1938   "Hastas (being a study of the elementary hand poses in

ancient Hindu dancing according to the Nātya Śāstra of Bharata Muni)," New Indian Antiquary 1 (Sept.), Bombay, pp. 345-361.

Naidu, Venkata Narayanaswami, Pasupuleti Srinivasulu Naidu, and Venkata Rangayya Pantulu
1936   Tandava Laksanam: or the Fundamentals of Ancient Hindu Dancing.   New Delhi: Munshiram Manoharlal, reprinted 1971.

Nakajima, Bun
1957   Japanese Etiquette.   Tokyo: Japan Travel Bureau, 222 pages.

Nandikesvara
1917   The Mirror of Gesture, Being the Abhinaya Darpana of Nandikesvara [translated by Ananda K. Coomaraswamy and Duggirala Gopalakrishnayya].   Cambridge: Harvard University Press, 52 pages.   2nd ed. , New York: E. Weyhe, 1936, 81 pages.

1957   Nandikesvara's Abhinayadarpanam; a Manual of Gesture and Posture used in Hindu Dance and Drama [translation by Manomohan Ghosh].   Calcutta: Mukhopadhyay, 152 pages.

Nash, Jeffrey E.
1973   "Cues or signs: a case study in language acquisition," with comments by R. Orin Cornett.   Sign Language Studies 3, pp. 79-98.

Nattiez, J. J.
1971   "Semiologie, linguistique, biologie (à propos d'une conférence de Roman Jakobson)," Cahiers Linguistiques d'Ottawa 1, pp. 51-73.

Natya Sastra see Naidu

Neal, A. J. , and M. S. Fry
[before 1942] The Language of the Silent Word.   Cardiff.

Neckel, G.
1935   "Über eine altgermanische Geste des Schmerzes," Archiv für das Studium der Neueren Sprachen und Literaturen 167, pp. 64-66.

Needham, Rodney
1974   Right and Left: Essays on Dual Symbolic Classification. Chicago: University of Chicago Press, 449 pages.

Needles, William
1959   "Gesticulation and speech," International Journal of Psychoanalysis, pp. 291-294.

Nekes, Hermann
    1912   "Trommelsprache und Fernruf bei den Jaunde und Duala
    in Südkamerun," Mitteilungen Desseminar für Orientalische
    Sprachen 15:3 (Berlin), pp. 69-83.

Nerbonne, Gary Patrick
    1967   "The identification of speaker characteristics on the
    basis of aural cues," Dissertation Abstracts 28, 4332B-33B.
    Michigan State University.

Neumann, Gerhard
    1965   Gesten und Gebärden in der griechischen Kunst.   Ber-
    lin: W. de Gruyter, 225 pages.

Neumann, Günter
    1966   "Zür chinesisch-russischen Behelfssprache von Kjachta,"
    Sprache 12, pp. 237-251.

Newell, William Wells
    1883   Games and Songs of American Children.   Reprinted,
    New York: Dover, 1963, 289 pages.

Newman, D. and R. Benton
    1964   "What's sexy?" Mademoiselle 59:1 (May), pp. 66-72.

Newman, Stanley S.
    1941   "Behavior patterns in linguistic structure: a case
    study," in Leslie Spier, A. Irving Hallowell, and Stanley S.
    Newman, eds. , Language, Culture, and Personality: Essays
    in Memory of Edward Sapir, pp. 94-106.   Menasha, Wis. :
    Sapir Memorial Publication Fund.

    1944   "Cultural and psychological features in English intona-
    tion," Transactions, New York Academy of Sciences Ser. II. 7,
    pp. 45-54.

    1946   "On the stress system of English," Word 2:3 (Dec.),
    pp. 171-187.   ['Expressive prosody. ']

Newman, Stanley S. , and Vera G. Mather
    1938   "Analysis of spoken language of patients with affective
    disorders, " American Journal of Psychiatry 94, pp. 913-942.

Nielsen, Gerhard
    1964   Studies in Self Confrontation: Viewing a Sound Motion
    Picture of Self and Another Person in a Stressful Dyadic Inter-
    action.   Copenhagen: Munksgaard; Cleveland: Howard Allen,
    221 pages.

Nierenberg, Gerard I. , and Henry H. Calero
    1971   How to Read a Person Like a Book.   New York: Haw-
    thorn Books, 180 pages.   Review by Edward A. Schmerler,
    ETC. , 29:2 (June 1972), pp. 215-217.

Niggemeyer, H.
1938-40 "Trommelsprache ohne Trommeln," Paideuma, pp.
191-192.

Nikolais, Alwin
1970 "A new method of dance notation," in Myron H. Nadel
and Constance Nadel, The Dance Experience. New York:
Praeger, pp. 145-150.

Nikolayeva, T. M.
1972 Zhest i mimika v lektsii. Moscow: Znanie. [Gesture
and mimics in lectures.]

Nilsen, Don L. F.
1970 "A linguistic analysis of humor," The English Record
20:3 (February), pp. 41-56.

Nilsson, O.
1964 "High frequency postural movements in man," Acta
Morphologica Neerlando-Scandinavica 6, pp. 9-16.

Nine-Curt, Judith [University of Puerto Rico]
"A partial listing of Puerto Rican gestures."

1976 "The role of non-verbal communication in teaching
Spanish speakers." Paper read at the conference of the English Language Institute, Ann Arbor, Michigan.

(in press) Nonverbal Communication among Puerto Ricans.
New York: Center for Bilingual Materials.

Nketia, J. H. Kwabena
The Poetry of Akan Drums. (Approaches to Semiotics
53) The Hague: Mouton.

1971 "Surrogate languages of Africa," Current Trends in
Linguistics 7. The Hague: Mouton, pp. 699-732.

1972 "Surrogate languages of Africa," Language Systems in
Africa 2, ed. by Sunday O. Anozie. New Paltz, N.Y.: Conch
Magazine, pp. 11-48.

Noël-Armfield, George
1931 General Phonetics: for Missionaries and Students of
Languages. Cambridge: W. Heffer. ["Peculiar noises":
kiss, sniff, snort, hiccough, p. 180.]

Nordenskiöld, Erland
1922 "Taubstumme Indianer und ihre Zeichensprache," Indianer und Weisse in Nordostbolivien. Stuggart, Chap. 25, pp.
204-215.

Norman, H. J.
    1943   "John Bulwer, the Chirosopher," Proceedings of the
    Royal Society of Medicine (May), pp. 589-602.

North, Marion
    1971   An Introduction to Movement Study and Teaching. Lon-
    don: Macdonald and Evans, 128 pages.

    1972   Body Movement for Children: an Introduction to Move-
    ment Study and Teaching. Boston: Plays, Inc., 104 pages.

    1972   Personality Assessment Through Movement. London:
    Macdonald and Evans, 300 pages.

    1973   Movement Education. London: Temple-Smith.

Northrop, F. S. C., and Helen H. Livingston, eds.
    1964   Cross-Cultural Understanding: Epistemology in Anthro-
    pology. New York: Harper and Row, 396 pages.

Norum, Gary A., Nancy Jo Russo, and Robert Sommer
    1967   "Seating patterns and group task," Psychology in the
    Schools 4:3 (July), pp. 276-280.

Nosek, J.
    1968   "Pauzovane opakování v moderní hovorové angličtiné,"
    Casopis pro Moderní Filologii 50:3, pp. 152-161. [Pause and
    repetition in modern spoken English.]

Noverre, Jean Georges
    1803   Letters on Dancing and Ballets. St. Petersburg.
    Trans. by Cyril W. Beaumont, 1930. Reprinted, New York:
    Dance Horizons, 1866. [P. 140, Diderot and d'Alembert's.]

Nummenmaa, Tapio
    1964   "The language of the face," Jyvaskyla Studies in Educa-
    tion, Psychology and Social Research 9. Jyväskylä, Finland:
    Jyvaskylan Yliopistoyhdistys.

Nummenmaa, Tapio, and Urpo Kauranne
    1958   "Dimensions of facial expression," Reports from the
    Department of Psychology 20 (Univ. Jyväskylä, Finland), pp.
    91-103.

Nyrop, Christopher
    1901   The Kiss: and Its History. London, 188 pages. Re-
    printed, Detroit, Mich.: Singing Tree Press, 1968.

                                - O -

O'Connell, Daniel C., and Sabine Kowal
    1972   "Cross-linguistic pause and rate phenomena in adults

and adolescents," Journal of Psycholinguistic Research 1:2, pp. 155-164.

O'Connell, Daniel C. , Sabine Kowal, and Hans Hörmann
1969   "Semantic determinants of pauses, " Psychologische Forschung 33, pp. 218-223.

O'Connor, John R.
1972   "The relationship of kinesic and verbal communication to leadership perception in small group discussion," Dissertation Abstracts 32, 6589A.

O'Connor, Lynn
ca. 1971   "Male supremacy," Mimeo.   San Francisco: The Women's Page (1227 37th Avenue, San Francisco), 8 pages.

Odom, Richard D. , and Carolyn M. Lemond
1972   "Developmental differences in the perception and production of facial expression," Child Development 43, pp. 359-369.

Oesterley, William O. E.
1923   The Sacred Dance: A Study in Comparative Folklore. Cambridge University Press, 234 pages.   Reprinted, Brooklyn, N.Y. : Dance Horizons, 1968.

Ogden, C. K. and I. A. Richards
1923   The Meaning of Meaning.   New York: Harcourt, Brace, and World, 363 pages.

Ohm, Thomas
1947   "Christus und die Gebetsgebärde," Benediktinishche Monatsschrift 23.

1947   "Die Gebetsgebärden in der Regel und im Leben des Heiligen Benedikt. " München.

1948   Die Gebetsgebärden der Völker und das Christentum. Leiden: Brill, 472 pages.

1949   "Die Gebetsgebärden des Gemens, " Benediktinische Monatsschrift 25.

Ohnuki-Tierney, Emiko
1972   "Spatial concepts of the Ainu of the northwest coast of Southern Sakhalin," American Anthropologist 74:3 (June), pp. 426-457.

Oldfield, Derek
1967   "The language of the novel: the character of Dorothea, " in Barbara Hardy, ed. , Middlemarch: Critical Approaches to the Novel.   Oxford University Press, pp. 63-86.

Olesen, Virginia L. , and Elvi W. Whittaker
1968   The Silent Dialogue: a Study in the Social Psychology
of Professional Socialization. San Francisco: Jossey-Bass,
312 pages.

Olofson, Harold
1974   "Hausa language about gesture, " Anthropological Linguistics 16:1 (January), pp. 25-39.

Olsen, Carroll L. [University of Toronto]
"Voice register and intonation levels in two dialects of
Spanish. " MS.

Olsen, Tillie
1970   "Silences: when writers don't write, " Women: A Journal of Liberation 2:1 (Fall), pp. 43-44.

Olson, Willard C.
1930   "The incidence of nervous habits in children, " Journal
of Abnormal and Social Psychology 25:1, pp. 75-92.

Ombredane, André
1933   "Le Langage: gesticulation significative mimique et
conventionnelle, " in Nouveau Traité de Psychologie; G. Dumas,
ed. Paris, pp. 363-458.

1944   Études de psychologie medicale: II, Geste et action.
Rio de Janeiro: Atlantica Editora.

Ono, Hiroshi, Albert H. Hastorf, and Charles E. Osgood
1966   "Binocular rivalry as a function of incongruity in the
meanings of stereoscopically fused facial expressions, " Scandinavian Journal of Psychology 7:4, pp. 225-233. [Third of
series; I, Osgood; II, Hastorf, Osgood, and Ono.]

Opie, Iona and Peter
1959   The Lore and Language of Schoolchildren. Oxford:
Clarendon Press, 417 pages. [...Research on the folklore-
games of children, rhymes, riddles, jokes, repartee, nick-
names, epithets, jeers, tricks, pranks, magical beliefs.]

Orione, Julio
1950   Teoria visual espacial. Buenos Aires: N. Zielony.

O'Rourke, Terrence J. , ed.
1972   Psycholinguistics and Total Communication: The State
of the Art. Washington, D. C. : National Association of the
Deaf, 134 pages. [11 chapts: Moores, Vernon, Meadow,
Lenneberg, Denton, Neesan, Bellugi, Stokoe, Schlesinger, Nem-
ser, Alatis.] Review by: Harry Markowicz, Sign Language
Studies 5 (1974), pp. 82-91.

Ortega y Gasset
1957 Man and People. New York: W. W. Norton. [Whole
vocabulary of glances: Goffman.]

Oseretzky/Ozeretsky see Allport and Vernon; Bouissac (pp. 158-
166); DaCosta; Davis, Martha (1972), Index, p. 185; Lassner

Oseretzky, N.
1931 "Psychomotorik: Methoden zur Untersuchung der Mo-
torik, " Beihefte zur Zeitschrift für Angewandte Psychologie 57.
Leipzig: Barth, pp. 1-162. [Institute of Child Research at
Leningrad. His plan for study of Psychomotorik: 1. Moto-
skopic--analyze and classify all movement, pp. 4-24; 2. Moto-
metric--measurements of movements, pp. 25-79, pp. 80-131;
3. Motographic--recording of them, pp. 132-158. Aim: development of age scale for determination of the motor matur-
ity of children.]

Osgood, Charles E.
1966 "Dimensionality of the semantic space for communication via facial expressions, " Scandinavian Journal of Psychology
7:1, pp. 1-30. [First of series; II, Hastorf, Osgood and Ono;
III, Ono, Hastorf, and Osgood.]

Osgood, Charles E. , and Albert W. Heyer, Jr.
1950 "Objective studies in meaning. II, The validity of posed
facial expressions as gestural signs in interpersonal communication, " American Psychologist 5, p. 298. (Abstract.)

Osgood, Charles E. , and Thomas A. Sebeok, eds.
1965 Psycholinguistics: A Survey of Theory and Research
Problems. Indiana University Press, pp. 84-92.

Osser, H. , and F. Peng
1964 "A cross-cultural study of speech rate, " Language and
Speech 7, pp. 120-125.

Ostrander, Sheila, and Lynn Schroeder
1970 Psychic Discoveries Behind the Iron Curtain. Englewood Cliffs, N.J. : Prentice-Hall, Inc. [Chap. 14, "Eyeless
Sight, " pp. 167-182--about Rosa Kuleshova, from the Ural Mt.
Nizhniy Tagil, who could identify colors by touch.]

Ostwald, Peter F.
1959 "When people whistle, " Language and Speech 2:3, pp.
137-145.

1960 "A method for the objective denotation of the sound of
the human voice, " Journal of Psychosomatic Research 4, pp.
301-305.

1960 "Human sounds, " in Dominick A. Barbara, ed. , Psychological and Psychiatric Aspects of Speech and Hearing.

Springfield, Ill.:   Charles C. Thomas, chap. 6, pp. 110-137.

1960   "The sounds of human behavior: a survey of the literature," Logos 3:1 (April), pp. 13-24.

1960   "Visual denotation of human sounds," Archives of General Psychiatry 3 (August), pp. 117-121.

1961   "Humming, sound and symbol," Journal of Auditory Research 3, pp. 224-232.

1961   "The sounds of emotional disturbance," Archives of
General Psychiatry 5 (Dec.), pp. 587-592.

1962   "Sound, music, and human behavior," Music Therapy,
E. H. Schneider, ed. Lawrence, Kans.: NAMT, pp. 107-125.

1963   "Sonic communication in medical practice and research,"
Journal of Communication 13:3 (Sept.), pp. 156-165.

1963   Soundmaking: The Acoustic Communication of Emotion.
Springfield, Ill.:   Charles C. Thomas, 186 pages.   ["Baby
Sounds," pp. 16-23, 46-48; "Listener Responses to Baby
Sounds," pp. 114-127.]

1965   "Acoustic methods in psychiatry," Scientific American
212:3 (March), pp. 82-91.

1967   "The interview," in The Correctional Community: An
Introduction and Guide; eds. Norman Fenton, Ernest G. Reimer,
Harry A. Wilmer.   University of California Press, pp. 95-106.

1968   "Symptoms, diagnosis, and concepts of disease: some
comments on the semiotics of patient-physician communication,"
Social Science Information 7:4 (August), pp. 95-106.

1970   "Greenson's remedy: review of a new book and some
comments about psychoanalysis," Semiotica 2:2, pp. 185-192.

1972   "The sounds of infancy," Developmental Medicine and
Child Neurology 14, pp. 350-361.

1973   "Musical behavior in early childhood," Developmental
Medicine and Child Neurology 15:3 (June), pp. 367-375.

1973   The Semiotics of Human Sound.   The Hague: Mouton,
422 pages.

Ostwald, Peter F., Daniel G. Freedman, and Joseph H. Kurtz
1962   "Vocalization of infant twins," Folia Phoniatrica 14,
pp. 37-50.

Ostwald, Peter F., and Philip Peltzman
1974   "The cry of the human infant," Scientific American
230:3 (March), pp. 84-90.

Ostwald, Peter F., R. Phibbs, and S. Fox
1968   "Diagnostic use of infant cry," Biologia Neonatorum 13,
pp. 68-82.

O'Toole, Richard, and Robert Dubin
1968   "Baby feeding and body sway: an experiment in George
Herbert Mead's 'taking the role of the other'," Journal of Personality and Social Psychology 10:1, pp. 59-65.

Ott, Edward Amherst
1892   How to Gesture.   New York: Hinds, Noble, and El-
drige, 126 pages.

Ott, John N.
1973   Health and Light: the Effects of Natural and Artificial
Light on Man and Other Living Things.   Old Greenwich, Conn. :
Devin-Adair, 208 pages.

Otterstein, Adolph W.
1942   The Baton in Motion: a Photographic Presentation.
New York: Carl Fischer, 59 pages.

Ovid [43 B. C. -A. D. 17?]
1954   The Metamorphoses.   Berkeley: University of California Press, 397 pages. [See p. 1 (phallic sign); p. 8 (nod);
p. 11-12 (covering head); p. 12 (stones tossed behind one's
back); p. 34 (beating one's breast); p. 34 (rending one's hair):
Hayes.]

Oxenford, Lyn
1951   Design for Movement: A Textbook on Stage Movement.
New York: Theatre Arts Books, 96 pages.

Ozeretsky   see   Oseretzky

- P -

Pack, Alice C.
1972   "Interpretations of kinesics are cultural not universal,"
TESL Reporter 6:1, pp. 6-7, 11.

Pack, Roger
1956   "Catullus, Carmen V: abacus or finger-counting?"
American Journal of Philology 77:305 (Jan.), pp. 47-51.

Paget, Sir Richard A. S.
1927   "The origin of language," Psyche 8, pp. 35-39.

1930   Babel: or the Past, Present, and Future of Human
Speech. London, 93 pages.

1930   Human Speech. London: Kegan Paul, Trench, Trubner; New York: Harcourt, Brace, 360 pages.

1935   "Sign language as a form of speech. " Paper read at
the Royal Institute of Great Britain (Dec. 13). [Compared ...
signs of Pitta-Pitta with the symbol representing the idea ...
cf. Indian sign language and deaf language. Refers to sign
language in Russian Armenia, the Caucasus ... by men only:
Critchley, pp. 49-50.]

1937   "Gesture language, " Nature 139 (Jan. 30), London,
p. 198.

1944   "The origin of language, " Science 99:2558 (Jan. 7), pp.
14-15.

1946   "Gesture as a constant factor in linguistics, " Nature
158 (July 6), p. 29.

Painter, Colin
1971   "Archetypal breath-groups and the motor theory of
speech perception: evidence from a register tone language, "
Anthropological Linguistics 13:7, pp. 349-360.

1975   "/m hm/, /!m!m/ and some forms of yes and no in
Gwa, " Anthropological Linguistics 17:1 (January), pp. 19-23.

Palmer, Robert D.
1973   "Desensitization of the fear of expressing one's own in-
hibited aggression: bioenergetic assertive techniques for behavior therapists, " in R. D. Rubin, J. P. Brady, and J. D.
Henderson, eds. , Advances in Behavior Therapy 4. New York:
Academic Press.

Panconcelli-Calzia, G.
1955   "Da Flüstern in seiner physio-pathologischen und
linguistischen Bedeutung, " Lingua 4, pp. 369-378.

Pandeya, Gayanacharya A.
1943   The Art of Kathakali.   Allahabad: Kitabistan, 163 pages.

Panek, David M. , and Barclay Martin
1959   "The relationship between GSR and speech disturbances
in psychotherapy, " Journal of Abnormal and Social Psychology
58, pp. 402-405. [Galvanic skin response.]

Pardoe, T. E.
1923   "Language of the body, " Quarterly Journal of Speech
Education 9 (June), pp. 252-258.

Parker   349

Parker, George Howard
  1922   Smell, Taste, and Allied Senses in the Vertebrates.
  Philadelphia: J. B. Lippincott, 192 pages.

Parker, Larry, and Russell L. French
  1975   "A description of student behavior: verbal and nonverbal," Language and Language Behavior Abstracts 9:2, 7501883.

Parkes, A. S.
  1963   "Olfactory and gustatory discrimination in man and animals," The Royal Society of Medicine, Proceedings 56 (Jan.),
  pp. 47-51.

Parrish, Wayland Maxfield
  1925   "The rhythm of oratorical prose," Studies in Rhetoric
  and Public Speaking in Honor of James Albert Winans, ed. by
  Alexander Magnus Drummond. New York: The Century Co.,
  [1962], pp. 217-231.

  1947   Speaking in Public. New York: Ronald Press.

Parsons, Elsie Clews
  1941   "Notes on the Caddo," American Anthropologist 43:3,
  Part 2. [Spitting, breath rites: pp. 28, 46.]

Paschall, Clarence
  1943   The Semasiology of Words Derived from Indo-European
  *nem-. University of California Publications in Linguistics 1,
  pp. 1-9.

Paschius, Georgius [1661-1707]
  1700   Inventa Novantiqua. Leipzig.

Passy, Paul Edouard
  1914   The Sounds of the French Language: Their Formation,
  Combination and Representation. Oxford: Clarendon Press,
  134 pages.

Patterson, Miles L., Sherry Mullens, and Jeanne Romano
  1971   "Compensatory reactions to spatial intrusion," Sociometry 34:I (March), pp. 114-121.

Patterson, Miles L., and Lee B. Sechrest
  1970   "Interpersonal distance and impression formation,"
  Journal of Personality 38:2 (June), pp. 161-166.

Pattison, E. Mansell
  1968   "Behavioral science research on the nature of glossolalia," Journal of the American Scientific Affiliation (Sept.), pp.
  73-86.

Payne, Buryl
  1968   "Extra-verbal techniques and Korzybskian formulations,"

ETC. 25:1 (March), pp. 7-15. [Esalen Institute, Big Sur ...
sensory awareness....]

Payne, P. S. B.
1935   "Trail-signs," Gypsy Lore Society Journal Ser. 3, 14
(Edinburgh), pp. 169-174.

Peale, O. F.
1932   "Sign language of deaf mutes," American Mercury 26
(Aug.), pp. 457-460.

Pear, Tom Hatherley
1931   Voice and Personality as Applied to Radio Broadcasting.
New York: Wylife; London: Chapman and Hall, 247 pages.

Pear, Thomas
1935   "Suggested parallels between speaking and clothing, "
Acta Psychologica 1, pp. 191-201.

Pearce, W. Barnett
1971   "The effect of vocal cues on credibility and attitude
change, " Western Speech 35:3 (Summer), pp. 176-184.

Pearce, W. Barnett, and Forrest Conklin
1971   'Nonverbal vocalic communication and perceptions of a
speaker," Speech Monographs 38:3, pp. 235-241.

Pearn, B. R.
1935   "Dumb-show in Elizabethan drama," Review of English
Studies 11:44 (Oct.), pp. 385-405.

Pécourt, Guillaume Louis [1653-1729]
1700   Chorégraphie ou l'art d'ecrire la danse, ed. Raoul Ager
Feuillet, q. v.

Pederson, Lee A.
1971   "Southern speech and the LAGS project," Orbis 20,
pp. 79-89.

Pei, Mario
1950   "Gesture language," Life (January 9), pp. 79-81.

Pei, Mario, ed. and chief contributor
1967   Language Today: A Survey of Current Linguistic Thought.
New York: Funk and Wagnalls, 150 pages. [Katharine Le Mée,
"Studies in Communication," Chap. 4, Paralanguage, Gestures,
Kinesics, Proxemics, pp. 98-127.]

Peled, T.
1967   "The sign language of the deaf: a comparative pilot
study," Working Papers, The Hebrew University of Jerusalem
1, pp. 1-12.

Penfield, Wilder, and Lamar Roberts
1959   Speech and Brain-Mechanisms. Princeton, N.J.:
Princeton University Press, 286 pages. Review by Eric
Lenneberg, Language 36:1 (1960), pp. 97-112.

Peng, Fred C. C. [International Christian University, Tokyo]
1974   "Communicative distance. " Language Sciences 31
(August), pp. 32-37.

        "The deaf and their acquisition of the various systems
of communication: a speculation against innatism. "

1974   "Kinship signs in Japanese sign language, " Sign Language Studies 5, pp. 31-47.

1975   "Sign language and its notational system. "

Pengniez, P.
1927   "Cinématique de la main: la main de prestidigatateur, "
Presse Medicale 35, pp. 123-125.

Penrod, James
1974   Movement for the Performing Artist. Palo Alto: National Press.

Penrod, James, and Janice Gudde Plastino
1970   The Dancer Prepares. Palo Alto: National Press.

Penzer, N. M.
1924-28 The Ocean of Story. 10 vols. London. [Bibliogra-
phy, Vol. 9, pp. 171-335; Index Vol. 10.] [See Vol. 1, p.
112; Vol. 3, p. 37, p. 150; Vol. 9, p. 162 ... fundamental
source for determining approximate number of centuries some
gestures have endured: Hayes.]

Perella, Nicolas J.
1969   The Kiss Sacred and Profane: An Interpretative History
of Kiss Symbolism and Related Religio-Erotic Themes. Berkeley: University of California Press, 356 pages.

Perju-Liiceanu, Aurora
1972   "The serenadical behaviour, " Cahiers de linguistique
théorique et appliquée 9, pp. 83-92.

Perrin, Noel
1962   "Old Macberlitz had a farm, " New Yorker (Jan. 27),
pp. 28-29.

Perrot, Marie-Catherine
1972   "La mimique et le langage gestuel chez les aphasiques, "
Rev. de Laryngologie, Otologie, Rhinologie, Rev. Portmann
93, p. 235.

Pesonen, Jaakko
    1968   Phoneme Communication of the Deaf: Theory and Ele-
    mentary Visio-Oral Verbal Education by Means of Individualized
    Visiophonemes. Helsinki: Suomalaisen Tiedeakatemian Toimi-
    tuksia Annales Academiae Scientiarum Fennicae, Ser. B. 151,
    207 pages.

Pesso, Albert
    1969   Movement in Psychotherapy. New York: University
    Press, 221 pages.

Peter, H. R. H. , Prince of Greece and Denmark
    1953   "Peculiar sleeping postures of the Tibetans, " Man
    53:230 (Oct.), p. 145.

Petersen, Gordon A. J. , and Marshall McClintock
    1942   A Guide to Codes and Signals; International Flag Code,
    Secret Ciphers, Weather Signals, Morse Code, Sign Language,
    Etc. , with Flags of All Nations. Racine, Wis. : Whitman,
    62 pages.

Peterson, Fred
    1957   "Of human laughter, " Mexico This Month 3:8. [Brief
    commentary on the ancient smiling and laughing carved mask-
    like faces found near Vera Cruz: Hayes.]

Peterson, Gordon E.
    1957   "Breath stream dynamics, " in L. Kaiser, ed. , Manual
    of Phonetics. Amsterdam: North-Holland Publishing Co. ,
    pp. 139-148.

Peterson, Gordon E. , and Harold L. Barney
    1952   "Control methods used in study of the vowels, " Journal
    of Acoustical Society of America 24:2 (March), pp. 175-184.

Petö, Endre
    1946   "Weeping and laughing, " International Journal of Psycho-
    analysis 27, pp. 129-133.

Petrov, P. M.
    1931   [Children's gestures in experiment], Pedalogia 2, pp.
    68-71. [Article in Russian.]

Pettigrew, John D. [California Institute of Technology]
    1974   "Seeing with an infant's eyes. " [Lecture at Caltech,
    Pasadena, Calif.]

Pfaff, Paul L.
    1954   "An experimental study of the communication of feeling
    without contextual material, " Speech Monographs 21, pp. 155-
    156. [Abstract.]

Pfaffmann, C.
1951   "Taste and smell" in Stanley S. Stevens, ed. , Handbook
of Experimental Psychology. New York: John Wiley and Sons,
1436 pages.

Philips, Susan U.
1974   "Warm Springs 'Indian Time': how the regulation of
participation affects the progression of events," in Richard
Bauman and Joel Sherzer, eds. , Explorations in the Ethnography of Communication. London: Cambridge University Press,
pp. 92-109.

Phillips, George L.
1951   "Toss a kiss to the sweep for luck," Journal of American Folklore 64:252 (April-June), pp. 191-196. [Lift your
hat, or toss a kiss to a sweep, or have the bride kissed at
the wedding by a sweep ... good luck: Hayes.]

Phillis, Judith A.
1970   "Children's judgments of personality on the basis of
voice quality," Developmental Psychology 3, Part 1 (November),
p. 411.

Phillott, D. C.
1906   "A note on the mercantile sign language of India,"
Journal of the Royal Asiatic Society of Bengal: Journal and
Proceedings, n. s. , 2:7 (July), pp. 333-334.

1907   "A note on sign-, gesture-, code-, and secret-language,
etc. amongst the Persians," Royal Asiatic Society of Bengal,
Journal and Proceedings, n. s. , 3:9 (Nov.), pp. 619-622.

Pickersgill, M. Gertrude
1936   Practical Miming. London: Sir Isaac Pitman & Sons,
117 pages.

Piddington, Ralph
1933   The Psychology of Laughter: a Study in Social Adaptation. London: Figurehead. Reprinted, New York, 1963.

Piderit, Theodor [1826-1898]
1867   Mimik und Physiognomik. 2nd ed. --Wissenschaftliches
System der Mimik und Physiognomik. Detmold, 1884, 212
pages. La mimique et la physiognomie, 1888.

Piderit, Theodor see also Boring and Titchener; Buzby; Fernberger; Guilford and Wilke; Jarden

Pierson, Donald
1951   Cruz das Almas: A Brazilian Village. Smithsonian Institution, Institute of Social Anthropology, Publ. no. 12, 226
pages.

Pike, Evelyn G.
    1949   "Controlled infant intonation," Language Learning 2
    (Jan. -March), pp. 21-24.

Pike, Kenneth L.
    1943   Phonetics: A Critical Analysis of Phonetic Theory and
    a Technic for the Practical Description of Sounds. University
    of Michigan Press, 1944, 182 pages. [Chap. I, "Marginal
    Sounds," pp. 5-31; Chap. II "Nonspeech Sounds," pp. 32-41,
    and throughout book.]

    1945   The Intonation of American English. Ann Arbor, Mich.:
    University of Michigan, 200 pages. [An etic system of voice
    quality, pp. 99-104.]

    1957   "Abdominal pulse types in some Peruvian languages,"
    Language 33:1 (January-March), pp. 30-35.

    1954-60   Language: In Relation to a Unified Theory of the
    Structure of Human Behavior. 3 vols. Glendale, Calif.:
    Summer Institute of Linguistics. ["Mode-like emic units and
    systems," vol. III, chap. 13.]

    1966   "Etic and emic standpoints for the description of be-
    havior," in Alfred G. Smith, ed., Communication and Culture:
    Readings in the Codes of Human Interaction. New York: Holt,
    Rinehart and Winston, pp. 152-163.

    1975   "On kinesic triadic relations in turn-taking," Semiotica
    13:4, pp. 389-394.

Piper, David
    The English Face.

Pitcairn, Tom K. [Centre Royaumont pour une science de l'homme]
        "Animal communication and human communication" [from
    the point of view of an ethologist].

Pitre, Giuseppe
    1877   "Gesti ed insegne del popolo siciliano," Revista di
    Letterature [Popolare] Moderne 1, pp. 32-43.

Pittenger, Robert E.
    1958   "Linguistic analysis of tone of voice in communication
    of affect," Psychiatric Research Reports 8, pp. 41-54.

Pittenger, Robert E., Charles F. Hockett, and John J. Danehy
    1960   The First Five Minutes: A Sample of Microscopic Inter-
    view Analysis. Ithaca, N.Y.: Paul Martineau, 264 pages.
    Reviews by Eric H. Lenneberg, Language 38:1 (1962), pp. 69-
    73; Helmut Richter, Word 21:3 (Dec. 1965), pp. 483-487;
    Robert P. Stockwell, International Journal of American Linguis-
    tics 28:4 (Oct. 1962), pp. 293-296.

Pittenger, Robert E. , and Henry Lee Smith, Jr.
   1957 "A basis for some contributions of linguistics to psychi-
   atry," Psychiatry 20:1, pp. 61-78. Reprinted in: Alfred G.
   Smith, ed. , Communication and Culture: Readings in the
   Codes of Human Interaction. New York: Holt, Rinehart and
   Winston, 1966. Reprinted in Bobbs-Merrill Reprint Series
   in Language and Linguistics, L-74. Partially reprinted as
   "Fundamentals of English structure," in Norman N. Markel,
   Psycholinguistics. Homewood, Ill. : Dorsey Press, 1969,
   pp. 80-108.

Pittman, A. T. , M. B. Parloff, and D. S. Boomer
   1965 "Facial and bodily expression: a study of perceptivity
   of emotional cues," Psychiatrist 28.

Playford, John
   1651 The English Dancing Master.

Plessner, Helmut
   1942 Lachen und Weinen, eine Untersuchung nach den Grenzen
   menschlichen Verhaltens. Arnhem: van Loghum Slaterus;
   Bern: A. Francke, 1950. Trans. as Laughing and Crying: a
   Study of the Limits of Human Behavior. Evanston, Ill. :
   Northwestern University Press, 1970, 172 pages.

Plutchik, Robert
   1962 The Emotions: Facts, Theories, and a New Model.
   Clinton, Mass. : Colonial Press, 204 pages.

Poiret, Maude
   1970 Bodytalk: The Science of Kinesics. New York: Award
   Books, 152 pages. Review by Edward A. Schmerler, ETC.
   29:2 (June 1972), pp. 215-217.

Pokorny, R. R.
   1959 Über die Ausdruckdeutung des Menschlichen Ganges.
   Wien-Stuttgart.

Polak, Paul R. , Robert N. Emde, and René A. Spitz
   1964 "The smiling response to the human face: I, methodology, quantification and natural history," Journal of Nervous
   and Mental Disease 139, pp. 103-109.

Polgar, Steven
   1960 "Biculturalism in Mesquaki education," American Anthropologist 62, pp. 217-235. [P. 232, Mesquaki children near
   Tama, Iowa, interpreted the normal loudness of voice and di-
   rectness of teachers as "mean-" ness and getting mad.]

Poling, Tommy Hugh
   1974 "Proxemic and kinesic behavior," Dissertation Abstracts
   International 35: 5132B.

Pollack, I. , H. Rubenstein, and A. Horowitz
1960   "Communication of verbal modes of expression, "
Language and Speech 3, pp. 121-130.

Pollack, Irwin
1967   "Language as behavior, " in Clark H. Millikan and F. L.
Darley, eds. , Brain Mechanisms Underlying Speech and
Language. New York: Grune and Stratton, pp. 89-102.

Pollenz, Philippa
1946   "Some problems in the notation of Seneca dances. "
M. A. thesis, Columbia University.

1949   "Methods for the comparative study of the dance, "
American Anthropologist 51:3 (July-Sept.), pp. 428-435.

Pollnow, Hans
1928   "Historisch-kritische Beiträge zur Physiognomik, "
Jahrbuch der Characterlogie 5, p. 159. [History of theories
of expression.]

Polti, Georges
1892   Notation des Gestes.   Paris: Albert Savine, 36 pages.

Polti, Georges   see also   Bouissac

Ponder, Eric, and W. P. Kennedy
1927   "On the act of blinking, " Quarterly Journal of Experimental Physiology 18, pp. 89-110.

Pool, I. , ed.
1959   Trends in Content Analysis.   Urbana: Univ. of Illinois
Press.

Poon, William, and Katherine G. Butler
1972   "Evaluation of intraverbal responses in five- to seven-
year-old children, " Journal of Speech and Hearing Research 15,
pp. 303-307.

Pope, Benjamin, Aron W. Siegman, and Thomas Blass
1970   "Anxiety and speech in the initial interview, " Journal of
Consulting and Clinical Psychology 35:2 (October), pp. 233-238.

Porta, J. B. P. (Giovanni Battista Della)
1586   De Humana physiognomonia.   Libri iiii, Vici AĒquensis.
[And other editions up to 1650, in Edinburgh.]

Porter, Euan, Michael Argyle, and Veronica Salter
1970   "What is signalled by proximity?" Perceptual and Motor
Skills 30, pp. 39-42.

Potter, Charles Francis
1949   "Gestures, " Standard Dictionary of Folklore, Mythology
and Legend, ed. Maria Leach.   New York, pp. 451-453.

Poulsson

Poulsson, Emilie
1893   Finger Plays: for Nursery and Kindergarten. Boston.
Reprinted, New York: Dover Publications, 1971, 80 pages.

Powell, Wilfred
1881   "Observations on New Britain and neighboring islands
during six year's exploration," Proceedings of the Royal Geographic Society n. s., 3:2 (Feb.).

1884   Wandering in a Wild Country: or Three Years Amongst
the Cannibals of New Britain. London. [14 good figures showing digital origin of numbers, pp. 252-261: Seton ... Hayes.]

Poyatos, Fernando
1970   "Kinésica del español actual," Hispania 53:3 (Sept.),
pp. 444-452.

1970   "Lección de paralenguaje," Filologia Moderna 39 (June),
pp. 265-300.

1970   "Paralingüística y kinésica: para una teoría del sistema
comunicativo en el hablante español," in Carlos Magis, ed.,
Actas del Tercer Congreso Internacional de Hispanistas (México), pp. 725-750.

1971   "Sistemas comunicativos de una cultura: nuevo campo
de investigación," Yelmo 1 (Aug. -Sept.), pp. 23-27.

1972   "The communication system of the speaker-actor and his
culture: a preliminary investigation," Linguistics 83 (May),
pp. 64-86.

1972   "Paralenguaje y kinésica del personaje novelesco: nueva
perspectiva en el análisis de la narración," Revista de Occidente 113-114, (August-September), pp. 148-170.

1972   "The Spanish speaker in the total context of his communicative activities: cultural approach to a foreign language,"
in M. Rubin, ed., Current Issues in Teaching Spanish. Philadelphia: Chilton Books.

1974   "Del paralenguaje a la comunicación total," Doce ensayos
sobre el lenguaje. Madrid: Fundación Juan March, Ediciones
Rioduero.

1974-75   "Cultura, comunicación e interacción: hacia el contexto total del lenguaje y el hombre hispánico," Yelmo 21-24,
Part I (October-November), pp. 23-26; II (December-January),
pp. 33-35; III (February-March), pp. 14-16; IV (April-May),
pp. 27-29.

1975   "Gesture inventories: field-work methodology and problems," Semiotica 13:2, pp. 199-227.

Praetorius, Johann
    1661   Ludicrum chiromanticum ... seu thesaurus chiro-
    mantiae...   2 pts. (in 1), Jenae.

    1667   De Pollice.   Leipzig, p. 101.

Prator, Clifford H., Jr.
    1951   Manual of American English Pronunciation.   Berkeley:
    University of California Press, 151 pages.

Prechtl, H. F. R.
    1958   "The directed head turning response and allied move-
    ments of the human baby," Behaviour 13, pp. 212-242.

Premack, David, and Ann James Premack
    1974   "Teaching visual language to apes and language-deficient
    persons," in Richard L. Schiefelbusch and Lyle L. Boyd, eds.,
    Language Perspectives: Acquisition, Retardation, and Interven-
    tion.   Baltimore, Md.: University Park Press.

Premakumar
    1948   The Language of Kathakali: a Guide to Mudras.   Allaha-
    bad: Kitabistan, 102 pages.

Prescott, Robin
    1975   "Infant cry sound: developmental features," Journal of
    the Acoustical Society of America 57:5, pp. 1186-1191.

Preston-Dunlop, Valerie
            Reader in Kinetography Laban.   London: Macdonald and
    Evans.

    1963   A Handbook for Modern Educational Dance.   London:
    Macdonald and Evans, 187 pages.

    1963   An Introduction to Kinetography Laban.   London: Mac-
    donald and Evans, 32 pages.

    1969   "A notation system for recording observable motion,"
    International Journal of Man-Machine Studies 1, pp. 361-386.

    1969   Practical Kinetography Laban.   London: Macdonald and
    Evans; Brooklyn, N.Y.: Dance Horizons, 216 pages.

Priest, Helen
    1937   "Dance notation," Dance Observer 4:4 (April), p. 39;
    4:5 (May 1937), p. 51.

Proshansky, Harold M., William H. Ittelson, and Leanne G. Rivlin
    1970   Environmental Psychology: Man and His Physical Set-
    ting.   New York: Holt, Rinehart and Winston, 690 pages.

Prost, Jack H. [University of Illinois at Chicago Circle]
"Expressive posture in humans. "

     "Filming body behaviour. "

1965 "A definitional system for the classification of primate
locomotion, " American Anthropologist 67:5, Part 1 (October),
pp. 1198-1214.

1974 "Varieties of human posture, " Human Biology 46:1
(February), pp. 1-19.

Ptacek, Paul H. , and E. K. Sander
1966 "Age recognition from voice, " Journal of Speech and
Hearing Research 9, pp. 273-277.

Ptolemy [Claudius Ptolomeus 127-151 A.D.]
1682 Harmonica, trans. by John Wallis. Oxford.

- Q -

Quackenbos, H. M.
1945 "Archetype postures: clinical impressions, " The Psychiatric Quarterly 19 (Oct.), pp. 589-591.

Quedenfeldt, M.
1887 "Pfeifsprache auf der Insel Gomera, " Zeitschrift für
Ethnologie 19, pp. 731-741.

1890 "Verständigung durch Zeichen und das Gebärdenspiel bei
den Marokkanern, " Zeitschrift für Ethnologie 22, Berlin.

Quinlan, Donald M. , and Martin Harrow
1974 "Boundaries disturbances in schizophrenia, " Journal of
Abnormal Psychology 83:5, pp. 533-541.

Quintilian, Marcus Fabius [A.D. c.35-c.95]
     Institutes of Oratory. Book 11, chap. 3, [Cited by
Critchley, chap. 14, pp. 94ff.]

Quinting, Gerd
1971 Hesitation Phenomena in Adult Aphasic and Normal
Speech. The Hague: Mouton, 73 pages.

Quirk, Randolph, Anne P. Duckworth, J. Svartvik, J. P. L.
Rusiecki, A. J. T. Colin
1964 "Studies in the correspondence of prosodic to grammatical features in English, " Proceedings of the Ninth International
Congress of Linguists. The Hague: Mouton, pp. 679-
691.

- R -

Rabanales, Ambrosio
1953   "Oral, escrita o somatolálica," in Introducción al estudio del Español de Chile. Santiago: Boletín de Filología,
Universidad de Chile, paragraphs 75-75b.

1954-55 "La somatolalia," Boletín de Filología 8 (Univ. de
Chile), pp. 355-378. [Treatise on g. with classification of
different types: expressive, communicative, descriptive, indicative, symbolic, active: Hayes.]

Ramsey, R. W.
1968   "Speech patterns and personality," Language and Speech
11:1 (January-March), pp. 54-63.

Rand, George, and Seymour Wapner
1967   "Postural status as a factor in memory," Journal of
Verbal Learning and Verbal Behavior 6, pp. 268-271.

Rands, Robert L.
1957   "Comparative notes on the hand-eye and related motifs,"
American Antiquity 22 (Jan.), pp. 247-257.

Ranson, Jay Ellis
1941   "Aleut semaphore signals," American Anthropologist
43:3, pt. 1 (July-Sept.), pp. 422-427.

Rasch, Philip J., and Roger K. Burke
1963   Kinesiology and Applied Anatomy. Philadelphia: Lea
and Febiger.

Rashevsky, Nicolas
1954   "Two models: imitative behavior and distribution of
status," in Paul F. Lazarsfeld, ed., Mathematical Thinking in
the Social Sciences. New York: Free Press, pp. 67-104.

Rasmussen, Holger
1963   "Das Fingerzeichen (at trække krog)," Ethnologie in
danischen Rechtsquellen. (Tidsskrift 5) Copenhagen: Folk
Dansk Etnografisk, pp. 283-286.

Rattray, Robert Sutherland
1916   "The drum language," Ashanti. London: Oxford University Press, [1923], pp. 242-286. [Congo.]

1923   "The drum language of West Africa," Journal of the
African Society, 22:87 (April), pp. 226-236.

Rawls, James
1972   "Personal space as a predictor of performance under
close working conditions," Journal of Social Psychology 86,
pp. 261-267.

Rawson, Philip
1968   Erotic Art of the East: The Sexual Theme in Oriental
        Painting and Sculpture. Intro. by Alex Comfort. New York:
        Prometheus Press.

Read, Allen Walker
1961   "The rebel yell as a linguistic problem," American
        Speech 36:2 (May), pp. 83-92.

Read, Charlotte Schuchardt
1963-64 "Communication as 'contact'," General Semantics
        Bulletin 30-31 (Institute of General Semantics, Lakeville, Con-
        necticut), pp. 39-40.

Redfern, Betty
1971   Introducing Laban Art of Movement. London: Macdon-
        ald and Evans, 32 pages.

Redican, William K.
1975   "Facial expressions in nonhuman primates," in Leonard
        A. Rosenblum, ed., Primate Behavior, vol. 4. New York:
        Academic Press, pp. 103-194.

Reece, Michael M., and Robert N. Whitman
1962   "Expressive movements, warmth and verbal reinforce-
        ment," Journal of Abnormal and Social Psychology 64, pp. 234-
        236.

Regnier, Yves
1961   "La main sur l'epaule," La nouvelle revue française
        9:106 (October), pp. 649-675.

Reik, Theodor
1949   Listening with the Third Ear. New York: Farrar,
        Straus, 514 pages.

Renneker, Richard
1960   "Microscopic analysis of sound tape," Psychiatry 23,
        pp. 347-355.

1963   "Kinesic research and therapeutic processes," in Peter
        Knapp, Expression of the Emotions in Man. New York: Inter-
        national Universities Press, pp. 147-160.

Rensky, Miroslav
1966   "The systematics of paralanguage," Travaux linguistique
        de Prague 2, pp. 97-102.

Requeno y Vives, Vincenzo [1743-1811]
1797   Scoperta della chironomia, ossia, dell' arte di gestire
        con le mani. Parma: Fratelli Gozzi, 141 pages.

Reuschert, E.
  1909   Die Gebärdensprache der Taubstummen und die
  Ausdrucksbewegungen der Vollsinnigen.   Leipzig: H. Dude.
  ["Reuschert devised a written form of deaf-mute sign language,
  based on the signs used at Berlin and Vienna deaf-mute institute": West, p. 85.]

Révész, Géza
  1944   Die menschliche Hand.   Basel: Karger.

  1946   Ursprung und Vorgeschichte der Sprache.   Bern, 280
  pages.

  1956   The Origins and Prehistory of Language.   New York:
  Philosophical Library; London: Longmans Green, 240 pages.
  ["The theory of expressive gestures and sounds"; "The theory
  of the priority of gesture language."]   Review by Douglas Taylor, Word 13:2 (1957).

  1958   The Human Hand: a Psychological Study.   London:
  Routledge and Paul, 138 pages.

Revill, P. M.
  1970   "Preliminary report on para-linguistics in Mbembe (E.
  Nigeria)," Appendix in K. L. Pike, Tagmemic and Matrix Linguistics Applied to Selected African Languages.   (Publications
  No. 23) Santa Ana, California: Summer Institute of Linguistics, pp. 245-254.

Reynault, Félix
  1898   "Le langage par geste," La nature 26:2nd, no. 1524
  (October 15), pp. 315-317.

Rheingold, Harriet L. , Jacob L. Gewirtz, and Helen W. Ross
  1959   "Social conditioning of vocalizations in the infant,"
  Journal of Comparative Physiology and Psychology 52, pp. 68-
  73.

Rheingold, Harriet L. , and G. C. Keene
  1965   "Transport of the human young," in Determinants of Infant Behaviour 3, ed. B. M. Foss.   London: Methuen; New
  York: Wiley.

Rhodes, Adele
  1937   "A comparative study of motor abilities of Negroes and
  Whites," Child Development 8, pp. 369-371.

Rialland, Annie
  1975   "Les langages instrumentaux, sifflés, ou criés en
  Afrique," Language and Language Behavior Abstracts 9:1,
  7500578.

Ribsskog, Oyvin
1945   Hemmelige Språk og Tegn: Taterspråk, Tivolifolkenes
språk, Forbryterspråk, Gateguttspråk, Bankespråk, Tegn.
Oslo: Vinkelog Punktskrift, 143 pages. [Secret language and
signs. Commun. devices used by ... gypsies, carnival people,
burglars, street urchins: Hayes.]

Rice, Charlie
1966   "Start to Finnish," This Week (Jan. 30), p. 18.

Rich, J. Dennis
1972   "National Theatre of the Deaf," Players 47, pp. 115-
119.

Riemer, Morris D.
1949   "The averted gaze," Psychiatric Quarterly 23 (Jan.),
pp. 108-115.

1955   "Abnormalities of the gaze--a classification," Psychiatric
Quarterly 29, pp. 659-672.

Riemschneider-Hörner, M.
1939   Der Wandel der Gebärde in der Kunst. Frankfurt.

Rigault, André, and Mary Gillis
1974   "Voiceless vowels and whispered speech in Japanese,"
World Papers in Phonetics: Festschrift for Dr. Onishi's Kiju,
pp. 463-503.

Rijnberk, Gérard Van
1954   Le langage par signes chez les moines. Amsterdam:
North Holland Publishing Co., 163 pages.

Rijnhart, Susie C.
1901   With the Tibetans in Tent and Temple. New York:
F. H. Revell, 400 pages.

Ringel, R. L., and D. D. Kluppel
1964   "Neonatal crying: a normative study," Folia Phoniatrica
16, pp. 1-9.

Ringwall, Egan A., Hayne W. Reese, and Norman N. Markel
1965   "A distinctive features analysis of pre-linguistic infant
vocalizations," in Klaus F. Riegel, ed., The Development of
Language Functions. University of Michigan, Center for Human Growth and Development, Language Development Program,
litho, 7 pages.

Rioch, David McK.
1959   "Problems of 'perception' and 'communication' in mental
illness," Archives of General Psychiatry 1 (July), pp. 81-92.

Ritzenthaler, Robert E. , and Frederick A. Peterson
    1954   "Courtship whistling of the Mexican Kickapoo Indians, "
    American Anthropologist 56, pp. 1088-1089.   ["Brief Commu-
    nications. "]

Roach, Mary Ellen, and Joanne Bubolz Eicher, eds.
    1965   Dress, Adornment, and the Social Order.   New York:
    John Wiley and Sons, 429 pages.

Roback, A. A.
    1930   "Meaning in personality manifestations, " Proceedings of
    the IX International Congress of Psychology.   Princeton: Psy-
    chological Rev. Co. , pp. 362ff.

Roberts, John M. , and Cecilia Ridgeway
    1969   "Musical involvement and talking, " Anthropological
    Linguistics 11, pp. 223-246.

Robinson, Louis
    1894   "On the anthropological significance of ticklishness, "
    Report, British Association of Advancement Science (London),
    p. 778.

Robson, Kenneth S.
    1967   "The role of eye-to-eye contact in maternal-infant at-
    tachment, " Journal of Child Psychology and Psychiatry 8,
    pp. 13-25.

Rochas, Albert de
    1899   "La mimique: enseignée par l'hypnotisme, " La Nature
    27:2 (Paris), pp. 252-254.

Rochas d'Aiglun, Albert de
    1900   Les sentiments, la musique et le geste.   Grenoble:
    H. Falque et F. Perrin, 279 pages.

Roderick, Jessie A. , and Joan Moyer
            "Nonverbal behavior of young children as it relates to
    their decision making: a report of research findings, " College
    Park: University of Maryland, College of Education, ED
    059764, PS 005373.

Rodríquez Arancibia, E.
    1950   La cueca chilena.   Santiago, Chile, 42 pages.   [Dance
    gestures.]

Roemer, Richard A. , Timothy J. Teyler, and Richard F. Thompson
    1973   "Neurolinguistics: brain correlates of language. "   Read
    at the 6th Annual Winter Conference on Brain Research, Vail,
    Colorado.

Rogers, Peter L. , Klaus R. Scherer, and Robert Rosenthal
    1971   "Content filtering human speech: a simple electronic

system," Behavior Research Methods and Instrumentation 3:1 (Psychonomic Journals, Austin, Texas), pp. 16-18.

Rogge, G. O.
1953 "Music as communication, with special reference to its role as content." University of California at Los Angeles, thesis.

Róheim, Géza
1921 "Das Selbst," Imago 7:1, pp. 1-39. [On spitting: Feldman, p. 243.]

1958 "The Western tribes of Central Australia: their sexual life," in Psychoanalysis and the Social Sciences, V. New York: International Universities Press, pp. 221-245.

Röhrich, Lutz
1960 "Gebärdensprache und Sprachgebärde," in Humaniora: Essays in Literature, Folklore, Bibliography Honoring Archer Taylor on his Seventieth Birthday, eds. Wayland D. Hand and Gustave O. Arlt. Locust Valley, N.Y.: J. J. Augustin, pp. 121-149.

1967 Gebärde - Metapher - Parodie: Studien zur Sprache und Volksdichtung. (Wirkendes Wort, Buchreihe 4) Düsseldorf: Pädagogischer Verlag Schwann, 238 pages.

Rolland, Eugène
1886-87 "Les gestes I," Mélusine 3, cols. 116-119. [Gestures from Turkey and France: Hayes.]

Rosa, Leone Augusto
1929 Espressioni e mimica. Milan: Hoepli. [Over 300 sketches of Italian gestures by an observant artist: Hayes.]

Rose, H. A.
1919 "The language of gesture," Folklore 30, pp. 312-315.

Rose, John, ed.
1965 Survey of Cybernetics: A Tribute to Dr. Norbert Wiener. London: Iliffe Books, 391 pages.

Rosekrans, Robert L.
1955 "Do gestures speak louder than words?" Collier's (March 4), pp. 56-57. [On Birdwhistell.]

Rosenberg, B. G., and Jonas Langer
1965 "A study of nonverbal symbolic behavior of schizophrenics," Journal of Clinical Psychology 21, pp. 243-247.

1965 "A study of postural-gestural communication," Journal of Personality and Social Psychology 2:4 (Oct.), pp. 593-597.

Rosenberg, S. , and A. Gordon
    1968   "Identification of facial expressions from affective
    descriptions: a probalistic choice analysis of referential am-
    biguity, " Journal of Personality and Social Psychology 10,
    pp. 157-166.

Rosenblith, Walter A. , ed.
    1961   Sensory Communication: Contributions to the Symposi-
    um on Principles of Sensory Communication (MIT).   New York:
    The MIT Press and John Wiley and Sons, 844 pages.

Rosenfeld, Howard M. [University of Kansas]
    1965   "Effect of an approval-seeking induction on interpersonal
    proximity, " Psychological Reports 17, pp. 120-122.

    1966   "Approval-seeking and approval-inducing functions of
    verbal and nonverbal responses in the dyad, " Journal of Per-
    sonality and Social Psychology 4:6, pp. 597-605.

    1966   "Instrumental affiliative functions of facial and gestural
    expressions, " Journal of Personality and Social Psychology 4:1,
    pp. 65-72.   Reprinted in Dean C. Barnlund, Interpersonal Com-
    munication: Survey and Studies.   Boston: Houghton Mifflin,
    1968, pp. 587-597.

    1967   "Nonverbal reciprocation of approval: an experimental
    analysis, " Journal of Experimental Social Psychology 3:1,
    pp. 102-111.

    1972   "The experimental analysis of interpersonal influence
    processes, " Journal of Communication 22:4 (December), pp.
    424-442.

    1973   "Time series analysis of mother-infant interaction. "
    Symposium on the Analysis of Mother-Infant Interaction Se-
    quences, Philadelphia.

Rosenthal, Robert
    1966   Experimenter Effects in Behavioral Research.   New
    York: Appleton-Century-Crofts.

    1967   "Covert communication in the psychological experiment, "
    Psychological Bulletin 67:5, pp. 356-367.

Rosenthal, Robert, Dane Archer, M. Robin DiMatteo, Judith Hall
    Koivumaki, and Peter L. Rogers
    1974   "Body talk and tone of voice: the language without
    words, " Psychology Today 8:4 (September), pp. 64-68.

Ross, John Robert
    1970   "On declarative sentences, " in Roderick A. Jacobs, and
    Peter S. Rosenbaum, eds. , Readings in English Transformation-
    al Grammar.   Waltham, Mass. :   Ginn and Co. , pp. 222-272.

Ross, William T.
1886   "Notation of gesture," Voice Culture and Elocution.
New York: Baker and Taylor, pp. 18-20.

Rossellius, Cosmas [also Cosimo Roselli, Cosma Rosellio, d. 1578]
1576   [A Florentine monk described three alphabets of sign
language in monastic communities: Critchley, p. 51.]

1579   Thesaurus Artificiosae Memoriae (ed. by D. Rossellius).
Venice.

Roth, H. Ling
1889   "On salutations," Journal of the Royal Anthropological
Institute 19, pp. 164-181.

Roth, Walter Edmund
1897   Ethnological Studies among the Northwest Central Queens-
land Aborigines. Brisbane, 199 pages. [Chap. IV, "The expression of ideas by manual signs: a sign language," pp. 71-
90.]

1929   Additional Studies of the Arts, Crafts and Customs of
the Guiana Indians. (Bulletin 91) Washington, D.C.: Bureau
of American Ethnology, 110 pages.

Rothschild, F. S.
1963   "Posture and psyche," in Lipman Halpern, ed., Problems of Dynamic Neurology: An International Volume: Studies
on the Higher Functions of the Human Nervous System. Jerusalem: Israel Academy of Sciences, pp. 475-509.

Rowe, Frederick B., Shirley Brooks, and Barbara Watson
1960   "Communication through gestures," American Annals of
the Deaf 105, pp. 232-237.

Rowe, Mary Budd
1974   "Pausing phenomena: influence on the quality of instruction," Journal of Psycholinguistic Research 3, pp. 203-
224.

Rowen, Betty
1963   Learning Through Movement. New York: Teachers
College Press, Columbia University, 77 pages.

Rowland, Beryl
1973   Animals with Human Faces: A Guide to Animal Symbolism. Knoxville, Tenn.: University of Tennessee Press.

Royal, D. C.
1959   "A multidimensional analysis of perception of emotion
from schematic facial expressions." Dissertation, University
of Michigan.

368 Bibliography

Rubenstein, L. , and D. E. Cameron
1968 "Electronic analysis of nonverbal communication,"
Comprehensive Psychiatry 9, pp. 200-208.

Ruckmick, Christian A.
1936 "The facial expression of emotion," The Psychology of
Feeling and Emotion. New York: McGraw-Hill, chap. 9.

Rudkin, Ethel H.
1934 "Collectanea: Lincolnshire folklore: witches and dev-
ils," Folklore 45, pp. 249-267. [G. used to protect oneself
against witches: Hayes.]

Rudolf, Heinrich
1903 Der Ausdruck der Gemütsbewegungen des Menschen.
Dresden: G. Kühtmann, 228 pages.

Ruesch, Jurgen
1953 "Synopsis of the theory of human communication,"
Psychiatry 16, pp. 215-243.

1955 "Nonverbal language and therapy," Psychiatry 18:4
(Nov.), pp. 323-330. Reprinted partially in Alfred G. Smith,
ed. , Communication and Culture: Readings in the Codes of
Human Interaction, 1966, pp. 209-213.

1957 Disturbed Communication; the Clinical Assessment of
Normal and Pathological Communicative Behavior. New York:
W. W. Norton, 337 pages.

1961 Therapeutic Communication. New York: W. W. Norton, 480 pages.

1966 "Social process," Archives of General Psychiatry 15,
(December), pp. 577-589.

1967 "The social control of symbolic systems," Journal of
Communication 17:4 (Dec.), pp. 276-301.

1972 Semiotic Approaches to Human Relations. The Hague,
Mouton, 804 pages.

Ruesch, Jurgen, and Weldon Kees
1955 "Approaches and leave-taking." 16mm. film, 12 min.
San Francisco: University of California, Langley Porter Clinic.

1956 Nonverbal Communication: Notes on the Visual Perception of Human Relations. Berkeley: University of California
Press, 205 pages.

Rump, E. E.
1960 "Facial expression and situational cues: demonstration

of a logical error in Frijda's report," Acta Psychologica 17, pp. 31-38.

Rush, James [1786-1869]
1827 The Philosophy of the Human Voice. Philadelphia: Lippincott, 648 pages.

Ruska, Julius
1917 "Zur ältesten arabischen Algebra," Sitzungsbericht der Heidelberger Akademia des wissenschafts Philos. -hist. Klasse, 2 Abh, pp. 82-92.

1920 "Arabische Texte über das Fingerrechnen," Der Islam 10, pp. 87-119.

Russell, William
1838 Rudiments of Gesture, Comprising Illustrations of Common Faults in Attitude and Action. Boston, 120 pages.

Russo, N. F.
1967 "Connotations of seating arrangements," Cornell Journal of Social Relations 2:1, pp. 37-44.

Ruwet, Jean-Claude
1972 Introduction to Ethology: The Biology of Behavior. New York: International Universities Press, 208 pages.

- S -

Sachs, Curt
1937 World History of the Dance. New York: Crown Publishers, 469 pages.

Sagan, Carl
1973 Communication with Extraterrestrial Intelligence. Cambridge, Mass.: MIT Press, 448 pages.

Sainsbury, Peter
1954 "A method of measuring spontaneous movements by time-sampling motion pictures," Journal of Mental Science 100, pp. 742-748.

1955 "Gestural movement during psychiatric interview," Psychosomatic Medicine 17:6, pp. 458-469.

Saint-Denis, Eugène de
1965 Essais sur le rire et le sourire des latins. Paris: Publications de l'Université de Dijon, 32, 304 pages.

Saint-Jacques, Bernard
1972 'Quelques aspects du langage gestuel en Japonais," in Festschrift to André G. Haudricourt, Langues et Techniques,

Nature et Société; Jacqueline M. C. Thomas, and Lucien Ber-
not, eds. Paris: Klincksieck, pp. 391-394.

Saint-Leon, Arthur
1852   Sténochorégraphy (La Sténochorégraphie).   Paris and St.
Petersbourg.

Saint-León (also St. León), Arthur   see also   Meunier, Antoine;
Stepanov; F. A. Zorn

Saitz, Robert L. , and Edward J. Cervenka
1962   Colombian and North American Gestures: A Contrastive
Inventory.   Bogota: Centro Colombo Americano, 90 pages.
Reprinted as Handbook of Gestures: Colombia and the United
States.   (Approaches to Semiotics 31) The Hague: Mouton,
1972, 164 pages.

Sajdak, Bruce T.
1974   "Silence on the Shakespearean stage," Dissertation Abstracts International 35:4455A.

Salisbury, Lee H.
1967   "Cross-cultural communication and dramatic ritual,"
in Lee Thayer, ed. , Communication: Concepts and Perspectives.   Washington, D.C.: Spartan Books, chap. IV, pp. 77-
95.

Salk, L.
1966   "Thoughts on the concept of imprinting and its place in
early human development," Canadian Psychiatric Association
Journal 11, pp. 295-305. [Heart-beat response of babies held
against mother's breast.]

Sallagoïty, Pierre
1975   "The sign language of Southern France," Sign Language
Studies 7, pp. 181-202.

Sallop, Marvin B.
1973   "Language acquisition: pantomime and gesture to signed
English," Sign Language Studies 3, pp. 29-38.

Samarin, William J.
"Correlates of expressive language in African ideo-
phones, " Journal of African Languages.

"Inventory and choice in expressive language, " Word.

1965   "Language of silence," Practical Anthropology 12, pp.
115-119.

1967   Field Linguistics: A Guide to Linguistic Field Work.
New York: Holt, Rinehart and Winston, 246 pages.

Samovar

1968   "The linguisticality of glossolalia, " The Hartford Quarterly 8:4 (Summer), pp. 48-75.

1969   "Forms and functions of nonsense language," Linguistics
50 (July), pp. 70-74.

1969   "Glossolalia as learned behavior, " Canadian Journal of
Theology 15:1, pp. 60-64.

1969   "The art of Gbeya insults, " International Journal of
American Linguistics 35:4 (October), pp. 323-329.

1971   "Evolution in glossolalic private language, " Anthropological Linguistics 13:2 (Feb.), pp. 55-67.

1972   Tongues of Men and Angels: The Religious Language of
Pentecostalism. New York: Macmillan, 277 pages. Review
by David Crystal, Language in Society 3 (1974), pp. 126-131.

1972   "Variation and variables in religious glossolalia, "
Language in Society 1:1 (April), pp. 121-130.

1973   "Glossolalia as regressive speech, " Language and
Speech 16, Part 1 (Jan. -March), pp. 77-89.

Samovar, Larry A. , and Richard E. Porter, eds.
1972   Intercultural Communication: a Reader.   Belmont,
Calif. : Wadsworth Publishing Co. [Part 4, "Nonverbal aspects," pp. 169-232.]

Sanford, Fillmore H.
1941   "Individual differences in the mode of verbal expression.
Harvard College Library (Unpub.). [Mentioned in "Speech and
personality: a comparative case study. "]

1942   "Speech and personality," Psychological Bulletin 39,
pp. 811-845.

1942   "Speech and personality: a comparative case study, "
Journal of Personality (Character and Personality) 10, pp. 169-
198. ["Hesitating sounds ("Uh" or "er")," p. 174.]

Sanford, Fillmore H. , and Lawrence S. Wrightman, eds.
1970   Psychology: A Scientific Study of Man.   Brooks/Cole
Pub. Co. , 736 pages. ["Study comparing pupillary reactions
of heterosexual and homosexual men to pictures of nude women. "]

Sanlecque, Le P. Louis de
1813   "Poème sur le geste, " in Boileau Despréaux, Oeuvres,
Troyes, Sainton, 348 pages. "Poeme sur les mauvais gestes, "
in Abbé Joseph-Antoine-Toussaint Dinouart, L'Eloquence du
corps, ou l'Action du prédicateur. Paris, 1761, 447 pages.

Sapir, Edward
    1910   "Song recitative in Paiute mythology," Journal of Amer-
    ican Folklore 23, pp. 455-472. Reprinted in David G. Mandel-
    baum, ed., Selected Writings of Edward Sapir: in Language,
    Culture, and Personality. Berkeley: University of California
    Press, 1968, pp. 463-467.

    1915   Abnormal Types of Speech in Nootka. (Canada, Geo-
    logical Survey, Memoir 62, Anthropological Series) Ottawa:
    Government Printing Bureau. Reprinted in David G. Mandel-
    baum, ed., Selected Writings of Edward Sapir: in Language,
    Culture and Personality. University of California Press, 1968,
    pp. 179-196.

    1921   Language: An Introduction to the Study of Speech.
    New York: Harcourt, Brace and World.

    1927   "Speech as a personality trait," The American Journal
    of Sociology 32:6 (May), pp. 892-905. Reprinted in David
    Mandelbaum, ed., Selected Writings of Edward G. Sapir: in
    Language, Culture, and Personality. University of California
    Press, 1948, pp. 533-543. Partially reprinted in Norman N.
    Markel, Psycholinguistics. Homewood, Ill.: The Dorsey
    Press, 1969, pp. 44-56.

    1927   "The unconscious patterning of behavior in society,"
    in E. S. Dummer, ed., The Unconscious: A Symposium.
    New York: Knopf, pp. 114-142. Reprinted in David G. Man-
    delbaum, ed., Selected Writings of Edward Sapir. Berkeley:
    University of California Press, 1968, pp. 544-559.

    1931   "Communication," Encyclopedia of the Social Sciences 4.
    New York: Macmillan, pp. 78-80. Reprinted in David G.
    Mandelbaum, ed., Selected Writings of Edward Sapir: in
    Language, Culture and Personality, pp. 104-109. Reprinted
    in John P. De Cecco, The Psychology of Language, Thought,
    and Instruction. New York: Holt, Rinehart, and Winston,
    1967, pp. 75-78.

    1949   Selected Writings of Edward Sapir: in Language, Cul-
    ture and Personality, ed. David G. Mandelbaum. Berkeley:
    University of California Press, 1968, 617 pages.

Sarles, Harvey B.
    1966   'New approaches to the study of human communication,"
    Anthropological Linguistics 8:9 (Dec.), pp. 20-26.

    1968   "Abstracts in human communication," International
    Journal of American Linguistics 34:4 (October), pp. 282-287;
    34:2 (April), pp. 137-141.

    1969   "The study of language and communication across spe-
    cies," Current Anthropology 10:2-3, pp. 211-215.

1974   "Facial expression and body movement," Current Trends in Linguistics 12. The Hague: Mouton, pp. 297-310.

Sartre, Jean Paul
1942   Being and Nothingness. New York: Philosophical Library, 1956. ["It is through our experience of the Look that we most directly apprehend another person as a being with consciousness and intentions of his own."]

Sathré, Freda S., Ray W. Olson, Clarissa I. Whitney
1973   Let's Talk: An Introduction to Interpersonal Communication. Glenview, Ill.: Scott, Foresman. [Chap. 7, "Nonverbal Communication," pp. 108-127.]

Satir, Virginia M.
1964   Conjoint Family Therapy: A Guide to Theory and Technique. Palo Alto, Calif.: Science and Behavior Books, 196 pages.

Satow, Sir Ernest Mason
1879   "Ancient Japanese rituals," Transactions of the Asiatic Society of Japan 7, Parts 2, 4, and 9, (and 1881). [See K. Florenz.]

Sattler, Jerome M.
1966   "Embarrassment and blushing: a theoretical review," Journal of Social Psychology 69, pp. 117-133.

Saunders, Ernest Dale
1960   Mudrā: a Study of Symbolic Gestures in Japanese Buddhist Sculpture. New York: Pantheon Books, 296 pages.

Saxl, F.
1932   Die Ausdruckgebärde der Bildenden Kunst. Jena.

Schäfer, T.
1934   "Über gebärdliche Verhaltensweisen, insbesondere bei Kindern," Archiv für die Gesamte Psychologie 91, pp. 1-48.

Schafer, R. Murray
1975   "The tuning of the world." MS in preparation.

Schaffer, H. R., and Peggy E. Emerson
1965   "Patterns of response to physical contact in early human development," in Paul Henry Mussen, John Janeway Conger, and Jerome Kagan, eds., Readings in Child Development and Personality. New York: Harper and Row, pp. 188-203.

Scheck, M. George
1925   "Involuntary tongue movements under varying stimuli," Iowa Academy of Science Proceedings 32, pp. 385-391.

Scheflen, Albert E.
    1963   "Communication and regulation in psychotherapy," Psy-
    chiatry 26:2 (May), pp. 126-136.

    1964   "The significance of posture in communication systems,"
    Psychiatry 27:4 (Nov.), pp. 316-331.

    1965   "Quasi-courtship behavior in psychotherapy," Psychiatry
    28, pp. 245-257.

    1965   Stream and Structure of Communicational Behavior:
    Context Analysis of a Psychotherapy Session. (Behavioral
    Studies Monograph #1) Eastern Pennsylvania Psychiatric Insti-
    tute. Reprinted as Communicational Structure: Analysis of a
    Psychotherapy Transaction. Bloomington, Ind.: Indiana Uni-
    versity Press, 1973, 378 pages.

    1966   "Natural history method in psychotherapy: communica-
    tional research," in Louis A. Gottschalk, and Arthur H. Auer-
    bach, eds., Methods of Research in Psychotherapy. New York:
    Appleton-Century-Crofts, pp. 263-289.

    1966   "Systems and psychosomatics: an introduction to 'Psy-
    chosomatic manifestations of rapport in psychotherapy,' [by E.
    Joseph Charney]," Psychosomatic Medicine 28:4 (Part I), (July-
    Aug.), pp. 297-304.

    1967   "On the structuring of human communication," American
    Behavioral Scientist 10, pp. 8-12.

    1968   "Human communication: behavioral programs and their
    integration in interaction," Behavioral Science 13:1 (Jan.),
    pp. 44-55.

    1970   "Communicational arrangements which further specify a
    meaning," Family Process 9:4, pp. 457-472.

    1974   How Behavior Means. New York: Anchor Books, 222
    pages.

Scheflen, Albert E., with Norman Ashcraft
    1976   Human Territories: How We Behave in Space-Time.
    Englewood Cliffs, N.J.: Prentice-Hall, 210 pages.

Scheflen, Albert E., Adam Kendon, and J. Schaeffer
    1970   "A comparison of video-tape and moving picture film in
    research in human communication," in Milton M. Berger, ed.,
    Videotape Techniques in Psychiatric Training and Treatment.
    New York: R. Brunner/Mazel.

Scheflen, Albert E., and Alice Scheflen
    1972   Body Language and Social Order: Communication as

Behavioral Control.   Englewood Cliffs, N.J.:   Prentice-Hall,
208 pages.

Schefold, Reimar
1973   "Schlitztrommeln und Trommelsprache in Mentawai
(Indonesien), " Zeitschrift für Ethnologie 98, pp. 36-73.

Schegloff, Emanuel A.
1972   "Sequencing in conversational openings, " in John J.
Gumperz and Dell Hymes, eds. , Directions in Sociolinguistics.
New York: Holt, Rinehart and Winston, pp. 346-380.

Schegloff, Emanuel A. , and Harvey Sacks
1973   "Opening up closings, " Semiotica 8, pp. 289-327.

Schenkein, James N.
1972   "Towards an analysis of natural conversation and the
sense of heheh, " Semiotica 6, pp. 344-377.

Scherer, Klaus R.
1970   Non-verbale Kommunikation.   Hamburg: Buske.

1972   "Judging personality from voice: a cross-cultural approach to an old issue in interpersonal perception, " Journal of
Personality 40, pp. 191-210.

1974   "Voice quality analysis of American and German speakers, " Journal of Psycholinguistic Research 3, pp. 281-298.

Scherer, Klaus, Judy Koivumaki, and Robert Rosenthal
1972   "Minimal cues in the vocal communication of affect:
judging emotions from content masked speech, " Journal of
Psycholinguistic Research 1, pp. 269-285.

Schiefelbusch, Richard L. , and Lyle L. Lloyd, eds.
1974   Language Perspectives: Acquisition, Retardation, and
Intervention.   Baltimore: University Park Press, 670 pages.

Schlauch, Margaret
1936   "Recent Soviet studies in linguistics, " Science and Society: A Marxian Quarterly 1 (New York), pp. 152-167.

Schlesinger, Hilde S.
1972   "Language acquisition in four deaf children, " Hearing
and Speech News (November-December), National Assoc. of
Hearing and Speech Agencies, Silver Spring, Md. , pp. 4-7,
22-28.

Schlesinger, Hilde S. , and Kathryn P. Meadow
1972   Sound and Sign: Childhood Deafness and Mental Health.
Berkeley: University of California Press, 265 pages.

Schlesinger, Itzhak M.
    1967   "Problems of investigating the grammar of sign lan-
    guage," Working Paper 2, The Hebrew University of Jerusalem,
    Israel, 13 pages.

    1971   "The grammar of sign language and the problems of
    language universals," in John Morton, ed., Biological and So-
    cial Factors in Psycholinguistics.   London: Logos Press,
    pp. 98-121.

Schlesinger, Itzhak M., E. Cohen, and L. Namir
        A New Dictionary of Sign Language.   (Approaches to
    Semiotics 50) The Hague: Mouton.

Schlesinger, Itzhak M., and Bina Presser
        "Compound signs in sign language."   Manuscript, The
    Hebrew University of Jerusalem, Israel.

Schlesinger, Itzhak M., Bina Presser, Einya Cohen, and Tsiyona
    Peled
    1970   "Transfer of meaning in sign language," Working Paper
    12, The Hebrew University of Jerusalem, Israel, 14 pages.

Schlosberg, Harold A.
    1941   "A scale for the judgment of facial expressions,"
    Journal of Experimental Psychology 29, pp. 497-510.

    1952   "The description of facial expressions in terms of two
    dimensions," Journal of Experimental Psychology 44:4 (Oct.),
    pp. 229-237.

    1954   "Three dimensions of emotion," Psychological Review
    61:2 (March), pp. 81-88.

    1959   "Woodworth scale values of the lightfoot pictures of
    facial expression," Journal of Experimental Psychology 60,
    pp. 121-125.

Schmais, Claire, and Elissa Q. White
    n.d., ca. 1974   "Hunter College dance therapy masters pro-
    gram." Final Report Grant #MH 12739, 61 pages.

Schmalz
    1838   Ueber die Taubstummen.   Dresden and Leipzig, [pp.
    214, 352.]

Schmidt, Leopold
    1953   "Die volkstümlichen Grundlagen der Gebärdensprache,"
    Beiträge zur Sprachlichen Volksüberlieferungen 2.   Berlin:
    Deutsche Akademie der Wissenschaften, pp. 233-249.

Schmidt, Wilfred H. O., and Terence Hore
    1970   "Some nonverbal aspects of communication between

mother and pre-school child," Child Development 41, Part 2 (September-December), pp. 889-896.

Schmitz, G.
1923   'Die Gebärdensprache der Kluniazenser und Hirsauer,"
Blätter für Taubstummenbildung 36, pp. 347-355, 362-364.

Schneider, John E.
1975   "Mind to mind communication: nonverbal influence?"
Language and Language Behavior Abstracts 9:2: 7501880. [The relationship between ESP and nonverbal communication.]

Schneider, Marius
1952   "Zur Trommelsprache der Duala," Anthropos 47, pp. 235-243.

Schneirla, T. C.
1956   'Interrelationships of the 'innate' and the 'acquired' in instinctive behavior," L'Instinct dans le comportement des ani- maux et de l'homme. Paris: Fondation Singer-Polignac, pp. 387-452.

Schreiber, Flora Rheta
1960   "The psychological factors affecting the development of speech in the early years," in Dominick A. Barbara, ed. , Psychological and Psychiatric Aspects of Speech and Hearing. Springfield, Ill. : Charles C. Thomas, pp. 42-68.

Schrero, Elliot M.
1972   'Intonation and moral insight: reading Henry James aloud," Oral English 1:3 (Summer), pp. 8-13.

1974   'Intonation in nineteenth-century fiction: the voices of paraphrase," Quarterly Journal of Speech 60 (October), pp. 289-295.

Schroeder, H. R. Paul
1899   Geschichte des Lebensmagnetismus und des Hypnotismus. Leipzig: Verlag A. Strauch.

Schubiger, Maria
1958   English Intonation. Tübingen: Max Niemeyer, 112 pages.

Schücking, Levin L.
1959   'Die Gebärde in englischen Dichtungen des Mittelalters, " Von Werner Habicht. (Abhandlungen, Neue Folge, Heft 46) München: Bayerische Akademie der Wissenschaften, Philo- sophisch-Historische Klasse, 168 pages. Review by Archer Taylor, Modern Language Quarterly 21:3 (Sept. 1960), pp. 281- 282.

Schuhl, Pierre-Maxime
1948   "Remarques sur le regard," Journal de psychologie normale et pathologique 41, pp. 184-193.

Schuhmacher, W. W.
1972   Cybernetic Aspects of Language.   The Hague: Mouton,
61 pages.

Schuler, Edgar A.
1944   "V for victory: a study in symbolic social control,"
Journal of Social Psychology 19 (May), pp. 283-299.

Schulman, David, and F. C. Shontz
1971   "Body posture and thinking," Perceptual and Motor
Skills 32:1, pp. 27-33.

Schultze, V.
1892   Zur Geschichte des Händefaltens.   Theologisches Litera-
turblatt, 591 pages.

Schurtz, Heinrich
1891   Grundzüge einer Philosophie der Tracht.   Stuttgart.

Schutz, William C.
1968   Joy: Expanding Human Awareness.   New York: Grove
Press, 223 pages.

Schützenberger, Anne Ancelin [Psychologie Lab. de Psychologie Social, Nice]
1962   "Sur quelques problemes de communication non verbale
et leur approche psychodramatique," Contribution à l'Etude des
Sciences de l'Homme 5 (Montreal), pp. 168-189.

(in press)   La communication non-verbale.

Schwartz, Andrew, Dana Rosenberg, and Yvonne Brackbill
1970   "Analysis of the components of social reinforcement of
infant vocalization," Psychonomic Science 20:6, pp. 323-325.

Schwartz, Irving
1967   "Patterns of communication in families with acting-out
children as compared to families with withdrawn children,"
Dissertation Abstracts 28, part 6, p. 4764 B, Order no. 68-
6103 (May-June 1968).   New York University, 298 pages.

Schwartz, Martin F.
1968   "Identification of speaker sex from isolated, voiceless
fricatives," Journal of the Acoustical Society of America 43:5
(May), pp. 1178-1179.

Schwartz, Martin F., and Helen E. Rine
1968   "Identification of speaker sex from isolated, whispered
vowels," Journal of the Acoustical Society of America 44,
pp. 1736-1737.

Scott, Christopher, and K. M. Goldney
1960   "The Jones boys and the ultrasonic whistle," Journal

of the Society for Psychical Research 40:703 (March), pp. 249-260.

Scott, Harry Fletcher, and Wilbert Lester Carr
1921   Development of Language. New York: Scott, Foresman.
["Use of Gestures," pp. 14-20.]

Scott, Hugh Lennox
1893   "The sign language of the Plains Indian," International
Folklore Congress 3d (Chicago), pp. 206-220.

1919   [Unpublished notes on sign language], Box 1799, Bureau
of American Ethnology Archives, [West, p. 104].

Scott, Hugh Lennox see also Seton; Weil, Elsie

Scott, Robert S.
1930   The Thumb of Knowledge. New York, 296 pages.
[Chap. 20.] [On the Finn's acquisition of magical knowledge
by sucking thumb: Hayes.]

Scott, Roland B., Angella D. Ferguson, Melvin E. Jenkins, and
Fred F. Cutter
1955   "Growth and development of Negro infants: V, Neuro-
muscular patterns of behavior during the first year of life,"
Pediatrics 16, pp. 24-30.

Scott, W. Clifford M.
1958   "Noise, speech, and technique," International Journal of
Psychoanalysis 39, pp. 108-111. [Burps, blathers, coughs,
finger-nail clicks, flatus, yawning, bopping, clapping, snoring,
sniffing, hum.]

Scott, W. R.
1844   The Deaf and the Dumb. 84 pages.

Scotto Di Carlo, Nicole
1973   "Analyse sémiologique des gestes et mimiques des
chanteurs d'opera," Semiotica 9:4, pp. 289-317.

Scovel, Tom
1971   "A look-see at some verbs of perception," Language
Learning 21:1, pp. 75-84.

Seaford, H. Wade, Jr.
1966   "The Southern syndrome. A regional pattern of facial
muscle contraction." Paper read at the Pennsylvania Sociological Society.

1975   "Facial expression dialect: an example," in Adam Kendon, Richard M. Harris, and Mary Ritchie Key, eds., Organization of Behavior in Face-to-face Interaction. The Hague:
Mouton, pp. 151-155.

Sebeok, Thomas A.
1962   "Coding in the evolution of signalling behavior," Behavioral Science 7:4, pp. 430-442.

1967   "On chemical signs," in To Honor Roman Jakobson, III.
The Hague: Mouton, pp. 1775-1782.

1968   "A selected and annotated guide to the literature of zoosemiotics and its background," Social Science Information 7:5,
pp. 103-117.

1972   Perspectives in Zoosemiotics.   The Hague: Mouton,
188 pages.

1974   "Semiotics: a survey of the state of the art," Current
Trends in Linguistics: Vol. 12, Linguistics and Adjacent Arts
and Sciences.   The Hague: Mouton, pp. 211-264.

Sebeok, Thomas A., Alfred S. Hayes, and Mary Catherine Bateson, eds.
1964   Approaches to Semiotics: Transactions of the Indiana
University Conference on Paralinguistics and Kinesics.   The
Hague: Mouton, 294 pages.

Sebeok, Thomas A., and Alexandra Ramsay, eds.
1969   Approaches to Animal Communication.   The Hague:
Mouton.

Sebeok, Thomas A., and Donna Jean Umiker-Sebeok
1975   Speech Surrogates: Drum and Whistle Systems.   2 vols.
The Hague: Mouton, 1456 pages.

Sechrest, Lee, and Luis Flores, Jr.
1971   "The occurrence of a nervous mannerism in two cultures," Asian Studies 9, pp. 55-63.

Sechrest, Lee, Luis Flores, and Lourdes Arellano
1968   "Language and social interaction in a bilingual culture,"
Journal of Social Psychology 76, pp. 155-161.

Sechrest, Lee, and John Wallace
1967   Psychology and Human Problems.   Columbus, Ohio:
C. E. Merrill.

Secord, Paul F.
1958   "Facial features and inference processes in interpersonal perception," in Renato Tagiuri and Luigi Petrullo, eds.,
Person Perception and Interpersonal Behavior.   Stanford University Press, pp. 300-315.

Secord, Paul F., William F. Dukes, and William Bevan
1954   "Personalities in faces. I: An Experiment in Social

perceiving," Genetic Psychology Monographs 49, pp. 231-279.

Seelye, H. Ned
    1966   "Field notes on cross-cultural testing," Language Learn-
    ing 16:1-2, pp. 77-85.

Seigel, Jerrold E.
    1965   "Ideals of eloquence and silence in Petrarch," Journal
    of the History of Ideas 26, pp. 147-174.

Seigel, Jules Paul
    1969   "The enlightenment and the evolution of a language of
    signs in France and England," Journal of the History of Ideas
    30 (January-March), pp. 96-115.

Selden, Samuel
    1941   The Stage in Action.   Carbondale: Southern Illinois
    University Press, 324 pages.

Seligmann, C. G., and A. Wilkin
    1907   "The gesture language of the Western Islanders," Cam-
    bridge Anthropological Expedition to Torres Straits, Reports 3,
    pp. 255-260.

Sella, I.
    1969   "Some impressions of an Israeli signer abroad," Work-
    ing Papers 10, The Hebrew University of Jerusalem, pp. 1-4.

Seneca
    1928   Moral Essays, trans. by John W. Basore.   London, 3
    vols. [See vol. 1, book 3, "De ira," for remarkable descrip-
    tion of the gestures of an angry man: Hayes.]

Seton, Ernest Thompson
    1918   Sign Talk: A Universal Signal Code, Without Apparatus,
    for Use in the Army, the Navy, Camping, Hunting, and Daily
    Life: The Gesture Language of the Cheyenne Indians: with
    Additional Signs Used by Other Tribes, Also a Few Necessary
    Signs from the Code of the Deaf In Europe and America, and
    Others that Are Established among Our Policemen, Firemen,
    Railroad Men, and School Children, in all 1,725, prepared with
    assistance from General Hugh L. Scott.   700 illus. New York:
    Doubleday, Page, and Co., 233 pages.

Seuss, Dr.
    1970   Mr. Brown Can Moo! Can You? New York: Random
    House.

Shaftesbury, Edmund
    ca. 1885   Lessons in Acting.   [100 line cuts to illustrate:
    Hayes.]

Shah, Iris S.
    1960   "An investigation of linguistic decision points and encod-
    ing segments in spoken English." Dissertation, Cornell Uni-
    versity.

Shands, Harley C.
    1970   Semiotic Approaches to Psychiatry.   The Hague: Mou-
    ton, 412 pages.

Shankweiler, Donald
    1971   "An analysis of laterality effects in speech perception,"
    in David L. Horton and James J. Jenkins, Perception of
    Language, pp. 185-200.

Shannon, Anna M.
    1970   "Perception of facial expression of affect in patients."
    Dissertation, University of California.

Shannon, B.
    1929   "What do your hands reveal?" World Today 53 (April),
    pp. 462-466.

Shapiro, Jeffrey G.
    1968   "Responsivity to facial and linguistic cues," Journal of
    Communication 18:1 (March), pp. 11-17.

Sharoff, Robert L.
    1960   "The deaf child," in Dominick A. Barbara, ed., Psy-
    chological and Psychiatric Aspects of Speech and Hearing.
    Springfield, Ill.:   Charles C. Thomas, chap. 20, pp. 440-455.

Sharpe, Ella Freeman
    1940   "Psycho-physical problems revealed in language: an
    examination of metaphor," International Journal of Psychoanaly-
    sis 21, pp. 201-213.

Sharpe, Margaret C.
    1970   "Voice quality: a suggested framework for description
    and some observations," in Stephen A. Wurm, and Donald C.
    Laycock, eds., Pacific Linguistic Studies in Honour of Arthur
    Capell.   Canberra: Pacific Linguistics, pp. 115-134.

Shawn, Ted
    1910   Every Little Movement: A Book about Francois Delsarte.
    M. Witmark & Sons.   Reprinted Pittsfield, Mass., 1954, 115
    pages; New York: Dance Horizons, 1963, 127 pages.

Shea, George E.
    1915   Acting in Opera: Its A-B-C, with Descriptive Examples,
    Practical Hints and Numerous Illustrations.   London: G.
    Schirmer, 90 pages.

Shearme, J. N., and J. N. Holmes
   1959   "An experiment concerning the recognition of voices,"
   Language and Speech 2:3 (July-Sept.), pp. 123-131.

Sheldon, W. H.
   1942   The Varieties of Temperament: A Psychology of Consti-
   tutional Differences.   New York: Harper and Brothers, 520
   pages.

Shen, Yao
   1969   "Two intonations in eight types of English questions,"
   Journal of English Linguistics 3 (March), pp. 66-81.

Sheppard, William Clarence, and Harlan L. Lane
   1965   "Development of the prosodic features of infant vocalizing," Report, Center for Research on Language and Language
   Behavior, Ann Arbor, Michigan, Journal of Speech and Hearing
   Research 11:1 (March 1968), pp. 94-108.

   1966   "Development of the prosodic features of infant vocalizing: II," Studies in Language and Language Behavior.   University of Michigan.

Sheppard, William Clarence, Jr.
   1968   "The analysis and control of infant vocal and motor behavior," Research in Education 3:9, p. 38.   Complete dissertation in: Supplement to Studies in Language and Language Behavior, Progress Report V, Sept., 1967, 69 pages.

Sheridan, Thomas
   1762   A Course of Lectures on Elocution: Together with Two
   Dissertations on Language.   Reprinted, New York: Benjamin
   Blom, 392 pages; Menston, Yorks: Scolar, English Linguistics,
   1500-1800, 1968, 262 pages.

Sherman, Lawrence W.
   1975   "An ecological study of glee in small groups of pre-
   school children," Child Development 46, pp. 53-61.

Sherman, Mandel
   1927   "The differentiation of emotional responses in infants:
   I; Judgments of emotional responses from motion picture views
   and from actual observation.   II, The ability of observers to
   judge emotional characteristics of the crying of infants, and of
   the voice of an adult," Journal of Comparative Psychology 7,
   pp. 265-284, 335-351.

Sherzer, Joel [University of Texas]
         "Greetings among the Cuna."

   1973   "Verbal and nonverbal deixis: the pointed lip gesture
   among the San Blas Cuna," Language in Society 2:1 (April),
   pp. 117-131.

Shipman, G. R.
    1953   "How to talk to a Martian," Astounding Science Fiction
    52:2 (October), pp. 112-120. [Now Analog Science Fiction--
    Science Fact.] Reprinted in Language: An Introductory Read-
    er, ed. by J. Burl Hogins and Robert E. Yarber. New York:
    Harper and Row, 1969, pp. 227-235.

Shipp, Thomas, and Harry Hollien
    1969   "Perception of the aging male voice," Journal of Speech
    and Hearing Research 12:4 (Dec.), pp. 703-710.

Shiver, Sam M.
    1941   "Finger rhymes," Southern Folklore Quarterly 5, pp.
    221-234.

Shopen, Timothy
    1972   "A generative theory of ellipsis: a consideration of the
    linguistic use of silence," Dissertation Abstracts 33, part 1,
    p. 299 A, Order No. 72-20, 473. University of California at
    Los Angeles, 511 pages.

Shor, Ronald E.
    1964   "Shared patterns of nonverbal normative expectations in
    automobile driving," Journal of Social Psychology 62, pp. 155-
    163.

Shunary, Jacob
    1968   "Hebrew finger spelling," Working Papers 6, The He-
    brew University of Jerusalem, pp. 1-8.

    1968   "The potentialities of visual communication systems for
    the rehabilitation of the deaf: double signs, a preliminary
    study, signs for mechanical terms and private names," Work-
    ing Papers 7, Hebrew University of Jerusalem, pp. 1-13; 8
    (1969).

Shunary, Jacob, and L. Miransky
    1970   "Comparison of adults' and children's signs," Working
    Papers 13, Hebrew University of Jerusalem, pp. 1-23.

Sibree, James
    1884   "Notes on relics of the sign and gesture language among
    the Malagasy," Royal Anthropological Institute of Great Britain
    and Ireland, Journal 13, pp. 174-183.

Sicard, Abbé Roch-Ambroise Cucurron [1742-1822]
    1803   Cours d'instruction d'un sourd-muet. Paris: Chez La
    Clere, 581 pages.

Siddons, Henry
    1807   Practical Illustrations of Rhetorical Gesture and Action,
    Adapted to the English Drama. London: R. Phillips, 387
    pages.

Si -Do-In-Dzou
1889   "Gestes de l'officiant dans les cérémonies mystiques
des sectes Tendai et Singon (Bouddhisme japonais)," Musée
Guimet, Annales, Bibliothèque d'Etude 8.

Siegman, Aron Wolfe, Thomas Blass, and Benjamin Pope
1970   "Verbal indices of interpersonal imbalance in the interview," Proceedings of the 78th Annual Convention, American
Psychological Association, pp. 525-526.

Siegman, Aron Wolfe, and Benjamin Pope
1966   "Ambiguity and verbal fluency in the TAT," Journal
of Consulting Psychology 30, pp. 239-245.

1972   Studies in Dyadic Communication.   Elmsford, N.Y.:
Pergamon Press, 336 pages.

Siegman, Aron Wolfe, Benjamin Pope, and Thomas Blass
1969   "Effect of interviewer status and duration of interviewer
messages on interviewee productivity," Proceedings, 77th Annual Convention, American Psychological Association, pp. 541-
542.

Siertsema, B.
1962   "Timbre, pitch, and intonation," Lingua 11, pp. 388-
398.

Silver, Archie
1952   "Postural and righting responses in children," Journal
of Pediatrics 41, pp. 493-498.

Silverman, Franklin H. , and Ellen-Marie
1971   "Stutter-like behavior in manual communication of the
deaf," Perceptual and Motor Skills 33, pp. 45-46.

Silverstein, Norman
1970   "Film semiology," Salmagundi 13, pp. 73-80.

Simkins, L.
1963   "Modification of pausing behavior," Journal of Verbal
Learning and Verbal Behavior 2, pp. 462-469.

Simmel, Georg
1921   "Social interaction: the definition of the group in time
and space," pp. 348-356; "Sociology of the senses: visual interaction," pp. 356-361, in Robert E. Park and Ernest W.
Burgess, eds. , Introduction to the Science of Sociology.   Chicago: University of Chicago Press.

1959   "Aesthetic significance of the face," in Kurt H. Wolff,
ed. , Georg Simmel 1858-1918.   Ohio State University Press,
pp. 276-281.

Simmons, Donald C.
    1955   "Efik iron gongs and gong signals," Man 60:117 (July),
    pp. 107-108.

    1960   "Tonality in Efik signal communication and folklore,"
    in Anthony F. C. Wallace, ed., Men and Cultures: Selected
    Papers of the Fifth International Congress of Anthropological
    and Ethnological Sciences (1956). Philadelphia: University of
    Pennsylvania Press, pp. 803-808. [Chao and Simmons discuss
    aesthetic aspects or oral use of phonemic tone: Hymes.]

Simms, T. M.
    1967   "Pupillary response of male and female subjects to
    pupillary difference in male and female picture stimuli,"
    Perception and Psychophysics 2, pp. 553-555.

Simpson, W. E., and Cynthia Capetanopoulos
    1968   "Reliability of smile judgments," Psychonomic Science
    12, p. 57.

Sinauer, Ernst M.
    1967   The Role of Communication in International Training and
    Education: Overcoming Barriers to Understanding with the De-
    veloping Countries. New York: Frederick A. Praeger, 155
    pages.

Singha, Rina, and Reginald Massey
    1967   Indian Dances: Their History and Growth. New York:
    George Braziller, 264 pages.

Singleton, W. T.
    1954   "The change of movement timing with age," British
    Journal of Psychology 45, pp. 166-172.

Siple, Patricia
    "Constraints for sign language from visual perception
    data," Studies in Sign Language.

Sittl, Karl
    1890   Die Gebärden der Griechen und Römer. Leipzig: B. G.
    Teubner, 386 pages.

Skelton, Robert B.
    1970   "Individuality in the vowel triangle," Phonetica 21,
    pp. 129-137.

Skelly, Madge, Lorraine Smith, W. Randall, and Rita Solvitz Fust
    1975   "American Indian Sign (Amerind) as a facilitator of
    verbalization for the oral verbal apraxic," Language and
    Language Behavior Abstracts 9.3: 7503026.

Skinner, E. R.
    1935   "A calibrated recording and analysis of the pitch, force,

and quality of vocal tones expressing happiness and sadness: and a determination of the pitch and force of the subjective concepts of ordinary, soft, and loud tones," Speech Monograph 2, pp. 81-137.

Skinner, R.
1970   "Those telltale executive gestures," Dunes 95 (March), pp. 66-67.

Skraup, K.
1892   Katechismus der Mimik und Gebärdensprache.   Leipzig.

Slama-Cazacu, Tatiana
1973   "Nonverbal components in message sequence," Ninth International Congress of Anthropological and Ethnological Sciences, Chicago.

1973   "Survey of research activity." Laboratory of Psycholinguistics, University of Bucharest.

Sloan, Thomas O. , ed.
1966   The Oral Study of Literature.   New York: Random House.

Slobin, Daniel I.
1969   "Universals of grammatical development in children." (Working Paper No. 22, Language Behavior Research Laboratory) Berkeley, California: University of California, 18 pages.

Smackey, T. R. , and Richard Beym
1969   "Tag questions: dangerous psycholinguistic territory for TESOL," International Review of Applied Linguistics 7, pp. 107-115.

Smith, Alfred G.
1966   Communication and Culture: Readings in the Codes of Human Interaction.   New York: Holt, Rinehart and Winston. [Chap. 13, "Intercultural communication."]   Review by Cecil Miller, Linguistics 46 (December 1968), pp. 115-117.

1969   "Nonverbal communication and communication theory." Paper read to SAA/ICA convention.

Smith, David E.
1971   "The use of gesture as a stylistic device in Heinrich von Kleist's Michael Kohlhaas and Franz Kafka's Der Prozess," Dissertation Abstracts 32.4634A.   Stanford University.

Smith, Edward W.
1972   "Postural and gestural communication of A and B 'therapist types' during dyadic interviews," Journal of Consulting and Clinical Psychology 39, pp. 29-36.

Smith, Frank, and George A. Miller, eds.
1966   The Genesis of Language: A Psycholinguistic Approach.
Proceedings of a conference on "Language development in
children." Cambridge: MIT Press, 400 pages.

Smith, George Horsley
1953   "Size-distance judgments of human faces (projected
images)," Journal of General Psychology 49, pp. 45-64.

Smith, Henry Lee, Jr.
1952   "Linguistic science and pedagogical application; an outline of metalinguistic analysis," Report of the 3rd Annual
Round Table Meeting on Linguistics and Language Teaching,
Georgetown University, pp. 59-67.

1952   "Voice qualifiers."

1953   "The communication situation," Department of State,
Foreign Service Institute.

1966-67 "The modalities of human communication," Bulletin
of General Semantics 32-33, pp. 6-17.

1967   "The concept of the morphophone," Language 43:1
(March), pp. 306-341.

1969   "Language and the total system of communication," in
A. A. Hill, Linguistics Today. New York: Basic Books,
chap. 9, pp. 89-102.

Smith, Kathleen, and Jacob O. Sines
1960   "Demonstration of a peculiar odor in the sweat of schizophrenic patients," Archives of General Psychiatry 2 (Feb.),
pp. 184-188.

Smith, McFarlane
1964   Spatial Ability. London: University of London Press.

Smith, Peter K., and Kevin Connolly
1972   "Patterns of play and social interaction in preschool
children," in Nicholas G. Blurton Jones, ed., Ethological
Studies of Child Behaviour. Cambridge University Press,
pp. 65-95.

Smith, T. C.
1972   "Glossolalia," Furman Studies 20:2, pp. 1-13.

Smith, W. John
1969   "Displays and messages in intraspecific communication,"
Semiotica 1:4, pp. 357-369.

Smith, W. John, Julia Chase, and Anna Katz Lieblich
1974   "Tongue showing: a facial display of humans and other
primate species," Semiotica 11:3, pp. 201-246.

Snell, Ada L. F.
1918   Pause: a Study of Its Nature and Its Rhythmical Function in Verse, Especially Blank Verse. Ann Arbor, Mich. Reprinted in Folcroft Library Editions, 1971.

Snyders, J.
1968   "Les tambours dans l'île de San Cristoval, Protectorat Britannique des Îles Solomon," Journal de la Société des Oceanistes 24, pp. 133-138.

Sokovnin, Vladimir Mihailovič
1974   The Natures of Human Communication: An Attempt at Philosophical Analysis [in Russian]. Frunze: "Mektep," 147 pages.

Sommer, Robert
1959   "Studies in personal space," Sociometry 22, pp. 247-260.

1961   "Leadership and group geography," Sociometry 24:1 (March), pp. 99-110.

1962   "The distance for comfortable conversation: a further study," Sociometry 25 (March), pp. 111-116.

1965   "Further studies in small group ecology," Sociometry 28, pp. 337-348.

1967   "Classroom ecology," The Journal of Applied Behavioral Science 3:4, pp. 489-503.

1967   "Small group ecology," Psychological Bulletin 67:2, pp. 145-152.

1968   "Intimacy ratings in five countries," International Journal of Psychology 3:2, pp. 109-114.

1968   "Proxemic notation." University of California at Davis.

1969   Personal Space: The Behavioral Basis of Design. Englewood Cliffs, N.J.: Prentice-Hall, 177 pages.

1969   "Planning 'notplace' for nobody," Saturday Review (April 5), pp. 67-69.

Sommer, Robert, and Franklin D. Becker
1969   "Territorial defense and the good neighbor," Journal of Personality and Social Psychology 11:2, pp. 85-92.

1971   "Room density and user satisfaction," Environment and Behavior 3:4 (December), pp. 412-417.

Sontag, Lester Warren, and Robert F. Wallace
    1935   "The movement response of the human fetus to sound
    stimuli, " Child Development 6, pp. 253-258.

Sontag, Susan
    1966   "The aesthetics of silence, " Styles of Radical Will.
    New York: Farrar, Straus, and Giroux, pp. 3-34.

Sorell, Walter
    1967   The Dance Through the Ages. ["Afternote: recording
    the dance. "] New York: Grosset and Dunlap, pp. 284-296.

Sorenson, E. Richard
    1967   "A research film program in the study of changing
    man, " Current Anthropology 8:5 (December), pp. 443-469.

Sorenson, E. Richard, and D. Carleton Gajdusek
    1966   "The study of child behavior and development in primi-
    tive cultures" (A research archive for ethnopediatric film in-
    vestigations of styles in the patterning of the nervous system),
    Pediatrics 37:1, pp. 149-243.

Soskin, William F.
    1953   "Some aspects of communication and interpretation in
    psycho-therapy. " Paper read at American Psychological Asso-
    ciation, Cleveland.

Soskin, William F. , and P. E. Kauffman
    1961   "Judgment of emotion in word-free voice samples, "
    Journal of Communication 11, pp. 73-80.

Spalding, A. C. B.
    1826   Portal to Rhetorical Delivery, with Questions, Exercises
    and Observations on the New System of Corporal Expression.
    Dublin, 224 pages.

Sparks, John
    1963   "Social grooming in animals, " New Scientist 19:350
    (August), pp. 235-237.

Speck, Frank G. , Leonary Broom, with Will West Long
    1951   Cherokee Dance and Drama. Berkeley: University of
    California Press, 106 pages. [The corn-dipping gesture:
    Hayes.]

Speer, Blanche C.
    1972   "A linguistic analysis of a corpus of glossolalia, " Dis-
    sertation Abstracts 32. 6960A. University of Colorado.

Speer, David C. , ed.
    1972   "Nonverbal communication" (special issue), Comparative
    Group Studies 3:4 (November).

Nonverbal Communication. Beverly Hills, Calif.: Sage Publications, No. 10.

Speier, Matthew
1973   How to Observe Face-to-Face Communication: a Socio-logical Introduction. Pacific Palisades, Calif.: Goodyear Publishing Co., 203 pages.   ✓

Spence, Donald P., and Carolyn Feinberg
1967   "Forms of defensive looking: a naturalistic experiment," Journal of Nervous and Mental Disease 145, pp. 261-271.

Spencer, Herbert
1858   Essays, Scientific, Political, and Speculative. ["The origin and function of music," p. 359.]

1860   Essays on Education, etc. ["On the physiology of laughter," Macmillan's Magazine (March).] Reprinted, New York: E. P. Dutton, 1949, pp. 298-309.

Spencer, Sir Walter Baldwin, and Francis James Gillen
1899   The Native Tribes of Central Australia. London: Macmillan, 500 pages.

1904   Northern Tribes of Central Australia. London: Macmillan. [Sign language, p. 525.]

1912   Across Australia. London: Macmillan, 390 pages.

1927-28   The Arunta: A Study of a Stone Age People. 2 vols. London: Macmillan. Reprinted, Oosterhout, 1972, 690 pages.

Sperling, Melitta
1954   "The use of the hair as a bi-sexual symbol," Psycho-analytic Review 41, pp. 363-365.

Spiegel, John Paul
1967   "Classification of body messages," Archives of General Psychiatry 17:3 (September), pp. 298-305.

Spiegel, John Paul, and Pavel Machotka
1974   Messages of the Body. New York: Free Press, 440 pages.

Spier, Leslie, A. Irving Hallowell, and Stanley S. Newman
1941   Language, Culture, and Personality. Menasha, Wis.: Sapir Memorial Publication Fund. Reprinted, University of Utah, 1960, 298 pages.

Spitz, René Arpad
1957   No and Yes: On the Genesis of Human Communication. New York: International Universities Press, 170 pages.

Spitz, René Arpad, with the assistance of K. M. Wolf
1946   "The smiling response: a contribution to the ontogene-
sis of social relations," Genetic Psychology Monographs 34,
pp. 57-125. [Survey of literature, p. 59; Is smiling response
universal?, p. 71; white, Negro, Indian.] Reprinted, New
York: Arno Press, as Facial Expression in Children: Three
Studies (includes R. W. Washburn, and Florence L. Goodenough), 1972.

Spreen, Hildegarde L.
1945   Folk-dances of South India.   Oxford University Press,
134 pages. [Madras.]

Stagner, Ross
1936   "Judgments of voice and personality," Journal of Educational Psychology 27, pp. 272-277.

Stählin, W.
1940   Form und Gebärde im Gottesdienst und Gebet.   Frauen-
hilfe.

Stanislavski, Constantin
1936   An Actor Prepares.   New York: Theatre Arts Books,
295 pages.

1949   Building a Character.   New York: Theatre Arts Books,
292 pages.

Stanistreet, Grace Marie
1944   "Pantomime is easy," Recreation 38 (May), pp. 72-74;
(June), pp. 137-138, 156-157.

Stankiewicz, Edward
1954   "Expressive derivation of substantives in contemporary
Russian and Polish," Word 10, pp. 457-468.

1964   "Problems of emotive language," in Thomas Sebeok, et
al., Approaches to Semiotics.   The Hague: Mouton, pp. 239-
264.

Stanley, Hiram M.
1898   "Remarks on tickling and laughing," American Journal
of Psychology 9, pp. 235-240.

Starkweather, John A.
1956   "The communication value of content-free speech,"
American Journal of Psychology 69, pp. 121-123.

1956   "Content-free speech as a source of information about
the speaker," Journal of Abnormal and Social Psychology 52,
pp. 394-402. Reprinted in Alfred G. Smith, ed., Communication and Culture: Readings in the Codes of Human Interaction,
1966, pp. 189-199.

1959   "Vocal behavior: the duration of speech units," Language and Speech 2, pp. 146-153.

1961   "Vocal communication of personality and human feelings," Journal of Communication 11:1, pp. 63-72.

1964   "Variations in vocal behavior," in David McK. Rioch and Edwin A. Weinstein, eds., Disorders in Communication. Baltimore: Williams and Wilkins, pp. 424-449.

1967   "Vocal behavior as an information channel of speaker status," in Kurt Salzinger and Suzanne Salzinger, eds., Research in Verbal Behavior and Some Neurophysiological Implications. New York: Academic Press, pp. 253-265.

1969   "Measurement methods for vocal information," in George Gerbner, Ole R. Holsti, Klaus Krippendorff, William J. Paisley, and Philip J. Stone, eds., The Analysis of Communication Content: Developments in Scientific Theories and Computer Techniques. New York: John Wiley and Sons, pp. 313-317.

Starr, R.
1893   "Sign language in print," Science 21 (May 26), p. 286.

Stass, John W., and Frank N. Willis, Jr.
1967   "Eye contact, pupil dilation, and personal preference," Psychonomic Science 7:2, pp. 375-376.

Stea, David
1965   "Space, territory, and human movements: territoriality, the interior aspect," Landscape 15:1, pp. 13-16.

Stead, R. Maillard
1941   "The secret 'V'" [condensed from a dispatch to the Christian Science Monitor], Current History and Forum 53 (June), p. 28.

Stearns, Marshall W.
n.d.   "Negro blues and hollers." [Recording.] Library of Congress, Recording Laboratory, AFS L 59.

Stebbins, Genevieve
1886   Delsarte System of Dramatic Expression. New York: Edgar S. Werner, 271 pages.

Stechler, Gerald, and Elizabeth Latz
1966   "Some observations on attention and arousal in the human infant," Journal of the American Academy of Child Psychiatry 5, pp. 517-525.

Steig, William
1942   The Lonely Ones. New York: Duell Sloan and Pearce, 102 pages. New York: Windmill Books, 1970, 88 pages.

1971   Male/Female. New York: Farrar, Straus and Giroux.

Stein, R. Timothy
1975   "Identifying emergent leaders from verbal and nonverbal
communication," Journal of Personality and Social Psychology
32:1, pp. 125-135.

Stein, W. , P. Ottenberg, and N. Roulet
1958   "A study of the development of olfactory preferences,"
Archives of Neurology and Psychiatry 80, pp. 264-266.

Steiner, George
1973   "The way to silence," Semiotica 8, pp. 94-96.

Steinmann, Alfred
1938   "Uber anthropomorphe Schlitztrommeln in Indonesien,"
Anthropos 33, pp. 240-259.

1938   "Die Verwendung von Baumwurzeln als natürliche
Gongs," Anthropos 33, pp. 656-657.

Steinthal
1851   "Uber die Sprache der Taubstummen," in Robert Eduard
Prutz, ed. , Deutsches Museum (Jan. -June), pp. 904ff.

Steinzor, Bernard
1950   "The spatial factor in face to face discussion groups,"
Journal of Abnormal and Social Psychology 45, pp. 552-
555.

Stent, Gunther S.
1972   "Cellular communication," Scientific American 227:3
(September), pp. 42-51.

Stepanov, Vladimir Ivanovitch [1866-1896]
1892   Alphabet des mouvements des corps humain. Paris:
Vigot.   Alphabet of movements of the human body: a study in
recording the movements of the human body by means of musical signs, translated by Raymond Lister. Cambridge: Golden
Head Press, 1958, 47 pages. Brooklyn, N.Y.: Dance Horizons, 1969.

Stephenson, Geoffrey M. , and D. R. Rutter
1970   "Eye contact, distance and affiliation: a re-evaluation,"
British Journal of Psychology 61:3, pp. 385-393.

Stephenson, Peter H.
1974   "On the possible significance of silence for the origin
of speech," with comments by G. W. Hewes, A. Kortlandt,
Current Anthropology 15:3, pp. 324-326.

Stern, D. N.
1971   "A micro-analysis of mother-infant interaction:

behavior regulating social contact between a mother and her
3-1/2-month-old twins," Journal American Academy of Child
Psychiatry 10, pp. 501-517.

Stern, Edith M.
1957   "She breaks through invisible walls," Mental Hygiene
41, pp. 361-371.

Stern, Karl, J. B. Boulanger, and Sheena Cleghorn
1950   "The semantics of 'organ language': a comparative
study of English, French, and German," American Journal of
Psychiatry 106 (May), pp. 851-860. [Comparative study to find
out how emotional conflicts are expressed in dysfunction of organs in three different languages... "I cannot stomach
it."]

Stern, Theodore
n.d.   "A provisional sketch of Sizang (Siyin) Chin." MS.
[Burma.]

1957   "Drum and whistle 'languages': an analysis of speech
surrogates," American Anthropologist 59 (June), pp. 487-506.
Bobbs-Merrill Reprint Series in the Social Sciences,
A-215.

Sternberg, W.
1909   "Die Kitzelgefühle," Zentralblatt für Physiologie 28
(Leipzig), pp. 865-869. [On ticklishness.]

1911-12   "Die physiologie der Kitzelgefühle," Zeitschrift für
Psychologie und Physiologie 60, p. 105. [The physiology of
ticklishness.]

Stetson, Raymond Herbert
1951   Motor Phonetics: a Study of Speech Movements in Action. Amsterdam: North Holland Publishing Co.,
212 pages.

Stetson, Raymond Herbert, and C. V. Hudgins
1930   "Functions of the breathing movements in the mechanism of speech," Archives Neerlandaises de Phonetique Experi-
mentale 5, pp. 1-30.

Stevens, Kenneth N., et. al.
1968   "Speaker authentication and identification: a comparison
of spectrographic and auditory presentations of speech material," Journal of the Acoustical Society of America 44, pp. 1596-
1607.

Stevens, S. S.
1956   "Calculation of the loudness of complex noise," Journal
of the Acoustical Society of America 28, pp. 807-823.

Bibliography

Stevenson, Merrill A., and Leonard W. Ferguson
   1968   "The effects on personality-impression formation of the cold-warm dimension, the frown-smile dimension, and the Negro-white dimension," Psychological Record 18:2, pp. 215-224.

Stirling, E. C.
   1896   "Gesture or sign language," Report on the work of the Horn Scientific Expedition to Central Australia. London and Melbourne, Part IV, Anthropology, pp. 111-125.

Stockwell, Robert P., J. Donald Bowen, and I. Silva-Fuenzalida
   1956   "Spanish juncture and intonation," Language 32:4 (October-December), pp. 641-665. Reprinted in Martin Joos, ed., Readings in Linguistics: the Development of Descriptive Linguistics in America Since 1925. New York: American Council of Learned Societies, 1957, pp. 406-418.

Stokoe, William C., Jr.
   1960   Sign Language Structure: An Outline of the Visual Communication Systems of the American Deaf. Studies in Linguistics: Occasional papers, No. 8, 78 pages. Review by Herbert Landar, Language 37:2 (1961), pp. 269-271.

   1966   "Linguistic description of sign languages," Georgetown University: Monograph Series on Languages and Linguistics 17th Annual Round Table No. 19, pp. 243-250.

   1969-70 "Sign language diglossia," Studies in Linguistics 21, pp. 27-41.

   1970   "CAL conference on sign languages," Linguistic Reporter 12:2, pp. 5-8.

   1970   "The study of sign language," Eric, EDRS ED 037719. Washington, D.C.: Center for Applied Linguistics, 38 pages.

Stokoe, William C., Jr., ed.
   Began 1972- Sign Language Studies. Review by I. M. Schlesinger, Language Sciences 29, (1974), pp. 33-35.

   1972   Semiotics and Human Sign Languages. The Hague: Mouton, 177 pages. Review by Bernard Tervoort, Semiotica 9:4 (1973), pp. 347-382.

   1973   "Sign syntax and human language capacity," Florida Foreign Language Reporter 11, pp. 3-6, 52-53.

   1974   "Classification and description of sign languages," Current Trends in Linguistics 12:1, The Hague: Mouton, pp. 345-371.

1974   "Motor signs as the first form of language," Semiotica
10, pp. 117-130.

Stokoe, William C., Dorothy C. Casterline, and Carl G. Croneberg
1965   A Dictionary: of American Sign Language on Linguistic
Principles. Washington, D.C.: Gallaudet College Press, 346
pages. Review by Sheridan E. Stasheff, Language Learning
16:3-4 (1966), pp. 228-230.

Stone, Gregory P.
1962   "Appearance and the self," in Arnold M. Rose, ed.,
Human Behavior and Social Processes: an Interactionist Approach. Boston: Houghton Mifflin, pp. 86-118.

Storper-Perez, D., and C. Veil
1968   "Observation des communications non verbales au sein
de petits groups," Bulletin de Psychologie 21, pp. 982-988.

Strang, Barbara M. H.
1963   Modern English Structure. New York: St. Martin's
Press. ["Suprasegmental," pp. 50-60.]

Stratton, Jean
1976   "The 'eye-music' of deaf actors fills stage eloquently,"
Smithsonian 6:12 (March), pp. 66-72.

Straus, Erwin W.
1951   "Rheoscopic studies of expression: methodology of approach," American Journal of Psychiatry 108 (Dec.), pp. 439-
443.

1954   "Der Seufzer: Einführung in eine Lehre vom Ausdruck,"
Jahrbuch für Psychologie und Psychotherapie II, pp. 113-128.

1966   "The sign," in Phenomenological Psychology: The Selected Papers of Erwin W. Straus. New York: Basic Books,
pp. 234-251.

Strehle, H.
1935   Analyse des Gebärdens: Erforschung des Ausdrucks der
Korpesbewegung. Berlin: Bernard U. Graefe, 223 pages.

Strehle, Hermann
1954   Mienen, Gesten und Gebärden. Analyse des Gebärdens.
München-Basel: E. Reinhardt, 174 pages.

Stringer, Peter
1973   "Do dimensions have face validity?" in von Cranach and
Vine, eds., Social Communication and Movement, pp. 341-385.

Stritch, Thomas M., and Paul F. Secord
1956   "Interaction effects in the perception of faces," Journal
of Personality 24, pp. 272-284.

Strongman, K. T. , and B. G. Champness
1968   "Dominance hierarchies and conflict in eye contact, "
Acta Psychologica 28, pp. 376-386.

Strowski, Fortunat Joseph
1934   Theatre et nous Paris.   Paris: Nouvelle Revue Critique,
219 pages.

Stuart, Don Graham, and John J. Godfrey
1970   "The specification of individual speech-voice characteristics, " in Georgetown University Working Papers on Languages
and Linguistics, No. 1, 127 pages.

Suci, George J.
1967   "The validity of pause as an index of units in language, "
Journal of Verbal Learning and Verbal Behavior 6:1, pp. 26-
32.

Sugar, N.
1941   "Zur Frage der mimischen Bejahung und Verneinung, "
Internationale Zeitschrift für Psychoanalyse und 'Imago' 26,
pp. 81-83. [On the mimic process of confirmation and negation.]

Sullivan, Harry Stack
1954   The Psychiatric Interview, ed. by H. S. Perry and M.
L. Gawel. New York: W. W. Norton, 246 pages.

Sulzberger, C. L.
1952   "Ethiopia approves area defense pact, " New York Times
(Dec. 21), p. 18. [Offers specific instructions on gestures
and postures necessary when entering or leaving the presence
of Haile Selaisse, the Elect of God: Hayes.]

Sutton, Valerie
1973   Sutton Movement Shorthand: Book I: The Classical
Ballet Key. Irvine, Calif. : The Movement Shorthand Society,
321 pages.

1974   "Sutton Movement shorthand: examples of notation of a
deaf sign language. " Irvine, Calif. : The Movement Shorthand
Society. [Pamphlet with examples from Rolf Kuschel's work,
q. v.]

1975   Sutton Movement Shorthand: Notation Supplement. Irvine, Calif. : The Movement Shorthand Society, 106 pages.

Sutton-Smith, Brian
1959   The Games of New Zealand Children. Berkeley: University of California Press.

Swadesh, Morris
1971   The Origin and Diversification of Language, ed. by Joel

Sherzer.   Chicago: Aldine Atherton, 350 pages.   Reviews by
Roger W. Wescott in Word; Sarah C. Gudschinsky, International
Journal of American Linguistics 39:1 (January 1973), pp. 52-
55.

Swan, Carla
   1938   'Individual differences in the facial expressive behavior
   of preschool children: a study by the time-sampling method,"
   Genetic Psychology Monographs 20, pp. 557-650.

Sweeney, Mary Anne
   1975   'Nonverbal communication: a study of selected characteristics of an individual in relation to his ability to identify information about human emotional states," Dissertation Abstracts
   International 36:2036A.

Swift, Jonathan
   1963   Swift's Polite Conversation: with Introduction, Notes,
   and Extensive Commentary by Eric Partridge.   Oxford University Press.

Szasz, Thomas S.
   1959   'The communication of distress between child and
   parent," British Journal of Medical Psychology 32, Part 3,
   pp. 161-170.

   1961   The Myth of Mental Illness.   New York: Hoeber-Harper.

                                - T -

Taboureau, Jean (Jehan Tabourot) see Thoinet Arbeau

Taboureau, Jean
   1938   Je lis dans les gestes; démarches, tics, mimiques.
   [Jean des Vignes Rouges, pseud.]   Paris: Les Editions de
   France, 80 pages.

Tagiuri, Renato, and Luigi Petrullo, eds.
   1958   Person Perception and Interpersonal Behavior.   Stanford, Calif.:   Stanford University Press, 390 pages.

Takala, Martti
   1953   'Studies of psychomotor personality tests, I," Annales
   Academie Scientiarum Fennicae Sarja-Ser. B Nide-Tom 81:   2,
   pp. 1-130.   Reprinted in Research Approaches to Movement
   and Personality, ed. Martha Davis.   New York: Arno Press,
   1972.

Tankard, James W. , Jr.
   1970   'The connotative meaning of the eye contact cue to a
   perceiver," Dissertation Abstracts 31. 2330B-31B, Stanford
   University.

Taylor, Allan Ross
    1975   "Nonverbal communications in native North America,"
    Semiotica 13:4, pp. 329-374.

Taylor, Archer
    1948   "Folklore and the student of literature," Pacific Specta-
    tor 2, pp. 216-223. Reprinted in Alan Dundes, ed., The
    Study of Folklore. Englewood Cliffs, N.J.: Prentice-Hall,
    1965, pp. 35-37.

    1956   "The Shanghai gesture," Folklore Fellowship Communi-
    cations, No. 166, Helsinki, 76 pages. [G. of thumbing the
    nose, its age, spread, names in several languages: Hayes.]

    1971   "Gestures in an American detective story," Estudios
    del Folklore 25. Mexico, D.F.: Universidad Nacional
    Autónoma de México, pp. 295-300.

Taylor, Harold C.
    1934   "Social agreements on personality traits as judged from
    speech," Journal of Social Psychology 5, pp. 244-248.

Taylor, Harvey M. [University of Michigan]
            "Misunderstood Japanese non-verbal communication."

    1974   "American and Japanese nonverbal communication,"
    Papers in Japanese Linguistics 3, ed. by J. V. Neustupný.
    Melbourne: Monash University.

    1974   "Developing student observational skills: using visual
    materials," Journal of the Association of Teachers of Japanese
    9:2-3, pp. 47-61.

    1974   "Japanese kinesics," Journal of the Association of Teach-
    ers of Japanese 9:1 (January), pp. 65-75.

    1975   "Beyond words: nonverbal communication in EFL."
    Paper read at the TESOL convention, Los Angeles.

    1975   "Training teachers for the role of nonverbal communica-
    tion in the classroom." Paper read at the ATESL session at
    the Foreign Student Affairs Conference, Washington, D.C.

Taylor, J. E. , R. R. Pottash, and Dorothy Head
    1959   "Body language in the treatment of the psychotic,"
    Progress in Psychotherapy 4, pp. 227-231.

Tchang Tcheng-Ming see Chang, Chêng-ming

Tedlock, Dennis
    1971   "On the translation of style in oral narrative," Journal
    of American Folklore 84:331 (January-March), pp. 114-133.

1971   "Silences in spoken narrative." Paper read at the
American Anthropological Association, CUNY, Brooklyn, New
York.

1972   Finding the Center: Narrative Poetry of the Zuni Indi-
ans. New York: Dial Press, 298 pages. Review by Stanley
Newman, International Journal of American Linguistics 39:4
(October 1973), pp. 261-263.

1972   "Pueblo literature: style and verisimilitude," New Perspectives on the Pueblos, ed. Alfonso Ortiz. University of
New Mexico Press, pp. 219-242.

Tegg, William
1877   Meetings and Greetings: The Salutations, Obeisances,
and Courtesies of Nations. London: William Tegg, 312 pages.

Teit, James A., ed. by Franz Boas
1927-30 "The Salishan Tribes of the Western Plateaus,"
Washington, D.C.: Bureau of American Ethnology, 45th Annu-
al Report. [The Coeur d'Alene, pp. 37-197; IX, "Sign
Language," pp. 135-150; The Okanagon, pp. 198-294; IX,
"Sign Language," p. 261; The Flathead Group, pp. 295-396;
VIII, "Sign Language," p. 373.]

Telford, C. W., and Arthur Storlie
1946   "The relation of respiration and reflex winking rates to
muscular tension during motor learning," Journal of Experimental Psychology 36, pp. 512-517.

Tennis, Gay H., and James M. Dabbs, Jr.
1975   "Sex, setting and personal space: first grade through
college," Sociometry 38, pp. 385-394.

Terango, Larry
1966   "Pitch and duration characteristics of the oral reading
of males on a masculinity-femininity dimension," Journal of
Speech and Hearing Research 9, pp. 590-595.

Tervoort, Bernard Th.
1953   Structurele Analyse van Visueel Taalgebruik binnen een
Groep Dove Kindern. 2 vols. Amsterdam: North-Holland
Publishing Co., 308 pages, 188 pages. [Summaries in English,
French, Spanish, German.] Review by B. Spang-Thomsen,
Word 12:3 (1956), pp. 454-467.

1958   "Acoustic and visual language communicating systems,"
Washington, D.C., The Volta Review 60 (September), pp. 374-
380.

1961   "Esoteric symbolism in the communication behavior of
young deaf children," American Annals of the Deaf 106, pp.
436-480.

1968   "You me downtown movie fun?" Lingua 21, pp. 455-465.

Tesch, Frederick E., Ted L. Huston, and Eugene A. Indenbaum
1973   "Attitude similarity, attraction, and physical proximity
in a dynamic space," Journal of Applied Social Psychology 3:1,
pp. 63-72.

Testelin, Henri
1696   Sentimens des plus habiles peintres.   Paris: Mabre-
Cramoisy, 40 pages.

Tetley, Glen
1948   "Status of notation-choroscript," Dance Observer 15:9,
pp. 116-117.

Thayer, Lee, ed.
1967   Communication: Concepts and Perspectives.   Washington, D. C.: Spartan Books.

Thayer, Stephen
An Eye for an Ear? Towards a Theory of Social Per-
ception: Nonverbal Communication and Deafness. New York:
Deafness Research and Training Center, New York University.

1969   "The effect of interpersonal looking duration on dominance judgments," Journal of Social Psychology 79, pp. 285-
286.

Thayer, Stephen, and William Schiff
1969   "Stimulus factors in observer judgment of social interaction: facial expression and motion pattern," American Journal of Psychology 82:1, pp. 73-85.

1974   "Observer judgment of social interaction: eye-contact
and relationship inferences," Journal of Personality and Social
Psychology 30:1, pp. 110-114.

Thie, Joseph A.
1964   Rhythm and Dance Mathematics.   Minneapolis, Minn.:
Joseph A. Thie, 101 pages.

Thiesen, Wesley
1969   "The Bora signal drums," Lore 19:3, pp. 101-103.

Thilenius, B., C. Meinhof, W. Heinitz
1916   "Die Trommelsprache in Afrika und in der Südsee,"
VOX 26, pp. 179-208.

Thiselton-Dyer, T. F.
1906   Folklore of Women: as Illustrated by Legendary and
Traditionary Tales, Folk-rhymes, Proverbial Sayings, Superstitions, etc. Chicago: A. C. McClurg. Reprinted, Detroit,
Mich.: Singing Tree Press, 1968, 253 pages.

Thomas, Lawrence L.
  1957   "The linguistic theories of N. Ja Marr," University of
  California Publications in Linguistics 14, pp. 1-176. [Bibli-
  ography--Hayes.]

Thomas, N. W.
  1928   "Counting on the fingers," Festschrift Publication Offerte
  au P. W. Schmidt, ed. W. Koppers. Vienna, pp. 726-733.

Thomasius, Jacobus
  1670   "De Ritu Veterum Christianorum Precandi versus
  Orientum." Dissertation, Leipzig.

Thompson, Diana Frumkes, and Leo Meltzer
  1964   "Communication of emotional intent by facial expression,"
  Journal of Abnormal and Social Psychology 68:2, pp. 129-135.

Thompson, Jane
  1941   "Development of facial expression of emotion in blind
  and seeing children," Archives of Psychology 37:264, 47 pages.

Thompson, Stith
  1955-58   Motif-Index of Folk-Literature.   Bloomington, Indiana:
  Indiana University Press. [See hand, finger, etc.]

Thorek, Max
  1946   The Face in Health and Disease.   Philadelphia: F. A.
  Davis, 781 pages.

Thorne, Barrie, and Nancy Henley, eds.
  1975   Language and Sex: Difference and Dominance.   Rowley,
  Mass.: Newbury House Publishers, 311 pages.

Thornton, G. R.
  1943   "The effect upon judgments of personality traits of varying a single factor in a photograph," Journal of Social Psychology 18, pp. 127-148.

Thornton, Samuel
  1971   A Movement Perspective of Rudolf Laban.   London:
  Macdonald and Evans, 134 pages.

Thorpe, W. H.
  1966   "A discussion on ritualization of behavior in animals
  and man," Royal Society of London, Philosophical Transactions,
  Series B, Vol. 251.

  1972   "The comparison of vocal communication in animals and
  in man," in R. A. Hinde, ed., Nonverbal Communication.
  Cambridge University Press, pp. 27-47.

Thorson, Agnes M.
  1925   "The relation of tongue movements to internal speech,"

Journal of Experimental Psychology 8:1 (February), pp. 1-32.

Thwing, Edward Payson
    1876   Drill Book in Vocal Culture and Gesture. New York:
    A. S. Barnes, 111 pages.

Tickell, S. S. C.
    1933   Speech and Movement: Corporal, Facial and Vocal Ex-
    pression. Swindon Press.

Tikkanen, Johan Jakob
    1913   "Zwei Gebärden mit dem Zeigefinger," Helsingfors:
    Druckerei der Finnischen Litteraturgesellschaft, 107 pages.
    Finska Vetenskaps-Societeten, Acta Societatis scientiarum
    Fennicae, Tomus 43, no. 2, "Studien über den Ausdruck in
    der Kunst. "

Timaeus, Ernst
    1973   "Some non-verbal and paralinguistic cues as mediators
    of experimenter expectancy effects," in von Cranach and Vine,
    eds. , Social Communication and Movement, pp. 445-464.

Tinbergen, E. A. , and Nikolaas Tinbergen
    1972   "Early childhood autism: an ethological approach,"
    Zeitschrift für Tierpsychologie. Berlin: Paul Parey, 53 pages.

Tindall, Ralph H. , and Francis P. Robinson
    1947   "The use of silence as a technique in counseling,"
    Journal of Clinical Psychology 3, pp. 136-141.

Tissie, Philippe
    1901   "La science du geste," Revue Scientifique ser. 4, 16
    (Paris), pp. 289-300. [Theory that all thought is transformed
    into some sort of movement, conscious or unconscious: West,
    p. 105.]

Tiwary, K. M.
    1975   "Tuneful weeping: a mode of communication," Working
    Papers in Sociolinguistics, No. 27, Austin, Texas, 10 pages.

Todd, Gibson A. , and Bruce Palmer
    1968   "Social reinforcement of infant babbling," Child Develop-
    ment 39, pp. 591-596.

Tomkins, Silvan S.
    1962-63 Affect, Imagery, Consciousness. 1: The Positive Af-
    fects, 2: The Negative Affects. New York: Springer Press.
    [Social significance of gaze-direction ... review of this topic
    ... reference to clay tablet, 3rd mill. B.C. : Kendon, p. 22.]

    1972   "The face as interface between brain and society. "
    Paper read at the American Psychological Association, Hawaii.

Tomkins, Silvan S. , and Robert McCarter
1964   "What and where are the primary affects? Some evidence for a theory," Perceptual and Motor Skills 18, pp. 119-159.

Tomkins, William
1926   Indian Sign Language: of the Plains Indians of North America together with a Simplified Method of Study, a List of Words in Most General Use, a Codification of Pictographic Symbols of the Sioux and Ojibway, a Dictionary of Synonyms, a History of Sign Language, Chapters on Smoke Signalizing, Use of Idiom, etc. and Other Important Co-related Matter. San Diego, 1929, 99 pages. Reprinted, New York: Dover Publications, 1969, 108 pages.

Tompa, József
1968   Ungarische Grammatik. The Hague: Mouton. [Pp. 348-355, on intonation.]

Tonkova-Yampol'skaya, R. V.
1973   "Development of speech intonation in infants during the first two years of life," in Charles Ferguson and Dan Slobin, eds. , Studies of Child Language Development. New York: Holt, Rinehart and Winston, pp. 128-138.

Topaz, Muriel, ed.
1966   Changes and New Developments in Labanotation. Fifth National Notation Conference.

Torrego, Esther
1972   "Lingüística y cinésica," Revista de Filología Española 54 (for 1971), pp. 149-159.

Tosi, Oscar, et al.
1972   "Experiment on voice identification," Journal of the Acoustical Society of America 51, pp. 2030-2043.

Toulouze, M.
1430   L'Art et instruction de bien danser. Paris. [About 1488; a facsimile in the Royal College of Physicians, London, 1936: Dyke.]

Tracy, Martin J. [University of California at Los Angeles]
1974   "The future of movement notation. " CORD Proceedings.

(in press) "Dance: movement analysis and notation," in Sally Sedelow, ed. , Modern Trends in Computer Usage in the Language Sciences. The Hague: Mouton.

Trager, George L.
1941   "The theory of accentual systems," Language, Culture, and Personality: Essays in Memory of Edward Sapir, ed. by Leslie Spier, A. Irving Hallowell, and Stanley S. Newman.

Wisconsin, pp. 131-145.

1958 "Paralanguage: a first approximation," Studies in Linguistics 13, pp. 1-12. Reprinted in Dell Hymes, ed., Language in Culture and Society. New York: Harper and Row, 1964, pp. 274-279.

1960 "Taos III: paralanguage," Anthropological Linguistics 2:2, pp. 24-30.

1961 "The typology of paralanguage," Anthropological Linguistics 3:1, pp. 17-21.

1962 "A scheme for the cultural analysis of sex," Southwestern Journal of Anthropology 18, pp. 114-118.

1964 "Language," section on Communication, Encyclopaedia Britannica 13, p. 695.

1964 "Paralanguage and other things," Le Maitre Phonetique 122, pp. 21-23.

1966 "Language and psychotherapy," in Louis A. Gottschalk and Arthur H. Auerbach, eds., Methods of Research in Psychotherapy. New York: Appleton-Century-Crofts, pp. 70-82.

Trager, George L., and Edward T. Hall
1954 "Culture and communication: a model and an analysis," Explorations 3 (August), pp. 137-149.

Trager, George L., and Henry Lee Smith, Jr.
1957 An Outline of English Structure. Studies in Linguistics, Occasional Papers 3. Washington, D.C.: American CLS, 91 pages.

Trân Dûc Thâo
1966 "Le mouvement de l'indication comme forme originaire de la conscience," La Pensee 128, pp. 3-24.

1969 "Du geste de l'index a l'image typique, I," La Pensée 147, 5 pages.

Tredgold, Alfred Frank
1908 A Text-book of Mental Deficiency (Amentia). Reprinted, Baltimore: The Williams & Wilkins Company, 1952, 545 pages.

Tremearne, Arthur John Newmann
1913 Hausa Superstitions and Customs. London, 548 pages. [See index: gesture, etc.]

Triandis, Harry C., Earl E. Davis, and Shin-Ichi Takezawa
1965 "Some determinants of social distance among American, German, and Japanese Students," Journal of Personality and

Social Psychology 2:4, pp. 540-551.

Triandis, Harry C. , and William W. Lambert
1958   "A restatement and test of Schlosberg's theory of emotion, with two kinds of subjects from Greece," Journal of Abnormal and Social Psychology 56:3, pp. 321-328.

Tricker, R. A. R. , and B. J. K. Tricker
1967   The Science of Movement. New York: American Elsevier, 284 pages.

Trim, J. L. M.
1967   "Cues to the recognition of some linguistic features of whispered speech in English," Proceedings of the 6th Congress of Phonetic Sciences, Prague.

Tringham, Ruth, ed.
1974   "Territoriality and proxemics: distribution patterns within settlements. " Mss. Modular Publications, New York.

Trojan, F.
1957   "General semantics: a comparison between linguistic and sub-linguistic phonic expression," in L. Kaiser, ed. , Manual of Phonetics. Amsterdam: North-Holland Publishing Co. , Chap. 28, pp. 437-439.

Tronick, Edward, Lauren Adamson, Susan Wise, Heidelise Als, and T. Berry Brazelton
1975   "The infant's response to entrapment between contradictory messages in face to face interaction. " Children's Hospital Medical Center and Harvard Medical School, Boston.

Troyanovich, John
1972   "Methodische Rundschau: American meets German, cultural shock in the classroom," Die Unterrichtspraxis 5, pp. 67-79.

Truby, H. M.
1970   "The perception and common misperception of infant pre-speech," Proceedings of the Symposium on Intonology Sponsored by the International Association of Phonetic Sciences, Prague, pp. 943-947.

Truby, H. M. , and John Lind
1965   "Cry sounds of the newborn infant," in John Lind, ed. , Newborn Infant Cry. Acta Paediatrica Scandinavica, Supplement 163, Uppsala, pp. 7-59.

Trueblood, Alan
1958   "El silencio en el Quijote," Nuevo Revista Filologia Hispanica 12, pp. 160-180.

Tubbs, Stewart L. , and Sylvia Moss
    1974   Human Communication: An Interpersonal Perspective.
    New York: Random House, 343 pages.

Turhan, M.
    1944   "An experiment concerning the interpretation of facial
    expression," Yayinlar 1941, Psychological Abstracts 18:149.
    Istanbul University.

Turkewitz, Gerald, Edmund W. Gordon, and Herbert G. Birch
    1965   "Head turning in the human neonate: spontaneous pat-
    terns," Journal of Genetic Psychology 107, pp. 143-158.

Turner, Ernest Sackville
    1954   A History of Courting.   England: Unwin Bros. , Gresham
    Press, 290 pages.

Turner, Paul R. [University of Arizona]
    "Laughter in faculty meetings. "   MS.

Turner, Pearl
    1968   "The tactile-kinesthetic technique in the teaching of
    Hebrew," Dissertation Abstracts 29:12 (June 1969). 4395 A-96 A,
    Order No. 69-9573. Kent State University.

Twain, Mark (Samuel Langhorne Clemens)
    1875   Sketches New and Old. New York: P. F. Collier.
    "The Petrified Man. " [For burlesque use of double Shanghai
    gesture, pp. 288-292.]

Tweney, Ryan D. , and Harry W. Hoemann
    1973   "Back translation: a method for the analysis of manual
    languages," with comments by William C. Stokoe, Jr. , and
    author's rejoinder, Sign Language Studies 2, pp. 51-80.

Tykulsker, Phillip
    1936   "Reference to the face in French drama before Racine,"
    Modern Language Notes 51, (June), pp. 381-386.

Tylor, Edward B.
    1865   Researches into the Early History of Mankind: and the
    Development of Civilization, ed. Paul Bohannan. Chicago:
    Phoenix Books, 1964, 295 pages.

    1871   Primitive Culture: Researches into the Development of
    Mythology, Philosophy, Religion, Language, Art, and Custom.
    New York: Brentano, 1924.

    1873   Religion in Primitive Culture, Part II of Primitive Cul-
    ture. New York: Harper Torchbooks, 1958, 539 pages.
    Originally published as Chapts. 11-19 of Primitive Culture.

- U -

Uklonskaya, R. , Basant Puri, N. Choudhuri, Luthura Dang, and
Raj Kumari
1960 "Development of static and psychomotor functions of infants in the first year of life in New Delhi, " Indian Journal of
Child Health 9, pp. 596-601.

Uldall, Elizabeth T.
1954 "[m?m], etc. , " American Speech (October), p. 232.

1960 "Attitudinal meanings conveyed by intonation contours, "
Language and Speech 3, pp. 223-234.

1962 "Ambiguity: question or statement? or 'Are you asking
me or telling me?', " Proceedings of the Fourth International
Congress of Phonetic Sciences, Helsinki, 1961. The Hague:
Mouton, pp. 779-783.

1964 "Dimensions of meaning in intonation, " in In Honour of
Daniel Jones, eds. David Abercrombie, et al. London: Longmans, Green, pp. 271-279.

Upshur, J. A.
1966 "Cross-cultural testing: what to test, " Language Learning 16:3-4, pp. 183-196.

Urbain, Marcel
1969 "The investigation of some extra-semantic features of
English intonation, " Revue de phonétique appliquée, pp. 45-54.

- V -

Valen, Leigh Van
1955 "Talking drums and similar African tonal communication, " Southern Folklore Quarterly 19:4, pp. 252-256.

Valsiner, Jaan, and Henn Mikkin
1974 "Nonverbal communication in dyads, " Studies in Psychology 3 (Tartu State University), pp. 110-127.

Vance, J. G.
1927 A Mirror of Personality. London: Williams and Nor-
gate.

Vance, Stuart-Morgan
1974 "Conversational alternation and the topic of conversation. " University of Chicago, dissertation.

Vanderbilt, Amy
1968 "Bad manners in America, " The Annals of the American Academy of Political and Social Science 378 (July), pp. 90-

98.   Reprinted in Reflections 4:1 (1969), pp. 12-23.

Vanderslice, Ralph
        1969   "The 'Voiceprint' myth, " Studies in Language and Lan-
        guage Behavior 8, pp. 386-406.

Van Deusen, Joan M. , and James Gunn
        1965   "An inventory of Mexican gestures, " in Harold Harris,
        et al. , eds. , Three Dimension. Kalamazoo, Mich. : Kalama-
        zoo College, pp. 47-56.

Van Ess, Dorothy L.
        1959   "Arab customs, " Practical Anthropology 6:5 (Sept. -Oct.)
        pp. 219-222.

Van Hooff, J. A. R. A. M.
        1962   "Facial expressions in higher primates, " Symposia
        Zoological Society of London 8, pp. 97-125.   ["Grooming
        talk. "]

        1970   "A component analysis of the structure of the social be-
        haviour of a semi-captive chimpanzee group, " Experientia 26,
        pp. 549-550.

Van Lancker, Diana, and Victoria A. Fromkin
        1973   "Hemispheric specialization for pitch and 'tone': evi-
        dence from Thai, " Journal of Phonetics 1, pp. 101-109.

Van Son, L. G.
        1968   "Deaf adolescent's ability to identify nonverbal and
        linguistic emotional expressions. " Thesis, Boston University.

Van Vlack, Jacques
        1966   "Filming psychotherapy from the view point of a re-
        search cinematographer, " in Louis A. Gottschalk and Arthur
        H. Auerbach, eds. , Methods of Research in Psychotherapy.
        New York: Appleton-Century-Crofts, pp. 15-24.

Vaschide, Nicholas
        1909   Essai sur la psychologie de la main.   Paris.

Vasey, George
        1877   The Philosophy of Laughing and Smiling.   London: J.
        Burns, 194 pages.

Vaughan, Victor C. , ed.
        [1967] Issues in Human Development: An Inventory of Prob-
        lems: Unfinished Business and Directions for Research.
        Washington, D. C. : U. S. Government Printing Office, n. d. ,
        [conference in 1967], 217 pages.

Vendryes, Joseph
        1921   Le Langage.   Paris.   Language: A Linguistic Intro-

Venkatachalam   411

duction to History.   New York, 1925.   [Chapter 1, on origin
of writing.]

1950   "Langage oral et langage par gestes, " Journal de
psychologie: normale et pathologique 43, pp. 7-33.

Venkatachalam, Govindraj
194?   Dance in India.   Bombay: Nalanda Publications, 131
pages.

Verneau, René
1923   "Le langage sans paroles, " L'Anthropologie 33, pp. 161-
168.   [Canary Islands: Classe.]

Verplanck, W. S.
1949   Panel on Psychology and Physiology: a Survey Report
on Human Factors in Undersea Warfare.   Washington, D. C. :
National Research Council, 541 pages.   [Section on gesture lg. :
Hayes.]

Very, Annette Gest
1935   "Island dwellers who talk by whistling, " New York
Times Magazine (March 3), p. 15.

1946   "Talking by whistling, " Natural History 55:8 (October),
pp. 360-365.

Vetter, Harold J.
1969   Language Behavior and Communication.   Itasca, Ill. :
Peacock.

1969   Language Behavior and Psychopathology.   Chicago:
Rand McNally.

Vetter, Harold J. , and Richard W. Howell
1971   "Theories of language acquisition, " Journal of Psycholinguistic Research 1:1, pp. 31-64.

Vierordt
1853   "Das Händefalten im Gebet, " Theologische Studien und
Kritiken 26, pp. 89-93.

Vinacke, W. Edgar
1949   "The judgment of facial expressions by three national-
racial groups in Hawaii.   I, Caucasian Faces, " Journal of
Personality 17, pp. 407-429.   Abstracted: "Judgment of facial
expression by Japanese, Chinese, and Caucasians in Hawaii, "
American Psychologist 4 (1949), p. 255.

Vinacke, W. Edgar, and Roberta Wat Fong
1955   "The judgment of facial expressions by three national-
racial groups in Hawaii: II, Oriental faces, " Journal of Social
Psychology 41, pp. 185-195.

Vine, Ian
     1970   "Communication by facial-visual signals: a review and
     analysis of their role in face-to-face encounters," in Social
     Behaviour in Birds and Mammals: Essays on the Social
     Ethology of Animals and Man, John Harrell Crook, ed. New
     York: Academic Press, pp. 279-354.

     1971   "Judgement of direction of gaze: an interpretation of
     discrepant results," British Journal of Social and Clinical Psy-
     chology 10, pp. 320-331.

     1973   "The role of facial-visual signalling in early social de-
     velopment," in von Cranach and Vine, eds., Social Communi-
     cation and Movement, pp. 195-298.

     1973   "Social spacing in animals and man," Social Sciences
     Information 12:5, pp. 7-50.

Voegelin, Carl F.
     1958   "Sign language analysis, on one level or two?" Interna-
     tional Journal of American Linguistics 24:1, pp. 71-77. Re-
     printed in Garrick Mallery, Sign Language among North Ameri-
     can Indians. The Hague: Mouton, 1972.

Voegelin, Carl F., and A. L. Kroeber
     1957   "Sign language of the Northern Great Plains Indians,"
     Report of the Committee on Research, Penrose Fund, Grant
     #2280, Yearbook of the American Philosophical Society, pp.
     418-419.

Voegelin, Carl F., and Florence M. Robinett
     1954   " 'Mother language' in Hidatsa," International Journal of
     American Linguistics 20:1, pp. 65-70.

Vogel, J. P.
     1920   "The sign of the spread hand or 'five finger token'
     (Pañcaṅgulika) in Pali literature," Nederlandse Akademie van
     Wetenschappen, Afdeeling Letterkunde, 5e Reeks (series) Deel
     4 (volume), pp. 218-235.

Vogelsang, R. W.
     1965   "The effects of student nonverbal reactions upon per-
     formances of lecturers on closed-circuit television." Thesis,
     Washington State University.

Voltz, P.
     1901   'Die Handauflegung beim Opfer," Zeitschrift für Alttesta-
     mentliche Wiss. 21.

Von Cranach see Cranach, Mario von

Voorhees, Oscar M.
     1945   The History of Phi Beta Kappa. New York: Crown

Voorhis   413

Publishers. [Sign of the society, p. 10; illustrating secret
handshake: Hayes.]

Voorhis, Paul H.
1971   "Notes on Kickapoo whistle speech," International Journal of American Linguistics 37:4 (October), pp. 238-243.

Vorwahl, H.
1932   "Die Gebärdensprache der Religion," Zeitschrift für
Religionspsychologie 5, pp. 121-128.

1932   Die Gebärdensprache im Alten-testament.   Berlin:
Ebering.

Vuillemey, Paul
1940   La pensée et les signes autres que ceux de la langue.
Paris: P. Foulon, 362 pages.

Vuillier, Gaston
1898   A History of Dancing, from the Earliest Ages to Our
Own Times.   London, 446 pages. [The art of miming and in
dance: Hayes.]

Vygotsky, L. S.
1934   Thought and Language, ed. and translated by Eugenia
Hanfmann and Gertrude Vakar.   MIT Press, 1969, 168 pages.

1939   "Thought and speech," Psychiatry 2, pp. 29ff.

                              - W -

Wachtel, Paul L.
1967   "An approach to the study of body language in psychotherapy," Psychotherapy 4:3 (August), pp. 97-100.

Wagner, Geoffrey
1968   "The many tongues of gesture," Cimarron Review 3
(Oklahoma State University), pp. 4-17.

Wagoner, L. C.
1925   "Speech as an indication of temperamental traits,"
Quarterly Journal of Speech Education 11, pp. 237-242.

Wagoner, Louisa C., and Edna M. Armstrong
1928   "The motor control of children as involved in the dressing process," Journal of Genetic Psychology 35, pp. 84-97.

Wainerman, Catalina H.
1969   "Estilos de 'tomar el piso': un estudio de habitos
verbales," Revista Interamericana De Psicologia 3:4, pp. 259-
272.

Wainwright, G. A.
   1961   "The earliest use of the Mano Cornuta, " Folklore 72,
   pp. 492-495.

Walker, Jerell R.
   1953   "The sign language of the Plains Indians of North America, " Chronicles of Oklahoma 31:2, pp. 168-177.

Walker, John
   1787   The Melody of Speaking Delineated: or Elocution
   Taught Like Music, by Visible Sign. London.

Walker, Kathrine Sorley
   1969   Eyes on Mime: Language without Speech. New York:
   John Day, 190 pages.

Wallace, Bruce R.
   1975   "Negativism in verbal and nonverbal responses of autistic children, " Journal of Abnormal Psychology 84:2, pp. 138-
   143.

Wallace, Karl R.
   1943   Francis Bacon on Communication and Rhetoric. University of North Carolina Press. [Pp. 9, 158: "emblem. "]

Walpole, Hon. F. T.
   1851   The Ansayrii and the Assassins. London. [Contains
   short paragraph on Ansayrii signs and salutes of recognition,
   Vol. III, p. 354: Hayes.]

Wandruszka, Mario
   1954   Haltung und Gebärde der Romanen. (Beihefte zur
   Zeitschrift für romanische Philogogie, No. 96) Tübingen: Max
   Niemeyer, 100 pages.

Wapner, S. , and I. Nachshon
   1967   "Effect of eye contact and physiognomy on perceived
   location of other person, " Journal of Personality and Social
   Psychology 7, pp. 82-89.

Ward, John Sebastian Marlow
   1928   The Sign Language of the Mysteries. London: Basker-
   ville Press. 2 vols. New York: Land's End Press, 1969.
   [Chronological listing of signs, Vol. II, pp. 193-237; Index,
   pp. 242-245: Hayes.]

Ward, John Sebastian Marlow, and W. G. Stirling
   1925   The Hung Society: or the Society of Heaven and Earth.
   London. [Chap. X, The Signs, pp. 108-121.]

Warman, Edward Barrett
   1892   Gestures and Attitudes: an Exposition of the Delsarte
   Philosophy of Expression, Practical and Theoretical. Boston:

Warner   415

Lee and Shepard, 422 pages.

Warner, Francis
1889   "Muscular movements in man and their evolution in the
infant," Journal of Mental Science 35, pp. 23-44.

Warner, William Lloyd
1937   A Black Civilization: a Social Study of an Australian
Tribe. Chicago, 594 pages.

Washburn, Ruth Wendell
1929   "A study of the smiling and laughing of infants in the
first year of life," Genetic Psychology Monograph 6:5-6, pp.
397-537. Reprinted, New York: Arno Press, 1972, as Facial Expression in Children: Three Studies (includes René A.
Spitz, and Florence L. Goodenough).

Washburn, S. L., J. B. Lancaster, and Louis Carini
1971   "On evolution and the origin of language," Current
Anthropology 12, pp. 384-86.

Wasz-Höckert, Ole, J. Lind, V. Vuorenkoski, T. Partanen, and
E. Valanne
1968   The Infant Cry: A Spectrographic and Auditory Analysis.
(Clinics in Developmental Medicine, No. 29) London: Spastics
International Medical Publications and Wm. Heinemann Ltd.
[Also Spanish version.]

Wathen-Dunn, Weiant, ed.
1967   Models for the Perception of Speech and Visual Form.
Proceedings of a Symposium. Cambridge: MIT Press, 470
pages.

Watson, David O.
1964   Talk with Your Hands. Menasha, Wis.: George Banta,
246 pages.

Watson, J. S.
"Orientation-specific age changes in responsiveness to
the face stimulus in young infants." Paper read at the American Psychological Association, Chicago.

Watson, O. Michael
1966   "An atlas of Navaho space." MS.

1969   "On proxemic research," Current Anthropology 10:2-3
(April-June), pp. 222-224.

1970   "Proxemic behavior: a cross-cultural study," Dissertation Abstracts 29. 854B-55B. University of Colorado. Approaches to Semiotics 8, The Hague: Mouton, 127 pages. Reviews by Weston La Barre, Semiotica 6:1 (1972), pp. 83-96;
Letizia Grassi, Semiotica 7 (1973), pp. 91-96.

1972   "Conflicts and directions in proxemic research," Journal of Communication 22:4, pp. 443-459.

1972   "Proxemics as non-verbal communication," in Samir K.
Ghosh, ed., Man, Language and Society. The Hague: Mouton,
pp. 224-231.

1972   "Symbolic and expressive uses of space: an introduction to proxemic behavior." Reading, Mass.: Addison-Wesley
Modular Publications, No. 20, 18 pages.

Watson, O. Michael, and Theodore D. Graves
1966   "Quantitative research in proxemic behavior," American
Anthropologist 68, pp. 971-985.

Watson, Sharon G.
1972   "Judgment of emotions from facial and contextual cue
combinations," Journal of Personality and Social Psychology
24, pp. 334-42.

Watzlawick, Paul
1964   An Anthology of Human Communication. Palo Alto,
Calif.: Science and Behavior Books, 63 pages.

Watzlawick, Paul, Janet Helmick Beavin, and Don D. Jackson
1967   Pragmatics of Human Communication: A Study of Interactional Patterns, Pathologies, and Paradoxes. New York:
W. W. Norton, 296 pages.

Waxer, Peter
1974   "Nonverbal cues for depression," Journal of Abnormal
Psychology 83:3, pp. 319-322.

Weaver, John see Raoul Auger Feüillet

Webb, James T.
1969   "Subject speech rates as a function of interviewer behaviour," Language and Speech 12, Part I (January-March),
pp. 54-68.

1972   "Interview synchrony: an investigation of two speech rate
measures," in Aron W. Siegman, and Benjamin Pope, eds.,
Studies in Dyadic Communication. New York: Pergamon Press,
pp. 115-133.

Webb, T. E.
1968   "Interpersonal behavioral styles and attention strategies
in decoding nonverbal affective communication." Thesis, University of Tennessee.

Webb, Walter Prescott
1931   "The sign language of the Plains Indians," The Great
Plains. Dallas: Ginn and Company, 1959, pp. 68-84.

Webb, Warren W., Adam Matheny, and Glenn Larson
1963 "Eye movements as a paradigm of approach and avoidance behavior," Perceptual and Motor Skills 16, pp. 341-347.

Weeks, Thelma E.
1971 "Speech registers in young children," Child Development 42 (December), pp. 1119-1131.

Weil, Elsie
1931 "Preserving the Indian sign language: General Scott's film to be a record of the Old Code of the Plains," The New York Times, Section 8 (July 5), p. 8. [See Hugh L. Scott.]

Weil, Pierre, and Roland Tompakow
1975 Votre corps parle. Verviers, Belgium: Marabout.

Weir, Ruth H.
1966 "Some questions on the child's learning of phonology," in Frank Smith, and George A. Miller, The Genesis of Language: A Psycholinguistic Approach. MIT Press, pp. 153-172.

Weisberg, Paul
1963 "Social and nonsocial conditioning of infant vocalizations," Child Development 34, pp. 377-388. Reprinted in Warner Modular Publications 162, Andover, Mass., 1973.

Weisgerber, Charles A.
1956 "Accuracy in judging emotional expressions as related to college entrance test scores," Journal of Social Psychology 44, pp. 233-239.

1957 "Accuracy in judging emotional expressions as related to understanding of literature," Journal of Social Psychology 46, pp. 253-258.

Weiss, Joseph
1952 "Crying at the happy ending," Psychoanalytic Review 39, p. 338.

Weiss, Paul
1943 "The social character of gestures," Philosophical Review 52, pp. 182-186.

Weitz, Shirley [New School for Social Research, New York]
"Sex role attitudes and nonverbal communication in same and opposite-sex interactions."

1972 "Attitude, voice, and behavior: a repressed affect model of interracial interaction," Journal of Personality and Social Psychology 24:1, pp. 14-21.

1974   Nonverbal Communication: Readings with Commentary.
New York: Oxford University Press, 351 pages.

Wenger, M. A.
1943   "An attempt to appraise individual differences in level
of muscular tension," Journal of Experimental Psychology 32:3,
pp. 213-225.

Welmers, William E.
1954   "Non-segmental elements in foreign-language learning,"
Report of the 5th Annual Round Table Meeting on Linguistics
and Language Teaching, ed. by Hugo J. Mueller. Washington,
D.C.: Georgetown University, pp. 130-36.

Werner, Heinz, ed.
1955   On Expressive Language. Papers presented at the
Clark University Conference on Expressive Language Behavior.
Worcester, Mass.: Clark University Press, 81 pages. Review by Roger Brown, Language 31 (1955), pp. 543-549.

Werner, Heinz, and Bernard Kaplan
1963   Symbol Formation: An Organismic-Developmental Approach to Language and the Expression of Thought. New York:
John Wiley.

Wescott, Roger W.
1962   Bini Phonology. United States Office of Education,
Washington, D.C.

1962   "Two Ibo songs," Anthropological Linguistics 4:3 (March),
pp. 10-15.

1963   "Ibo phasis," Anthropological Linguistics 5:2 (February),
pp. 6-8.

1966   "Introducing coenetics: a bio-social analysis of communication," The American Scholar 35:2 (Spring), pp. 342-356.

1967   "The evolution of language: reopening a closed subject,"
Studies in Linguistics 19, pp. 67-81.

1967   "Strepital communication a study of non-vocal sound-
production among men and animals," The Bulletin of the New
Jersey Academy of Science 12:1, pp. 30-34.

1969   The Divine Animal: an Exploration of Human Potential-
ity. New York: Funk and Wagnalls, 340 pages.

1970   "Man without speech: speculations on hominid proto-
culture," Anthropological Journal of Canada 8:2 (Ottawa, Ontario), pp. 27-32.

1971   "Linguistic iconism," Language, 47:2 (June), pp. 416-428.

1972   "The origin of speech." Paper presented at the American Anthropological Association.

Wespi, Hans Ulrich
1949   'Die Geste als Ausdrucksform und ihre Beziehungen zur Rede, Darstellung anhand von Beispielen aus der französischen Literatur zwischen 1900 und 1945." Bern: A. Francke. Romanica Helvetica 33, 171 pages. Also issued in part as thesis, Zürich, 1949.

West, LaMont, Jr.
1960   The Sign Language: an Analysis. Indiana University dissertation, vol. I, 128 pages; vol. II, 170 pages.

Wexley, Kenneth N., Stephen S. Fugita, and Michael P. Malone
1975   "An applicant's nonverbal behavior and student-evaluators' judgments in a structured interview setting," Psychological Reports 36, pp. 391-394.

Wheeler, Alva
1967   "Grammatical structure in Siona discourse," Lingua 19, pp. 60-77.

Whiffen, Thomas
1915   The North-West Amazons. New York: Duffield, chap. 15, pp. 190-205. [On dance.]

Whitaker, H. A.
1969   "On the representation of language in the brain," Working Papers in Phonetics 12, University of California at Los Angeles.

White, Edwin C., and Marguerite Battye
1963   Acting and Stage Movement. New York: Arc Books, 181 pages.

White, J. H., J. R. Hegarty, and N. A. Beasley
1970   "Eye-contact and observer bias: a research note," British Journal of Psychology 61, Part II (May), pp. 271-273.

White, Leslie A.
1949   "The symbol: the origin and basis of human behavior," The Science of Culture: A Study of Man and Civilization. New York: Farrar, Straus and Cudahy, chap. 2, pp. 22-39. Reprinted in Bobbs-Merrill Reprint Series in the Social Sciences, A-239.

White, Ralph G.
1972   "Toward the construction of a lingua humana," Current Anthropology 13:1, pp. 113-117.

White, William Alanson
    1921   Foundations of Psychiatry. New York: Nervous and
    Mental Disease Publishing Company, 136 pages.

Whitehall, Harold
    1951   Structural Essentials of English.   New York: Harcourt,
    Brace and World. [Especially p. 2.]

Whitmire, Laura G.
    1927   "A course in pantomime, " Quarterly Journal of Speech
    Education 13, pp. 110-118.

Wickes, Thomas A. , Jr.
    1956   "Examiner influence in a testing situation, " Journal of
    Consulting Psychology 20, pp. 23-26.

Widvey, Harold W.
    1972   "A study to examine the relationship of kinesic nonverb-
    al activity to selected processes of decision emergence in
    small groups, " Dissertation Abstracts 32. 4157A.   University
    of Nebraska.

Wied-Neuwied, Prince Maximilian von
    1832-34, 1841 [A list of Indian sign language], Reise in das
    Innere von Nordamerika, vol. II, pp. 645-653.

Wiener, Harry
    1966   "External chemical messengers. I: Emission and re-
    ception in man, " New York State Journal of Medicine   66:24
    (December), pp. 3153-70.

    1969   "A model of schizophrenia, " Transactions: Journal of
    the Dept. of Psychiatry 1:2 (Marquette School of Medicine),
    (Fall), pp. 29-33.

Wiener, Morton, Shannon Devoe, Stuart Rubinow, Jesse Geller
    1972   "Nonverbal behavior and nonverbal communication, "
    Psychological Review 79:3 (May), 185-214.

Wiener, Morton, and Albert Mehrabian
    1968   Language Within Language: Immediacy, a Channel in
    Verbal Communication.   New York: Appleton-Century-Crofts,
    214 pages.

Wiener, Norbert
    1948   Cybernetics: or Control and Communication in the Ani-
    mal and the Machine.   Cambridge, Mass.: MIT Press, 212
    pages.

    1950   The Human Use of Human Beings: Cybernetics and So-
    ciety.   Boston: Houghton Mifflin, 241 pages.

Wigdorsky, Leopoldo [Universidad Católica de Chile]
1972   "An inventory of Chilean Spanish lexical items and a research on speed of speech and its relation to vocabulary diver-
sity. " Paper read at the 3rd International Congress of Applied
Linguistics, Copenhagen.

Wigman, Mary
1966   The Language of Dance.   Middletown, Conn.: Wesleyan
University Press, 118 pages.

Wilkins, John
1641   "Mercury, or the secret and swift messenger," Mathematical and Philosophical Works, Volume 2, London, 1802;
An Essay Towards a Real Character and a Philosophical
Language, 1668; reprint, London, 1970.

Williams, F. , and Barbara Sundene
1965   "Dimensions of recognition: visual vs. vocal expression
of emotion," Audiovisual Communication Review 13, pp. 44-52.

Williams, Frederick, and John Tolch
1965   "Communication by facial expression, " Journal of Communication 15:1 (March), pp. 17-27.

Williams, Judy
1968   "Bilingual experiences of a deaf child. " Washington,
D. C.: Gallaudet College.

Williams, Thomas R.
1966   "Cultural structuring of tactile experience in a Borneo
society, " American Anthropologist 68:1, pp. 27-39.

Willis, Frank N.
1966   "Initial speaking distance as a function of the speakers'
relationship," Psychonomic Science 5, pp. 221-222.

Wilton, K. M. , and F. J. Boersma, with an introduction by H.
Macworth
1974   Eye Movements, Surprise Reactions and Cognitive Development. Netherlands: Rotterdam University Press, 69
pages.

Winick, Charles, and Herbert Holt
1961   "Seating position as nonverbal communication in group
analysis," Psychiatry 24, pp. 171-182.

1962   "Eye and face movements as nonverbal communication
in group psychotherapy," Hillside Hospital (Journal) 11 (New
York), pp. 67-79.

Winitz, Harris
1960   "Spectrographic investigation of infant vowels, " Journal
of Genetic Psychology 96, pp. 171-181.

1969   "Prelanguage articulatory development," in Articulatory
Acquisition and Behavior. New York: Appleton-Century-Crofts,
chap. 1, pp. 1-54.

Wise, C. M., and Lily Pao-Hu Chong
1957   "Intelligibility of whispering in a tone language," Journal
of Speech and Hearing Disorders 22, pp. 335-338.

Wiseman, Cardinal
1855   Essays on various subjects. London. [Volume 3, pp.
533-555, on Italian gestures.]

Witte, O.
1930   "Untersuchungen über die Gebärdensprache: Beiträge
zur Psychologie der Sprache," Zeitschrift für Psychologie 116,
pp. 116, 225-308.

Witte, P. A. von
1910   "Zur Trommelsprache bei den Ewe Leuten," Anthropos
5, pp. 50-53.

Witzleben, Henry D. von
1958   "On loneliness," Psychiatry 21, pp. 37-43. [On silence.]

Wolf, J. J.
1969   "Acoustic measurements for speaker recognition,"
M. I. T. Research Laboratory of Electronics Quarterly Progress
Report 94, pp. 216-22.

1970   "Choice of speaker recognition parameters," M. I. T.
Research Lab. of Electronics Progress Report 97, pp. 125-33.

Wolf, Jared J.
1972   "Efficient Acoustic Parameters for Speaker Recognition,"
Journal of the Acoustical Society of America 51, pp. 2044-2056.

Wolff, Charlotte
1934   "Expression: excerpts," Review of Reviews 85, London
(February), p. 37.

1943   The Human Hand. London, 198 pages.

1945   A Psychology of Gesture. London: Methuen, 225 pages.
Translated, Psycologica del Gesto, La Paz, Bolivia. Reprinted by New York: Arno Press, 1972.

1951   The Hand in Psychological Diagnosis. London, 218
pages.

Wolff, J. G.
1971   "The influence of finger spelling on the development of
language, communication, and educational achievement in deaf
children," The Teacher of the Deaf 69, pp. 334-38.

Wolff, Peter H.
1959   "Observations on newborn infants," Psychosomatic Medicine 21, pp. 110-118.

1963   "Observations on the early development of smiling," in B. M. Foss, ed., Determinants of Infant Behaviour II. New York: John Wiley, pp. 113-138.

1964-65   "The development of attention in young infants," Annals of the New York Academy of Science 188, pp. 815-830.

1969   "The natural history of crying and other vocalizations in early infancy," in B. M. Foss, ed., Determinants of Infant Behaviour IV. London: Methuen, pp. 81-109.

Wolff, Peter, and Joyce Gutstein
1972   "Effects of induced motor gestures on vocal output," Journal of Communication 22, pp. 277-88.

Wolff, Sulammith, and Stella Chess
1964   "A behavioural study of schizophrenic children," Acta Psychiatrica Scandinavica 40, pp. 438-466.

Wolff, Werner
1933   'Involuntary self-expression in gait and other movements: an experimental study," Character and Personality 2, pp. 328-344.

1943   The Expression of Personality: Experimental Depth Psychology. New York: Harper, 334 pages. Reprinted, New York: Johnson Reprint Corporation, 1971.

Wolfram, Walt
1973   "Aspects of glossolalia," Working Papers in Sociolinguistics 1:1, Georgetown University (February), pp. 29-74.

Wood, Lucie A., and J. C. Saunders
1962   "Blinking frequency: a neurophysiological measurement of psychological stress," Diseases of the Nervous System 23, pp. 158-163.

Woodmansee, J. J.
1970   "The pupil response as a measure of social attitudes," in G. F. Summers, ed., Attitude Measurement. Chicago: Rand-McNally, pp. 514-533.

Woodward, James C., Jr.
1973   "Some characteristics of pidgin sign English," Sign Language Studies 3, pp. 39-46.

Woodward, James C., and Carol Erting
1975   "Synchronic variation and historical change in American Sign Language," Language Sciences 37 (October), pp. 9-12.

Woodward, Mary F.
1957   Linguistic Methodology in Lip Reading.   Los Angeles.

Woodworth, Robert S., and Harold Schlosberg
1954   Experimental Psychology, revised from Woodworth's
1938 edition.   New York: Holt, Rinehart and Winston.   [Chap-
ter 5, "Emotion I: Expressive movements," pp. 107-132.]

Wooster, Harold, Paul L. Garvin, Lambros D. Calimahos, John
C. Lilly, William O. Davis, Francis J. Heyden
1966   "Communication with extraterrestrial intelligence,"
IEEE Spectrum 3:3, (March), pp. 153-163.

Wooten, Betty Jane
1964   "Spotlight on the dance: gesture, a kissin' cousin,"
Journal of Health, Physical Education, Recreation 35:5 (May),
pp. 77-78.

Worth, Sol
1966   "Film as a non-art: an approach to the study of film,"
The American Scholar 35:2 (Spring), pp. 322-334.

1968   "Cognitive aspects of sequence in visual communication,"
AV Communication Review 16:2 (Summer), pp. 121-145.

1969   "The development of a semiotic of film," Semiotica 1:3,
pp. 282-321.

1974   "The uses of film in education and communication," in
Media and Symbols: The Forms of Expression, Communication,
and Education, 73rd Yearbook of the National Society for the
Study of Education, chap. 11, pp. 271-302.

Worth, Sol, and John Adair
1972   Through Navajo Eyes: An Exploration in Film Communication and Anthropology.   Bloomington, Ind.: Indiana University Press, 286 pages.

Wright, R. H.
1964   The Science of Smell.   New York: Basic Books.

1966   "Why is an odour?" Nature 209 (February 5), pp. 551-
554.

Wundt, Wilhelm
1911   The Language of Gestures.   Translated from Völkerpsychologie, 2nd chapter, and articles by Karl Bühler and George
Herbert Mead, introduction by Arthur L. Blumenthal.   The
Hague: Mouton, 1973, 149 pages.

1911   Völkerpsychologie: eine Untersuchung der Entwicklungs-
gesetze von Sprache, Mythus und Sitte.   "Die Sprache."   Leipzig.

1912   Elements of Folk Psychology: Outlines of a Psychological History of the Development of Mankind.   London, 1916,
532 pages.

Wyburn, G. M. , R. W. Pickford, and R. J. Hirst
1964   Human Senses and Perception.   London: Oliver and
Boyd.

- Y -

Yahraes, Herbert
1947   What Do You Know about Blindness?   New York, 32
pages.   [Gestures of the blind.]

Yngve, Victor H.
1969   "On achieving agreement in linguistics," Papers from
the Fifth Regional Meeting of the Chicago Linguistic Society,
eds. Robert I. Binnick, et al.   University of Chicago, pp. 455-
462.

Young, Paul Thomas
1943   Emotion in Man and Animal.   New York: John Wiley
and Sons, 422 pages.

Yousef, Fathi S.   [California State University at Long Beach]
"Inter-cultural communication: aspects of contrastive
social values between North Americans and Middle Easterners. "

1976   "Nonverbal behavior: some intricate and diverse dimensions in cross-cultural communication. "

Yousef, Fathi S. , and Nancy E. Briggs
1975   "The multinational business organization: a schema for
the training of overseas personnel in communication. "   Paper
read at the International Communication Association, Chicago.

Yutang, Lin
1935   My Country and My People.   New York: Halcyon House.

- Z -

Zahl, Paul Arthur
1950   Blindness.   Princeton University Press, 576 pages.

Zaidel, Susan F. , and Albert Mehrabian
1969   "The ability to communicate and infer positive and negative attitudes facially and vocally," Journal of Experimental Research In Personality 3:3, pp. 233-41.

Zalk, Mark
1969   "Movement behavior in the theatre: a study. "   MS,

Columbia Teachers College, 22 pages. (Copies from Dance Notation Bureau, 8 East 12th Street, New York.)

Zeidler, M. Melchior
1673   Exercitatio Theologica de Conversione Orantium, ceu Ritu Ecclesiae iam Olim Usitato. Königsberg.

Zeligs, Meyer A.
1957   "Acting in: a contribution to the meaning of some postural attitudes observed during analysis," Journal of the American Psychoanalytic Association 5, pp. 685-706.

1961   "The psychology of silence: its role in transference, countertransference and the psychoanalytic process," Journal of the American Psychoanalytic Association 9, pp. 7-43.

Zelkind, I., and J. Sprug
1974   Time Research: 1172 Studies. Metuchen, N.J.: Scarecrow Press, 248 pages.

Zemp, Hugo, and Christian Kaufmann
1969   "Pour une transcription automatique des 'langages tambourines' mélanésiens (un exemple kwoma, Nouvelle-Guinée)," Homme 9:2, pp. 38-88.

Zerffi, William A. C.
1957   "Male and female voices," American Medical Association Archives of Otolaryngology 65, pp. 7-10.

Zibucaite, E.
1967   "K voprosu ob èmocionalnosti," Kalbotyra 18, pp. 99-108. [Emotionality vs. expressiveness.]

Zimbardo, Philip G., George F. Mahl, and James W. Barnard
1963   "The measurement of speech disturbance in anxious children," Journal of Speech and Hearing Disorders 28:4 (November), pp. 362-370.

Zimmerman, Don H., and Candy West [University of California at Santa Barbara]
        "Conversational order and sexism: a convergence of theoretical and substantive problems."

Zimpfer, Forest Adam
1974   "Attitudes of selected office personnel toward nonverbal communication symbols and actions," Dissertation Abstracts International 35:7600A.

Ziskin, J. H.
1962   "An effect of verbal conditioning on nonverbal behavior." Thesis, University of Southern California.

Zivin, Gail [University of Pennsylvania]
1975   "Preschoolers' facial-postural status messages."

Zlutnick, Steven, and Irwin Altman
1972   "Crowding and human behavior," in J. F. Wohlwill,
and D. H. Carson, eds., Environment and the Social Sciences:
Perspectives and Applications. American Psychological Association, pp. 44-60.

Zons, Franz Bernhard
1933   Von der Auffassung der Gebärde in der mittelhochdeut-
schen Epik. [Dissertation. Studie über 3 Hauptarten mal.
Gebärdendarstellung.] Münster: Fähle.

Zorn, Friedrich Albert
1887   Grammatik der Tanzkunst. Leipzig: Verlag von Weber.
Translated as Grammar of the Art of Dancing: Theoretical
and Practical: lessons in the arts of dancing and dance writing (choregraphy) with drawings, musical examples, choregraph-
ic symbols and special music scores, edited by Alfonso Josephs
Sheafe. Boston: Heintzemann Press, 1905, 302 pages. Reprinted, New York: Burt Franklin, 1966.

Zorn, John W. , ed.
1968   The Essential Delsarte. Metuchen, N.J.: Scarecrow
Press, 205 pages.

Zubek, John P. , W. Sansom, and J. Goving
1961   "Perceptual changes after prolonged sensory isolation
(darkness and silence)," Canadian Journal of Psychology 15,
pp. 83-100.

Zubek, John P. , W. Sansom, and A. Prysiaznuik
1960   "Intellectual changes during prolonged perceptual isolation (darkness and silence)," Canadian Journal of Psychology
14, pp. 233-243.

Zuk, Gerald H.
1966   "On the theory and pathology of laughter in psychotherapy," Psychotherapy: Theory, Research and Practise 3, pp.
97-101.

Zung, Cecilia S. L.
1937   Secrets of the Chinese Drama: a Complete Explanatory
Guide to Actions and Symbols as Seen in the Performance of
Chinese Dramas: with synopses of fifty popular Chinese plays
and 240 illustrations. Shanghai, Hong Kong, Singapore: Kelly
and Walsh, 299 pages. Reprinted, New York: Benjamin Blom,
1964, 324 pages.

Zwicky, Arnold M.
1971   "In a manner of speaking," Linguistic Inquiry 2:2
(Spring), pp. 223-233.

1972   "On casual speech," Chicago Linguistic Society 8, pp. 607-615.

1974   "Hey, Whatsyourname!" Papers from the Tenth Regional Meeting, Chicago Linguistic Society, pp. 787-801.

NOTES

Chapter 1

1. Thomas Carlyle, Journal (18 May 1832), quoted in James T. R. Ritchie, The Singing Street. Edinburgh: Oliver and Boyd, 1964, p. 1.

2. Margaret Schlauch, The Gift of Language. New York: Dover, 1955, pp. 214-217.

Chapter 2

3. Most of the ideas in this section appear in my article on the relationship of verbal and nonverbal communication (1974b).

4. In the 1974b article I gave several other references, among them, John Robert Ross, "On declarative sentences," in Roderick A. Jacobs, and Peter S. Rosenbaum, eds., Readings in English Transformational Grammar. Waltham, Mass.: Ginn and Co., 1970, pp. 222-272; and Paul Kiparsky and Carol Kiparsky, "Fact," in Danny D. Steinberg, and Leon A. Jakobovits, eds., Semantics: an Interdisciplinary Reader in Philosophy, Linguistics and Psychology. Cambridge University Press, 1971, pp. 345-369.

5. Isadora Duncan, My Life. New York: Liveright Publishing Corporation, 1927, p. 10.

6 Elizabeth Camp and Millicent Liccardi, Vocabularios Bolivianos, No. 6 Itonama, Castellano e Ingles. Beni, Bolivia: Riberalta, 1967.

7. I wish to acknowledge the generosity of Don Walter, of the UCLA Brain Research Institute, for sharing his expertise by reading and commenting on this section. He is not responsible, of course, for my "mistakes."

8. Quoted in MS Magazine (April 1973), p. 15.

9. Quoted by Macdonald Critchley, 1961, p. 252.

10. Los Angeles Times (November 16, 1974).

11. Ralph G. Martin, Jennie: the Life of Lady Randolph Churchill:
    the Romantic Years 1854-1895. Englewood Cliffs, N.J.:
    Prentice-Hall, 1969, p. 325.

12. Junichiro Tanizaki, The Key, translated from the Japanese by
    Howard Hibbett. New York: Alfred A. Knopf, 1961.

13. Louis Untermeyer, ed., A Concise Treasury of Great Poems:
    English and American. New York: Pocket Books, 1965,
    p. 296. Michelsson used this quotation at the beginning
    of her dissertation on the cry of newborn infants.

14. See methodology on the monolingual approach; for example,
    Chapter 7, "Field Procedures," in Eugene A. Nida,
    Morphology. Ann Arbor: University of Michigan Press,
    1949.

15. Robert H. de Coy, The Nigger Bible. Los Angeles: Hollo-
    way House, 1967, p. 153.

16. I used this diagram in a paper presented to the American Dia-
    lect Society in 1971. It was later published with an ab-
    stract (1974) and also is included in my other book on
    nonverbal communication (1975b).

17. Will Durant, The Story of Philosophy. New York: Simon and
    Schuster, 1953, p. viii.

18. See such works as: Hubert M. Blalock, Causal Inferences in
    Nonexperimental Research. University of North Carolina
    Press, 1964; Abraham Kaplan, The Conduct of Inquiry.
    San Francisco: Chandler, 1964; Thomas S. Kuhn, The
    Structure of Scientific Revolutions. University of Chicago
    Press, 1970; Ernest Nagel, The Structure of Science.
    New York: Harcourt, Brace and World, 1961.

19. I want to express my appreciation to three generous scholars
    who brought to my attention or helped me find these il-
    lustrations: Franz Bäuml, Antonio Tovar, and the late
    Archer Taylor. The first is from Oskar Moser, p. 765;
    the second is from Herbert Fischer (Plate V), and is
    originally from H. R. Paul Schroeder, Geschichte des
    Lebensmagnetismus und des Hypnotismus. Leipzig, 1899,
    p. 157; the third is from de Jorio; the fourth is from
    Herbert Fischer (Plate VIII).

20. Quoted in Fortune (November 1974), p. 162.

21. Jerome S. Bruner, Jacqueline J. Goodnow, and George A.

Austin, <u>A Study of Thinking</u>. New York: John Wiley, 1962, p. ix.

22. I included the full communication in an informal newsletter, "Nonverbal components of communication: paralanguage, kinesics, proxemics," No. 5, which I distributed in 1973.

23. <u>The New Yorker</u> (December 16, 1972), p. 125.

24. Victoria A. Fromkin, "The non-anomalous nature of anomalous utterances," <u>Language</u> 47:1 (March 1971), pp. 27-52.

Chapter 5

25. Robert A. Hall, Jr., <u>Introductory Linguistics</u>. Philadelphia: Chilton Books, 1964, p. 67.

26. Thomas Hardy, <u>Time's Laughingstock and Other Verses</u>. London: Macmillan, 1909. First published in <u>Harper's Weekly</u> (November 8, 1902).

27. Katharine Anthony, <u>Catherine the Great</u>. New York: Alfred A. Knopf, 1926, p. 229.

28. Daniel G. Brinton, <u>The Philosophic Grammar of American Languages: as Set Forth by Wilhelm von Humboldt</u>. Philadelphia, 1885, p. 19.

29. Mary Ritchie Key, <u>The Grouping of South American Indian Languages</u>. The Hague: Mouton, in press.

30. Mary Haas, "Tunica," extract from Franz Boas, <u>Handbook of American Indian Languages</u>, Vol. 4, BAE-Bulletin 40 (1941), p. 110.

31. <u>100 of the World's Most Beautiful Paintings</u>. R. T. V. Sales, Inc., 1966, No. 59.

32. Quoted in <u>Eleanor Roosevelt's Book of Common Sense Etiquette</u>. New York: Macmillan, 1962, p. 486.

33. Jarcho, p. 44.

34. Thomas Benfield Harbottle, <u>Dictionary of Quotations</u>. New York: Frederick Ungar, 1958, p. 493.

35. Kahlil Gibran, <u>The Prophet</u>. New York: Alfred A. Knopf, 1923 [1973], p. 15.

36. Quoted in <u>World</u> (7/3/73), p. 71.

37. Juan Tuggy, <u>Vocabulario Candoshi de Loreto</u>. Peru: Summer

Institute of Linguistics, 1966, pp. 247-248.

38. Mildred L. Larson, Vocabulario Aguaruna de Amazonas.
     Peru: Summer Institute of Linguistics, 1966, pp. 101-
     102.

39. "Comment," Dance Index 1:3 (March 1942), pp. 39-40.

Chapter 7

40. These sketches were used in, Mary Ritchie Key, "A language-
     category test from a composite culture," duplicated for
     the Orange County Department of Education, TESOL Con-
     vention, Anaheim, California, Spring 1971.

41. Robert A. Hall, Jr., "Linguistics and music," Introductory
     Linguistics. Philadelphia: Chilton Books, 1964, pp. 411-
     415. "La struttura della musica e del linguaggio,"
     Nuova Rivista Musicale Italiana 7 (1973), pp. 206-225.
     See also Alain Danielou, "The relationships between mu-
     sic and language according to Hindu theory," The World
     of Music 17:1 (1975), pp. 14-23, International Institute
     for Comparative Music Studies and Documentation
     (UNESCO), Berlin.

42. John Steinbeck, East of Eden. New York: Bantam Books,
     1952 [1962 printing], p. 25.

43. Jean-Paul Sartre, "The room," in Germaine Brée, ed.,
     Great French Short Stories. New York: Dell Publishing
     Company, 1960, p. 237.

44. 100 Selected Poems by e. e. cummings. New York: Grove
     Press, 1959, p. 44.

45. Ruth Slenczynska, Music at Your Fingertips. New York:
     Doubleday, 1961. Reprinted, New York: Da Capo Press,
     1974, pp. 62-63.

46. Naturwissenschaftliche Schriften, Goethes Werke, Band XIII.
     Hamburg: Christian Wegner Verlag, 1955, p. 17.

Chapter 8

47. Index of Economic Articles in Journals and Collective Volumes
     9 (1967), p. vii.

INDEX

Abipon 102
abstract 76-79
acoustical 92
acquisition of language 17, 27-
35, 120, 123-124; see also
infant
adult 8, 122-124
affection 112
affective see emotive
affirmative 16, 34, 120-121
Africa 94, 136
age 35, 122-124; see also
adult; child; infant
aggressive/aggression 20, 112
Aguaruna 60, 115-116
air (direction, source, amount)
31, 93, 99-100; see also
breath; ingressive
alphabet 56
American 12, 136
American Indian 12, 42, 82-
86, 99, 102, 133-134, 136;
see also Indian Sign Language
American Sign Language 54;
see also deaf
analysis 46-50, 55
anecdote 48
animal 36-37, 106, 128
animal call 119
animal mimicry 119
animal noises 119
antithesis/antithetical 20, 41
aphasia 11, 18
applied 48
Arab/Arabic 136
Arabela 60
Arawak 60
Argentina 102
artifacts 116-117
arts/artist 87, 104, 122,
129-133

Asia/Asian 136
athlete/athletics 72, 110, 122,
126; see also physical education; sports
auditory see sensory
Australian 66
autistic/autism 21, 122-123
automatic reflex 100, 101; see
also reflex
Aymara 99

Baby talk 119
Bali 45
Bedoins 45
belch 112
bent knee 101-102
bibliographies 53, 135
Bini 96
biological rhythm 10-11
biological sciences 13
birth see childbirth; reproduction
Black English 12, 42, 136-137
blind 134-135
blushing 113
body elimination 109-112, 128
body language see kinesics
body movement 61-62, 101, 107-
110; see also kinesics
body movement and intonation
62
brain 15-18, 107
Brazil 126
breath 71, 94, 99, 109-110;
see also air
Breton 83
By-Element 93, 116-117

Caingang 102

Campa 60
Candoshi 115-116
categories 33, 34, 49; see
  also grammatical categories
Ceylon 102
Chama 102
chemical 92
child/children 28, 42, 120,
  122-124; see also age;
  infant
childbirth 104, 109-111, 125;
  see also reproduction
chimpanzee 36
China/Chinese 94
Chippewa 85
choke 112
chronemics 10, 114-116;
  see also time; temporal
classical 45, 53, 89; see
  also Romans
classification 48-49
clearing throat 112
click 93, 129
clothing 116-117
clubs 122, 127
cognitive/cognition 16, 21,
  26, 29, 33
combinatory 101
comedian 22, 95, 129, 132
communication 1, 47, 112;
  see also human communication
comparative 36-37, 41, 42, 72,
  101
consonants 16
context of situation 25, 135
continuum 30
control of air movement see
  air
conversation 21, 24, 112, 120
cough 28, 112, 129
counter-example see anecdote
courting/courtship 99, 107
cross-cultural 19, 25, 51,
  54, 56, 95, 104-105, 122,
  136-139
cross-disciplinary 47, 51
cry 29, 30-31, 35, 93, 97-99,
  123
Culina 60
cultural dialects 122, 125-133
cutaneous 113

dance 12, 54, 55, 70, 71-72,
  80, 82-86, 89-91, 94, 99,
  101, 109-110, 116-118, 129,
  131-132
deaf 42, 53, 65, 76-79, 134-
  135
deictic 34, 120; see also
  pointing
descriptive act/gesture 119-
  120
dialect 122-139
dialogue 23; see also conversation; interaction
"different" 49
direct communication 1
directive/directional 21
discourse 6
distance 133-134
distinctive feature 30, 33
dominance 37
drama 129, 131
drinking 109
drum 133-134
dyad 24

eating 109
education 90, 122, 126
electrical 92
electromyograph 88
elements used in kinesics 101
elements used in paralanguage
  92-93
embellishment 100
emblem 41, 49
emic 50, 56
emotion/emotional 6, 16, 19,
  20, 60, 94, 120, 135-136
emotive 9, 33; see also expressive
English 8, 11, 25, 56, 95
ethnic 72, 82-86
ethnomusicology 72
etic 50, 56
etiquette 40, 125
etymon 42
Europe/European 45
exclamation 119; see also interjection
expressive 22; see also emotive
extra-terrestrial 37
eye 18, 69, 94, 101, 106-107;

see also   gaze; optical

face/facial expression 16, 54, 65,
   67-71, 94, 100-01, 104-07
face-to-face 24, 38
falsetto 42, 93, 97
faucalization/faucialization 93
feedback 38
female 18, 25, 28, 122, 124-25
film 56, 88-89, 129, 133
Fine Arts 12, 54
Finland 126
folk gesture 122, 127-128
formal 26
French 11, 94, 95, 137
fricative 92
fronting and backing see sound
   placement
function (of communication) 21

gaze 69; see also eye
general systems theory 46
genitals 36, 42, 45
geographic 122-123
German/Germany 11, 17, 94,
   95, 137
gesture 42, 86, 100
gong 133-134
grammar/grammatical see
   syntax
grammatical categories 7;
   see also categories
Greece/Greek 45, 137
greetings 36, 112, 120
group behavior 122-125
gymnastics 72

haiku 21
hair 116-117
hand 16, 18, 94, 101, 107-
   109
haptics see tactile
head 107
hearer 24
Hebrides 99
hesitation 2, 9, 57, 92, 93,
   94-96; see also pause
hiccup 112
historical reconstruction 41-
   45

history of ideas 37-41, 89-91
homosexual 125
Huichol 94
human communication 20-27,
   46, 50
humming 93
Hungarian 19, 94, 137
hunting 96, 126

iconic 80
idiomovement 123
idiosyncratic 123
imitative behavior 20, 26, 28-
   29
imprinting 28
India 20, 53, 89, 94, 101,
   102, 137; see also Sanskrit;
   Natya Shastra
Indian see American Indian
Indian Sign Language 66, 79;
   see also American Indian
indirect communication see
   direct communication
individual behavior 122-123;
   see also idiomovement; idiosyncratic; personality
infant 11, 18, 28-35, 70, 99,
   123-124; see also child
informal 26
informative 21
ingressive air 99
innate 27, 28
instinctive 101
instruments 29, 76, 89, 100;
   see also electromyograph;
   Psychological Stress Evaluator
insult 8, 128
intelligence 104
intention 1
interaction/interactional 6, 10,
   12, 17, 21, 22, 23-27, 32,
   38, 47, 50, 52, 62, 73, 74-
   76, 117, 120; see also turn-
   taking
interjection 119; see also
   exclamation
International Phonetic Alphabet
   30, 33, 90-91
interpretation 49
interruption 9, 25
intonation 2, 11, 18, 19, 31,

55, 58-61, 62, 90, 93-94,
100; see also length; pitch;
stress; suprasegmental
intonation and movement   62
intonation and music   129
involuntary   see   instinctive;
reflex; voluntary
Iran   102
Italy/Italian   5, 25, 66, 95,
136, 137
Itonama   12

Japan/Japanese   27, 45, 94,
137
jaw   120
Jews   25, 136
Jivaro   60, 115-116
journalist   22, 53
jumping   109-110
juncture   93;   see also   hesitation; pause

kinesic act   119-121
kinesics   5, 61-70, 72-74,
100-112, 129
kinesiology   62
King's X   42, 44
kiss   93, 96-97

Labanotation   57, 72, 81, 90
labialization   93
language   21
language element modification
93
language sounds   92-93
language substitutes   122, 133-
135;   see also   surrogate
lapses   50, 94
laryngealization   93, 94
laugh   30-31, 93, 97-99, 129
learned behavior   27, 28, 112
leave taking   120
left   15, 17-18, 107
left hemisphere   15-16
length   93
lie detector   49
Lingua Franca   122, 133-134
literature   129-130, 132
locomotion   109-110;   see
also   walking

lying down   101-102, 110

male   18, 25, 28, 122, 124-
125
marriage   125-126
mask   104
meaning   see   semantics
measurement   119, 128-129
measuring movement   62
media/medium   38, 129-133
Melanesia   102
mentally ill   135-136
metaphor   135
Mexico   20, 105
micromomentary expression
104
mime   131
mimicry   119;   see also   animal, noise,   speech mimicry
model   46-50
modifications   93
monolingual approach   35
morpheme   56, 79
mouth   101, 107, 120-121
movement   see   kinesics
Movima   107
Mummer Talk   99
muscle constriction   9, 93
music   10, 12, 18, 86-87, 94,
129, 132

nasal   92
nasalization   93, 94
Natya Shastra   19, 94
Navaho   8, 94
negation/negative   16, 34, 120-
121
Newfoundland   99
Nias   45
noise   14, 101, 127
noise/sound mimicry   119
non-cry vocalization   30
non-language modification   93,
97
non-language sounds   93, 96-
100
nonverbal act   119-121
nonverbal coded substitutes   122,
133-135
nose   40, 101, 107, 128
notation system   33, 55-91;

see also transcriptions
noun 17

obscene 8, 128
occupation 112, 122, 126
olfactory 16, 76, 113
one-legged position 102
opposites see antithesis
optical 92; see also eye
oral literature 132
orator/oratory 38, 54, 62, 90, 129, 132
order 31-32, 50
origin of language 45-46
outcries 119
out-of-awareness 17, 19, 28

palatalization 93
Papua 45
paragraph 6
paralanguage 2, 5, 92-100, 129
paralinguistic 57-61, 72-74, 80, 88
pasimology 2
pause 93; see also hesitation; juncture
perception/perceptual 16, 18, 20
performance 122, 129-133
performative verbs 7
personality 90, 122-123; see also idiomovement; idiosyncratic; individual behavior
pharyngealization 93
phatic communication 26
Philippines 99
phonetic/phonetician 30, 45, 92
physical education 90; see also athlete; sports
physicist 47
physiology/physiological 5, 12-18, 25, 94, 100-101, 109-112
pitch 93; see also intonation
play 112
pointing gesture 120; see also

deictic
Polish 12
politician 95
Portuguese 137
posture 67, 86, 101-104
power 19
prelinguistic see infant
prosody see intonation; suprasegmental
proxemics 74-76, 113-114; see also space
psychological/psychology 19-20, 94, 97, 135-136
Psychological Stress Evaluator 100

quantitative 119, 128-129
quantity see length

radio 129, 133
rate of speech 11, 93, 96; see also speed
Rebel Yell 42
recording 55, 76-89
recreation 112
reflex 19, 100-101
regulators 24
relationship of nonverbal and language 5-10
religion/religious 54, 122, 127, 133-134
reproduction 109-111; see also childbirth
response signal 24
responsibility 26
rhythm 10-12, 62, 73, 93, 126
right 15, 17-18, 107
right hemisphere 15-16
Rites of Passage 112, 122, 125-126
ritual 112, 120, 127
Romans 45, 120; see also classical
Russian 94, 102, 137

"same" 49
Sanskrit 89
schwa 95
science of motion 88

science/scientific method 46-50
scratch 112
secret language 126, 127
segmental 92-93
semantics 1, 6, 7, 9, 13,
21, 22, 56, 59, 79, 100
semiotics 2
sensory 1, 18, 20, 51, 92,
113
sentence 6
sex 25, 122-125
sexual 99, 109-111
sigh 112
sign language 54, 66, 126,
133-135
silence 26, 57, 94, 95, 117,
127, 133-134
simultaneous conversation 26
singing 18
Sioux 85
sitting 101-102, 110-111
sketch 81-88
Slavic 102
sleeping 102, 109-110
slips 50, 94
smile 68-70
sneeze 112
snoring 110
societies 122, 127
socioeconomic 122, 125;
see also status
solo (performance) 122, 129,
132
sound mimicry see noise
mimicry
sound placement 93
South America 102, 110, 115-
116
Soviet Union 126
space/spatial 16, 21, 62,
113-114; see also proxemics
Spanish 5, 11, 25, 66, 94,
95, 128-129, 137
speaker identification 100
speech mimicry 119
speech surrogate see language
substitute
speed 93, 96
spelling 56
spit 112
split-brain 17
spoken language 9, 10, 38;
see also written language

spontaneous physiological act
101, 112
sports 109; see also athlete;
physical education
standing 101-102
startle reflex 19; see also
reflex
status 122, 125; see also
socioeconomic
stick figure 81-86
stops 92
stress 93; see also intonation; suprasegmental
stretch 112
stutter 18
submissive/submission 37
sucking 42, 112
suprasegmental 62, 93-94;
see also intonation
surrogate 5, 122, 133-135
swallowing 112
Swiss-German 99
symbol/symbolic 21, 76-87,
119-120
syntax/syntactic 69

taboo 120
Tacana 102
tactile/tactual 16, 18, 35, 51,
71, 74-76, 92, 112-113
television 38, 129, 132-133
temporal 62, 122; see also
chronemics; time
terminology 2, 48
theory 46-50
thermal 76
third party 27
thought and movement 41
Tibet 119
tickling 112
time 21, 93, 114-116; see
also chronemics; temporal
Toba 102
tongue 107
Totonac 102
touch see tactile
transcription 58, 129; see
also notation
Trappist 133
trill 93
Tunica 102
turn-taking 24, 27; see also

interaction

unified field theory   47
United States   126, 127
universals/universality   50-51
unvoiced/voiceless   93

V for Victory   41, 120
ventriloquism   93, 97
verb   16
videotape   101
visual   see   optical
voice disguiser   93
voice quality   57-58, 93, 97
voiceless/unvoiced   93
voiceprints   56, 100
voluntary   17
vowel   93

walking   21, 109-110;   see
    also   locomotion
warfare   112, 122, 127
weeping   see   cry
West Africa   94
whisper   3, 93
whistle   93, 96, 133-134
written language   9, 10, 38,
    129-130;   see also   spoken
    language

yawn   28, 112
yell   42, 93, 96-97, 127

Zaparo   60
Zulu   17